This book is dedicated to

Cordelia, Olivia, Alfred, Georgiana, Tamara and Cicily –
my darling great grandchildren.

Cartoons - Robert Duncan
Cover - Chris Perfect
Artwork - BJ Press Ltd, Truro

Whilst every effort has been made to obtain permission for the use of photographs, the author wholeheartedly apologises for any omissions.

ISBN 978-0-9561108-0-0

First published 2008

Printed and bound in Great Britain by TJ International Ltd. Padstow, Cornwall

CONTENTS

Foreword by Lady Mary Holborow, Lord-Leiutenant of Cornwall

I am delighted to write a foreword for this book by Bettye for more than one reason.

Firstly, it gives a fascinating insight into the story of Newquay over the last century and how it has developed and changed. Probably if anyone outside Cornwall was asked for the name of a town in the county they had heard of they would mention Newquay. However, and perhaps because it is such a tourist attraction, many of us in Cornwall know little about its history, particularly its social history, and this book tells a great deal.

It is also a remarkable story of a family and how they have influenced so many of the hotels, mainly in the Newquay area but also elsewhere in the county. They have gone through hard times but have overcome all the obstacles. All of us in Cornwall owe Bettye and her family a great deal in that our tourism industry has been helped so much by what they have achieved.

Over the years we have appreciated knowing Bettye and her family and have enjoyed their hospitality and their company. We started off our married life in Feock; Bettye lived in Feock for many years; Tommie Gray lived near us in Ladock and Bettye joined him there when they married – and so many of the functions I go to as Lord-Lieutenant take place in the hotels which are owned by her family. We even had the pleasure of going to her 90th birthday party and joining in the dancing which she was leading!

I know that all that read this book will be fascinated – and will need to read to the end to learn how three generations have done so much to rise to the challenges of what visitors to Cornwall expect and welcome. It must be unusual and a great credit to their parents and grandparents that the present generation are continuing their involvement with the tourist industry – congratulations.

Well done Bettye!

Mary Holborow
May 2008

"Oh Get On!"

Why a second edition?

Firstly, I wish to make it quite clear that this is the same story related in 'Oh my dear life!'. So why, readers might ask, another edition? Well, for one thing it takes the story almost ten years on, and they have been exceedingly eventful years for Newquay and my family.

Secondly, one of my grandchildren read the first edition word for word, pencil in hand and when I next saw their copy some years later I found the margins scattered with 'whys and wherefores' and I realised what serious gaps had been left in the telling of the story. In this second edition I have attempted to fill some of those gaps.

My family has been deeply involved with tourism in Cornwall for a hundred years and this is the story of how it came about and what happened on the way. Now in my ninety-second year, and surely nearing the departure lounge, I have felt somewhat less inhibited about telling it so here goes! Incidentally in this edition some of the original hotel stories have been deleted and/or abridged.

But first a little more about early Newquay.

The White House
Veryan
2008

Newquay at the beginning of the 20th Century

In the 19th century the main industry in Newquay was pilchard fishing and towards the end of the century that was beginning to decline, as was the industrial use of the harbour which was not deep enough to accommodate the larger steam cargo vessels then being built. Nearby, also on the Towan promenade, were the public baths where hot and cold sea water baths were available, and the unsightly steam laundry, opened in 1895, which constantly belched black smoke and steam.

The Par to Newquay railway line was opened in 1876 amid great rejoicing. The first passenger train arrived on 20th June that year and its arrival was a gala occasion. The station was decorated with flags and bunting. A large welcoming committee of local nobs and

Opening of the Par to Newquay branch line in 1876.

dignitaries in full regalia was on the platform while outside a huge throng of excited spectators waited. As the train drew into the station the town brass band struck up the National Anthem, the coastguards presented arms and the crowd cheered lustily. Newquay was on its way. The following year, 1877, the first town guide appeared printed by F. Warren, a Newquay printer, and those were the first two steps towards Newquay's development as a holiday resort.

By the beginning of the 20th century Newquay was just becoming known as a rather exclusive watering place, a delightful little seaside town with really high-class shops and before long several large hotels were being built. The first was the Atlantic, in 1892, and The Headland, Victoria, Edgcumbe, and Watergate Bay, four miles up the coast, soon followed. There were two or three coaching inns and several smaller unlicensed hotels and boarding houses. Many of the locals offered 'apartment with attendance and cooking' and it was very popular until the mid-1930s, but the arrangement seems rather quaint today. The landlady let two or three bedrooms and a sitting room to the visiting family. They bought their own food which the landlady cooked and served to them. Families usually stayed for several weeks or a month. In those days there were no short breaks and all the bookings were weekly

Many of the large houses in Newquay, including the ones on Narrowcliff, were holiday homes for the gentry who came with their servants for the month of August and sometimes they let the houses furnished when they were not using them. The same families came year after year; there were always many happy reunions, and lifelong friendships were forged. The seasons were very short — ten weeks at the most. The beaches were completely undeveloped, apart from the bathing machines which were pulled up and down to the sea by ponies, and the odd few private tents which would appear in August. There was very little organised entertainment. In the main the visitors simply

Bathing machines on Towan Beach, circa 1909. - *Courtesy of Sandra Vingoe.*

enjoyed the therapeutic bathing, the bracing air, the beaches, the coastline, and the company of their friends. Family picnics and rambles were the order of the day.

The Newquay Golf Club Pavilion was opened in 1895 and the club soon became the social hub of the town. It was exclusive: the Committee would black-ball any potential member they thought 'not quite'. Artisans and tradesmen were not acceptable but they did accept temporary members if they belonged to an accredited club and had a handicap. In those days the masses did not play golf; it was a game for the privileged few. As the Narrowcliff area of Newquay developed in the 1930s and became cluttered with hotels the western end around the golf club became the elite residential part of the town and very much the place to live. After the Second World War all that was to change. The club opened its doors to the world and his wife and amalgamated with the Newquay tennis club which moved from the top of Trenance Hill. Today it flourishes and is very popular with locals and visitors alike. It is well in tune with modern Newquay but it no longer has the cachet it once had.

The branch railway lines from Newquay to Truro were opened in 1905. The trains stopped at many little halts along the route: Trerice and Trewerry Halt, Shepherds, Goonhavern, Perranporth, Goonbell, St Agnes, Mithian with a change at Chacewater Junction for Truro.

Newquay Railway Station 1910.

For some thirty years the branch lines were well used regularly by locals living in the outlying hamlets around Newquay. Weekly runabout tickets were available at 10s. (50p). They were valid for train journeys anywhere between Liskeard and Penzance on any train except the Cornish Riviera and for many visitors in those days excursions by train were part of the holiday. The branch lines served the country folk well for almost sixty years until 1964 when they were axed by Dr Beeching. In the 1920s Newquay had not yet been discovered by the masses and was just emerging as an up-market seaside resort. There were no paid holidays and Cornwall was a long way from the industrial regions of the country, but even in those days the town was beginning to attract tourists in ever increasing numbers. Most people did not yet own cars, they arrived by train and it is interesting to reflect that the journey from Newquay to Paddington in the 1930s took some six hours. It can take longer today because there are very few through trains. Seventy years ago the third class fare from Paddington was £2.6s.9d. (£2.34), which seemed expensive at the time[1]. A row of jingles stood outside the station ready to take visitors to their hotels or lodgings and Mr Hoyte, the town carrier, would bring the luggage along later in his handcart. In the early 1930s the jingles were replaced by motor taxis. In those days the visitors usually explored the county by train or charabanc.

Luggage was mostly leather and heavy. It was not possible to 'travel light' and wheelie cases had not been invented. Within a few years the Great Western Railway was offering an excellent service — "Luggage in Advance". Once one had bought one's ticket one could pay 2s. extra per item and the cases could be sent on two or three days ahead. They would then be delivered to the holiday address to await the owners' arrival. It worked well and was in general use for many years.

A jingle from the railway station followed by Mr Hoyte with the luggage in his cart.

[1] In the 1920s and 1930s a working man's wage was £2-£3 per week.

Going to a concert, August 1896, gentleman on the left is Sir Richard Tangye
Courtesy Moira Tangye.

In the early days concerts were held several times a season in the vast banqueting cavern at Porth at low spring tides. The cavern itself was awe-inspiring, 200ft long and 60 ft wide with a very high roof which had a hole right at the top. The acoustics were marvellous. For the concerts, which lasted just an hour, a small harmonium would be trundled across the sandy beach, manoeuvred carefully over the rocks and through the tiny entrance. In the 1930s Miss Tessie Horler played the piano. Folk simply flocked there and there was space for everyone.

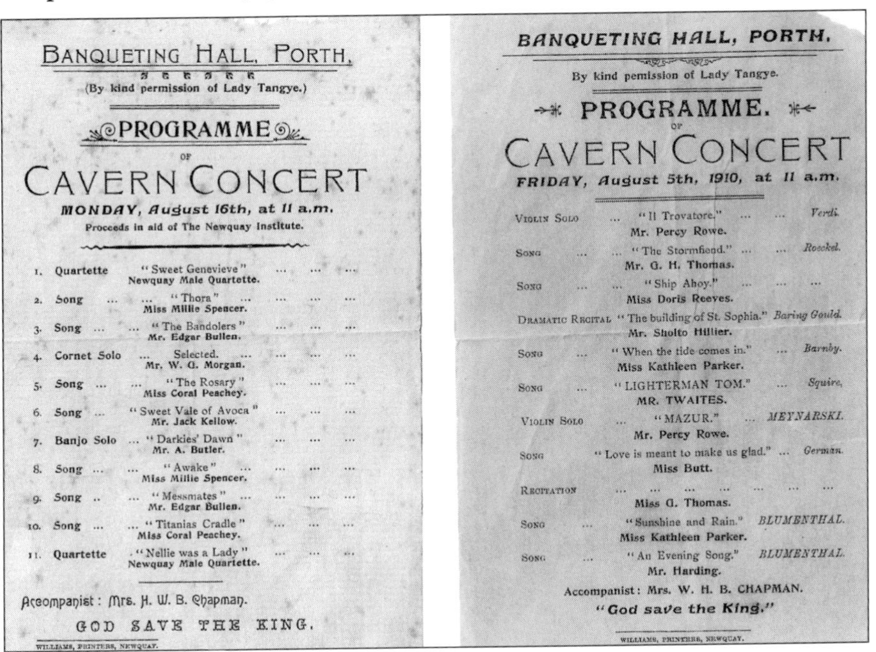

BANQUETING HALL, PORTH.

(By kind permission of Lady Tangye.)

PROGRAMME

OF

CAVERN CONCERT

MONDAY, August 16th, at 11 a.m.

Proceeds in aid of The Newquay Institute.

1. Quartette ... "Sweet Genevieve" ... Newquay Male Quartette.
2. Song ... "Thora" ... Miss Millie Spencer.
3. Song ... "The Bandolers" ... Mr. Edgar Bullen.
4. Cornet Solo ... Selected. ... Mr. W. G. Morgan.
5. Song ... "The Rosary" ... Miss Coral Peachey.
6. Song ... "Sweet Vale of Avoca" ... Mr. Jack Kellow.
7. Banjo Solo ... "Darkies' Dawn" ... Mr. A. Butler.
8. Song ... "Awake" ... Miss Millie Spencer.
9. Song ... "Messmates" ... Mr. Edgar Bullen.
10. Song ... "Titanias Cradle" ... Miss Coral Peachey.
11. Quartette ... "Nellie was a Lady" ... Newquay Male Quartette.

Accompanist: Mrs. H. W. B. Chapman.

GOD SAVE THE KING.

WILLIAMS, PRINTERS, NEWQUAY.

BANQUETING HALL, PORTH.

By kind pemission of Lady Tangye.

PROGRAMME.

OF

CAVERN CONCERT

FRIDAY, August 5th, 1910, at 11 a.m.

VIOLIN SOLO ...	"Il Trovatore." ... Mr. Percy Rowe.	Verdi.
SONG ...	"The Stormfiend." ... Mr. G. H. Thomas.	Roeckel.
SONG ...	"Ship Ahoy." ... Miss Doris Reeves.	
DRAMATIC RECITAL	"The building of St. Sophia." Mr. Sholto Hillier.	Baring Gould.
SONG ...	"When the tide comes in." ... Miss Kathleen Parker.	Barnby.
SONG ...	"LIGHTERMAN TOM." ... MR. TWAITES.	Squire.
VIOLIN SOLO ...	"MAZUR." ... Mr. Percy Rowe.	MEYNARSKI.
SONG	"Love is meant to make us glad." ... Miss Butt.	German.
RECITATION ...	Miss G. Thomas.	
SONG ...	"Sunshine and Rain." Miss Kathleen Parker.	BLUMENTHAL.
SONG ...	"An Evening Song." Mr. Harding.	BLUMENTHAL.

Accompanist: Mrs. W. H. B. CHAPMAN.

"God save the King."

WILLIAMS, PRINTERS, NEWQUAY.

Programmes of Cavern Concerts in the Banqueting Hall. – *Courtesy Moira Tangye.*

Some would bring a candle which they would put in a niche in the cave, and a camp stool or rug to sit on. As can be imagined the music, the setting and the atmosphere were magical. They were popular concerts for many years until the late 1930s.

On lifeboat day crowds would gather on the Headland to watch the lifeboat being launched down the slipway – and as it went a hearty cheer went up.

The highlight of the season was lifeboat day — Bank Holiday Monday, the first Monday in August. Farm workers worked a seven day week with a half day on Sunday and lifeboat day was one of their few whole summer days off, and they made the most of it! On that day of days the shops were closed and special excursion trains were laid on to bring the country folk to town from the outlying villages, and all the little 'halt' stations bustled with activity. Whole families came, they wore their Sunday best, and many carried baskets with their home-made pasties, baked at the crack of dawn by mother. At Newquay they thronged onto the streets and beaches. Some climbed into the waiting horse-drawn jingles outside the station where there was a granite drinking trough for the horses.[2] The streets were lined with people and the Newquay Town Band, in all its glory, was out in force. In memory the sun always shone and the visitors and locals enjoyed the fun together. It was a joyous day

The main event of the day was the launching of the lifeboat down the slipway on the Headland, after which it would be dragged up on Towan Beach by six handsome, bedecked shire horses. In the 1920s and the 1930s at the Central Square the artistes from the Cosy Nook Theatre clambered aboard with a small piano and gave an impromptu concert, to the delight of the milling crowd, while a collection was taken in aid of the lifeboat. The whole parade would then move on to the next stop where there would be another performance outside the

[2] The drinking trough from outside Newquay station now stands by the Riviera Hotel, holding plants.

Lifeboat with artistes from the Cosy Nook Theatre. The pianist can clearly be seen at the piano.

Victoria Hotel, and so on through the town to Narrowcliff. The last stop was outside the Great Western Hotel.

Another highlight of the season was the Gannel regatta which was held every year on a high spring tide, when crowds would picnic on the grassy banks overlooking the estuary while enjoying the simple water sports; rowing, swimming, greasy pole, etc. It was always a busy and highly profitable day for the jingles. In the late 1920s and early 1930s there was much discussion locally about damming the river at its narrowest point to flood the area up to Trevemper Bridge which would have made a large lake for dinghy sailing, etc. It was a very

Graham, Mrs Farmer, Gwen Farmer and Olive Whittington setting off to the Gannel regatta.

controversial scheme, but it almost came off. The plans were scuppered when the owner of a small boat yard at Penpol Creek moored his sizeable boat *'The Ada'* above the proposed dam and pointed out that if the dam were built he would not be able to get his vessel out to sea, and that was the end of the matter. In fact *'The Ada'* never moved. It was there for at least 20 years. After the Second World War for a short time it became a small museum and eventually it disintegrated and was removed.

Gannel Regatta. The banks on the Newquay side of the Gannel have long been covered with expensive houses. *Cornish Studies Library.*

The leisure area of Trenance evolved very slowly over a long period. Trenance Gardens were originally laid out in 1906 in what had been known as Tolcarne Valley. They ran along the valley under the viaduct with a stream and giant gunnerii and a little oval pond where small boys would sail their boats. The gardens remained unchanged for many years. There was an attractive round thatched summer house, two or three gardeners' cottages, and beyond was a swamp which ran towards the river Gannel.

The hard tennis courts and bowling green at Trenance were made in 1917. There was also a very popular Tennis Club with eight grass

Trenance Tennis Courts. The tennis courts and bowling green made in 1917. Today the whole area in the background is covered in houses. – *Cornish Studies Library.*

courts at the top of Trenance Hill where the infant school now stands and many regular visitors became temporary members year after year. There were lively weekly tournaments all through the season. The garb was long cream flannel trousers for the men and skirts to their ankles for the ladies.

For many years the Victoria Hall, as it was known, behind the central square was Newquay's only general purpose hall and every activity was held there: dances, auctions, whist drives, concerts, bazaars, political meetings, beauty contests, baby shows, flower shows, and the like. In those early days there was also the Cosy Nook Theatre on Towan Promenade above Towan beach. It was really little more than a tent; just a wooden frame covered in canvas which was erected for about ten weeks — late June to early September. It seated approximately 150 people in deck chairs and when there were high spring tides and rough seas the canvas on the sea side had to be rolled up. Simple Pierrot type summer shows were put on and were much appreciated by the visitors. Impromptu children's matinees were sometimes arranged on wet afternoons.

Original Cosy Nook Theatre, steam laundry and public baths pre – 1914.

The Pavilion picture house was built in 1912 above Towan Beach. It showed the latest talkies. During the 1930s it became a theatre for the 10 week summer season when touring repertory companies put on London plays for one week only. The companies brought their own scenery and effects which had to be dismantled and packed up on Saturday nights and sent to the next town where they would be appearing the following week. Bettye recalls her first serious, date aged seventeen, in 1933. A handsome twenty year old boy invited her to the Pavilion to see Noel Coward's 'Private Lives'. She wore a long dress and they sat in the third row and held hands — she felt very grown up! To this day the music from 'Private Lives' takes her back to that exciting evening in her youth. Later the Pavilion was completely

The Pavilion, built in 1912, in the 1930s it became a repertory theatre during the season. *Cornish Studies Library.*

destroyed by fire. It was rebuilt and enlarged to seat eight hundred people. It then became the Camelot Cinema until it was sold in 1999 and its image changed completely — but that is a story that will come later.

In August 1919 there was a major disaster in the town when there was a serious fire and one of the town's leading hotels was destroyed. It was the original Hotel Edgcumbe, which stood on Narrowcliff at the top of Ulalia Road, where the Hotel Bristol now stands[3]. The name, of course, was to have great significance for the family in later years. The Hotel Edgcumbe was a narrow, but deep, four storey building which had been built at the turn of the century. It accommodated fifty to sixty guests and in 1919 was owned by Mr Purchas of Truro. When the fire broke out in the kitchen at 2.30 a.m. it was discovered by the staff sleeping behind the kitchen on the ground floor. There was a strong wind blowing which fanned the flames, which quickly took hold. The hotel was full of guests who were aroused by the staff and escaped in their night-clothes. They all crowded into the Bella Vista Private Hotel across the road, where they were given hot drinks and shelter for the night, but no alcohol — the owner of the hotel was a rabid teetotaller! The local newspaper of the day reported: "All the guests managed to escape without their belongings: the majority of them only in their night attire. They were calmly directed by Miss Strutt, the Manageress, who was quite composed throughout. It is said of her, indeed, that she called her dog saying it had better be muzzled as there was certain to be a policeman outside, and later the

[3] Adjoining it on its east side was Newquay College, a privately owned boys' school for the sons of gentlemen — the owner and Headmaster was Dr. Oswald Parker, a family friend.

Advert for the first Hotel Edgcumbe, 1918.

dog was seen running around with its muzzle on." The fire alarm was raised, but it took the firemen some time to arrive on foot from the fire station in Crantock Street, at the other end of the town. They had to manually pull their fire tender which consisted of a trolley with a ladder and a few leaky hosepipes. When they arrived the fire was well away and after much discussion in the road, and a great deal of

The gutted Hotel Edgcumbe on Narrowcliff, August 1919.

Torpoint Fire Engine circa 1920 – unfortunately Newquay's fire tender was a much smaller and simple affair, pulled manually by the firemen until 1926.
Cornish Studies Library.

shouting and blowing of whistles, they decided they had better turn the water on at the mains, but by then it was too late — far too late. Nothing they could do could save the hotel, it was completely gutted. There was just one casualty; a man who was forgotten jumped from a first floor window on to the roof of a small shed at the back and broke his ankle.

Fortunately, the hotel was fully insured, but it was never re-built. All through the 1920s the space where it had stood was used as a council car park. So, from 1919, when the Hotel Edgcumbe was burnt down, to 1926, when Olive Whittington and Tom Farmer bought 4 Colchester Villas in Edgcumbe Avenue, there was no Edgcumbe Hotel in Newquay. But it was destined to rise again, as the reader will hear. Incidentally, Newquay did not get a proper fire engine for another seven years until 1926. Until then the firemen had to haul their equipment about manually while the council argued and discussed whether they should buy a new one or a second-hand one. Eventually they bought a new Leyland Motor Fire Engine which remained in service until about 1950. When it was replaced, control of the service was taken over by the Cornwall County Fire Brigade.

Nagajanka, Narrowcliff
1908 – 1930s

Narrowcliff from the east, 1919. From the left: Bella Vista, Nagajanka, private house, Cliffdene, private house (Dr. Gadston), Marina, St Brannocks, private house, Penolver Boarding House, Beresford, Runnymede, private house.
Cornish Studies Library.

It has always been thought that the first member of the family to be in the tourist business in Newquay was Graham Farmer, when he opened Tolcarne Hotel on Narrowcliff in 1922. In fact, that is not quite accurate for Eliza Farmer's younger sister, Mrs Minnie James, Graham and Olive's aunt, great aunt to Bettye, Peter and Lorna and grandmother of Sally Hooper (née James) and Ann Rollings, had been running a boarding house, "Nagajanka", on Narrowcliff sea front since 1908. Will and Eliza's children often stayed with "Auntie Min", as she was known to the family.

Mr and Mrs James.

"Nagajanka" was a substantial granite faced double fronted house with ten bedrooms. Auntie Min rented it from her wealthy nephew, Joe Congdon, a retired tea planter who then lived in St Keyne. He had had "Nagajanka" built at the turn of the century as a holiday house, and when he no longer needed it he

Nagajanka Boarding House. Note there is nothing showing as a board outside announcing the fact.

rented it to Auntie Min for £52.00 per annum. She ran it as a boarding house from 1908 to the early 1930s with one old Cornish retainer, Emma, and a little extra help in the season. She advertised "en Pension". At that time, most of the houses on Narrowcliff were private residences and Mrs James' establishment was very genteel — no flashy board in the garden — in fact, nothing to say it was a boarding house.

From the left: Emma, Auntie Min, James, Cissie Wangford, her daughter, and husband and son.

Emma, utterly devoted to her mistress, who she always referred to as "The Missus", wore a voluminous black dress to her ankles, covered by a huge white apron and a white cap. She rarely wore her teeth and she sported a fine, black moustache! She was an excellent plain cook, and always seemed to have a fresh batch of saffron cakes just out of the oven, which she offered children visiting Auntie Min, with a "Would 'ee like some saffron cake, m'andsome?" And her pasties were quite something! She slept in a cubby hole under the roof.

Emma's domain was a spacious kitchen dominated by a large, old black Cornish range with brass knobs and trimmings which she kept gleaming. There was a large well scrubbed wooden table by the window, where she would sit drinking copious cups of strong tea when she had finished her cooking and her chores, until 'the Missus' rang the bell for attention.

The summer paying guests all sat at one large table in the dining room which ran from the front to the back of the house, and a second table came into play in July and August. The tables groaned with plain, wholesome 'Cornish fare'. The other front room was the guests' lounge, and the room behind, known as the morning room, was kept as the private family sitting room.

Auntie Min at her upper floor bedroom window, circa 1946.

Auntie Min, like many of her generation, was a real old Wesleyan Victorian humbug, who didn't approve of Sunday papers or drink —

Family group outside Nagajanka circa 1921
Centre back: Minnie James, on her left her son Dick, a friend and Graham Farmer
Seated: Eliza and Will Farmer and Olive Whittington
In front Susie James (later Sue Hardwick).

but she always kept a bottle of whisky in the bottom of the wardrobe "for medicinal purposes, my dear", which she offered to her visitors if they were sufficiently important. She spent the last ten years of her life in the first floor front bedroom at "Nagajanka" waited on hand and foot by Emma. In the summer she spent hours sitting at her open window overlooking Narrowcliff, acknowledging her friends as they walked passed. She died in 1947 aged eighty-three. When 'the Missus' died Emma retired and went to live with her son in Liskeard. By that time Nagajanka was the last remaining private house on Narrowcliff. Later it became part of the next door Bella Vista Hotel, which had already been converted into a four storey building with a flat roof.

So Auntie Min was really the early pioneer in the family but it was Graham Farmer who, when he got going in 1922, showed the family and the rest of Newquay what exciting possibilities there were in the hotel business — and that was the real beginning.

The Family
- and how they came to settle in Cornwall

The Cornish side of the family came from St Keyne, Liskeard. Bettye and her brother Peter's maternal grandmother, Eliza Jane Skinner Broad, was born on Killcrew Farm, St Keyne on 7th September 1862. Killcrew is still farmed by members of the Broad family. Eliza had four younger sisters, Minnie, Janie, Bessie and Nellie. Uncle Albert Clogg, a wealthy retired tea planter, built a substantial house in St Keyne called "Dhoolie" and lived there until his death. Incidentally, today, Dhoolie is the well-known Well House Hotel. It was sold in 2006.

In 1885, at the age of twenty-three, Eliza Broad left Cornwall when she married William Farmer, who had gone to London from Leicester to seek his fortune. Life in the early years of William and Eliza Farmer's marriage was happy but very hard. They had a small drapery shop at 200 Old Kent Road, which was a working class but, at that time, thriving and flourishing district in South East London[1]. William Farmer was successful and prospered. In those days the hours were long, the work was hard, and on Saturday nights the shop didn't close

The family, Autumn, 1914.

[1] The Old Kent Road was badly bombed in the Second World War and never recovered so that by the middle of the twentieth century it had become a very run down slum area. Nearly seventy years on the Old Kent Road is becoming prosperous again, although it will always be a working class district. It is in the heart of London's East End.

until 11.00 p.m. There were stalls outside lit by naphtha flares. The street thronged with bustling people, the air was thick with cheerful Cockney banter and sometimes in winter with a real 'pea-souper' of a fog that came down like a blanket.

Bettye and Peter's mother, Olive Ellen Beatrice, was born in the flat above the shop on 5th February 1887 — the year of Queen Victoria's Golden Jubilee. She was the second child, the eldest being William, who died aged eight after piercing his head with a rusty nail and then developing meningitis. In 1889 came Arthur, then in 1892, Graham, Gwen, in 1896, and when Tom was born in 1900, their family was complete. Nellie, Eliza's youngest sister, had never married so lived with them and helped with the growing family.

Gradually William Farmer was able to buy the properties adjoining his, and eventually he had a large department store, 200-210 Old Kent Road, which sold most of the goods the department stores sell today — but there were no furniture or food departments. At the beginning of the twentieth century W.A. Farmer & Sons Ltd. was the department store in the Old Kent Road.

William Farmer & Sons Ltd., 200-210 Old Kent Road, London.

William Farmer was, in fact, a contemporary, and friend of Gordon Selfridge who was busy establishing his department store at Marble Arch — what a pity the Farmer business turned out to be in the wrong area! The Farmer family flourished and the children were sent to good London day schools — St Olaves and Alleyns. When they left school Arthur, Olive and Graham all became involved with W.A. Farmer & Sons. Arthur went into the Accounts Department, Olive into the Millinery Department and Graham was all over the place and always full of bright ideas!

There was a private entrance at the side of the building and a dining room for the staff. Upstairs, on the top floor, was a private sitting room cum dining room for the family where luncheon was served every day, and where after lunch they sank into comfortable chairs for an afternoon nap, a habit in which even the younger working members of the family indulged.

Olive Farmer ran the hat department, the Millinery Department, as it was called. She eventually became the millinery buyer and made regular visits to the quality hat makers of the day; Hitchcock Williams in St Paul's Churchyard in the City of London and others, to buy the stock for her department. In those days no-one ever went out without a hat, so they were very important and Olive was enthusiastic about her work.

Eliza Farmer missed Cornwall greatly and whenever possible would take her family to visit their Cornish cousins at Nagajanka, her sister's boarding house on Narrowcliff, Newquay, and they always went to stay there at Easter.

Inglewood, St James's Road, Sutton, Surrey, where Bettye and Peter were born.

In 1910 the family moved to Sutton, when W.A. Farmer bought Inglewood, in St James' Road, a detached house with five bedrooms on the first floor and two bedrooms for maids on the second floor. There was a drawing room which ran from the front to the back, and a good sized square dining room, with a large table covered by a red chenille cloth in the fashion of the day. There was a good range of kitchen, scullery, pantry, larders, etc., and a pleasant garden which overlooked fields — alas, now long all built over.

Olive's marriage.

Monty and Olive's wedding,
16th September 1915,
at St Nicholas Parish Church, Sutton, Surrey.

In 1915 Olive Farmer retired from the family business when she married Montague James John Whittington at St Nicholas Parish Church, Sutton, Surrey, on 16th September, at noon. She wore a cream gabardine two-piece coat and skirt, ankle length in the fashion of the day, and a large cream hat trimmed with osprey feathers. This was her chosen garb because it could be worn afterwards for special occasions; she always had a parsimonious streak which never left her. The bride's mother did not approve of the match, she thought Monty was too much of a playboy, and she looked rather stern throughout the ceremony. Olive was her favourite child. The wedding breakfast was held at Inglewood where long tables were laid out in the garden, for it was an elaborate cold meal with a huge ham and roast beef, trifles, fruit salad with Cornish cream especially sent from Cornwall, and a stilton cheese. Later there was a cream tea with saffron cake. Really a Cornish Edwardian Feast!

Afterwards, Olive changed into a navy gabardine coat and skirt. A hansom cab, booked in advance from the row that stood outside Sutton station, pulled by a sleek dark bay horse with the driver up on his box in a bowler hat, and the luggage piled on the back, took the happy couple on the first leg of their long honeymoon journey. First by train from Sutton to Waterloo, another hansom cab across London to Kings Cross and then a long train journey to Llandudno, where they stayed at the Grand Hotel for fourteen days.

An early sign of the incompatibility that would eventually break the marriage was already there. As a wedding present Monty bought his bride a beautiful diamond and sapphire brooch which he could probably ill afford, and Olive, showing signs of the carefulness with money which she would have for the rest of her life, decided they really could not afford it and promptly sent it back! Getting their home together was much more important to her; she felt the money could be put to better use.

The Whittingtons set up home at Parkwood, a four bedroom semi-detached house with a large garden in Broomfield Lane, opposite Broomfield Park in Palmers Green, London, N.13, within striking distance of Monty's business. The firm was "Whittington Bros.", a large furniture emporium in nearby Wood Green, occupying a corner site on several floors, where he was in partnership with his brother, Horace.

Monty was a hard worker, as his son Peter was to be, but he also liked to play hard, and this was later to cause trouble in the marriage. He was clever, good company and an extrovert who loved to entertain and show off; he also loved women. It would be difficult to think of a couple more incompatible than he and Olive. Looking back, the marriage must have been doomed from the beginning. Olive was quiet, home loving, careful and had a giggly sense of fun. In fact, all she really wanted was a quiet domestic life with her children, and all that went with it.

At the outbreak of World War One in September 1914, Monty and his brother had turned the upper floors of their premises to the manufacture of black-out blinds. This was considered to be war work and they were therefore exempt from joining the armed forces. In fact, during the war years this make-shift factory flourished, enabling them to keep the business together so that early in 1919 they were able to pick up where they had left off — selling furniture, and sometimes antiques. They were clever and hard working and they worked well together.

Every now and then, if the sales of furniture became too slack, they would rent an empty house, furnish it with everything and anything they could lay hands on — especially items from the shop which had proved difficult or impossible to sell, and hold an auction sale. This really must have been the forerunner of the dubious practices carried out in many of the auction rooms today — but shops do have to sell their stock one way or the other, and it does still happen at auctions, even upmarket ones.

Monty and Olive's two children were born at Inglewood in Sutton; Bettye in 1916 and Peter in 1919. Just before Peter was born Olive engaged Miss Jarvis, a mother's help, the equivalent of a modern day 'au pair' but more long term — very much more long term! Miss Jarvis, the daughter of a Merchant Navy Captain, was a rather plain spinster of about forty whose fiancé had been killed in the Great War.

Olive Whittington, with Peter, age 6 months, and cousins Cissie and Wang, and Olive's mother, Eliza Farmer.

She never had another beau and she seemed to have no friends. Her entire life was to be with the Whittingtons. She had just a half day off on Sundays when she would take a bus 'up West', have tea and listen to the orchestra at Lyons Corner House in Piccadilly, and then go to the service in St Martins in the Fields Church by Trafalgar Square. She was paid 12s. 6d. per week (62p) and her keep. She was devoted to Olive and the children; Peter was her 'blue-eyed boy'. Miss Jarvis was a tower of strength for seventeen years until she suddenly became crippled with very aggressive rheumatoid arthritis and had to retire when she was fifty-seven.

Arthur and Joan Farmer's wedding, 1920. Graham Farmer on the right and Bettye as bridesmaid, sitting left.

But back to the Farmers. They prospered and by 1916 life in Sutton had become very agreeable. Will Farmer travelled to the Old Kent Road daily by train and every summer they went to Newquay for their summer holidays where they took a furnished house for a month. In 1920 Arthur married Joan Barling, a barrister's daughter, and that proved to be a very happy marriage.

In 1921 William Farmer bought a large Ruston Hornsby Open Tourer motorcar. It was a great barouche with a glass windscreen between the front seats and the back to protect the rear passengers from the weather. He had a garage built at the side of Inglewood for the car and from then on the Farmers always travelled to Newquay by road. The journey took two days and they usually stayed overnight at the Grosvenor Hotel in Shaftesbury. Incidentally, no-one was allowed to speak to the driver while he was driving in case they distracted him. By the early twenties the whole family had a long association and a great affection for Newquay.

William and Eliza Farmer on holiday in Cornwall, circa 1922, in the Ruston Hornsby.

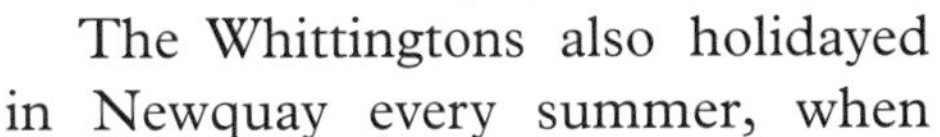

The Whittingtons also holidayed in Newquay every summer, when Olive and Monty took a furnished house. She took the children, with Miss Jarvis, and Monty would usually join his family for part of the holiday. When the big day came there was an early morning bustle in the house. Miss Jarvis cut sandwiches for their picnic lunch, wrapped in greaseproof paper and tied with cotton. They had a taxi to Paddington station where they caught the Cornish Riviera Express at 10.30 a.m. In those days children under three years of age travelled free. Peter had always been very small for his age, and Olive made the most of it; she did not buy a ticket for him until he was nearly five. When the ticket inspector came Olive would grab Peter and, despite his protests, ram a white bonnet on his head and sit him

1919 Family picnic on grassy slope at back of Tolcarne Beach (then known as Crigga Beach).?, Monty and Olive Whittington, Bettye on Grannie's knee. In front: Gwen Farmer (later to be struck down with schizophrenia), on the left Auntie Min from Nagajanka and in the middle her younger daughter, Susie, in the brown school gymslip of Thelma School, Pentire (later Sue Hardwick). At the back, her elder sister Cissie and husband and standing Miss Jarvis, the Whittington's factotum.

on her lap, while Miss Jarvis kept the fidgety Bettye quiet. How exciting those journeys were! The thought of them is so nostalgic — even the smell of those old steam trains evokes memories.

In 1920 Graham Farmer went to Newquay to stay with his Aunt at Nagajanka on Narrowcliff. While there, on Tolcarne beach, he met a tall, slim, pretty girl called Winnie Brooks, daughter of a well-to-do colliery director who lived in Desford, just outside Leicester. They fell deeply in love and he proposed to her.

Although Graham's mother was Cornish and had been brought up on the farm at St Keyne, Graham, who had lived in the Old Kent Road all his life, was no country lad. He was a slick young Londoner of twenty-seven, debonair, a natty dresser, oozing charm, brimming with confidence and ambition. Graham was a persistent suitor, he wooed Winnie Brooks ardently, showering her with presents and paying her great attention.

Winnie's parents did not approve of him, they thought he was too clever by far, and since their daughter was under age, they refused to consent to the marriage until she was twenty-one. But Graham was tenacious and finally the wedding was arranged for June 1921. In the meanwhile he set about buying a house in Surrey for them; a four bedroom detached house in Sandy Lane, Cheam. Graham and Winnie were married at Desford Parish Church in June 1921, and travelled by train to Newquay for their honeymoon. They seemed indeed a "golden couple" and the future looked promising.

Graham and Winnie Farmer's wedding at Desford Parish Church, June 1921.

While in Newquay on their honeymoon Graham saw for sale, for £2,000, a double fronted house in the middle of Narrowcliff with nine bedrooms. It interested him greatly. He thought it would make a good hotel and he began thinking seriously about it.

They returned to London to begin their married life in Cheam and their path seemed set. Graham travelled daily by train to the Old Kent Road, but he did not adapt easily to suburban married life. He found it restricting and soon became restless; his thoughts kept turning to the house he had seen for sale in Newquay. By early 1922 he had firmly made up his mind he intended to buy that house and start an hotel.

Winnie from the beginning was not keen on the idea; she did not want to move to Newquay. Her first baby was due that May. She loved her home and the orderly way of life suited her, but Graham was determined to move his family to Cornwall.

He told his father he wished to leave the family business and set up on his own, and asked if some capital might be made available to him. This did not come as a great surprise to his parents for from an early age Graham had shown signs of being a budding entrepreneur. While at school he had kept chickens in the back garden and sold the eggs, and he was always thinking up money-making schemes. His father agreed to give him some capital from the family business. Graham bought the house on Narrowcliff for £2,000 and called it Tolcarne Hotel.

Their first son, John, was born in May of that year and Winnie remained in Cheam for the summer, while Graham spent most of his time in Newquay getting his business going. Graham loved children and was very proud of his son but he paid little attention to his family. He was completely absorbed by what he was doing in Newquay.

In the meanwhile, Olive and Monty Whittington's marriage was beginning to run into serious trouble. Monty had discovered Westcliff-on-Sea, about an hour from London on the south coast, and he wanted Olive to join him there for weekend jollies with his friends. She preferred to stay at home with her children. Before long he was spending many of his weekends and much of his money on his own with his friends in Westcliff, and he had an eye for the girls. Surely a recipe for disaster?

By 1923 Olive's marriage was going from bad to worse. Monty was frivolling and the household bills were not being paid. Olive went back to being the millinery buyer in W.A. Farmer & Sons and travelled daily by bus from Palmers Green, leaving Bettye and Peter with Miss Jarvis. Graham had already left the business and taken off for Newquay and her father was very glad to have her back, and for her it was therapy. She enjoyed her work and did not find it a hardship. It also helped pay the bills. Her salary was £3. 10s. 0d. (£3.50) per week. Life at home was becoming increasingly difficult for her but she loved her home and children and was absolutely steadfast. At that time she was still hopeful she and Monty would manage to work things out. Sadly it was not to be.

In 1923 there was a major catastrophe in the family when Graham and Olive's father died suddenly of a heart attack at the age of sixty-three.[2] His will, leaving W.A. Farmer & Sons equally to his three sons, proved to be invalid because there was only one witness to it. The law at the time decreed that his eldest son was therefore entitled to claim the family business, and Arthur, aided and abetted by his barrister father-in-law, did so, in spite of his father's written wish that his three sons should share it equally. This came as a serious blow to the whole family, and particularly to Graham who was struggling to find capital to get his projects in Newquay going.

Arthur claiming the business left a deep family rift that lasted until the end of his life and was never to be healed. His brothers and sister never spoke to him again, not even when he turned up for his mother's funeral ten years later. It was tragic. That was the last time they saw him. At the time the family breach seemed not to matter so much and certainly not to Arthur: happily married with three children and in the bosom of his prosperous in-laws, he just cut himself off and all the brothers got on with their lives. But some twenty years later great tragedy befell Arthur when his beloved wife, Jean, died, age forty-two, from a blood disorder and his three children all died in their twenties during Second World War. For the rest of his life he was friendless and alone.

Later, after the war Arthur faced further troubles. The Old Kent Road was badly bombed during the war and the district went into a serious social and economic decline[3]. In the early 1950s the business failed and Arthur went bankrupt. He lived with his in-laws until they died but he was a broken man. It seems he had paid the price for ignoring his father's wishes about the will, but there was no going back. He died alone and friendless of lung cancer in a London hospital in 1956 aged sixty-seven years. Surely a tragic story? Incidentally, Arthur's death had a very profound effect on Bettye. She vowed then that however difficult she found her brother, Peter, — and they did find each other very difficult at times — she was never going to fall out with him permanently and she never did. So although it must be said that during their middle years they did not always see eye to eye, they never became completely estranged.

---

[2] W.A. Farmer was buried in Northwood Cemetery in March 1923, as was his wife, E.J.S. Farmer, in 1933.
[3] In 2008 Old Kent Road is once again a flourishing, bustling district, but is unlikely ever to be what one might call classy – but who knows?

Tolcarne Hotel
1922 – 1945

Graham Farmer opened Tolcarne Hotel on Narrowcliff in early July 1922. It was just a double fronted house with nine bedrooms and it took twenty guests. It was never part of Graham's plan that he actually ran it himself and he engaged a Manageress for the short eight or nine week season.

Tolcarne Hotel, 1922 – just a double fronted house.

Graham was full of enthusiasm for his new project and in that year in partnership with his younger brother, Tom, he also took a lease on Crigga Beach below his new hotel, but more about that later. He spent much of that year in Newquay dealing with the newly acquired hotel and beach leaving his wife, Winnie — barely twenty-two years old — alone in Surrey with their new baby son, John. In Graham's book the business had to come first. When he returned to Surrey in September he was delighted with the way the season had gone and his head was full of ideas for the following year, but first he had to raise some more capital.

That winter Graham was offered Oxford House which adjoined Tolcarne Hotel and he was determined to buy it. He spent most of the winter unsuccessfully trying to raise extra capital and he became desperate to find the money. In the spring of 1923 he treated his wife shamefully. He sold the marital home in Sandy Lane, Cheam, without consulting Winnie or even telling her. He simply told her he had sold it and they were moving to Cornwall. Poor Winnie was very upset, in fact outraged, and she never forgave him. Graham was unrepentant. He had got his capital to buy Oxford House, and to him that was all that mattered. He was a most inconsiderate husband.

They gave up possession of the house in Cheam in January 1923 when John was just eight months old and moved to Newquay lock, stock, and barrel. Graham took a lease on Clifton Villa in Cliff Road for them. Much more important to him, he bought Oxford House for £1,800 and linked it to the Tolcarne so that when Tolcarne Hotel opened for the season in 1923 it had eighteen bedrooms and accommodated forty guests. It also had a new Manageress. Tolcarne Hotel and the beach were well and truly underway.

Tolcarne Hotel 1924, showing the Oxford House addition on the right, and on the left the entrance to the new ballroom. – *Cornwall Studies Library.*

In November 1924 Graham and Winnie's twin sons, Bobbie and Tony, were born at Clifton Villa, Newquay. They then had three children under two and a half years — think what that must have been to cope with! Fortunately the hotel and beach were doing well and the Farmers were soon able to engage a fully trained Nannie. Nannie was known as Nurse Harper and she stayed with the family for some years, which was just as well, for in January 1927, Graham and Winnie's fourth and last child was born — a girl, Lorna.

From the beginning Tolcarne Hotel was a great success. Graham's first major innovation was the creation of the ballroom with maple floor. It was the first proper ballroom in Newquay — even the Headland did not get its famous silver and black ballroom with its sprung floor until the early 1930s. Bettye remembers as a small child going to the opening of the Tolcarne Hotel ballroom: it was a big social event in Newquay in the summer of 1924. The ballroom enabled Graham to advertise nightly dancing to a "London Resident Orchestra" with Cabaret Artistes. Of course, soon the other hotels followed and by the late thirties many of the hotels had ballrooms or at least "dance rooms", meaning a room where one could dance! But Tolcarne led the way, and in Graham Farmer's day the Tolcarne ballroom was very stylish; and certainly the dances were the liveliest and most popular in the town. In fact it was the only 'ballroom' and there was no public dance hall.

THE MAGNIFICENT NEW BALLROOM
AT THE TOLCARNE HOTEL
A SWIMMING POOL will be built at the end of this ballroom

Ballroom, 1932, with exotic new decoration.

By the mid twenties Tolcarne was without doubt the leading hotel of its type in Newquay, possibly in Cornwall, but it had one drawback. There was no space for a garage and in those early motoring days provision of a garage for cars was very important; almost as important as private bathrooms were to become. Motors simply did not stand out in the open as they do now.

In 1924 Graham managed to acquire a substantial plot of land immediately behind the hotel and build two large garages that would hold some thirty or forty cars. He installed petrol pumps and inspection pits, all very important, and advertised them as amenities of the hotel. Again, Tolcarne was the first to offer these facilities.

Graham and his family were still living in Clifton Villa, in Cliff Road. The plot of land behind the hotel had frontage on to Edgcumbe Gardens and there, behind the garages, he built 8 and 10 Edgcumbe Gardens, two semi-detached, four bedroom houses, each with a garage. His wife and family moved into one, which they called "Tolcarne Lodge", and his recently widowed mother, Eliza Farmer, rented the other as a holiday home for the summer holidays. She decided to call hers "Cheam", as at that time her Surrey house was in Cheam and she thought by so doing she would not have to have her linen re-marked! She still retained her comfortable house in Surrey, to which most of the family returned for much of the winter. The seasons in Newquay were still very short, roughly from mid June to mid September, and the winters were long and dreary and to be avoided if possible — or so the family thought! The Tolcarne Hotel and the beach were going great guns. Graham leased land from The Great Western Railway and built a row of five shops beside the station. He called it Station Parade and rented the shops to stable, long-term tenants. It seemed that everything Graham Farmer touched turned to gold and his family and others watched his success with fascination.

In the 1920s Tolcarne Hotel was the leading holiday hotel and the rest of Newquay was following. In 1926 Graham bought an hotel boat; a 15ft clinker built craft painted red, white and blue, with an outboard motor. She was called *Brighter Newquay*. He engaged a young, attractive, well educated, entertainment hostess for the hotel who arranged bridge, tennis and ping-pong, etc. She was given a single room and a table in the dining room but was paid only £1.00 per week. Weekly ping-pong tournaments were held with a silver cup for the winner. Soon they were copied by many Newquay hotels — in fact some hotels are still running them seventy years later! Today, of course, it is known as table tennis.

From the outset Graham Farmer seemed to be having it all his own way but soon he was to have serious competition. In 1927 Mr and Mrs Howard Young arrived in Newquay and took over Newquay College on Narrowcliff. They rented the school from Dr. Parker, the owner and Principal, for £300 per annum with an option to buy it for £6,000. They converted the school into a forty-bedroom hotel and called it The Hotel Bristol, and it was not to be long before they would be giving Graham Farmer at Tolcarne a run for his money.

In the 1920s and 1930s tourism in Newquay was gathering pace: in September 1928 the old canvas Cosy Nook Theatre on Towan Beach was dismantled for the last time and during the winter of 1928-1929 the new Cosy Nook Theatre was built on the same site. It seated three hundred and eighty people and there was a Gala opening on 9th July 1929 with an invited audience of local "nobs and dignitaries" — all dressed "to the nines".

New Cosy Nook, 1933 (opened in 1929). – *Cornwall Studies Library.*

Opening night of Cosy Nook Theatre on Towan Beach, 9th July 1929.

Note. Some well known locals include:- 1st row centre block left Mr and Mrs Knight and their daughter, Joan – Beachcroft Hotel; Mr and Mrs Thompson Philpotts – Towan Blystra; Mrs Borland – Lisbon House. 3rd row centre block from left Mr and Mrs E.M. Trembath – Town Clerk later Publicity Officer. Immediately behind Mrs Trembath is Auntie Min's daughter, Sue Hardwick; next to her, on the aisle, is Arnold Pearce later the family builder, 5th row left hand block Mr and Mrs Buller Knight and Ivy Knight – Trebarwith Hotel. 9th row centre block right aisle Carl Walters – Newquay Council Surveyor.

In the early 1930s Graham took out a three year lease on the new Cosy Nook Theatre where he arranged first class concert parties. The artistes came every season for several years and were welcomed by the locals as celebrities. Of course, Graham hob-nobbed with them; he was a showman and while he was the lessee of the Cosy Nook he was constantly entertaining the theatrical folk he booked for the summer shows. There were some well-known names, Naunton Wayne, Bert Brownbill are two that come to mind, and there were others. In their contracts was a clause binding them to weekly cabarets at Tolcarne Hotel. That gave the hotel a boost, but it didn't do Graham any good. There was too much partying, usually at his expense. At Tolcarne in those days, champagne was offered at 11.00 a.m. to anyone who cared to blow in and of course people sponged on him. Soon he was surrounded by sycophants and hangers on and was drinking too much. Sadly later that was to get him into serious trouble but in the early 1930s Graham was just a popular and successful fellow and life was one long party, but marital difficulties were looming.

In 1930 the roofs of the Tolcarne Hotel and the adjoining Oxford House were ripped off and a third storey with a flat roof was added. The hotel, in the middle of Narrowcliff sea front, then had fifty bedrooms, catered for one hundred guests and towered above its neighbours on either side, which were of course still just small double fronted private hotels. There was no planning authority in those days and the new Tolcarne dominated Narrowcliff, but not for long. In the next couple of years St Brannocks and Penolver, on either side of Tolcarne, copied Graham and squared up their roofs and added an extra storey. Gradually most of the other hotels followed and soon Narrowcliff became the row of flat-roofed, four storey box-like buildings it eventually became.

All through the 1920s and early 1930s Graham Farmer was Newquay's Golden Boy. Where he led Newquay followed and he is still remembered by older residents as "the man who put Newquay on the map." He enjoyed a flamboyant lifestyle with a large car bearing his insignia on the side and a chauffeur.

"THE MAN WHO PUT NEWQUAY ON THE MAP."

and who set it all going, family-wise!

He and Winnie lived very comfortably with a cook, trained nanny and other help. In the autumns they travelled abroad spending holidays in the South of France and several times they cruised on the *Arrandora Star*, Cunard's flagship at the time, always first class, of course! But sadly they were not really getting on and even in those days drink was becoming a problem. When they returned Winnie would often say the holiday had been marred by Graham's drinking and behaviour.

Graham Farmer's grand days.

Graham applied several times for a liquor licence for Tolcarne Hotel but his applications were refused. At that time there were only about six large licensed hotels in Newquay and about the same number of public houses. All the other hotels, including those on Narrowcliff, were unlicensed and there were no licensed restaurants in the town. The drink laws in this country have always lagged a long way behind those in Europe, and before the Second World War they were archaic.

In the early 1930s Graham and Tom Farmer still had good incomes from Tolcarne Beach, but they were both drinking too much. Graham, who had already borrowed from his mother, was always trying to raise more money and his financial problems were becoming bothersome — but he was still full of big and bright ideas for the Tolcarne Hotel. In 1932 he was advertising a swimming pool on the roof of the hotel — that would certainly have been quite something in the thirties. There wasn't to be a pool of any sort in Newquay for at least another thirty years. But it was just talk; he was beginning to lose his grip — too much frivolling!

In the meantime the Young family at the Hotel Bristol were flourishing and catching up fast. In 1932 they bought the car park adjoining the hotel, which had been the site of the original Hotel Edgcumbe, from the local council for £3,500, and extended the Bristol on to it. Hotel Bristol then had one hundred bedrooms and interestingly only three had private bathrooms. The dining room was magnificent. They also managed to obtain a liquor licence which really was a feather in their cap. Graham Farmer had led the way for ten years but as his star began to wane Mr and Mrs Howard Young's was undoubtedly in the ascendancy and their day was coming.

By 1934 Graham, Tolcarne Hotel, and the Beach were seemingly still on the crest of a wave but beneath the surface there were sounds

pages ten and eleven

Est. 1920 TOLCARNE HOTEL Extended 1930

TOLCARNE is essentially
the LEADING EARLY
HOLIDAY HOTEL

Book Early !

POPULAR INCLUSIVE "ALL-IN"
TERMS
from
MARCH-MAY
3 gns. per week, 10/6 per day
JUNE
3½ gns. per week, 11/6 per day
JULY
4½ gns. per week, 15/- per day
AUGUST
5 gns. per week, 16/6 per day
SEPTEMBER
3½ gns. per week, 11/6 per day
OCTOBER
3 gns, per week, 10/6 per day

Tolcarne is the premier Motorists' Hotel on the Narrowcliff Sea - Front, having PRIVATE GARAGE. Garage in the Hotel Grounds for 50 Cars, FREE to guests except during the high season. Petrol Pump. Hotel Mechanic etc.

DAY AND NIGHT SERVICE

Illustrated Tariff Booklet - Apply MANAGER

Sole Founder and Proprietor
G. Graham-Farmer

Advertisement from Town Guide 1932 – and the first talk of a swimming pool. In fact, the first swimming pool in Newquay was opened in 1960!

Graham Farmer and his sons, circa 1934.

of ominous rumblings and he ignored them. He put his head in the sand and opened another bottle. Success takes its toll and needs handling. Graham Farmer's success had come quickly and overwhelmingly and he had tried to go too fast. As time went by he and Winnie became utterly incompatible, in fact, openly hostile to each other. He was gregarious; an extrovert who liked to entertain and have parties and she, with four young children, preferred a quiet well ordered home life with her family. For Graham the money had rolled in too easily and there were too many parties, pretty girls and other distractions. Tolcarne and the Beach were flourishing, but he was "playing about" and he began neglecting his family and businesses.

Unhappy at home, he spent too much time in the pubs. His marriage was crumbling, and his creditors began to hound him. He was always borrowing more money from everyone and anyone; the bank, his relations, his in-laws and others. It is very easy to borrow money for an obviously successful venture but it has to be repaid plus interest. Later as he got into deeper water the people from whom he had borrowed, notably the bank, clamoured for their money back. Then he began robbing Peter to pay Paul and that is a highly dangerous game.

His behaviour was greatly upsetting his family and poor Winnie, a really conscientious mother, was having a dreadful time with her four young children to look after and creditors constantly banging at the door. By the end of 1934 she could stand no more. She left him and moved with the children into a bungalow in Eliot Gardens, Newquay.

Graham was devastated at the loss of his children. He loved them dearly — but what did he do? He opened another bottle and had another party.

The final blow for Graham Farmer came in 1936. The bank wanted their money back and threatened to foreclose. This was a catastrophic blow and was only averted by Graham's in-laws bailing him out and putting money into Tolcarne and Winnie, with great reluctance, agreeing to move back into the hotel and take over. Poor Winnie, it was very hard on her. Their four children were aged nine to thirteen years old. The bank barred Graham from ever setting foot in the hotel again. He had lost everything, his wife, family, the beach, the hotel, and his other businesses. He was homeless. His reign was over. He was only forty-three years old.

Graham was overwhelmed by despair and all his "fine weather" friends deserted him. He was utterly alone and then he made what was perhaps his biggest mistake of all — he turned to the bottle for solace and so began the slippery slide into dipsomania.[1] His was a sad story of triumph and disaster in just fifteen years. Between 1921 and 1936 Graham Farmer had made and lost a fortune. How could it be that he was effectively down and out in 1936?

He had made three fatal mistakes during his successful years, apart from the drink. He borrowed too much money, did not give the business enough attention, and he tried to go too fast. It is one thing to have bright ideas but a business will not run itself. It has to be managed properly and he turned his back on it and left it to others to cope. All the time he was borrowing, borrowing, borrowing — and as he got into deeper water everybody wanted their money back. By 1936 the party was over and the bubble had finally burst. It was a tragedy of the first order.

There was one other deep, underlying cause which brought about Graham's downfall; his unhappy marriage and home life. Certainly he had been cruelly inconsiderate to his wife in the early days of the marriage when she was young and inexperienced, but as she matured Winnie became a capable, strong woman with many talents, but she was difficult and very bitter. She had never wanted an hotel, or Newquay, and she held the move to Cornwall against Graham for the rest of their lives. If they could only have worked together and she could have helped him, the story might have been very different.

---

[1] For the uninitiated, a dipsomaniac is one who goes into violent drinking bouts that go on for days and in which the drinker becomes quite paralytic. These bouts are interspersed with periods of complete abstention from drink. Some people manage to overcome it and the price to be paid is that never, never must they have another drink or they risk it all happening again. Poor Graham never managed to conquer it until, in his old age, he had a stroke, and then it was too late.

Poor Graham, how foolish he had been. By 1937 he was virtually penniless and his standard of living slowly deteriorated as the years went by. At first he stayed at The Nare Hotel, Veryan, for six months. The second winter he lived at Falmouth Hydro on the sea front. His sister, Olive, who had a deep affection for him, sometimes invited him to stay with her for long periods — as long as he remained sober! Sadly, his visits always ended in disaster when he fell off the wagon once again and had to go to be dried out. His situation was hopeless. He was forever trying to raise money. In the early days he sold his personal possessions one by one; first his gold cigarette case, then his Gold Benson pocket watch and chain. He sold a large diamond ring for just £10, and finally his gold ring was sold. He had lost everything and he drifted in and out of lodgings and hospitals for the next twenty years. He was to be a tortured soul for the rest of his life and became obsessed with the idea that everyone had done him down. Today, no doubt, he could, and would, have claimed all kinds of benefits but in the 1930s there was no Welfare State to provide for failures and drop outs. There was the dole, which was fifteen shillings per week (75p), but for which Graham Farmer was not eligible as he had never been officially employed, and there was a state pension of ten shillings (50p) weekly from the age of sixty five years, but he was still in his early forties.

Tolcarne Hotel in 1936.

1936-1945
Tolcarne Hotel under Winnie Farmer

When Graham was officially banished from the hotel by the bank in 1936, his wife, under pressure, took over the running of it — poor dear, she had no choice! She and their four children had to move back into the hotel because "Tolcarne Lodge" and "Cheam" were no longer available. Tolcarne Lodge had become the hotel annexe and the rooms were booked and Cheam had been sold. In the summers Winnie and her daughter Lorna shared a small hot back first floor room with bunk beds over the kitchen in the hotel, and the three boys squashed into a ground floor room in the annexe. For the long summer holidays they were packed off to stay with their maternal Grannie in Leicester. Life was very difficult for all of them. Imagine running a fifty bedroom hotel and living in a couple of rooms in the corner with four school children — no easy task. The seasons in those days were still very short and the winters long and uncomfortable for there is little comfort to be found in a large north facing hotel, without heating, on the cliffs when it is closed. Fortunately Winnie had a good loyal aide, Miss Grigg, who gave her unfailing support for years.

Although Winnie lacked Graham's flair she had other talents. She was good at figures and paperwork; she worked hard and coped with it all well and under her the hotel flourished. She was attractive, personable, extremely well dressed and greatly to her credit she kept the hotel going successfully, until the outbreak of war, although she would have much preferred not to have had to take it on. It is not really surprising that when the war was over she had no wish to resume such a life style. It could not have been foreseen how different life for all of them would have been had she done so.

Meanwhile up the road the Hotel Bristol was going from strength to strength. By the mid-thirties they were arranging cricket matches, beach sports, picnics at Treyarnon Bay — all with cream teas. There were weekly tennis tournaments at Trenance. Ralph Hunt and his five piece orchestra played in the dining room for luncheon and dinner and in the evenings it was all black ties, long dresses and dancing. By the late '30s the Bristol had overtaken Tolcarne as Newquay's leading hotel, notwithstanding the stuffy four star Headland. The Hotel Bristol was destined for even greater success after the war as the reader will hear.

When the war broke out in 1939 Winnie's three sons quickly went into the RAF straight from school. Graham Farmer was called up, and during the war he 'floated' in and out of various war-time jobs. He went first into the Catering Corps in the Army as a Private and later into the Air Force. At one time he was in charge of a Government run British Restaurant, but nothing lasted very long. His affliction was upon him — drink.

The 1940 season did not materialise, which was disastrous for everyone. Winnie Farmer was much relieved when Tolcarne Hotel was requisitioned by the Ministry of Defence in 1941. They paid £500 per annum rent for it and for the duration of the war the building was used as a billet for soldiers. All the hotel furniture, carpets and chattels were moved into a store in Crantock Street and she and Lorna, aged fifteen, were given just forty-eight hours notice to move out with all their personal belongings. Winnie was an orderly soul and to her it was a nightmare, but she managed to rent an unfurnished house, 25 Edgcumbe Avenue, and moved in a great rush. She lived there throughout the war and for some years beyond.

With the war over, in 1945 Tolcarne Hotel was de-requisitioned badly knocked about and with graffiti on many walls. It was in a most dilapidated state. The war office paid £5,000 compensation for the damage. Poor Winnie Farmer then had to make a very difficult decision. Should she take it on again or should she put it on the market? She was embittered and difficult and did not feel she could work with her children. Fifty years later perhaps it can be said she made the mistake of her life and therefore deprived her family of what surely would have been a prosperous future, but the reader can be assured it was not as straight forward as it now seems.

When all the hotels in Newquay were de-requisitioned suddenly in July 1945, it was a nightmare for the proprietors. Many of the buildings had been used as barracks for the troops for four years and as can be imagined they had been badly damaged, in fact, vandalised. Some had become just battered empty shells. When the furniture and all the chattels were brought back they were dumped in heaps in the various rooms — with woollen carpets and blankets all riddled with moth. It is no wonder that so many of the pre-war owners felt unable to face the task of getting going again. It was to be a mammoth undertaking: nothing could be replaced properly, even tea towels and furniture were "on coupons" and there was very little labour to be found.

Winnie Farmer had no-one to help her get the hotel back into good order; her children were not quite old enough. Her own family, the Brooks, and her brother-in-law, Frankie Franklin, a successful accountant, had all put money into Tolcarne Hotel ten years before to save it from bankruptcy. They now wanted their money back and were advising her, indeed, pressing her, to sell although they were affluent and not in urgent need of the money. Perhaps most significantly of all, nobody at that time realised what a terrific boom Newquay was about to enjoy for the next thirty years. The seasons were to be entirely different; much longer and busier; in fact the town faced a complete metamorphosis.

Winnie's decision to sell was catastrophic for her family's finances. The capital was scattered and the Farmers came out of it with very little money but she was by no means the only hotelier in Newquay who made that mistake. In 1945 Tolcarne was sold for £25,000 and the new owners claimed the £5,000 compensation paid by the War Department. Winnie could not have known that within a couple of years it would have been worth much more than double that sum. After the sale, when the debts had all been paid, there was little money left for anybody.

Poor Winnie, she was to be comparatively poor for the rest of her life; she had to take a job and earn her living, which was surely hard. For years she held a responsible position with a London firm and when she retired she returned to Newquay and lived very modestly in a bungalow at Porth. Aged eighty-five she moved to a residential home in Chobham and her bungalow had to be sold to pay the fees; it fetched £38,000. She lived in the home for five years and died when she was ninety; and her capital had almost all been spent on the home fees, and once again her children were deprived of even that small legacy. Life had not been kind to Winnie but she was a dedicated mother and her family all turned out well. She was justifiably proud of them. The tragedy was she never seemed to realise what a difference a little family cooperation would have made to all their lives. It is very sad to reflect that although Graham had given his family such a hard time while they were growing up, he had created a potentially valuable business which would have set them all up for life. It was Winnie who ultimately denied them their birthright by selling Tolcarne in 1945 — a tragic story indeed.

Winnie Farmer, circa 1938.

The Farmer Children

The Farmer children's childhood was a roller coaster ride blighted by their father's erratic life style. Although their mother remained steadfast while they were growing up it was she who ultimately decided to sell the Tolcarne Hotel after Second World War and so denied them the right to take it on. The hotel would have given them all a start in life. As it was they had to make their own way. However, greatly to their credit, they all made stable lives for themselves and enjoyed successful long-term marriages.

John Farmer's life was virtually wrecked by his wartime injuries. He had joined the Royal Air Force after a short spell in a civilian job in London. He was a handsome young Pilot Officer, a Battle of Britain fighter pilot. He married his childhood sweetheart, Dulcie Mallet, the daughter of a well-known Newquay family, in 1942 before he was twenty-one, and their only child, Julie, was born in January, 1944.

John was shot down in his Spitfire in 1943 when he was twenty-one. He bailed out but the wires of his parachute wound tightly around his left arm and destroyed the nerves so that gradually the arm withered. He also suffered head and eye injuries from which he never recovered; his eyes never focused properly again. He had a disability pension for the rest of his life.

Gradually over the years his injuries caused a slow deterioration and his health declined. He became an old man before his time. His wife was devoted to him. She was caring and supportive and spent her life looking after him and it was a tragedy that she died before him. He then lived in an RAF Residential Home for his last five years, and he died there in early 1992, aged seventy. His war injuries had virtually killed him fifty years later.

Bobby and Tony, Winnie's younger twin sons, went into the Royal Air Force straight from school at the age of sixteen as boy apprentices. They were only twenty-one when Tolcarne was being de-requisitioned and both were posted overseas at the time.

The twins stayed in the RAF after the war and both served a further thirty years. Bobby was attached to a bomb disposal unit and he married Marie Walters, from Norfolk, in 1951. They bought a house in Norwich near her parents where they lived until he died in September 2000. They enjoyed service life in the RAF. Bobby retired as Squadron Leader in 1978 when he became Managing Clerk to a Norfolk firm of Solicitors where he worked until he finally retired in 1993. They had two children, Sue and David.

Tony, Bobby's twin brother, served in the Pay Master General's Department. He married Beryl Walden, from Coombe Martin, in

1950, and when he retired from the RAF as Warrant Officer in 1974 he took up an appointment in the accounts office of the Hospital Service in Oxford until he finally retired in 1989. Tony and Beryl bought a house at Carterton, near Oxford, which they called "Trelawney" where they still live. They have a son, Nicholas, and a daughter, Sarah, both unmarried.

Towards the end of the war Graham and Winnie's daughter, Lorna, was just old enough to join the WRENS. She loved it! After a spell as an hotel receptionist she joined BOAC as an Air Hostess — in the days when they really were Air Hostesses! She married Peter Bicknell, a BOAC Steward, in 1957. They were then both in British Airways for many years; he eventually became a Director of Cabin Services and Lorna became a 'Ground Auntie' — looking after unaccompanied children at Heathrow. When they retired Peter became flats manager at Dolphin Square, London, where he had a second successful career for some twelve years.

Now the Bicknells have an enviable 'perk' for life: heavily discounted worldwide travel with British Airways. Jolly well merited, too! They had three sons, John, Richard, and Peter. John and Richard are doing well, but Peter, the youngest, who suffered from severe bipola disorder and realised he had no future — he took his own life in February 2007. Really it was an act of great courage. But his going has left a gap in Peter and Lorna's lives which can never be filled.

Graham and Winnie Farmer's surviving children, Tony and Lorna, are both now enjoying a well earned retirement, although less affluent than they might have been. Individually they have made a success of their lives in spite of the ups and downs of their childhood — after all, money is not everything!

Tolcarne Beach under the Farmer Brothers 1922 – 1936

Graham Farmer had flair, foresight and business acumen in full measure and in 1922 he and his younger brother, Tom, managed to negotiate a fourteen year lease for Crigga Beach with Sir Robert Edgcumbe, at a rent of £52.00 per annum. The beach was just an undeveloped stretch of sand with natural grassy terraces under the cliff at the eastern end with only a few bathing machines and one or two private tents in the summer. For many years locals had enjoyed bathing and picnicking there. It was immediately below the new Tolcarne Hotel on Narrowcliff.

The beach was renamed "Tolcarne" and the success of Tolcarne Hotel and Beach and was to go hand in hand all through the 1920s and beyond. Narrowcliff quickly became the *Promenade des Anglais* of Newquay and by the early 1930s the town's smartest hotels were established there. They were Hotel Bristol, Bella Vista, Cliffdene, Marina, St Brannocks, Tolcarne, Penolver, Beresford and Runnymede, and on the cliff edge opposite was Trenarren.[1]

1920 Family picnic on grassy slope at back of Tolcarne Beach (then known as Crigga Beach) with Bettye and Peter, aged nine months.

1 A list of these hotels, their owners and what happened to them is to be found at the end of the book.

WHERE TO STAY AT NEWQUAY.

Finest, Safest and most Select Bathing in England.

TOLCARNE Beach

Season 1922. NEWQUAY.

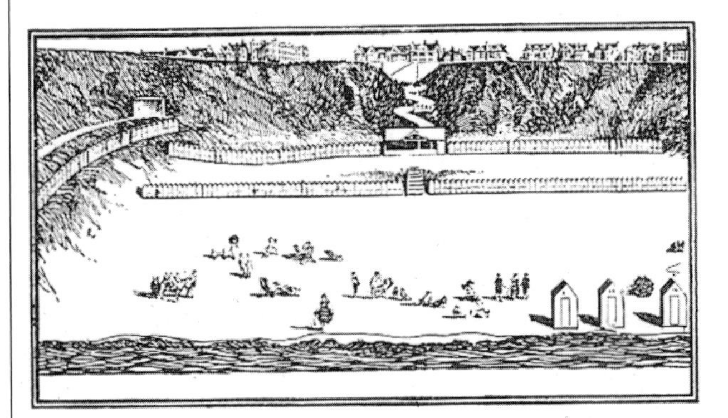

Where the Visitors Bathe.

WRITE NOW and reserve your Family Bathing Tent (fitted with Deck Chairs, etc.) on these Sands.

Sole Proprietors—
FARMER BROS.

Overlooking the centre of this Beach.

TOLCARNE Private HOTEL

Finest English Catering only. Newly Decorated and Furnished. Golf, Tennis, Dancing, Boating, ∴ ∴ Picnics, etc. ∴ ∴

Special Early Season Terms from 3 gns.

Write: PROPRIETRESS.

In 1922 Graham Farmer was advertising the Tolcarne Beach as the safest and most select in England, and he was offering dancing in his 'Private Hotel', at that time unheard of.

Before long a wooden beach shop and a large café, known as the Pop Café, were built from which tea trays, lunches and soft drinks were available. Adjoining the Beach Shop was a homely little booking office presided over by Miss Thomas, a pleasant, middle-aged spinster. She sat facing the door at a wooden table with the front covered by a huge Union Jack and on the wall beside her was a large booking chart for all the huts and tents, which increased in number every year.

Tolcarne Beach Shop with Susie James and her cousin in charge. The door on the right is Miss Thomas's office where the children hid under her desk, which was a table draped with the Union Jack, when they played hide and seek.

Miss Thomas loved children and she was their friend. Under her Union Jack was a favourite hiding place when they played hide and seek — she did not mind a bit. She was also the cashier and all money had to be paid in to her office at the end of every day. Where it went after that is anybody's guess! The Farmer brothers built beach huts on

Narrowcliff circa 1922. From the right, Runnymede, offering the all-important 'garages', Beresford, Penolver Private Hotel, Tolcarne Private Hotel, St Brannocks, where the Whittingtons had stayed in 1919, Marina, Cliffdene (a private house), Nagajanka and Bella Vista. – *Cornish Studies Library.*

John Farmer and Nanny on Tolcarne Beach 1923. Note Queenie's summer stable on the grass at the far right of the picture.

the natural terraces and erected tents on the beach. There was a sturdy chestnut pony called Queenie, who lived in a stable on a grassy bank under the cliff for the summers. Queenie pulled the wooden bathing machines up and down to the water each day according to the tides. Visitors paid 6d. (2p) to undress in them, and leave their clothes in them while they bathed. It was unthinkable in those early days that bathers would walk down to the beach uncovered. The smarter hotels on Narrowcliff offered 'Bathing direct from the hotel' and often one would see bathers making for the beach in their robes or Mackintoshes and paddling shoes, with a towel over their arm, going for their daily swim straight from their hotel bedrooms.

The Farmers also hired out deck chairs, and Queenie pulled a wooden wheeled flat trolley around the beach every morning setting them out and later, when people were sitting in them, the beach man would tour the beach collecting the money and issuing tickets. In the evening Queenie would collect the chairs to be stored at night under a green canvas sheet in the middle of the beach. Happy, carefree days when one did not have to carry one's own chair, long before self-service was introduced.

Queenie, with the Farmer boys up.

There were three beach donkeys called Pip, Squeak and Wilfred to give the children rides on the sands. They grazed on the grassy banks around Queenie's stable in the summer and they, and Queenie, had winter quarters at Quintrell Downs where they were looked after by Jack Sparkes, the long-term Beach Foreman.

Tom Farmer was never really an active partner. He was not very bright and left it all to brother Graham. He did little apart from taking the money to the bank occasionally, and then retiring to the pub.

The Summer Theatre above Tolcarne Beach. A small family show called the "Bix Six" came for many years. In the early 1930s 'The White Notes' took over, starring Albert H Grant and Harry Huston, for whom a wealthy Newquay spinster built the New Theatre on Narrowcliff, circa 1935. – *Cornish Studies Library.*

In 1923 the Summer Theatre was built on the site of an old quarry on the path down to the beach. It was a simple wooden building, really little more than a large hut with SUMMER THEATRE painted in large white letters right across its sloping roof. Below the Summer Theatre was a small group of privately owned huts. The land, natural grassy terraces, belonged to the Council and they charged a nominal rent for the sites. A handful of local families erected their own huts, each quite individual; some small and some large. The owners formed a regular summer colony and year after year there was a

Harry Huston from The White Notes of the New Theatre, and friends.

gathering of friends and many life long friendships were forged during those happy beach days.

There always seemed to be a great deal of activity on the beach in the late twenties. The bright young things of the day brought their ukuleles with gaily coloured ribbons tied to the keys and sat on the sand in groups strumming away and singing wordy little songs. History was to repeat itself forty years later when, in the sixties, the young brought their guitars to the beach and sat in groups on the sand and twanged happily, although the second time round it seemed not quite so socially agreeable — it was louder! and the whole scene was more crowded and noisier with radios blaring in competition with the guitars — not quite the same tranquil atmosphere!

John Staffieri, "Johnnie Ice Cream" as he was known, would drive across the beach at low tide with his pony and little cream and green cart, with four shiny brass barley sugar twist poles at each corner which held a canopy to shield him from the sun. He would sell ice creams to all and sundry and the children would crowd around him clutching their pennies. He was their friend and is remembered with affection by generations of children. It was proper vanilla home made ice cream — vanilla cornets for 1d. and wafers for 2d., or a really large one was 3d. — a far cry from today's factory made frozen confections.

Johnnie Ice Cream with his usual queue of children.

In the 1920s the favourite beach game was hockey. It was serious hockey with good players and a hard ball — at low tide of course, and in those days there was space, plenty of space. Later beach cricket with a soft ball was the great thing and there were regular weekly inter-hotel cricket matches with rows of deckchairs laid out for the spectators, much enjoyed by everybody.

Giant push ball with the Farmer boys.

Surfing began to be popular in the late twenties and young and old took to it. Almost everyone had their surfboard — a lightweight plywood plank about ten inches wide and four feet long and there are still older regular visitors to Cornwall who arrive every year with their original surf boards — known these days as belly boards. In fact, there is still one in the family — it occasionally gets an airing!

Graham also had a giant push ball on the beach, six feet in diameter, boldly emblazoned with the "Tolcarne Hotel" — surely an early forerunner to the hot air balloons used for advertising today? He installed a little wooden switchback ride in the middle of the beach for the children, which cost 2d. (less than 1p) a go!

The Farmers gradually erected more and more huts on the grassy banks at the east side of the beach. In front of them on the sand was a long row of tents, eventually nearly two hundred of them, some with gaily coloured tops no doubt copied from Graham's autumn holidays on the beaches in the South of France.

There was one character who was always on the beach in the 1930s during the high season. He was a solicitor in his fifties or sixties who lived in Plymouth and had a holiday house in Newquay. He had short grey grizzled hair and a tidy grey beard and he always wore long grey flannel shorts which came below his knees. Every day he would arrive early and set up his 'Tenniquoit' net on the dry sand and then he would scour the beach for young people to play tenniquoits with him — often three or four a side. He was affectionately known among the local young as 'old man Jago'. They, of course, were much too busy with their own activities — surfing, rock climbing, fishing, playing hide and seek or just lazing on the warm dry sand talking, but there was much giggling among the girls about 'old man Jago' being after them. In fact he was a dear old boy who just loved tenniquoits and young people.

NEWQUAY — Official Booking Form For . . **RESERVING IN ADVANCE**

BATHING TENTS AND LOCK UP HUTS

ON THE

TOLCARNE BEACH

Proprietors and Lessees:
GRAHAM FARMER. THOS. FARMER.

(Patronized by Royalty and Society).

No holiday at Newquay is complete without YOUR OWN FAMILY TENT or LOCK UP HUT on these famous sands with its Selectness and absolute SAFETY BATHING. Each Tent and Hut is furnished with **2 Deck Chairs, Mirror, Footbath,** and **includes Attendance.**

Bathing Costumes, Towels, etc., may always be left in the Tents or Huts. Attendants on duty day and night.

200 Tents.

50 Lock up Huts.

60 Bathing Machines.

1000 Deck Chairs.

Donkey Rides.

BOOK EARLY.

Refreshment Pavilion.

ORCHESTRA.

Chocolates.

Teas.

Cigarettes.

BOOK EARLY.

TOLCARNE BEACH—NEWQUAY'S BATHING RENDEZVOUS.

TERMS PER WEEK.

Inclusive for Bathing Tent, 2 Deck Chairs, Mirror, Footbath and Attendance.

(For the exclusive use of not more than 4 persons)

	Front Row.	Bank Row.		Front Row.	Bank Row.
MAY and JUNE	10/-	—	AUGUST	25/-	—
JULY	15/-	12/6	SEPT. 4th—30th	15/-	10/-

Terms per Week for LOCK UP HUTS.

JUNE ... 15/- JULY ... 20/- AUGUST ... 35/- SEPTEMBER ... 20/-

No Tent or Hut will be reserved without remittance or deposit of 50%.

During AUGUST TENTS and HUTS will only be reserved on receipt of FULL PAYMENT.

By the late 1920s Graham Farmer was offering 200 tents, 50 lock-up huts, 60 bathing machines, 1,000 deck chairs, and donkey rides. What progress!

In the thirties the first stage of surfing's development as a serious sport began. Until then it had been nothing more than a simple little bathing past-time, but surfing has come a long way in the last sixty years. In 1934 a young Australian, Alan Secombe, arrived on Tolcarne Beach with a new type of surf board. It was made of very thick, firm rubber about twenty-one inches wide and thirty inches long and was called a Surf-O-Plane. It became immensely popular, although many older surfers stuck to their old fashioned boards. Every year until the Second World War Alan was on the beach hiring out his Surf-O-Planes. He must have had about two hundred of them. The young local bucks became very skilful on them and would wait for big seas when the tide was in so they could show off and impress the visitors, especially the girls, with their prowess — and they sometimes surfed in mountainous seas. How the holiday makers enjoyed their displays; they would gather on the shore at high tide to watch. There were no wet suits in those days and no red flags or professional lifeguards with loud speakers telling people when and where they could bathe, and the author has no memory of drownings,

John Murray, the life guard, with a pile of Surf-O-Planes.

Jean Young (Hotel Bristol), Rona Marshall and a friend, with their surf boards circa 1930.

Surfers – note the old surf boards and the Surf-O-Planes.

no-one seemed to get into difficulties and the spectators loved it. Neither were there security guards or dogs to ensure folk didn't go on the beach after dark. Oh what fun the late night bathing parties were! John Murray, Bettye's, and Peter's life long friend, was for some four years before the war the "Beach Boy" in charge of the Surf-o-Planes. He was also one of the lifeguards, although in those free and easy days it was only an honorary, glamorous title, which was just as well for John really couldn't swim! What a figure he cut, how the girls admired him—and how he lapped it up! John died in 1998 aged eighty.

Graham Farmer outside the office on Tolcarne Beach at the height of his success.

All through the twenties and early thirties Narrowcliff, Tolcarne Beach, and Tolcarne Hotel were the fashionable places for visitors to Newquay. There was a freedom in those days which is denied us now. Dogs were welcome and there was no fuss about them. Vandalism was not a problem. Buckets and spades, surf boards, towels and bathers, etc., could safely be left in the tents overnight. The rampant petty pilfering that we all suffer today did not set in until after the war. There were rogues, of course, but in the main there seems to have been a stricter code of decency than rules now. Hotel Bristol also put on a very good show in the '30s. Not only did they have regular cricket matches there, but also beach sports for their guests with the pitch marked out and rows of deck chairs for spectators. The porters would arrive at 4.00 p.m. bearing cream teas in enormous wicker hampers for the guests. It was done with such style and the rest of the beach enjoyed the spectacle and watched enviously — and wished they were staying there!

In 1935 the Farmer brothers faced a major financial disaster. The lease on Tolcarne Beach expired, and the Edgcumbe Estate refused to renew it. They did not think Graham Farmer had been behaving at all well. Graham and Tom could not, or would not, raise the £10,000 to buy the freehold and so it was put on the market and sold to an outside private buyer, Garfield Daniel, from St Ives. The new owner offered the Farmer brothers a very fair price for the beach huts, tents and deck chairs, and all the beach paraphernalia, which they foolishly refused. Consequently all their beach goods and chattels were sold by auction on the beach in November 1935 and fetched very little, for who would want quantities of deckchairs, foot baths, tea trays, etc., in November? They were virtually given away.

It was a sad day for the Farmer brothers. For years Tom and Graham had each had a comfortable income from the beach, much of it straight into their pockets, and when that income stopped it was a dire financial blow from which neither of them ever recovered. It was but the first of Graham's serious setbacks and mounting difficulties.

Garfield Daniel already owned a very successful beach in St Ives and he really did shake Tolcarne up. He acquired the land below the Summer Theatre from the Council and built four tiered, concrete terraces with concrete cabins and concrete steps to the sands. The beach had lost its early charm in the name of progress; no longer were there huts on grassy banks with space between them — they were all crammed together cheek by jowl, but they were very popular and well booked from one year to the next, except for the war years. Wilfred Daniel, Garfield's cousin, was the long term manager. He ran the beach well and it flourished for the next forty years. Garfield Daniel later also acquired Lusty Glaze beach which was smaller and more intimate but also very successful and that was managed by another cousin, Lorna.

So much for Tolcarne Beach pre the Second World War.

Edgcumbe Private Hotel, Edgcumbe Avenue 1926 – 1936

In the early 1920s, while Graham seemed to be going from strength to strength with his projects in Newquay, his sister, Olive Whittington, was in London wrestling with her worsening marital problems. By the early summer of 1925 she had finally made up her mind she had had enough. She was essentially peace-loving and would go to extreme lengths to avoid confrontation with anyone and so she quietly made her plans. When she went to Newquay for her usual summer holiday with her children she would not return.

In July 1925 she, Bettye and Peter, with Miss Jarvis, departed for their holiday. Monty saw them off at Paddington. There were no rows or recriminations. No doubt his head was full of the lovely weekends he would be free to enjoy in Westcliffe. Little did he know he would never see his family again. In Newquay they stayed with Grannie at "Cheam", 8 Edgcumbe Gardens, and Olive simply wrote to Monty from there and told him she would not be returning. It must have been an agonising decision for her for she loved her home and it was to be several years before she, Bettye and Peter were to have a proper home of their own again.

When Olive Whittington and her children with Miss Jarvis finally left London and arrived in Newquay for good they were welcomed with open arms by the family. After a short holiday Olive helped her brothers for that one year on Tolcarne Beach, which was booming. She supervised the cream teas etc., in the cafe and the children had a glorious summer holiday on the beach — the first of many.

Tolcarne Beach – showing the hut the Whittingtons were given by Uncle Graham. Note Queenie pulling deck chairs and her stable in the top left hand of the picture.

Graham Farmer gave the Whittingtons the use of the hut nearest the private ones for the next ten years, and so Bettye and Peter had a base on the beach near their chums. They were allowed to fetch a free tea tray every day from the back door of the Pop Café. Their mother would usually join them, arriving at 4.00 p.m. after she had had her afternoon rest. For the Whittington children there was just one fly in the ointment. Olive Whittington insisted that they had to go home for lunch every day and be there by 1.00 p.m. In her view growing children had to be fed properly and sandwiches etc. would not do. Bettye and Peter would dash up the steps for lunch and be back again in forty minutes! Very occasionally they would be allowed to take a picnic and that was a treat. They envied their friends, Laurie and Dennis Francis, from the Hotel Bristol, who were also always on the beach. They brought a picnic every day — the lucky chaps! After lunch the older members of the families would arrive on the beach, bringing cream teas and saffron buns. There were always cream teas — they were part of the scene. Slimming and calorie counting was not yet fashionable!

Monty Whittington, in London, was deeply upset when he realised his family would not be returning and he begged Olive to change her mind but she would have none of it. She was absolutely firm in her resolve to remain in Cornwall. There was no financial settlement, divorce, or even legal separation. He and Olive never met again; he had lost his wife and children, and they their father. It was very sad for them all. When the marriage broke up Olive's mother cut every single photo of Monty out of the family pictures. Mrs Farmer felt strongly that her son-in-law had behaved extremely badly.

With the break up of her marriage, 1925 had been a traumatic year for Olive Whittington. She was thirty-eight years old and with great courage she had succeeded in closing the door on a life that had become quite untenable. She was very apprehensive about the future; she knew it was not going to be easy but was determined to make a life for herself and her children in Cornwall. She had brought them back to the roots of her forebears and Cornwall was to be home to them for the rest of their lives.

The move from London to Cornwall seemed to have no impact on Bettye and Peter. Olive in her wisdom gave them no explanation; at the end of the summer she simply told them they were all staying in Newquay and they would be going to school there. Their father had never given them a great deal of attention, they had a devoted mother and the loyal Miss Jarvis and they felt secure within Granny's warm family circle. Both children loved Newquay so when told they were not going back to London they were delighted - and for them that was the end of the matter.

When the 1925 season finished in September the question of life for Olive was, what next? She had two children, no home and no income, but she did have the whole-hearted moral and financial support of her mother and a well-heeled brother who was busy setting Newquay alight! As can be imagined there was much talk around the family table that summer about their future. It was finally decided that she and her younger brother, Tom, who was already a partner in the Tolcarne Beach project, should follow Graham's footsteps and go into the hotel business together. Apart from anything else by so doing Olive felt it would at least put a roof over their heads.

It was arranged that Olive and her family would live at 'Cheam' in Edgcumbe Gardens for the time being, with Miss Jarvis in charge. Next door at Tolcarne Lodge was the prosperous Farmer family. The Whittingtons were very much the poor relations and Olive felt that keenly, although Graham, then in his hey day, was very supportive. He was most generous and kind to his impoverished sister and he behaved like rich Uncle Graham with jaunts and trips to the races, etc., for Olive, and treats and presents for Bettye and Peter. He bought Bettye her first bicycle.

In September 1925 Bettye and Peter went to local schools in Newquay; Bettye to Albany, in Tolcarne Road, where the police station now stands, and Peter to a small private school for boys called Finnart, on the corner of Edgcumbe Gardens, which today is part of the Eliot-Cavendish Hotel. It was run by Mr Cresswell Payne, a well-known Cornish historian. Peter, although he was nearly seven, had not yet started school because his mother believed that too much learning was bad for small children. It taxed their brains, she thought, so Finnart was his first school — mornings only, so that he could have a rest in the afternoons!!

Olive Whittington and Tom Farmer then had a busy time in front of them searching for suitable premises for their proposed hotel. They had very little capital although Tom, a bachelor of twenty-five, had his share of the income from Tolcarne Beach. However they hoped they would be able to buy a suitable house for about £2,000 and they searched hard. They considered Larus Hotel on Porth Beach, now called Sand Piper Hotel, but thought it too far out of town. These days it would be considered too far in!

Finally the choice was between Cliffdene on Narrowcliff sea front and 4 Colchester Villas in Edgcumbe Avenue, which they were offered

4, Colchester Villas, NEWQUAY.

Superior Apartments.

Excellent Cuisine.

Large and Lofty Rooms; Bath (h. & c.). Beach and Station one minute. Good open position. Lovely scenery. Close to Tennis Courts and Bowling Green. Terms according to season.

Mrs. PENGILLY,
Proprietress.

Colchester Villas – Advert. 1922.

on rental with an option to buy, and they decided on the latter to preserve their meagre capital to build extra bedrooms on the back garden. No one could possibly have foreseen what a far reaching effect that decision was to have for Olive's family. That nine bedroom terrace house was to spawn every hotel the family has owned to this day.

4 Colchester Villas was a double fronted terrace house with nine bedrooms, five on the first floor, and four attic rooms at the top. It had three, large well proportioned reception rooms. There was a largish back garden on which they planned to build extra bedrooms. The house had been run for many years as an apartment house by Mrs Pengilly from whom they managed to rent the property, with an option to buy it later for £2,000.

They took over in the spring of 1926 and named it Edgcumbe Private Hotel. They considered that they were fortunate to be allowed to do so. As has been explained, the former large Hotel Edgcumbe on Narrowcliff, which had been destroyed by fire in August 1919, had not been re-built, and the site was being used as a car park.

Tom and Olive immediately knocked two of the reception rooms together which made a dining room seating fifty people. On the other side of the front door was a comfortable lounge. The reception office was little more than a cupboard under the stairs.

The Edgcumbe Private Hotel opened in June 1926 with one guest — a spinster, Miss Burgess. During her stay she took nine year old Bettye and six year old Peter for a cream tea at the Fernpit Tearooms on Pentire. The Fernpit Tearooms flourish today, seventy years later, run by the same Northey family, still offering splendid cream teas. What wonderful family continuity!

Tom and Olive's partnership was unbalanced from the beginning; there was no equality about it. In all partnerships, indeed in all relationships, there must be a balance and between the brother and sister there was none. Olive had two fidgety children who were no doubt tiresome; she had no income and, at that time, no proper home. She was very much the under-dog. Tom, who had always been the duffer in the family, had never had a job or worked properly and was getting too much money into his pocket from Tolcarne beach, which was going great guns. Apart from anything else he was already drinking too much and spending most of his time in the pubs and before very long that was to become a serious problem for him and those around him. So it must be said the Edgcumbe Hotel did not get off to a very auspicious start. However Olive had affection for Tom, and was essentially peace loving and they managed to get along only because of her extreme tolerance. The real trouble was to come when Tom married; then there were to be serious squalls of which more later.

The seasons in Newquay were still extremely short, only about ten weeks. Tom and Olive engaged a Manageress, Miss Worthington, a ladylike spinster of indeterminate age, tall and thin with frizzy carroty hair, who came every summer from mid-June to mid-September to run the hotel. She arrived with a huge green canvas trunk and had to be given the best single room on the first floor. To the young Bettye and Peter she was fearsome! She was professional, honest, and hard working and Olive learnt a great deal from her. She kept the catering on a very tight rein insisting that four prunes was the portion for breakfast, and when it came to roast beef the Yorkshire pudding was the size of a postage stamp! One wag wrote in the remarks column of the visitors' book, "When ordering Yorkshire pudding, ask for a small portion!" No wonder the Edgcumbe didn't exactly take off in those days! Incidentally, after the war Bettye made Miss Worthington's bedroom into a small double and it brought in a lot of money!

The Edgcumbe got going very slowly. Miss Thomas came from Tolcarne Beach daily for a couple of hours to type the letters and make out the bills and there was an old woman who cooked quite well but very plainly. She was paid £2.5s. (£2.25) for a seven day week and she was known as Cook Beavrill. The Head Waiter was paid £1.00 per week for a seven day week. No seasonal hotel worker had a day off in the twenties and thirties — or for many years to come.

In 1928 Olive and Tom decided to build the planned extra

bedrooms on the back garden and a flat roof extension was built, but that did not keep them in Newquay for the winter! They simply engaged an architect and builder, approved the plans and went back to Sutton. There were no planning or building regulations in those days but a dispute soon arose with the neighbours about ancient lights rights. The new back wing was to provide seven rooms on the first floor and five on the ground floor, one of which was to be the cook's. The ancient lights rights dispute meant the new building had to be kept so many feet back from the boundary, which of course reduced the size of the new rooms. Olive and Tom had to pay their neighbours twenty-five shillings annually (£1.25) for the privilege of having windows overlooking the adjoining back garden — all very tiresome. That annual sum was still being paid when the hotel was sold in 1958 — thirty years later!

During the winter of 1928-29 with no telephone in Sutton contact was by letters, which flew to and fro constantly. The partners did not really give the hotel much attention or take it very seriously. To them, at that time, it was just a means to an end — keeping a roof over their

R. S. RAWLINGS, F.F.A.S.,
Architect & Surveyor.

3, Acland Gardens,
Newquay, Cornwall.
Jan. 4th. 192[illegible].

Dear Mr Farmer,

I am in receipt of your letter of the 2nd inst, enclosing copy of letter received from Mr Rickard with reference to additions, at the rear of the Edgcumbe Private Hotel. You probably received mine at the same time.

I note that you will not be returning to Newquay for a few weeks, and I will therefore get Mr Clemens to sign his part of the Contract and forward to you for your signature.

I have noted your remarks with reference to the clearing out of the rooms, and I will see Mrs Whittington about this.

I see from your letter that Mr Rickard and Mr Ennor called to see you last week. (it was Mr Edward Ennor I believe). I should have thought that they would have made it their business to see me when they found that you were not at home. I have been reading up the question of light and air, but not sufficiently yet to give an opinion, and really it is a Solicitors job, as it involves all sorts of questions, and personally I think that you would be well advised if you would allow me to consult a solicitor on your behalf in connection with the matter, for advice It is also very necessary to know if Mr Rickard has any special easements of light in his Lease, and also for myself, or if you instruct a Solicitor to have a sight of your Lease, and I should be glad if you could arrange for this. As far as I can see now, and without the knowledge of any special easements which he may possess that we are quite in order, the only difficulty in my mind being the addition of the smoke room. I do not see that he can prevent you extending out at least to the extent of the present conservatory. As far as my reading of the law goes with regard to overlooking windows he cannot do anything in the matter, the only thing that he can do is to erect a screen in front of them in his own right, and that of course he is quite welcome to do as it ould effect him more than it would you.

I shall be glad to get full instructions from you with regards to this matter.

Yours faithfully,
R. S. Rawlings

T. Farmer, Esq.

Letter re ancient lights.

R. S. RAWLINGS, F.F.A.S.,
ARCHITECT & SURVEYOR.

3, ACLAND GARDENS,
NEWQUAY, CORNWALL.

August: 28th. 1928.

Thomas Farmer, Esq.
Edgcumbe Private Hotel.
Newquay.

DR TO

R.S.Rawlings.

1928.

TO PROFESSIONAL SERVICES RENDERED in measuring and preparing plans and specifications for alterations and additions to the Edgcumbe Private Hotel, submitting same in duplicate to the Newquay Urban District Council and obtaining their approval Visiting Sir Robert Edgcumbe and obtaining terms and approval. Obtaining tenders from Contractors, typing contract and including meeting to sign contract. Supervision of work during erection.
2½% of Contract price £1545. £38. 12. 6.

Re Ancient Lights question.
Jan: 9th. Consultation with Mr Strutt and yourself
Jan: 10th. Consultation at Solicitors Office in morning, on site in afternoon. Preparing plan to obviate objections.
Jan: 11th. At Hotel re above
Jan: 12th. " " " "
Jan: 13th. " " " "
Jan: 14th. At Hotel in morning. Accompanied you to Truro in afternoon to consult Messrs Coulter Hancock & Thrall.
Preparing sketches re Ancient Lights, 3. 3. 0.
Jan: 14th. At Hotel in morning re lights.
Feb: 24th. Discussing question of alteration of Bathrooms and W.C. writing you and enclosing two paper tracings. Discussing question with Mr Rickard.
Feb: 25th. Preparing extra plans re ancient lights, enlarging site plan and supplying Mr Carpmael with three copies of each, all coloured. 1. 1. 0.
Feb: 29th. Discussing question of alteration of rooms with Mr Rickard re terms. Wire to you 3/- Telegram 3/-
Mar: 1st. Saw Messrs Clemens, Rickard & Carpmael re alterations. Working on amended plans for Council.
Mar: 2nd. Working on amended drawing
Mar: 3rd. Printing and colouring amended drawings took three copies to Mr Carpmael re

Bill re building works, 1928.

heads, paying the food bills and providing a little something. Eliza Farmer's house in Sutton remained the family home.

Later when "Cheam" in Edgcumbe Gardens was sold the Whittingtons had to move into Edgcumbe Hotel, which meant "tucking away" in the summer and rattling round the cold, draughty hotel without heating in the winter. Not the most comfortable of living arrangements but there was no alternative.

By 1928 after Bettye had been at the County School at Albany in

Tolcarne Road for two years, her mother felt it was having an adverse effect on her and she was becoming wild and uncouth. (Heaven knows what Olive would have thought of the large comprehensive schools with over one thousand pupils in Newquay today!) It was then arranged for Bettye to live with her grandmother in St James Road, Sutton as there was a good girls' public day school nearby, while Peter remained at school in Cornwall looked after by Miss Jarvis. Bettye went to Sutton High School GPDST, (Girls Public Day School Trust) from September 1928 until 1933 when her grandmother died. She was an inattentive pupil and did not apply herself to her lessons. Later in life she was to regret that greatly, but at the time her mother held a firm view that children's brains must not be over-taxed, therefore she was less than encouraging about homework, etc. She need not have worried on Bettye's behalf, for never would she have overworked her brain with schoolwork! She was completely disinterested and idle about it. In school she would sit bored out of her mind, gazing out of the window dreaming of what she would do when she escaped, at times utterly oblivious to what was going on about her. She never did her homework properly and was in constant trouble about it.

Bettye was her grandmother's favourite and the arrangement worked well; she was company for Grannie, she went to a good school and it was financially helpful in view of her mother's circumstances, but it was a strange environment for a lone teenage girl. The household consisted of Grannie, a mentally disabled aunt who muttered to herself and ranted round the house at times, and Bettye. There was one live-in servant (a cook general) and a "daily woman" twice a week for cleaning. No visitors ever came to the house other than family.

At first Bettye was lonely and begged to be allowed to have a dog.

Bettye, aged 16, and Bunny.

She was given a Pekinese called Bunnie who became her constant companion and she wept when she was not allowed to take him to Cornwall for the Easter holidays — happily, he always went with her in the summer. Bunnie gave Bettye her life long love of dogs. Pekes can be turned into cushion dogs or sporting lion dogs depending how they are treated. Bettye was a tomboy and accordingly Bunnie became the most courageous lionhearted fellow. She loved him dearly.

During these years Peter stayed at school in Newquay and Miss Jarvis looked after him. They joined the family in Sutton for the whole of the Christmas holidays and very jolly Christmases they were. The large dining table was piled high with good food cooked by Daisy, the long term cook general who was an excellent cook, and as can be imagined with Tom and Graham around— the cellar was well stocked, and the liquor flowed.

Peter Whittington, Christmas circa 1932.

Bettye was always delighted when Uncle Graham arrived; he brought the party spirit with him. He would sit down at the piano and belt out all the latest tunes of the day and there would be cheery sing-songs. He taught her to do the Charleston, clutching the back of a chair. Bettye referred to him as her "Hot Uncle" (today the term would be "Cool Uncle"), and he would sometimes take a box at the Croydon Empire and treat the whole family to the current variety show. To Bettye and Peter those theatre jaunts were pure magic — they felt so posh — being chauffeur driven to the theatre they were overcome by the grandeur of it all. Even the dark interior of the theatre, all gilt and red plush with enormous chandeliers and a full orchestra in the pit was exciting and being in a box made them feel frightfully grown up and grand. No wonder Bettye loved Uncle Graham's visits! His wife seldom came with him to Sutton — things were already getting difficult between them at home.

During those Christmas holidays Olive would take her children to London for the day. They would catch an early morning train from Sutton to London Bridge — about half an hour. First they would go to Gamages in Holborn where Peter was ever keen to see the latest gadgetry, then to Bourne and Hollingsworth in Oxford Street where Olive and Bettye would have a quick look for sale bargains. Olive sometimes brought a little packed lunch on these jaunts and they would find a quiet seat in a park or nearby square and eat their picnic; sandwiches, some fruit and perhaps sweet biscuits. Then came the excitement of the Christmas show — usually a pantomime — or Peter Pan — with an ice cream in the interval. Afterwards they travelled wearily home on the train; they had had a lovely day! It mattered not that lunch was a picnic in the park in January, which was all Olive's slender resources would run to. After all children don't need the Ritz to enjoy themselves — these days what better than Burger King or McDonalds?

The Easter and summer holidays were spent in Newquay — a perfect arrangement, thought Bettye. Basically Olive and her children lived very comfortably under Grannie's financial umbrella during those difficult years.

In Newquay by the 1929 season the new rooms had been built and the Edgcumbe had twenty letting bedrooms plus one for the cook. With children's beds in the large rooms it could take about forty-five people. There was no running water in the bedrooms, the chambermaids had to carry enamel jugs of hot water to the rooms mornings and evenings, and every bedroom had a chamber pot in the bedside cupboard. There were only two bathrooms and three WCs in the building, but that was quite usual and acceptable at the time. How impossible it sounds today! For the thirteen years from 1926-1939 the Tolcarne and Edgcumbe were the two family hotels in Newquay. The Tolcarne was doing very well and the Edgcumbe just plodded along — its turn would come!

In the early 1930s the boating lake at Trenance was dug out — by hand with unpaid, voluntary labour. It was the town's first serious tourist development. Unemployed local men on the 'dole' were invited to volunteer to do the work and about twenty chaps applied. There was no compulsion about it. The Foreman was Bill Slater[1], and his son, Charles, was one of the team. They worked a five day week and although they were not paid for their toil they still drew their 'dole', which was about 15/- (75p) per week and they were given a pasty every day for lunch and half a pound of tea per week. The task took the whole winter.

---

[1] Bill Slater was Mrs Burt's grandfather, and Charles Slater was her father.`

Visit of HRH Prince of Wales during the digging out of Trenance boating lake by volunteers, 1933. – *Courtesy Newquay Old Cornwall Society.*

The Prince of Wales visited them twice during the winter, which was very important to the volunteers. What a splendid community spirit must have prevailed in those days! One cannot imagine such a scheme getting off the ground today. The boating lake was Newquay's show piece and the town was very proud of it. For the Jubilee of King George V and Queen Mary in 1935 the lake was the centre of the town's celebrations with many coloured lights and an evening water gala. It was an important leisure area and for a few years it was floodlit on summer evenings. There was even a dance hall built, called Tony's,

COUNCIL CHAMBERS,
NEWQUAY,
31st May, 1933.

THE MEMBERS of the NEWQUAY URBAN DISTRICT COUNCIL desire to place on record their appreciation of the services voluntarily rendered during the winter of 1932-33, by:

H. BARBERRY,
T. J. BRAY,
B. L. BURDEN,
W. H. CARVER,
R. COOK,
R. EARL,
W. EDWARDS,
E. ELSWORTH,
H. HOWARD,
R. MOFFATT.
F. J. NILES,
E. PASCOE,
C. PEARCE,
L. REYNOLDS,
L. ROSSI,
W. C. SLATER,
W. J. SLATER,
J. SMITH,
E. SPEAR,
C. K. STEPHENS,
R. SWEET,
K. TAMBLYN,
A. E. TREMBATH,
E. TRETHEWEY,
W. WARREN,
H. WATTERS,
H. WEBB,
G. WILTON.

in preparing the site for the TRENANCE BOATING LAKE.

Their work was honoured by the personal inspection of H.R.H. THE PRINCE OF WALES, DUKE OF CORNWALL, on the 1st of February last, and His Royal Highness in commending their efforts expressed the hope that the lake would be of benefit to the town.

EDWARD J. ENNOR, *Chairman.*
FRANCIS CARPMAEL, *Clerk.*

List of the names of the men who dug the boating lake at Trenance.

overlooking the lake which was later converted into holiday flats.

Ever since the 1930s Trenance Lake has offered self drive motor boats, rowing boats, children's paddle boats and other craft, and for generations of children when all else fails it has been "Let's go and feed the ducks at Trenance".

In 1931 Alan Cobham brought his touring air show "Cobham's Flying Circus" to Newquay in August. He landed in the field at the top of Hilgrove Road where the Medical Centre now stands. From there he offered joy rides to all and sundry. He gave 15 minute flips around the bay for 5s. (25p) a head and people queued to have a flight. Bettye and Peter Whittington were thrilled when Uncle Graham gave them a trip in the aeroplane. It was the most exciting treat of their summer holiday. Alan Cobham brought his air show to Newquay again in 1933 when they flew from Trebelzue big field. It later became part of St Mawgan Airfield. His chief girl pilot was Pauline Gower.

Alan Cobham giving 'flips' around the bay.

When Eliza Farmer died in Sutton in January 1933 aged 71 it was not completely unexpected as she had been ailing for some time, but it was the end of an era. She had been a widow for almost ten years and had maintained her large nine bedroomed house. She and her home had been the cornerstone for the whole family. Her mentally disabled younger daughter Gwen, then in her 30s, lived with her often with a paid companion or minder. Bettye lived with them during the term times and Tom Farmer, unmarried, lived at home some of the time. However when she died it emerged that for ten years Eliza Farmer had been living beyond her means. She had never seemed to realise that after her husband had died and Arthur, her eldest son, had claimed the business in South London, her income was seriously reduced. She had been living largely on capital. A trust fund had been set up to provide an income for the mentally disabled Gwen and after that had been taken care of there was very little money left. It was a great shock to the family. Arthur turned up for his mother's funeral. His brothers did not speak to him and from then on he was completely alienated from his family and none of them ever saw him again.

Of course there was a mighty family upheaval. The family house had to be sold. Gwen had to be taken care of and was moved into a private wing of the mental hospital at Coulsdon, Surrey. Bettye had to leave Sutton High School and that posed a problem — what next? Her mother saw an advertisement in the magazine "The Lady" for a little private boarding school in Iver, Bucks., near Windsor, in need of a pupil teacher and arranged for Bettye to go there on reduced fees.

Westfield School, owned and run by two genteel old girls, Miss Overton and Mrs Fitzpatrick, had just three senior boarders and about twenty day pupils aged five to eight. Bettye was to teach the little ones in the mornings and have tuition herself in the afternoons. She hated it. After the hustle and bustle of Sutton High, with its six hundred girls, it seemed a potty little affair. She begged her mother to take her away after one term. From then on the whole family was permanently based in Newquay. The house in Sutton, detached on a large corner site, proved difficult to sell and fetched just £1,500 and an auction sale of the contents was held on the premises. Later it was sold for a huge sum for its site value, and today a block of flats stands where the house once stood.

As can be imagined it was a serious blow to Graham when he realised there was very little money to come from his mother's estate. He had already borrowed from her and so owed the estate money which was never to be properly repaid. As the reader has heard he and the Tolcarne Hotel were already getting into deep trouble: trouble with the bank, trouble with the marriage and worst of all, trouble with the demon drink. The bank realised he was playing up and drinking and began making threatening noises. And to make matters worse very soon his wife was to leave him.

In March, 1933 there was another big change in the family. Tom married the receptionist who worked in the Edgcumbe office. She was a train driver's daughter from Par, an attractive but pernickety little thing aged about twenty three — ten years younger than he, but there is no doubt she thought she was doing well. Was she not marrying the boss? Tom seemed very affluent to her. Her name was Winifried Luscombe — the family called her Lusty. He had brought her to Sutton to his mother's house one earlier Christmas. That must have been a shock for her to say the least — what with a mentally unbalanced sister Gwen, and Olive with her two children.

Tom bought a detached bungalow in Edgcumbe Gardens and Lusty spent much time and money making it attractive and when they married he hired a huge Studebaker car and driver to take them on their honeymoon tour to Brighton where they stayed at the Hotel Metropole. Bettye, not yet seventeen but even then perceptive, thought "How could she marry him? He'll want her to spend all her time drinking in pubs with him. He'll never take her to a dance or a party!"

Tom Farmer and Lusty on their honeymoon tour to Brighton standing by the large Studebaker.

In 1933 Tolcarne was still leading the way but beneath the surface trouble was brewing and the Edgcumbe was progressing slowly — very slowly, in fact it was just marking time!

Olive Whittington and Tom Farmer managed to arrange three garages for their little establishment. They rented the stables at the back of Nagajanka from Auntie Min. Until the mid thirties it was possible to buy a car, get a driving licence from the General Post Office for 5/- (25p) with no questions asked, and take to the road. Therefore many of the 'motorists' arriving in Newquay by car in those days had not learned to reverse. In fact, they couldn't really drive by today's standards. The stables at Nagajanka were very awkwardly placed at right angles to the lane and many guests could not manoeuvre their cars into them. Bettye and Peter Whittington earned many pennies for ice creams by garaging guests' cars for them. They thought it great fun! From time to time they would also earn a few extra pennies by shelling peas for the hotel. They were paid 3d each (1.5p) for shelling a small sack of peas — they were very happy with it. Splendid, they thought. A bar of chocolate was a penny (one half-pence).

By the 1933-34 winter Tom and his new wife were ensconced in "Carn Brea", Edgcumbe Gardens, but Olive and her children, with the faithful Miss Jarvis, had to live in the cheerless Edgcumbe Hotel, without heating. The atmosphere between Olive Whittington and the Farmers was worsening; it was a very difficult time for all of them.

Bettye, a rather plain headstrong girl in her teens couldn't wait to get on with her life although she had no clear idea of what she wanted to do. Above all she couldn't see how she was ever to escape from the dreary Newquay winters. All that first winter she travelled three times weekly by bus and train, a journey of more than an hour each way, to St Austell Secretarial College where she took a shorthand and typing course and for the 1934 season she dealt with the hotel bookings — very haphazardly. She was a sun worshipper and if the sun came out she would dash to Tolcarne Beach to top up her tan and the bookings would have to wait! Then, if necessary, she would work half the night catching up. Her office "uniform" was a navy blue Crysede[2] silk dress. She was paid 10/- (50p) per week.

Bettye and Peter Whittington with Lilo on Tolcarne Beach, circa 1932.

[2] Crysede was one of the high quality shops in Newquay in the 1930s. It was a St Ives firm headed by a talented designer. It sold hand printed silk fabrics with modern designs in wonderful colours. Alas such quality and style has long disappeared from the Newquay scene.

Olive's legacy from her mother's estate was about £1,500, some of which she spent on a three bedroom semi-detached house, "Granham", 5 Edgcumbe Gardens, and she managed to move her family into it after the 1934 season. It had a small two room asbestos chalet at the bottom of the garden where Bettye and Peter slept in the summer so that their bedrooms could be used for 'sleepers' from the hotel. It was their first proper home Olive and her children had had since leaving London in July 1925. Most of the remainder of her inheritance went on sending Peter to Truro Cathedral School, where he was from 1933 to 1936. He was a dark, intense, earnest, clever little chap who worked hard, unlike his sister, and he did very well at school and passed all his examinations properly, which is more than can be said for Bettye. He also won the boxing championship and the divinity prize, although it would seem the religious education was somewhat overdone. He was to say later "church three times a day was too much" and he became a confirmed atheist. Olive really had no income beyond what Edgcumbe Hotel would provide, which at that time was very little. They were difficult years for her financially but she was content that at last she, Bettye and Peter had their own home.

In early 1935 Graham Farmer by then separated from Winnie and on the wagon was staying with his sister, Olive, at "Granham", Edgcumbe Gardens, when he decided he must go to London to see his solicitor in Sutton. All his energies in those days were engaged in 'raising the wind'. It was decided that nineteen year old Bettye should accompany him as minder/companion. She understood her role — she was not to let him out of her sight!

They travelled by train and stayed at the Cock Hotel in Sutton for a few days. All was well and Graham's visit to the solicitor must have been successful for when it was time to return to Cornwall he decided to buy a car and motor back. He explained to Bettye it would really be cheaper than the train fares (which of course had already been paid for!). She thought it a splendid idea! He bought an old Austin 12 Open Tourer for £12. 10s. (£12.50) and they set off in it for Cornwall via Torquay where, unbeknown to Bettye, he planned to look up a girlfriend.

They arrived in Torquay, had lunch at the Grand Hotel, and later motored to Plymouth where they were to stay the night at the Royal Hotel. They had dinner, went to a boxing match with ring-side seats and afterwards disaster struck. He gave Bettye the slip! When she caught up with him again he had met some pals, was well "under the weather", and had run out of money. He borrowed her last two pounds. The next day they returned to Newquay broke and before long poor Graham had to be "dried out" once again.

By 1935 Tom's marriage was getting into difficulty. Sadly he was already a chronic alcoholic — and Bettye had been right — the main recreation since they had married was 'pubbing' — it was hopeless! The marriage was a terrible mis-match and was running into deep trouble, which made Tom drink even more. He, in fact, was never really sober and just went through life in a ginny haze.

Olive and her new sister-in-law did not see eye to eye. Olive Whittington, above all, liked to live peacefully, and in the family at that time she was still very much the underdog. Nineteen year old Bettye on the other hand was naturally outspoken and she stuck up for her mother. As can be imagined this caused more difficulty and there were battles royal. Relations became very strained and were worsening all the time. Miss Worthington, the Manageress, returned to the Edgcumbe for the last time and ran the hotel for the ten weeks season but the partners gave it scant attention. Little progress was made; in fact there was much talk about dissolving the partnership and selling the hotel.

What would have happened is anyone's guess but Tom Farmer died suddenly in March 1936 aged thirty-six, of influenza aggravated by alcoholism. He had been married about three years. His poor little widow was still in her mid twenties. It had been a short and unhappy marriage. He had been a chronic alcoholic for several years, which meant that he was never drunk and never sober, but went through life in an alcoholic haze. His greatest concern was when the next drink was coming up. After he died the inspection pit beneath his car in the garage was found to be half full of empty miniature whisky bottles — hundreds of them. It was tragic — it was such a waste of a young life.

Tom's death in 1936 completely changed the scene. The partnership arrangements had to be sorted out and Olive Whittington and her sister-in-law fought a bitter battle for possession of Edgcumbe Hotel. Eventually it was decided by the solicitors that, as Olive was the surviving partner, the business legally came to her, and the widow's half share had to be paid out. It was valued at £1,300. In the end Olive had to sell her little house in Edgcumbe Gardens and arrange a second mortgage on the hotel, which she did with great difficulty — and again she and her children had no proper home. Tom's bungalow in Edgcumbe Gardens was sold for £1,000. His widow left Newquay and the family had no further contact with her.

Despite Tom's death in March 1936, the hotel had to be run through the season while the battle for possession raged. The season was full of difficulties. Fortunately Cook Beavrill returned, as she had every summer for years. She had her single room on the ground floor which was next to the kitchen and she always brought her old smelly white Pomeranian dog with her. In the middle of the summer the dog began to die of old age in her bedroom. The stench was frightful and the dog lingered for about a week. Bettye knew that the cook mixed everything with her hands and promptly went on a diet of bananas and boiled eggs for a time. Cook Beavrill was distraught — the dog was everything to her. She wept and wept and asked Olive Whittington if it could be buried in the garden of the little house in Edgcumbe Gardens, for which the buyer had yet to be found. "Yes," said Olive, "put him in a box and we'll arrange it."

Olive Whittington had no intention of allowing the dog to be buried in her back garden — she would not even allow her children's dogs to be buried there — rather ridiculously she always thought another dog would come and dig up the corpse. So she wrote a note for the dustbin men to call at Edgcumbe Gardens on their next round. Unfortunately, Cook Beavrill saw the note, realised what it was about and immediately went on strike. She said "I am not cooking another meal here unless my dog's body is brought back." Consternation! Olive 'phoned the Council Offices to see where the rubbish had been taken. "The tip at Trevemper Bridge" she was told "and by now it might be under many tons of rubbish".

Although she had no car, undaunted, Olive called a taxi, put Bettye in it and told her to go to the tip and find the box containing the dog. She was lucky; Bettye arrived at the dump to find the load carrying the dog had just been tipped and after a short search the box was located. In the waiting taxi Bettye sped back to the hotel with it. History doesn't record what then happened to the dog in the box — but the dinner was cooked and came up on time so the 50 guests were fed — but it was a near thing!

Peter left Truro Cathedral School in July, 1936 and started work in the office of John Julian & Co. Ltd., House Agents in Victoria Parade, Newquay. He was paid 5/- (25p) per week and he stayed there for about six months. He then joined the GPO as an engineer, which he found much more interesting.

And so it was that by June 1937 Olive Whittington had become the sole proprietor of the Edgcumbe Private Hotel in Edgcumbe Avenue — although it was mortgaged to the hilt. From then on the hotel was to be taken a great deal more seriously — and Bettye was more than ready to play her part.

A new beginning — Olive Whittington and Bettye at Edgcumbe Hotel, Edgcumbe Avenue 1937 - 1939

When Olive became the proprietor in 1937 there had been no improvements to Edgcumbe, apart from building the rear wing of bedrooms. For almost ten years it had just stood still. If owners are disinterested and the business is not flourishing it will stagnate and eventually peter out. In the case of Edgcumbe in the 1930s that very nearly happened. It was narrowly averted in 1937 when Olive was joined by Bettye, then aged twenty. Bettye had enthusiasm for the hotel and was full of bright ideas — sensible and otherwise!

After the settlement with Tom Farmer's widow, Olive Whittington's financial state was dire in the extreme. Edgcumbe was already heavily mortgaged and she had no money or other assets, except the semi-detached house in Edgcumbe Gardens which did not prove easy to sell. The Midland Bank refused to advance any more money and it looked as though the hotel might have to be sold after all. Fortunately J.A.N. Ralph, the most successful solicitor in Newquay at the time and a long term family friend who had helped Graham out financially several times, managed to arrange a second mortgage on the Edgcumbe with one of his wealthy clients. Olive sold her house eventually for £700 and in that way the necessary capital was raised. But it had been a very near thing and the Edgcumbe story might well have ended there. As it was, it was just about to take off! By the time the legal arrangements were finalised there was little time to do anything but open the doors and get on. The family were going to have to tuck away again. Olive and Bettye shared a room on the ground floor and Peter slept at the end of the three foot wide corridor with a door slung across as a screen. There was much catching up to be done, the Edgcumbe had fallen sadly behind and had become shabby and outdated.

Bettye worked hard and was very enthusiastic, but she was impetuous and determined that the Edgcumbe was no longer going to be the dull little Private Hotel it had been for the previous ten years. She was going to follow in Uncle Graham's footsteps and the Edgcumbe was going to be a mini version of the Tolcarne!

Although the season was almost upon them she immediately arranged for three of the small ground floor bedrooms with small windows to be gutted, doors blocked up and a little narrow bench seat put along one wall, and voila! Edgcumbe had a recreation/dance room with room for a table tennis table, an upright piano in one corner, and a very up to date second hand cabinet radiogram that played eight records automatically in the other. The floor was just rough boards, but nobody seemed to mind. Bettye was determined to emulate everything that Uncle Graham had done at Tolcarne. A trio was booked two nights weekly for dancing. Ken Langmaid was the pianist and he recalled that they were paid 10/- (50p) each per night 8.30 - 12.00 midnight. Weekly table tennis tournaments were held with a silver cup for the winner, à la Uncle Graham.

Olive Whittington, tolerant as usual, gave Bettye her head about all this although she really thought much of it unnecessary and a waste of money. One week when there were very few people she decided they didn't really need a dance and took down the notice in the hall announcing it. She then cancelled the trio without telling the guests. When they discovered there was to be no dance that evening they were livid and Olive had a near riot on her hands. So Bettye, at the last moment, was despatched in a taxi to find the band and persuade them to come and play. Reluctantly, and in a huff, they came and all was well. After that the weekly entertainments became a permanent fixture.

Bettye could type quite ably but could neither do paperwork, balance the money properly, nor keep the petty cash straight! She was inclined to overbook the rooms but she could charm the guests with her enthusiasm and exuberance. In those days all the bookings were done by letter and there was little use of the telephone. Later she was fortunate in being to able to employ people more efficient than she to take charge of the office. However, she quickly became expert at managing 'difficult' guests who did not find their rooms to their liking and since the rooms were so varied and lacked running water, and bearing in mind the guests didn't always get the room they had booked, that happened fairly frequently!

The difficulty was that the rooms in the original house were enormous, the second floor rooms were attics with sloping roofs, and the new rooms were small. By that time most hotels had installed hot and cold water in the bedrooms and it was becoming a very important facility. At the Edgcumbe, however, with its twenty bedrooms and two bathrooms, hot water still had to be carried to the bedrooms morning and evening, and this was fast becoming quite unacceptable to the guests and staff. The bedrooms in the extension, built in 1928, were somewhat cramped, and also lacked the increasingly important running water. That made more difficulties, as can be imagined.

Olive and Bettye's first season was not an easy one. Although they managed without a Manageress, they did find it hard but 1937 was very busy and the first really good season the Edgcumbe had ever had.

In the autumn of 1937 with a great effort Olive managed to buy their first car, a brand new Austin Seven Ruby saloon, DRL3, which cost £150, to be shared and driven by Bettye and Peter. In the first twelve months they drove thirty-one thousand miles between them in that little car, but with constant squabbling about whose petrol was in it and whose turn it was to have it! They always seemed to want to go in opposite directions. Bettye and Peter had found it impossible to share the little Ruby Saloon. During the following summer Bettye managed to buy her own car. She scraped up £30 and bought a splendid little navy blue open two-seater Austin 7. She was inordinately proud of it and spent several sunny afternoons driving it round the lanes for sheer pleasure.

In December 1937 Bettye married Rodney May, a local boy three years older than she who she had met at the badminton club four years earlier. He was her first boyfriend and they had become engaged on her eighteenth birthday. She had been just seventeen when he had taught her to drive his little £100 Morris Minor. He was the son of a local business man, and had been to Dunheved College at Launceston and for his twenty-first birthday present he was given a brand new sports car; a two seater, bright yellow Austin 7 Swallow. That was a big attraction!

They were married in Kenwyn Parish Church, Truro, and, after a wedding reception for thirty people at Edgcumbe Hotel, spent their honeymoon of a few days at Budock Vean Hotel in Mawnan Smith. They began their married life in a rambling two bedroom flat at the top of a large house in Richmond, for which the rent was 18/- (90p) weekly. Rodney had a lowly job as a manager for Rothmans and they jogged along for a couple of years with very little money. Bettye's mother, convinced they would not feed themselves properly, sent them a weekly Cornish food parcel, a fresh chicken, a saffron cake, a half a pound of butter, and a half pound tin of cream with a sugar lump in the middle to keep it sweet.

Even in those early days Bettye had little interest in acquiring domestic skills — beyond developing a passion for cake making. She had a morning woman who came for two hours every Saturday and was paid 1/9d. (about 10½p per hour). She cleaned right through and left the flat gleaming. Bettye spent much of her time at nearby Richmond Ice Rink learning to skate and walking her dog in the park.

Her other great interest was scouring the junk shops for treasures for the flat, usually clutching about half a crown (12½p) in her hot little hand! Looking back, it is extraordinary that it did not occur to her to get a job but in those days married women just did not go out to work. But each summer she returned to Newquay for the short season to help her mother at Edgcumbe.

Bettye later told friends it was a foolish marriage, but at the time she felt it unlikely that anyone else would want to marry her and she couldn't see how she was ever going to escape the boredom of life in Newquay in the winter. The appeal of being a Mrs Somebody, having a white wedding and then a flat in London was too much and she succumbed. It was youthful foolishness in the extreme. In fact the marriage was based on friendship with very few sexual connotations and as the modern reader will understand, it really stood no chance. It lasted barely three years.

For the 1938 season Olive managed to rent "Ashby", a seven bedroom terrace house opposite the hotel in Edgcumbe Avenue, for £52 per annum. She called it the annexe, and filled it with 'sleepers' which gave the Edgcumbe extra bedrooms, plus quarters for the family. Things were beginning to look up!

Although living in Richmond Bettye already had a keen interest in the hotel and her heart was in Newquay. During the winter she was in constant touch with her mother. By the time the hotel opened in June 1938 she had got the bit

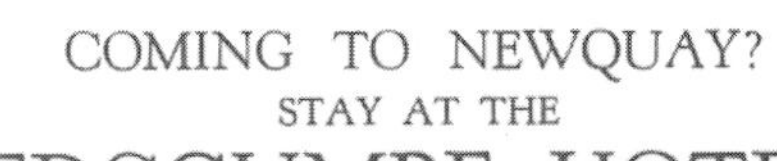

Bettye Whittington's first attempt at an advertisement – already full of big ideas – talking of Entertainments by London Artistes and Talkies, 1938.

between her teeth and had produced a new brochure which was really very successful. Fortunately there were no 'trading standards officers' in those days. Pencil sketches were used instead of photographs and there was much artistic licence about it.

As has already been said, young Bettye sometimes got carried away by enthusiasm and went too far. Edgcumbe was just a double fronted terrace house, and after someone wrote saying they would like a room overlooking the tennis court (the houses adjoining the hotel having been left out in the pencil sketch) Olive Whittington wrote in "Houses

Olive Whittington did her best to modify her daughter's wild exaggeration in making the house appear detached.

adjoining" by hand on every brochure sent out. However the brochure did bring in the bookings; it was used even after the war until it was possible to do a new one — and the new post-war one also used pencil sketches which stretched the imagination somewhat. The Edgcumbe was coming to life, copying faithfully all the exciting things that Uncle Graham had been doing for the previous fifteen years, although in a rather more homely way. In those days the only advertising necessary was in the Town Guide and Holiday Haunts, published by Great Western Railway.

The little recreation room made in 1937 had been very popular and so for the 1938 season it was enlarged, and a maple floor was laid. Another bedroom and the corridor were knocked in and a large square

TARIFF

(Inclusive Weekly Terms)

From 2½ to 4½ Guineas per person, according to Season and Rooms selected.

NO REDUCTION FOR TEMPORARY ABSENCE.

HOURS OF MEALS.

Weekdays.		Sundays.	
Breakfast	9 to 9.30 a.m.	Breakfast	9 to 9.30 a.m.
Luncheon ...	1. 0 p.m.	Dinner	1. 0 p.m.
Afternoon Tea ...	4. 0 p.m.	Afternoon Tea	4.30 p.m.
Dinner	7.15 p.m.	Supper	8. 0 p.m.

Luncheon Sandwiches are provided free for Guests away during the day.

EXTRAS.

Meals in Bedroom	1/- per person.
Early Morning Tea	4d. per person.
Baths—Hot	1/- each.
,, Cold	6d. each.

HOTEL NOTICES.

Our Guests are respectfully requested to sign the Hotel Register immediately on arrival.

The Proprietress cannot hold herself responsible for Monies or Valuables, unless deposited at the Hotel Office for safe keeping.

Cheques accepted in payment of accounts only if presented FOUR CLEAR DAYS in advance of departure.

Bedrooms must be vacated by NOON on day of departure.

Edgcumbe Pre-war Tariff. £2.62½ per person per week for four meals daily – including afternoon tea.

bay window built out which made a stage for the musicians. All the windows were given coloured leaded light glass, in 1920s style. Then the Edgcumbe was able to advertise a new Dance Room. Even Bettye couldn't quite bring herself to call it a Ballroom! — that would come later!

Arrangements were made for some evening entertainment. "Evening entertainment" meant, apart from the dancing twice a week, self employed entertainers who came in — conjurors, a palmist, a singer or two, who passed the hat around at the end of the performance and took a silver collection, usually 6d. (2½p) or 1/- (5p). The hotel paid nothing! The Edgcumbe really was beginning to get going!

One of the favourite entertainers in those days was "Madame Roma" who told fortunes — a palmist! She was a squat dark haired woman with a white round moon face and straight black hair with a heavy fringe and she always wore black. She was very popular but one sometimes felt the guests were laughing at her rather than with her — but they thoroughly enjoyed her. She had to be given a quiet corner and she charged 2/6d. (12½p). She was a riot; the guests all sat around waiting their turn and as each one emerged they regaled those waiting with what they had been told. When one said he had been told he would be incarcerated, and he got the word slightly muddled with another beginning with 'c' they rolled on the floor with laughter. It was hilarious. Madame Roma's husband, Charlie, made the bookings, took the money, and sat around while she read the palms. He often kept her at it until far into the night. Then there were would be fireworks between them. More entertainment for the guests! Her act was very popular and she worked around the Newquay hotels for many years.

In the 1920s and 1930s most visitors arrived in Newquay by train and in the early days there were many excursions available by charabanc. As the number of visitors increased year by year, so did the demand for sight seeing tours and by 1930s coach tours were big business and very popular. In Newquay there were two main companies, Newquay Motor Company and Hawkey's Tours. For many years they ran daily trips all over the county. The Manager of Newquay Motors, Edgar Pope, a very personable man long known to the family, would go around the Edgcumbe dining room at breakfast and again at lunchtime (everyone had a full blown luncheon in those days) booking his tours.

"Good morning Madam, can I interest you in a trip to St Mawes this afternoon?" etc. The guests would pay at reception and the coach would pick them up at the hotel. It was a good service and it worked

Day trips around Cornwall, 1930s.

well. What didn't work was Bettye with the paperwork and the money. She was supposed to collect the money, keep it separately, take 10% commission, and settle up at the end of the season. One year when the time to settle came the money was £38.00 short (say £500 today). Olive Whittington had to make good the deficiency which, typically, she did without recrimination, but Edgar Pope gave the young Bettye the ticking off of her life. He said, "If you go on like this my girl, you will end up like your Uncle Graham." She was mortified, not so much by the loss of the money, but by the ticking off by this man she rather admired.

Olive Whittington did little to curb her headstrong daughter's enthusiasm. At that time Bettye was keen on cooking and loved making cakes, etc., so in the summer of 1938 she set up a little kitchen for herself at the back of Ashby where she could spend her mornings making scones, maids of honour, fruit cakes, sponges, etc. for the guests' teas. Several mornings a week she would spend cooking there until she wearied of it and the teas reverted to what they had been before. Olive Whittington wisely allowed her to realise for herself that making home-made cakes almost daily for fifty people who were paying very little, 2½ guineas (£2.62½) per week for full board including afternoon tea was, to say the least, silly nonsense!

Bettye was always determined to copy the big hotels and that summer in one of her more exuberant moments, aping the Hotel Bristol, she decided to give Edgcumbe guests cream teas on the beach.

She only did it for a few weeks. Of course, she had to do it all herself and she soon tired of it but the visitors simply loved it!

By 1938 Bettye yearned for a sportier car. She saved her money all the season; no doubt sometimes a little petty cash found its way into her kitty — not so difficult in those free and easy days — and she bought a blue 1937 MGT two seater, CRL 360, for £99. Hire Purchase did not occur to her, she paid what she could and made an arrangement with the garage that she would pay the balance the following season, which she did. Shortly after, Peter also managed to buy his own car; a 1933 Riley 9, a two-seater open March Special, for which he paid £70 and which he kept and ran for several years after the war. It was a lovely car — today it would be called an "interesting car"! Peter, aged nineteen, and working as an engineer in the General Post Office in Truro, had little or no interest in the hotel at that time, fiddling with cars or machinery was more up his street.

The next winter, 1938-1939, a few rooms were given hot and cold running water and the 1939 season got off to a very good start. All was going well in August when it became clear that there was about to be a war. Most of the guests fled to their homes and the season collapsed abruptly. It was a severe financial loss. This really came as a great shock to Olive Whittington and Bettye; although there had been so much talk of war, they, struggling to get a small business going, had not paid attention and therefore had not realised the war was really going to happen. They had rather put their heads in the sand and thought that somehow it would be averted — or if it came, they didn't realise the enormous impact it would have on every aspect of life in this country. At a drop of a hat life changed completely and it was never to be the same again. Afterwards it was to be not only a "new leaf" but for many people, and certainly for Bettye, "a new book".

War Time Newquay 1940 – 1945

When war was declared in September 1939 Bettye was in Cornwall helping her mother at Edgcumbe and she and her husband immediately gave up the flat in Richmond and brought all their possessions to Cornwall.

With the outbreak of war many young people did not know what to expect and the whole country waited with bated breath. Immediately the lights went out all over England and a complete blackout was in force for almost six years. Every window had to be blacked out after dark and very soon Air Raid Wardens, volunteer local businessmen wearing tin hats, patrolled the streets after dark to make sure no chinks of light were showing. Some were over zealous about it — rather like some of the present day Traffic Wardens! They caught Olive Whittington with chinks of light showing several times, quite a serious offence in those days and she was fined. The truth was she could not afford to have proper blackout curtains made — she simply bought pieces of blackout material, cheap black cotton, and roughly pinned them up at the windows with drawing pins and they were constantly falling down — hence the chinks and fines!

In September 1939 petrol rationing was officially introduced and everyone dashed to fill their cars with petrol before stocks ran out. Peter Whittington, always ready to go one better, filled every container he could lay hands on (polythene had not yet appeared) and then tried to persuade his garage to fill several galvanized baths with petrol for him. Very sensibly they refused to do so. Thousands of cars were soon to be laid up for the duration of the war. Bettye sold her M.G. — her most cherished possession!— to a friend, Colin Rickeard, for about £70. After the war he sold it for £450, the equivalent of about £9,000 today. What one would call a 'good buy'!

All that first winter the country was preparing for what it might have to face. Air Raid Shelters were being built, gas masks — to be carried at all times — were issued to the entire population, buildings were packed around with sand bags, and brown paper was pasted over windows against blast from bombs. By the end of November 1939 a million men aged between twenty-one and forty-one had been called up and sent to centres all over the country for training. Later the age was reduced to eighteen. In January 1940 food rationing was introduced and was to get ever tighter as the war progressed.

By early 1940 Bettye realised her 1937 marriage was hollow and had been a big mistake. They had nothing in common and she made up her mind it must be sorted out. They had no children, their home had been packed up, and as Bettye later explained they were both in their twenties, young enough to start again and that is exactly what happened. When Rodney went into the Army in January, 1940 the marriage was virtually over. He trained at Shrivenham, Wiltshire and was then posted to Iceland for the rest of the war. They were divorced in 1943 and never met again.

In the spring of 1940, with bombing and invasion imminent, the Government evacuated thousands of children between the ages of about eight and twelve years from the East End of London to Cornwall. Most had never been away from their mothers before and they were bewildered and unhappy. They were marshalled at Paddington station with labels attached to them and cardboard gas mask boxes on strings round their necks. Many clutched teddies. Special trains were laid on and soon the children were on their way to the West Country and safety, although neither they nor their parents knew to where they were being taken. In Cornwall every householder who had a spare room had to take them in — there was NO choice and Olive Whittington had to take two. She was to be paid 10/6d. (52½p) per week for the first child and 8/6d. (42½p) per week for the second child.

When the children arrived in Newquay they were transferred en masse to the Salvation Army Hall at the bottom of Crantock Street and from there volunteer drivers were to take them to the addresses where they were to stay. Bettye was one of the drivers. She was driving Peter's Riley March Special and her mother asked her to bring back two little boys. When she arrived at the hall an amazing sight met her eyes. Hundreds of dejected, bewildered children, some clutching older siblings' hands, some snivelling silently, were waiting to be taken to their temporary homes. At that moment they were the sorry victims of the war.

Bettye, who has always had a soft spot for blonde children, chose a blonde curly headed boy and his companion and took them home. They were both about eight years old and were called Geoffrey and Tony. They had never seen the sea or a cow before and their clothes were utterly unsuitable. Peter immediately put them in his car and took them to Trinimans, the local outfitters, and fitted them out with grey flannel shorts and shirts and striped belts with snake clasps. That was small boys' garb at the seaside in those days.

Olive Whittington coped with the boys as well as she could — but it did not last very long. A few months later a policeman was at the door. It turned out that gangs of evacuees had been stealing from Woolworths and Geoffrey and Tony were the ring leaders. They were smartly packed off back to London and were never heard of again.

As the 1939-1940 winter wore on it became clear that the 1940 season was not going to materialise — it didn't and it was extremely worrying: how were the mounting bills to be paid? That year the town was peopled by folk who had evacuated themselves from the big cities to escape the bombing but there was no holiday season. The call up became serious. Girls became land girls working on the farms, or nurses, and many went into factories. Everyone had to be involved and only mothers with small children and the elderly were exempt.

In May 1940 the Local Defence Volunteers (LDV) was formed, later to be re-named the Home Guard. Bettye joined and was detailed to report for duty in the Drill Hall at Crantock Street at 7.30 a.m. several mornings a week to man the telephone. It didn't ring! She found that incredibly boring. She was still doing voluntary driving.

Peter was still at home working as a General Post Office (GPO) Engineer in Truro, a reserved occupation. He travelled daily by car. One day he arrived home with a hundredweight bag of sugar which had 'fallen off the back of a lorry'! His mother was horrified and terrified and told him to get rid of it. He hid it under the frill of the bench seat in the Edgcumbe dance room and forgot about it. Months later when he looked for it again it had 'fallen out of there' and was never found.

Gradually the petrol shortage worsened and petrol was only available for essential services — doctors, ambulances, fire engines, etc. Fuel for private motoring all but dried up and there were very few cars on the roads. Peter could no longer get to Truro GPO by car and so rented "Greenbank", a small furnished thatched cottage in Feock — more about that later. Travelling by car became almost impossible and travelling by train was a nightmare. The trains were absolutely packed with servicemen and women on leave. Even on the night trains the corridors were stuffed with them slumped on their kit bags trying to sleep, there was no room for them even to lie down on the floor.

The invasion was expected at any minute and all through the late spring of 1940 there were feverish anti-invasion precautions going on. Fistral and Crantock beaches were mined; Towan and Great Western beaches were closed to the public and concrete anti-tank defences were built to prevent invading enemy landing craft leaving the beaches. Lusty Glaze beach was used as a practice firing range and was also closed for the duration. The only Newquay beach available to the public was Tolcarne. Many open spaces were staked out with heavy wooden poles to prevent enemy aircraft landing. All station names and road sign posts were removed to confuse invaders and more and more air raid shelters were being built. At the eleventh hour the country was feverishly preparing for what might come — there was a national panic.

At the Edgcumbe and Tolcarne, and no doubt many other hotels, with no prospect of a season the bills kept coming and the debts mounted. It was a constant worry to Olive Whittington. Fortunately, the government acted to prevent small businesses being made bankrupt by bringing in a law called the Liabilities Adjustment Act. The Act decreed that no-one could be declared bankrupt if they had lost their business because of the war and all outstanding debts must be set aside to be dealt with when the war ended. That of course was an immense relief to all the small businesses in Newquay whose customers had disappeared almost overnight, but with no season many of their owners were still left without an income.

In June, 1940 came the famous Dunkirk débâcle. A vast number of the rescued soldiers of the British Expeditionary Force arrived by train at Newquay station, en route for Penhale Army camp at Holywell Bay. They were the Dunkirk survivors. They were a war-weary, bedraggled, pathetic sight; they had lost everything and had spent days on the French beaches sheltering from incessant German bombs and machine gun fire awaiting rescue by an armada of all kinds of craft. They had had to wade waist deep in water to get into the boats and it was a miracle that they had escaped.

At Newquay station they were met by voluntary drivers, Bettye among them, who then drove them in relays to Penhale camp at Holywell Bay. The Women's Voluntary Service (WVS) worked flat out providing comforts and the Newquay people treated them like heroes plying them with tea, food, and cigarettes. The soldiers stayed at Penhale for a week or two resting and in fact Bettye and Molly Murray

June 1940. Cream tea on Tolcarne beach for the survivors of Dunkirk, with Bettye Whittington and Molly Murray and Peter Whittington's dog, Buster.

"did their bit". For several days they gave one or two of the soldiers cream teas on Tolcarne Beach! What Cornish comfort for the troops!

As the summer wore on and the Battle of Britain began Bettye, still doing voluntary work and manning the telephone that never rang, wondered what to do next. With no season she had no proper occupation and no money. When the Western National Bus Company began advertising for girls to drive the buses to replace the men who were all being called up she applied and was given a driving test on a bus around Truro. She passed with flying colours and was about to become a wartime bus driver when fate took a hand. She was invited to a weekend house-warming party outside Bristol and while there was persuaded by her friends to join Bristol Air Raid Precautions (ARP) as an ambulance driver, and that changed her life. She was not to return to Newquay, except when on leave, for the next five years.

All through the winter of 1940-1941 horrendous bombing of the cities in this country continued night after night and thousands and thousands of civilians were killed. There was a blitz on Plymouth all through the spring of 1941 and the city suffered a spate of heavy enemy air raids. The Cornwall Auxiliary Fire Services (AFS) were constantly called upon for reinforcements. In April, 1941 with the blitz at its height the Newquay detachment of the AFS was sent for. By the time they arrived the city was ablaze and they had not even reached the pumps before their fire tender received a direct hit and five Newquay members of the crew were killed. They were Bob Whiting, Guy Featherstone, E.S. Old, B.A. Phillips and S.H. Vineer. The whole of Newquay grieved for those five brave local chaps. That night 1,000 incendiary bombs rained on Plymouth. The whole city burned. In all seventeen firemen were killed and the centre of Plymouth had finally been completely destroyed.

By the autumn of 1941 almost every building of any size in Newquay had been requisitioned by the War Ministry for the duration of the war. Many of the hotels were occupied by Royal Air Force personnel and many thousands of Air Cadets trained in Newquay. There were several Elementary Flying Training Schools (EFTS) units in the town, and the Commanding Officer's headquarters were at Trebarwith Hotel. The Summer Theatre above Tolcarne Beach became a NAAFI canteen.

Coniston and Kilbirnie Hotels were both taken over by the RAF and were used as Initial Training Wings (ITWs). Cadets were billeted there for an eight week course learning the rudiments of navigation before being transferred to EFTS elsewhere for further instruction to become

322/102/Q C/422 ARMY FORM W 3068.

AN AGREEMENT made the 21st day of October

1941 BETWEEN Mrs. O E B Whittington

of Edgcumbe Avenue, Newquay, Cornwall
of the one part and *HIS MAJESTY'S PRINCIPAL SECRETARY OF STATE FOR THE WAR DEPARTMENT* (hereinafter called "the Department") of the other part.

Insert Description of Land. WHEREAS the Department has taken possession of Edgcumbe Hotel, Newquay, Cornwall

pursuant to the powers conferred on it by the Defence Regulations 1939 by reason of which compensation is or will be payable to the said Mrs. O E B Whittington

under the provisions of the Compensation (Defence) Act 1939

IT is hereby agreed between the parties hereto that the Department shall pay and the said Mrs. O E B Whittington shall accept payment at the rate of £ 275. 0. 0 per annum payable quarterly on the usual quarter days in satisfaction of the sums which may be payable pursuant to section 2 (1) (*a*) and of interest thereon under section 10 of the said Act

AS WITNESS the hands of the parties hereto

Witness to the signature of Mrs. O.E.B. Whittington — O. E. B. Whittington.

Witness to the signature of G.W. Wilkinson — G. W. Wilkinson

A Spicer

on behalf of His Majesty's Principal Secretary of State for the War Department.

Agreement for the requisitioning of Edgcumbe Hotel, signed in October 1941.

pilots. The large car park, then by the side of the Coniston, was used as a parade ground and the cadets were drilled there every morning.

Several of the hotels became private schools which were evacuated from vulnerable areas of the country. Benenden School in Kent took over the Bristol, and St Ursuline Convent, a Roman Catholic school from Forest Gate, London was based at Cliffdene Hotel on Narrowcliff. Greshams boys' school from Norfolk was at the Pentire Hotel, and Micklefield girls' school from Seaford, Susssex was at the Eliot Hotel in Edgcumbe Avenue. There was also a school at Penhallow Hotel in Trebarwith Crescent. The Grantham Hotel became an RAF Officers' club and it was the brightest spot on the Newquay scene throughout the war as can be imagined!

The Headland Hotel was an RAF hospital, the Atlantic and Victoria hotels were general hospitals. St Rumons was also a hospital. Many local girls joined the Voluntary Aid Detachment (VAD) and worked as nurses throughout the war.

Negotiations with the War Office about the requisitioning took the whole summer of 1941 but when it came it happened very quickly and the owners of most of the hotels were only given forty-eight hours to give possession after the arrangements were settled. It was a great relief to Winnie Farmer and Olive Whittington when the Tolcarne and Edgcumbe were finally taken off their hands. The Government only paid unfurnished rentals for the requisitioned properties but at least they now both had fixed incomes, however small, and all their debts were set aside to be settled when the war was over. Winnie was paid £500 per year for Tolcarne; Army personnel were billeted there. The Edgcumbe became an Army Sergeants' Mess. The £275 per year paid by the War Department as rental was Olive Whittington's sole official income. She moved into "Ashby" opposite the hotel. All furniture etc., from the hotel was removed and was stored in the large knitting factory in Crantock Street where it remained until August 1945. When it was returned, almost as quickly as it had been removed, it was just dumped anywhere in a heap; the woollen carpets and blankets were all riddled with moth and had to be replaced, but that is another story.

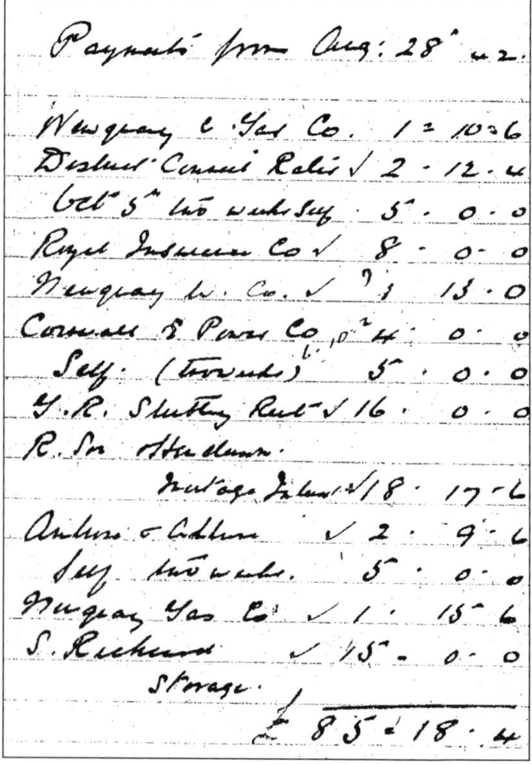

Payments from Aug: 28th 42.

Newquay & Gas Co.	1	10	6
District Council Rates ✓	2	12	4
Oct 5th two weeks self	5	0	0
Royal Insurance Co ✓	8	0	0
Newquay W. Co. ✓		13	0
Cornwall E. Power Co	4	0	0
Self (towards)	5	0	0
Y. R. Shutting Rent ✓	16	0	0
R. Sn Headdown. Mortgage Interest ✓	18	17	6
Ambrose & Addison ✓	2	9	6
Self two weeks.	5	0	0
Newquay Gas Co ✓	1	15	6
S. Richmond ✓ Storage.	15	0	0
£	85	18	4

A copy of Olive Whittington's three-monthly accounts submitted to the Liabilities Adjustment Accountants. Interestingly, she only allowed herself £2.10s. 0d. (£2.50) per week.

Throughout the war accounts had to be carefully kept and submitted every three months to the Liabilities Adjustment Accountants who closely monitored the outgoings. In order to supplement her small income, Olive let part of "Ashby", which was a sizeable house, to an Englishman with a French wife. She shared the kitchen with them, and that must have been very tricky with the extremely tight food rationing because he was the local Food Officer in charge of the Food Office in Newquay. But they somehow survived until the war ended. Olive also rented rooms to Micklefield School, evacuated to the Eliot Hotel across the road, as sleeping quarters for members of the staff and in this rather haphazard way she survived the war financially. Of course she always kept a spare room for when Bettye or Peter could get home on leave.

In the autumn of 1943 the Americans arrived and a division of U.S. Air Transport command was stationed at St Mawgan. Their Officers' Mess was at the Great Western Hotel, Newquay. The Commanding Officer issued a booklet of information to his officers - below are extracts from it.

Billeting. *Your billet whilst at this base will be the Great Western Hotel. The service charge at the hotel is 5/- (25p) per night.*
Messing. *You will eat at the Officers' Mess at the Great Western Hotel. However, meal tickets for each meal must be obtained at the desk in the hotel.* ***Bars.*** *The usual drinks are bitters, lager, ale and whisky. A ration card may be had for spirits at the hotel by applying for same at the desk.*
Security. *Be sure you get a security pamphlet, but most important of all don't tell where you have been or where you are going.*
Currency. *While you are in England you will only be able to spend British currency. The rates of exchange follow:*

British	***U.S. dollars (approx.)***
Half penny	*.01*
Penny	*.02*
Threepence	*.05*
Sixpence	*.10*
Shilling (12 pence)	*.20*
Two shillings (florin)	*.40*
Half crown	*.50*
10 shilling note	*2.00*
One pound note	*4.00*

General. *Remember you are here on serious business not a Roman holiday. As a uniformed member of the U.S. Forces your dress conduct and deportment will either bring credit or discredit upon the United States. The standards of dress, conduct and military courtesy here are very high.*

Remember you are now in a country that has had over four years of hardships of war. Don't expect or demand the impossible. You are not immune to disciplinary action should ***you*** *make it necessary.*

Signed: Charles W. Steinmetz, Colonel Air Corps, Commanding

The instructions from the American Commanding Officer to his officers on how to behave!

All through the war there were three cinemas in Newquay. The New Cinema on Narrowcliff, the Victoria behind the Central Hotel and the Pavilion above Towan Beach; they were well patronised by the troops. The Blue Lagoon in Cliff Road had long been Newquay's one public dance hall and was very popular with hoi polloi. Of course during the war, with thousands of troops in the town, it really came into its own and the servicemen and local dolly birds flocked to it. The dance hall was unlicensed in those days and so the chaps would "tank up" in the Great Western Hotel nearby and then make their way to the Blue Lagoon.

The RAF Officers' Club at the Grantham Hotel, Edgcumbe Gardens was the rendezvous for all the officers in town. The weary air crews from St Mawgan and St Eval would gather there and sit at the bar with "the hangar doors open" talking shop and swapping flying yarns; their triumphs and their near misses, with many stories of the "there was I hanging upside down waiting to die" variety. Later, mellowed, they would let their hair down and dance and there would be merriment and high jinks far into the night. Briefly, the morrow was forgotten — it would be another day!

This then, was the war-time Newquay. Gradually everyone became involved in the war in one way or another and the face of Newquay changed from that of a select holiday resort to a garrison town. For the next four years thousands of troops, mostly RAF, were stationed there. When the war was over they were to return in droves bringing their families with them but by then, of course, it was to be a different Newquay — and a different world.

Bettye and Michael's War 1940 – 1945

Michael's family, the Henslows

In October 1940 Bettye went to the weekend housewarming party of friends who had taken a furnished cottage outside Bristol. There she met a young design engineer called Gordon Bedson who had a car for sale. It was a 1926 Austin 7 "Chummy", an open tourer called "Minnie", taxed and ready for the road. He wanted £5.00 for it. Insurance seemed unimportant in those days! Bettye bought Minnie for £4.00 without a battery — she would buy that later — second hand! Having an old 1926 engine with a magneto the car needed no battery to start it or run it. It could be started by winding the brass handle at the front or giving it a gentle push, or even by being scooted like a scooter. The battery was only needed for lights at night and they were not important. As part of the national blackout during the war car headlights had to be completely covered by cardboard and then a small slit was made about one inch deep which just let through a glimmer of light. Minnie was a sturdy little tub painted muddy grey with a canvas hood that was little more than an awning and ill fitting side screens that were rarely used, but she had a sound engine and went like a bird.

Minnie – 1926 Austin Seven Chummy, which Bettye bought for £4, with Gordon Bedson at the wheel, 1940.

As the reader has heard during the weekend Bettye's friends persuaded her to join the Bristol Air Raid Precautions (ARP) Ambulance Service as a driver. Thus in November 1940 at the height of the Bristol blitz she became an Ambulance Driver stationed at Shirehampton, Bristol, which was the dépôt guarding Avonmouth

Docks. When she reported for duty on 5th November 1940 she arrived in style — in Minnie!

The ARP dépôt in Shirehampton was a large empty house with all the windows boarded up and standing in its own grounds. In charge was Mr Shepherd and there were two despatch officers under him. Men drivers worked shifts, 24 hours on 24 hours off and were paid £3 weekly. Girl drivers worked alternate days from 3.00 p.m - 8.00 a.m. for 30/- (£1.50). The girls slept about eight in a room on very small camp beds on bare boards and there was a canteen that opened at 6.00 a.m. for breakfast — white bread and butter which they toasted on the gas fire and smeared with marmalade, when it was available. For supper beetroot and cheese sandwiches were often on offer and Heinz carrot soup (which replaced tomato soup for the duration). The canteen closed at midnight.

One of the drivers at the dépôt was a tall, handsome man called Michael Armstrong who was immediately intrigued by this girl who had arrived, wearing thick woollen patterned stockings and a tweed coat with a hood, in a little old car. He invited her to play table tennis and offered to help her with some necessary tinkering on the car! He came from Devon and when she told him that she proposed to drive down to Cornwall in the little car to spend Christmas with her mother he offered to show her the way. He was going home to Devon for Christmas on his motorbike. Bettye's little car still had no battery or lights, and wouldn't go more than about 40-45 miles an hour. She planned to get as far as she could before the light failed and then to stay in a pub for the night, and resume her journey the next day.

A few days before Christmas they set off at lunch time from Shirehampton with Michael leading the way on his motor bike. When they stopped at about 4.30 p.m. at the public house in Bow, Devon, a village very near his mother's house, Bettye asked him to go in and see if they could give her a single room for the night. Instead he rang his mother, told her he had a 'stranded girl' with him and Mother promptly invited Bettye to spend the night at their home. Home was an attractive long low thatched cottage — The Mill House, Down St Mary, seven miles from Crediton, Devon.

When Michael and Bettye arrived there they were frozen to the marrow, but there was the biggest log fire she had ever seen burning on a vast hearth and the living room was lit by several oil lamps and glowed with warmth and welcome. The room was dominated by a large dining table and at one end of it tea was laid; home-made raspberry jam, honey, coarse country bread and butter and boiled eggs. She had probably been saving her entire month's rations for when Michael came home. Never was a feast more welcome. In Bristol they hadn't seen an egg for weeks!

Although Michael's mother gave Bettye a very warm welcome that cold night in 1940 she must have been less than pleased when Michael arrived home with his travelling companion in a little rag tag car. She was not impressed with Michael's new friend. Married, blonde at the time, with painted nails and smoking cigarettes — although fifty years ago most people smoked and it was not the social gaffe it is today. In fact Michael also smoked when not at home! But what was far worse Bettye was "Trade" — which was quite beyond the pale. What were things coming to? After a convivial evening Bettye said goodbye to her hosts the next morning and set off in her little car for Cornwall to join her mother and brother, Peter, for Christmas and New Year.

In Newquay Olive Whittington was delighted to have Bettye and Peter home for Christmas and after a quiet but festive few days Bettye had to get back to the ARP depot. Her mother made her some turkey sandwiches, wrapped them in greaseproof paper, tied them with cotton, and added a mince pie and some fruit; then Bettye set off for Bristol with her little picnic lunch on the seat beside her.

In those days, before by-passes and motorways, one had to go through the centre of every village and town on the way and the journey from Newquay to Bristol in Minnie took about 5 hours. Bettye had only got as far as Axbridge, about an hour's run from Bristol, before dark so she found a 'B & B' in the village at the foot of the Mendips; she planned to resume her journey the following morning at first light. First light was not early enough as she had to be back by 9.00 a.m. She drove without lights in near darkness for an hour and was stopped in Bristol by a policeman who said "You haven't got your lights on, Miss". "Thank you, officer", said Bettye. She fiddled at the dashboard and shot off into the gloaming before there could be further talk about it. She managed to be on duty on time but decided she really must do something about getting a battery for Minnie. At the depot Michael, already on duty, was waiting for her.

When Michael and Bettye first met he had digs in St Paul's Road, Clifton. His landlady was an old crone called Stella who drank. She spent her nights in the crypt under the nearby church to escape the bombing. Bettye was staying with a friend and colleague, Jennifer Jackman, at 15 Mortimer Road, Clifton. Jennifer's doctor father was in the Army and her mother and younger sister had been evacuated to Wells. Jennifer and Bettye lived on the ground floor and the cook lived on the top floor, but she didn't cook for the girls. Michael paid many illicit visits there when out on duty runs from the Shirehampton dépôt. He once found himself in trouble. His duty car — a large Studebaker parked outside — wouldn't start. He was off his official route and it took ages to get the car going. In the morning he was late back and 'on the mat' being asked to account for himself.

From that first Christmas Michael and Bettye were seldom apart and Minnie gave them virtually the first taste of freedom either of them had ever known. Freedom from the constraints of the narrow life they had lived before the war. There must have been thousands of young people to whom that applied. Certainly they were driving ambulances and doing their bit, but they 'played up' and were incorrigible in the matter of going sick, having appointments and not being where they should be at the right time. ARP was a civilian organisation and the rules were much more lax than in the services. Rather like the modern emergency services, being on duty meant long hours hanging around, drinking tea, talking, playing table tennis until the emergency happened — but when it did in the war-time blitz — Oh my dear life! It was mayhem! During that winter of 1940-1941 much of the centre of Bristol was destroyed and Michael and Bettye were in the thick of it.

The Revd. and Mrs L.R. Henslow and family, Zeals Rectory, Wilts.
Michael's mother is in the top left hand corner.

Now a little about Michael's family. Michael's mother had been born Agatha Sybil Henslow in 1876, one of eleven children of Leonard and Susan Henslow. Her father was the dearly loved Rector of Zeals, Wiltshire, for forty four years and her grandfather was Professor J S Henslow, life-long friend and mentor of Charles Darwin.

The Henslow family consisted of:

Eltheda	Died young.
Katherine	Died young.
Geoffrey	Parish Priest who married a Bishop's daughter and who was later defrocked.
Veronica	Much loved GP in Bath for fifty years. She married John Christie, the Rector of Batheaston. She became John Armstrong's Godmother.
Lancelot	Colonel in the Wiltshire Regiment. He was Commandant of the Physical Training School, at Aldershot.
Leonora	A nun who died in her middle years.
Ginevera	Headmistress of St Swithun's Junior School, Winchester.
Agatha	Michael's mother, married Henry William Armstrong, an Irish widower of fifty-seven.
Raymond	Went to Cambridge and achieved nothing other than a little occasional tutoring — a brilliant raconteur.
Cyril	Became a Roman Catholic Priest and was disowned by the family — quite 'beyond the pale'.
Hermione	Spinster, who lived quietly in Zeals. She became Mary Armstrong's Godmother.

The Henslows were a distinguished family in the nineteenth century and Michael had illustrious forebears, with several eminent botanists in the family. John Stephens Henslow (1796-1861) was Regius Professor of Botany at Cambridge University. He was Darwin's tutor and mentor and a life-long friend. It was he who proposed Darwin for the famous voyage of the *Beagle* which sailed from Plymouth in December 1831 and lasted for five years. John Henslow's son, George, was a lecturer in botany at St Bartholomew's Medical School, 1866-90.

Sir Joseph Hooker, Michael's great uncle who brought the first Rhododendron to England from the Himalayas, was the director of Kew Gardens for twenty years from 1865-1885 and was knighted in

1877. There is a memorial to him in Westminster Abbey where the Abbey honours Modern Science.[1]

Joseph Hooker married Frances Henslow, eldest daughter of Professor John Henslow, in 1851 and when he died in 1911 at the age of ninety-four he left £38,800, quite a lot of money in those days!

Another Henslow ancestor was Henry Addington who was for eleven years Speaker of the House of Commons during Pitt's premiership of 1783-1800. Addington followed Pitt and was Prime Minister from 1800-1807. He was a well meaning but not eminent statesman whose relationship with Pitt was expressed in the couplet "Pitt is to Addington what London is to Paddington" — not a particularly successful Prime Minister. Later he became the first Lord Sidmouth with a family seat at Ottery St Mary, Devon. Henry Addington died in 1844.

Agatha Henslow was the beauty of the Henslow family; six feet tall, intellectual and autocratic. On 5th June 1905 at the age of twenty-nine she married a clergyman, the Revd. Henry William Armstrong, Rector of the neighbouring parish of Lacock. He was a well connected Irish widower aged fifty-six, son of Colonel William Andrew Armstrong, 1st Battalion of the 14th Regiment. It was a large and fashionable country wedding and the bride's uncle, Sir Joseph Hooker, the Director of Kew Gardens, arranged for the flowers to be sent from Kew to decorate the church and the rectory. After the wedding they travelled in a specially chartered train to their reception

Agatha Henslow,
Michael Armstrong's mother.

[2] Whilst researching the life and letters of Sir Joseph Hooker for this book the author came across a description of Dartmouth written by him in 1899:
"Dartmouth harbour is charming, but the town beastly, swarming with dirty children and a population of loutish men and distressingly plain women. The predominance of dirty little lolly pop shops is a feature of the place."
(Today that description might well apply to many seaside resorts.)

held at the Arachne Club in Russell Square, London. There was a party for the villagers in Lacock in the evening. Their honeymoon was spent on the edge of the New Forest, in a house loaned to them by friends. History does not record how they reached it. They returned to live in the Rectory at Lacock where their son, Henry Michael Andrew Armstrong, was born on 19th February, 1906. He was to be their only child. As his mother explained to Bettye — she wasn't having any more of "that"!

Henry William Armstrong, as a young man.

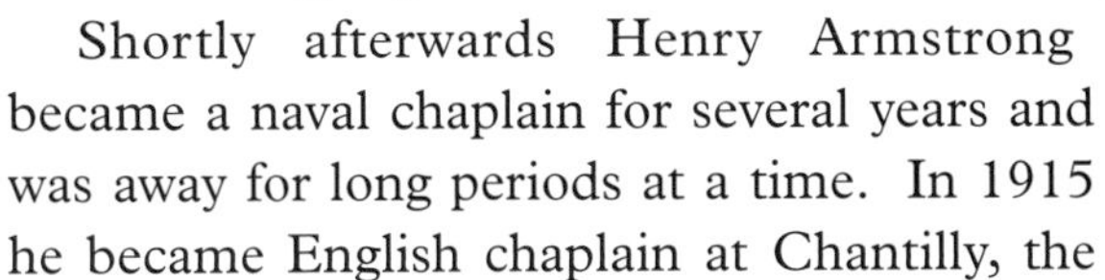

Shortly afterwards Henry Armstrong became a naval chaplain for several years and was away for long periods at a time. In 1915 he became English chaplain at Chantilly, the charming little French racing town on the edge of the forest about twenty five miles south of Paris. He was joined by his family and there the Armstrongs lived in the parsonage until 1924, when they returned to England. They made good and lasting friends among the leading families of the racing fraternity. Michael went to school in Paris and spoke fluent French. He hobnobbed with the stable lads and picked up fluent colloquial French too! For the rest of his life he retained a keen interest in racing.

Michael Armstrong, with his grandfather, Revd. Henslow.

On their return to England Henry Armstrong accepted the living at Down St Mary, Devon, where they lived in the rectory. When they arrived in Down St Mary Michael was eighteen and apart from his fluent French his education had been sketchy so he had no academic qualifications which would take him further. There was little money beyond Henry Armstrong's stipend. In his parents' view there was only one option for their son — the church. Michael had a deep and abiding faith which never left him but he did not want to go into the church — he would have

The Rectory, Down St. Mary, Devon.

charmed his parishioners but he would have made an erratic parson and a dog collar would not have become him. He had a passion for flying and a burning ambition to go into the Royal Air Force. His parents would not hear of it — to them, especially to his aged father, the RAF was a suicide squad but apart from that in those days one needed a private income to go to Cranwell and funds would not have run to it. There was deadlock between Michael and his parents and so for the next few years he did little.

Henry W Armstrong, Michael's father, Rector of Down St Mary 1925-1934.

By 1930 his parents were seriously concerned about his future and under pressure from them he reluctantly agreed to go into the church. So in 1931 he enrolled at Clifton Theological College in Bristol and in fact once there he did well and was enjoying it. But a career in the church was not to be. He had what in those days was a fast motor bike and in 1932 he had a very serious crash on his bike and was nearly killed; he fractured his skull badly. He took a long time to recover from his injuries and spent months recuperating. He never went back to college and he was to suffer severe headaches for the rest of his life.

Clifton Theological College, 1932. Michael Armstrong is 3rd from left, 3rd row from front.

By 1932 Henry Armstrong's eyesight was failing badly — in fact his wife had been writing his sermons for him for some time; early in 1933 he was almost blind and forced to retire when he was eighty-four years old. They moved from the rectory to The Mill House, Down St Mary, where he died the following year. He is buried in the churchyard at Down St Mary.[2]

The Mill House had a thatched roof with three large rooms on the ground floor, four bedrooms in a row upstairs with a staircase at each end. It nestled under a hill about a mile from the village of Down St Mary. It was attractive but primitive — no sanitation at all, no electricity or gas and not even a cold water tap in the house. Water was drawn from a well a few yards away from the kitchen door by dunking a bucket in it. Milk had to be fetched daily in a jug from the farm which was half a mile away. There was not even an 'Elsan'[3]. In fact as Bettye, a 'townie at heart', was to discover later the Mill House was picturesque but extremely uncomfortable, draughty, damp and overrun with mice. They scampered along the dado rail during supper and were ignored even by the cat and dog! The only means of cooking was in a tin box which had to be balanced on the open log fire. Hot water was provided by a black iron kettle which swung above the fire on a stout black chain.

There is no doubt that the Armstrongs had found life difficult since Michael's father had died and his income with him! After his father's death Michael continued to live with his mother at the Mill House but

---

[2] His wife, Agatha, was also buried there in 1949.

[3] Chemical lavatory.

at that time there were no pensions for clergy widows and when Henry died her income ceased. She had no private means, what family money had come their way from time to time had long since gone. She was virtually penniless and extremely proud. For a long time she refused to accept the tiny state pension of 10/- (50p) per week to which she was entitled. Seventy years on it is difficult to understand how they got into such financial straits. Michael worked and minded not in the least what he did. It has to be understood that to his mother 'trade' was a dirty word and so any work that Michael did was done in the spirit of the Rector's son kindly helping the parishioners, which really meant he was never paid properly. They would be grateful to him and perhaps give him a little something — a couple of rabbits, maybe a dozen eggs or a bunch of flowers for his mother — but for him to have given anyone a proper bill would have been unthinkable. Even when the Armstrongs first arrived in Devon from Chantilly and Michael, aged eighteen or nineteen, sometimes won the high jump in the sports events held during the summer in surrounding Devon villages, on no account had he been allowed to accept a monetary prize. If given one he had to return it. Gentlemen did not accept money! And so they struggled on selling a family treasure to raise funds now and then.

Despite her straitened circumstances, Agatha Armstrong had delusions of grandeur which never left her and she carried her impoverishment with great dignity. She would happily throw an old shawl over a teapot to keep it warm but spurned tea cosies as frightfully middleclass. She was a stoic resourceful old lady typical of her breed and era and it was amazing what splendidly nourishing country meals she could produce under such conditions and with war time rationing. She was an expert at improvising — she needed to be. The all important thing was "one must keep one's end up, my dear."

Mrs Armstrong's situation was something that Bettye had never encountered before. Certainly the Whittingtons had never had any spare money but the little Edgcumbe Hotel had housed and fed them. Although it made no profit there was always a "little something" to be produced in an emergency but Michael's mother lived from hand to mouth. If Michael mended a wireless for someone and they paid him there would be money to buy meat from the butcher tomorrow otherwise the menu would be leek and potato soup and baked apples — all from the garden. But it was all enormously dignified. If a charity donation was requested it would be given even if that meant no meat tomorrow. "Amour-propre" had to be preserved at all costs. But when

Michael was accepted by Air Transport Auxiliary (ATA) and was properly and regularly paid he was very good to his mother, and was able to help her and life became somewhat more comfortable for her. Michael was an only child and his Mother idolised him. She was wise but sometimes even the most devoted mothers have to accept their children's decisions in matters of the heart and she to her credit, when it came to it, accepted Bettye graciously. In fact Bettye was to say later she learnt a great deal from her mother-in-law.

In 1936 with the Second World War looming the Government had introduced a scheme for teaching young people to fly. It was called the Civil Air Guard (CAG) and flying clubs around the country then offered subsidised flying lessons for 2/6d. per hour (12½p). Michael was delighted and immediately joined the CAG at Exeter Flying Club. He took to it like a duck to water. He worked hard at his 'odd jobs' to earn the money for the flying lessons; at times he was a car salesman and demonstrator for Stanfield and White in Exeter. He gave driving lessons; he dabbled with wirelesses and motor engines in a desultory fashion. He became an electrician and sometimes drove coaches but he nursed his ambition and the only thing he really wanted to do was fly.

Before long he had gained his pilot's licence and from then on all his spare time, money, and energy were spent at the flying club. In fact that was to stand him in good stead later because it was his flying experience that enabled him to get in to the ATA. There is no doubt that had his parents allowed him to go into the RAF in the 1930s he would have made a big success of it for, when he eventually became a ferry pilot during the war, he was a very good one. Whether he would have survived the war is another matter!

At the beginning of the war he tried to enlist for flying duties in the RAF but was turned down on medical grounds. He would not accept a ground job and was still desperate to get into flying. In 1940 he applied to ATA but at that time he had not enough hours in his log book and so in June of that year while waiting to get into ATA he had joined the ARP in Bristol as an ambulance driver.

Michael, who was knowledgeable about mechanics, soon realised that Bettye's little car, Minnie, the Austin 7 Chummy would run on tractor vaporising oil, known as TVO, once the engine was warm; but it had to be started with petrol, so with a little ingenuity he fixed a plum tin which held about 1½ pints of petrol under Minnie's bonnet, put a switch on the dashboard so that she could be started on petrol and when the engine had warmed up he could switch on to TVO. It

"Up to no good" !

was highly illegal of course, but TVO was un-rationed, much cheaper than petrol, and it worked. He and Bettye travelled thousands of miles in that little car, often in extreme discomfort; there was no heater. They draped rugs over the ill fitting side panels, but still the wind howled around and Bettye sat huddled in her little bucket seat with a rubber hot water bottle on her lap and a rug around her knees, — but oh, what fun they had! They toured all round the West Country. Amid all the miseries and deprivations of war there was a carefree happy-go-lucky air — a sort of "let's live for today for tomorrow may never come" — and for many, sometimes, it didn't. Like thousands of other young people they were doing their bit and having fun.

They had little money but what did they care? They were together, they had Minnie, and she never let them down. They dossed on friends' floors, stayed in cottage 'B&Bs' and whenever possible went to Feock, where Peter, working in a reserved occupation in Truro as a GPO engineer, was renting "Greenbank", a thatched furnished cottage for which he paid £1.00 per week. He shared it with Wilfred Hancock, who also worked for the GPO. Incidentally, Wilfred and his wife were later to be the owners of Trevelgue Hotel, Newquay.

"Greenbank", Feock, rented by Peter Whittington 1941 - 1943.

The cottage in Feock was also extremely primitive — an outside cold tap, no electric light, and an 'Elsan' in a hut in the garden, emptied once a week by a man who wanted the contents to fertilise his violets. The bath was a tin affair in an outhouse, to which hot water had to be carried in kettles. There was a little oil cooker on which Bettye, when she visited, made delicious soups with vegetables often obtained by hopping over the hedge and picking them in the fields around, and skimmed milk fetched from the farm in a large jug for 1d. (less than ?p). There was a dire shortage of everything except potatoes, bread, and fish, which was expensive. Rationing was very strict. Each adult was allowed, per week, 4 ozs. bacon and ham. Meat to the value of 1s. 2d. (6p). Sausages, made mostly of bread, were not rationed but difficult to get; offal was officially unrationed but sometimes formed part of the meat ration. 2 ozs. of butter, cheese, and tea. 4 ozs. of margarine and cooking fat, 8 ozs. of sugar. 1 shell egg a week if available but at times dropping to 1 every two weeks. Dried eggs — 1 packet each 4 weeks. Preserves 1lb. every two months. Milk 3 pints weekly. Sweets 12 ozs. per month (approx. one small chocolate bar per week). It was frugal but everyone managed somehow.

One day in 1942 Bettye and Michael, while staying with Peter in the cottage at Feock, decided they would all drive over to Newquay to have Sunday lunch with Bettye and Peter's mother. They got as far as Shortlanesend when they ran out of petrol and they were stuck for it was quite impossible to get more. Fortunately they were near the pub and

Peter knew the landlord. He dashed in and somehow persuaded him to empty the paraffin oil out of the lamp on the bar counter. They went happily on their way, belching paraffin fumes.

Peter Whittington as an Officer Cadet in the Royal Corps of Signals, off to India.

Peter and Wilfred gave up the Feock cottage when Peter was called up in January 1943. He went into the army and was sent to Catterick, Yorks, for training. In late 1943 he was posted to India and sailed from Southampton to Bombay as an Officer Cadet. In India he was attached to the Royal Corps of Signals and worked closely with the Americans keeping the lines of communication open. He returned to the UK as Captain Whittington at the end of 1946 and vowed never to go to India again. He hated it!

Looking back, Michael and Bettye's existence while waiting to be called up for ATA was perhaps a war time version of the modern 'gap year' which so many young people enjoy today when they backpack around the world before facing up to the realities of life, although they did not realise it at the time of course. They had briefly escaped from reality and they had no thought of the morrow, let alone what they might do when the war was over. The height of their ambitions was to camp in a tent on the Mendip Hills — which they never achieved, and to get into ATA, which they did! But they lost themselves or found themselves, which ever way one cares to look at it. They lived for the day — and in between they drove ambulances in Bristol.

Recently one of Bettye's grandsons said to her "Grannie I've been reading your book again and although you write of you and Grandpa having your first taste of freedom during the war and you likened it to a 'gap year' you didn't say what you actually did or where you went. In a gap year people travel the world and you didn't tell us much about the ARP dépôt and the Bristol blitz although you were in the thick of it." Bettye pondered on this and realised her recollections of those momentous days were hazy because the overwhelming thing at the time was that she and Michael Armstrong had fallen in love. She was on 'cloud nine' and everything else — even the bombs, blitz and the war itself faded into insignificance; the truth is, of course, that they were up to no good at all, but she has no wish to give this family saga a 'Jilly Cooper' touch. Enough to say that they, like many thousands of young people, had for the first time escaped the constraints of the narrow lives they had lived before the war and they made the most of it. They lived for the day.

Of course the war itself imposed enormous restrictions on everyone. It was impossible to get petrol, everything was in short supply; there was rigid rationing and many government controls. The finest restaurants in the land could only charge 5/- per meal, and the Savoy Hotel in London offered a special rate for service men of five guineas (£5.25) per night and the chaps made the most of it. Many took their wives or girlfriends there whenever they could get away — it was the thing to do. Unfortunately Michael Armstrong could not afford it but he and Bettye were quite happy with their little country cottage 'B & Bs', which cost 5/- (25p) and they had found a freedom they had never known before — or since. For many, many people normal life was suspended from 1940-1945 but there was great camaraderie; everyone was in the same boat and even the political parties buried their differences and worked together in a coalition.

ATA was a wartime civilian organization set up by Gerard d'Erlanger at the outbreak of the Second World War. It was a Ferry Pilot Service and its main function was ferrying aircraft around the country to and from the factories and Maintenance Units (MUs) to the airfields for the RAF. The original pilots were an elite band of aviators with a hundred hours in their log books. Some had their own planes before the war. Later, less experienced flyers were accepted, which was when Michael Armstrong joined. ATA could only have men who for one reason or another were not eligible for the RAF on medical grounds or perhaps age. There were some First World War pilots, and there were also disabled pilots, several with only one arm, but they all seemed to cope most ably. Later girls were recruited to train ab initio and Bettye was one of the first five to be accepted. Later some girls managed to transfer from the RAF to train as pilots. In all ATA had over six hundred pilots and about one hundred of these were women. They flew all types of planes without radio or instruments. ATA limits were 2,000 yards visibility and a height of 800 feet. If owing to weather that was not possible they did not fly. Amy Johnson[4] and her husband Jim Mollison, both with great record-breaking flying achievements

---

[4] Amy Johnson was killed in ATA in January 1941 while ferrying an Oxford from the north of England. It was poor weather and she was advised not to take off, but she was over-confident and she replied "I can smell my way round England." She crashed into the Thames and her body was never found.

behind them, John Cobb, the pre-war racing driver and Philip Wills, later British Gliding champion, were all pilots in ATA. There were also MT drivers, engineers and ground staff — some 1,500 in all. This then was the organization Michael was determined to join and he was tenacious about it. A splendid atmosphere prevailed rather like a large flying club and many, like Mike Armstrong, were dismayed when ATA was finally disbanded in November 1945. They had loved it!

When Michael was eventually invited to present himself at ATA Headquarters at White Waltham, near Maidenhead, for an interview and flight test, he passed with flying colours. Bettye also went along to enrol as an MT Driver. At first they wouldn't have her, so she went to the Labour Exchange and was told ATA didn't need drivers, but they did need clerks. She shuffled in as a clerk in the Catering Office where she spent about two weeks pushing papers around and checking the prices of jam and other boring items; she hated it. However she soon sought out the Manager of the MT department and with her talk of driving Western National buses and ambulances she was quickly transferred to driving — much more her line! Once they had joined ATA it was another story. Michael especially was conscientious to a degree and life took on a serious aspect — their salad days were over. He was a reliable pilot, flew long hours, and worked hard. ATA suited him well, and he it. He felt his patience and persistence about joining had been justified.

By late 1942, ATA were getting seriously short of pilots and decided to invite girls who were already in the organisation to apply for ab initio training as pilots. Three hundred immediately applied; many of them drivers. Michael was keen for Bettye to apply, but she sat back and considered and listened to how the other applicants got on. The requirements were age twenty-one to twenty-seven, 5ft 6ins tall, unmarried and with school certificate. The girls were all turned down, mostly over the school certificate question. When Bettye applied she was determined to give Pauline Gower, the Women's Commandant, the right answers. She wrote home for details of her brother's school certificate, so with a little bending of the rules (which, incidentally, she has always thought are for bending) she sailed through and was one of the first five girls accepted out of three hundred who applied for ab initio flying training. Michael was so proud of her and promised her an emerald ring when she made her first solo flight. She had to wait some twenty-six years for the emerald ring — he couldn't afford it at the time, but he gave her one for their silver wedding in 1968.

Bettye and Michael were married in Reading on 23rd July, 1943 at Reading Registry Office, with a Blessing afterwards by the Bishop of Reading. She wore a navy blue bouclé suit from Wollands, for which she had scrounged coupons from all her friends, with a matching small navy blue hat. Owing to the difficulties of war time travel no member of either family was able to be there, and there were no photographs taken, they had no cameras. There were just two witnesses, Eve Longmore, who became Mary's Godmother, and John Pippet, both in ATA. Afterwards they had luncheon and a bottle of champagne at the Great Western Hotel by the station in Reading; a typical war time wedding. The Hotel was later demolished. In the afternoon Michael had to return to duty and Bettye and Eve went shopping. Bettye and Michael then had a three day honeymoon at the Thames Hotel, Maidenhead.

Michael and Bettye Armstrong, at Down St Mary, in their wedding garb, 1943.

Soon after they were married, Michael was posted to No.2 Ferry Pool at Whitchurch Aerodrome, Bristol. Although Bettye was enjoying flying and was doing well, there was no question but that she would go to Bristol with him; they had been waiting for some two-and-a-half years for her divorce to go through, so she resigned from ATA. However, they were both to regret later that she did not go a little further with the flying. She would have liked to have progressed to Spitfires and Hurricanes. Ever since when "What did you do in the war?" crops up, the first question she is asked is "Did you fly Spitfires?" It would have been much more dashing to have been able to reply "Yes!"

A.T.A. No. 2 Ferry Pool, Whitchurch, Bristol. The C.O., Commander Len Leaver is the third from the right, sitting.

Manor Farm – From the left - Michael and Bettye's sitting room, third window was their kitchen. Their bedroom was the room over the kitchen.

The newly married Armstrongs moved to furnished quarters at one end of a large manor farm house in Corston, three miles from Bath. At Manor Farm they had a large sitting room, with open fireplace, lit by oil lamps, and a small adjoining makeshift kitchen which was dominated by a large table. There was no sink or even cold water tap. All the water had to be carried in and out in buckets and the cooker was a flimsy, freestanding oil affair which flared up from time to time and covered the room in black smitch. There was no electricity in the house and an oil lamp stood on the kitchen table.

Their daughter, Mary, was born in the maternity wing of the Forbes Fraser Hospital in Bath on 6th May 1944. Every morning before Michael left for the aerodrome he drew a bucket of cold water from the pump outside and fetched another bucket of hot water from the other end of the farmhouse where the farmer and his family lived for Mary's morning bath — in a tin bath on the kitchen table!

Michael collecting water from the other end of the farmhouse.

They only had one bedroom. Michael adored his little daughter, but he was a man of his time and unlike many fathers today. He never changed a nappy and when Mary cried in the night he simply moved out of the bedroom and slept on the

Bath time on the kitchen table at Manor Farm, Corston. Note the washing up bowl in the background.

divan in the corner of the sitting room. Bettye was so desperate at one point that she rang the Quaker Matron of the maternity unit at Forbes Fraser and asked her if she would take the baby back for a few weeks to sort her out. Eventually, of course, it all settled down. For the first two months Mary could not go out because they had been unable to buy a pram. Such items were no longer in the shops. Eventually Michael managed to buy a second hand one by fighting his way to the head of a queue of twenty-four pregnant women who wanted it! He was proud of himself about that — but it was his only contribution about helping with the baby.

Michael managed to buy a pram.

In Corston there was no village shop or bus service and, of course, Michael needed the car every day and so having given up flying and an exciting life, Bettye found herself stranded in the country without mod. cons., telephone or transport and often, with a screaming baby. Such is life.

What happened to Minnie? They regretfully sold her for £10 as soon as they got into ATA and could afford something a little more 'presentable'. Michael bought a dashing little two seater bright green sports car — an Austin 'Swallow' with a beetle back, which they ran happily until 1944. When Mary was born he had to change the sports car for a small family car which would take a carrycot and all the paraphernalia that goes with a baby. It was a dull little Morris 8 saloon. He didn't mind in the least!

In June 1945, Michael was seconded to the Ferry Pool at Ratcliffe, near Leicester for two weeks and he took the car, leaving Bettye stranded at Manor Farm with their baby. That was more than she could bear and so as soon as she had waved him off she made her own arrangements. She packed an overnight bag, mostly with baby clobber, slung her baby over one shoulder (papooses and the like had not yet been invented), and carrying them both walked the half mile or so to the main Bristol-Bath road. There she hitched a lift with a lorry driver to Temple Meads Station, where she caught a train for Newquay. Her mother, of course, was delighted to see them. Michael collected them two weeks later, and took them back to Corston. Bettye and Mary had had a lovely unexpected summer holiday in Newquay.

Michael and Bettye stayed at Manor Farm until November 1945 when ATA was disbanded and then packed up their paraphernalia, including a table tennis table! and moved back to Newquay. They had no home and so for that winter they joined Olive Whittington at Ashby in Edgcumbe Avenue. Like so many others they were about to begin a new chapter in their lives.

Michael Armstrong — and Spitfire!

Edgcumbe Hotel, Edgcumbe Avenue, re-opens 1945 – 1948

By late 1944 there were signs that the war might soon end and the Armstrongs had long discussions about their future. The choice seemed to be between taking on the Edgcumbe Hotel in Edgcumbe Avenue, which Bettye's mother was thinking of selling, and Michael going into the Fleet Air Arm as a pilot on a short service commission, which would have lasted about five years. He was then thirty-nine years old. They decided they would take on Edgcumbe if there was a proper family arrangement with Bettye's mother. That was to prove a very fortunate choice for the future of their family.

By early 1945 Olive Whittington had made up her mind that when the Edgcumbe Hotel was de-requisitioned, she would not take on the responsibility of running it again. It was understandable. She was nearly sixty years old, had been retired and living quietly for five years. She put the hotel on the market and very soon was offered £6,000, exactly double what it had been valued at before the war. She was very tempted to accept it, but Bettye and Michael were offering to take it on, and Peter sent a cable from India saying "do not sell Edgcumbe". She turned down the offer — and thus the family fortunes arrived at a turning point.

The war in Europe ended in May 1945. The lights came on and the whole country went wild with excitement. Michael had two weeks leave from ATA in late July 1945 and he and Bettye went down to Newquay with Mary, aged fourteen months. They were looking forward to lazing on Tolcarne Beach for a fortnight. When they arrived, they found Newquay in a frenzy. All the hotels had been de-requisitioned with a rush, the town was a-buzz with activity and milling with people seeking accommodation.

At Edgcumbe all the furniture had been brought back and dumped in various rooms in heaps. The carpets and blankets — pure wool of course, were riddled with moth from four years storage in a warm factory building. The furniture was solid, old fashioned and heavy, including wardrobes. None of the flimsy chipboard produced these days. The beds were not light-weight divans, they had heavy wooden ends with iron sides which went between them and had to be properly put together and screwed up tightly with a bed spanner, then the base and mattress had to be mounted on them. It was a two-man job. There was very little labour to get it sorted — it was a mammoth task, impossible really, for a lone, elderly woman. Bettye's mother was in despair. She had just one girl of low mentality to help her and she could not begin to cope.

Michael and Bettye set to work with a will, all thoughts of Tolcarne Beach forgotten. They shoved the furniture around, slapped down carpet squares without underfelts and stained the surrounds with Dark-o-Line. It was virtually impossible to find labour, but Olive found an old man to help put up the beds. Meanwhile she sorted out the linen and soft goods which had been dumped in the dining room in bales and she also dealt with the steady stream of callers at the front door clamouring for rooms. It was utter chaos.

In a few days they managed to take in a few guests — even at that early stage Bettye couldn't say No! As can be imagined it was all very rough and ready, but no-one seemed to mind. One family arrived, a couple with an eleven year old son, pleading for a room. Apparently they had booked at a small guest house with six bedrooms on Mount Wise. When they arrived they found there were seventy-five people staying, most of them sleeping in houses up and down the road, and there were three sittings for every meal. Michael and Bettye promised to prepare a room for them by the next day. They worked long and late to get it ready. That family, the Trathens from Enfield, were to be regular guests at Edgcumbe Hotel for the next thirty years.

Bettye's mother took on the catering and she found it extremely difficult. Rationing was strict; it was almost impossible to get hold of any un-rationed extras. She was unskilled at improvisation, or foraging for food, consequently the menus were very basic: Brown Windsor soup, Spam salad, scrambled dried eggs and bread sausages with a dash of meat featured strongly. But when VJ day

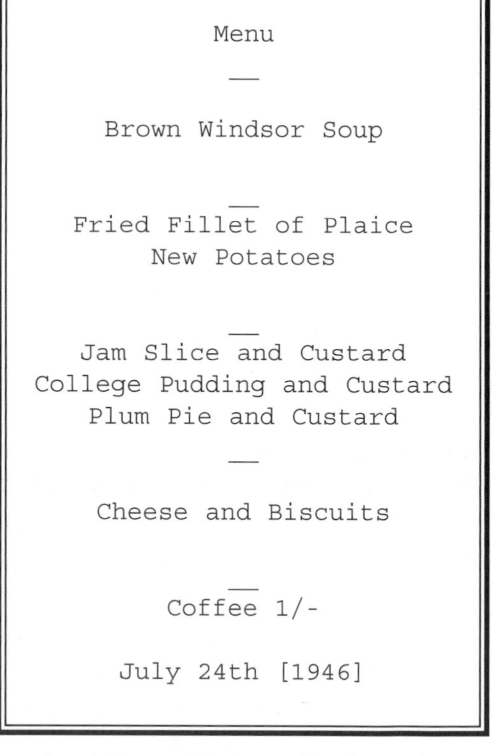
Menu

—

Brown Windsor Soup

—

Fried Fillet of Plaice
New Potatoes

—

Jam Slice and Custard
College Pudding and Custard
Plum Pie and Custard

—

Cheese and Biscuits

—

Coffee 1/-

July 24th [1946]

Lunch Menu 1946 - it was illegal to make Cornish cream.

was announced and the World War was finally over they did manage a celebratory dinner with roast Cornish chicken as the main course and a little illicit Cornish cream on the pudding! all washed down with almost undrinkable Algerian wine which cost 8/- per bottle (40p)! It was much appreciated by the guests: an air of elation prevailed. At last after nearly six years of separation, deprivation, and hardship, the war was really over and the country went mad.

Looking back one wonders how they ever managed to open the hotel — even for a few people for a few weeks! The staff must have been dragged off the streets in a hurry. One night Michael and Bettye, too tired to put their bed up, were asleep on a mattress on the floor on bare boards with furniture piled around them when their bedroom door opened and a torch shone on them. It was a friendly policeman on night patrol who had found the front door open and had come in to see if everything was all right. On being assured it was, he said "Goodnight Sir" and went on his way.

When Michael had to report back for duty in Bristol, Bettye stayed to help her mother for a few more weeks. They seemed to be having a mini season and the money was much needed. All the debts which had been set aside in 1940-41 now had to be paid. The outstanding bills were owed chiefly to local shopkeepers and Olive Whittington was anxious to settle them so that Edgcumbe would face the 1946 season with a "clean slate". She dealt with this in her own way. She persuaded Bettye to see the local creditors and negotiate a settlement — and get a discount for cash, if possible, even after five years! She was teaching her daughter! So, before she returned to Bath in mid-September, Bettye scuttled around the town on foot — no car or petrol — and paid the outstanding bills from the failed 1940 season, mostly with discount for cash. Thus the pre-war debts were settled. It meant another lean winter for Olive Whittington, but Edgcumbe was out of debt although mortgaged to the hilt. However, Bettye soon discovered there were repercussions. Edgcumbe had lost its credit worthiness. In 1946 a shop in Newquay, John Julian, refused to allow her to take goods worth £12.00 from the shop without payment. She was mortified and outraged and it was to be many years before she set foot in that shop again. Once the 1946 season got under way, although money was to be tight for many years, there were no more difficulties of that kind.

Next the compensation claim for damage to the hotel had to be submitted to the War Office. The building had been used as a sergeants' mess for five years. The new maple dance floor had been swabbed daily with water, smashed lead-light windows were boarded up, there were cracked basins and loos and broken locks, missing cupboard doors and the whole place was a shambles. It needed redecorating throughout.

Olive Whittington was unable to cope with the complicated form filling. She had engaged Fred Luxon, a local man, to act as her agent in getting the claim settled. He was a clever, wealthy chap with a well established business. He was also personable, and sharp! When Bettye met him first she was disconcerted to discover that her mother was in thrall to Mr Luxon. He was telling her what should be done and she was in "Yes, Mr Luxon. No Mr Luxon, my big toe Mr Luxon." mode. He was clearly in charge and he wasn't going to talk to Bettye who also had firm ideas about what should be done, and in what order. She wasn't going to join the Luxon fan club either. A battle ensued, chiefly about what could or could not be done before the painters took over.

The War Office finally agreed to pay £750 damages (perhaps £10,000 today). Luxon received the cheque as Mrs Whittington's agent and put it straight into his coffers. Then he arranged for his firm to carry out the repairs. That was actually illegal because the agent and builder were not allowed to be the same firm. He also acted for others hotels in the town, including the Headland. However, in the post-war scramble to get ready for the 1946 season everyone seemed to ignore the rules and Luxon's men carried out the basic repairs. All the walls were slapped with cream distemper and the woodwork was painted dark brown just as it had been before the war.

Many people, like Olive Whittington, were relieved when he didn't send a bill as soon as the work was finished, nor at the end of the following season, but they were in for a shock about three years later when the bills arrived. He didn't account for the monies he had collected as agent; he simply said in effect "You owe me so much" without any detail about how the figure had been arrived at. Even the accountant couldn't get figures out of him. If the bill wasn't settled smartly he threatened court proceedings. The Armstrongs refused to pay and asked for details. When none was forthcoming they invited Luxon to sue them. He never did so they didn't pay — but many smaller business owners were intimidated and so paid up and were done down. It was the smart big boy bullying the little chaps — and some not so little!

Looking back how fortuitous it was that the Armstrongs had by chance arrived home on leave in 1945. Had they not done so Bettye's mother, alone and unable to cope, might well have sold Edgcumbe and retired and the outcome would have been very different. As it was the whole chaotic scene they had found had stimulated them and fired their enthusiasm. They returned to Bath with their minds firmly made up — they were going into the hotel business in Newquay. Their path was set and they couldn't wait to get going with it, but first they had other matters to attend to.

In November 1945 ATA was finally disbanded and the Armstrongs, with Mary, aged eighteen months, packed up their clobber in Corston, outside Bath, and returned to Newquay for good. They lived for that winter in "Ashby", with Bettye's mother, who was delighted to have her little grand daughter with her.

In January 1946 Michael and Bettye set to work with a will. They had a busy winter trying to get Edgcumbe shipshape for the coming season. Immediately after the war and for some time to come even furniture and bedding were rationed. There was a great demand for second hand goods (incidentally Bettye still loves buying second hand; she thinks she caught the bug in 1946 when nothing could be bought in the shops). Michael and Bettye as "young marrieds" were entitled to coupons to help them set up home; their coupons went on new dining room chairs for the Edgcumbe! Home had to wait — the hotel had to get going first! Of course there were carpets, blankets etc. to be replaced. There was a great deal of work to be done, but very little money or labour with which to do it. They managed to get the vital hot and cold running water in one or two bedrooms, although it was to be several years later before they were all so equipped.

When the war ended, overnight it seemed to the locals the Newquay hotels were being bought and sold like pounds of apples. It was said 'Northerners' came with their pockets weighed down with coppers from their war years of running amusement arcades and fruit machines in Blackpool. Maybe, but it is a fact that most of the hotels of any size changed hands, some several times, in the years immediately after the war. The main exceptions were the Hotel Bristol, Penolver, Great Western, Trenance, Beachcroft and Trelawney. There were one or two other medium size hotels which remained in the same ownership, Trevone being one, but they were certainly in the minority. In Edgcumbe Avenue the Armstrongs struggled to get their little project off the ground.

Like everything else in Newquay, the beaches faced an exciting new future and it all got going with a tremendous rush. Soon Johnnie Ice Cream was back with his pony and cart. Wafers had gone up to 6d. (2.5p), cornets were 3d, and for some years many of the pre-war families returned to the beach and all went on much as before. There were a few changes, of course — not all for the better. Self-service had arrived and Queenie wasn't there to haul the deck chairs and bathing machines about. The machines were still used for a few years but were static. Visitors had to collect their own deck chairs and return them to get their deposits back. Today they have to bring their own chairs. It was a bright new world — and a new generation of modern young people was going to enjoy it to the full.

Johnnie Ice Cream was back on the beaches with his pony and cart. – *Courtesy Mrs Staffiere.*

At a Christmas party in December 1945 Bettye and Michael met a personable girl, Maggie Dyer, who had just come out of the ATS as a Regimental Sergeant Major. Like many other people at the time she was wondering what to do next. It was arranged that she would become a member of the Edgcumbe team for the 1946 season. Maggie Dyer really had no skills, but she had a good sense of humour and personality, was an experienced driver, and had a talent with people. In ATS she had been one of the Army staff who had taught Princess Elizabeth (now HM Queen Elizabeth II) to drive. She was prepared to have a go at anything providing it wasn't in the kitchen!

From January 1946 Newquay was hectic; the town was inundated with postal enquiries, Newquay had never known anything like it. The bookings and deposits rolled in; mostly in postal orders or cash (a deposit of two guineas (£2.10) per person was charged). In those free and easy days before VAT, deposits could go straight into a bank account and be used — and how useful they were! For years to come many Newquay families scraped along, living from hand to mouth, on the deposits from January until the season began. These days it is against the rules. Most of the commandeered buildings had been de-requisitioned and were in a deplorable state, badly knocked about, but it was almost impossible to get materials and labour — even unskilled labour was at a premium and cowboy builders were rampant. Clearly the coming season was going to be a boomer and of course everyone wanted to be ready for it. It was just cover the cracks, slap distemper on the walls, flop down lino on rough floors — or at best a carpet square with Dark-o-line around the edges, and paint everything in sight.

By mid-April '46 the Edgcumbe was fully booked for the whole season with weekly bookings Saturday to Saturday, for full board, with a child's bed or cot tucked in every available corner — it was a piece of cake! After the hotel was opened hundreds of enquiries continued to flood in and many went unanswered. There was no receptionist and Bettye just couldn't cope.

Immediate post-war guests at Edgcumbe.

When the Armstrongs started up in January 1946 Michael had no experience at all and Bettye had helped her mother for only two or three seasons. They had no money, but they had great enthusiasm for what they were about to tackle and they just put the little hotel together as best they could, and opened their doors, but they had to find themselves a long-term builder. They were very fortunate when they took on Arnold Pearce, a Newquay man who had inherited his father's firm. Arnold Pearce was completely honest, trustworthy, and full of integrity and he did all the Armstrongs' building work for the next twenty five years. They worked together in complete harmony and he never let them down. He was something of an entrepreneur himself, and at one stage he asked Bettye to go into partnership with him in a camping site which was being sold just outside Newquay, but she felt too committed to what she was doing to take on anything else at the time. A great pity!

Edgcumbe Hotel opened in April 1946 with eight guests and went like a bomb from the beginning. It was a rip-roaring season. No longer had guests to be wooed — they were fighting to get in. Thousands of service men had discovered Newquay while stationed there during the war, now they brought their wives and families to show them what a beautiful place it was. They had their gratuities in their pockets, their demob suits on their backs, and they were determined to have fun — and what fun they had! Maggie Dyer proved to be a great asset and was very popular with the guests. She and Olive Whittington did the housekeeping between them. The bed linen and tablecloths were only changed once a week on Saturdays; the tablecloths in the dining room were turned over on Wednesdays. The dining room seated fifty guests — twelve rectangular tables for four arranged tea-shop fashion and one for two. There were just two waitresses who worked a seven day week and were paid 15/- (75p).

Maggie only stayed the one season at the Edgcumbe and then departed to do other things. Michael and Bettye were sorry she wouldn't stay but it was too hectic for her; the nights too late, and worse, the mornings too early! But she and the Armstrongs were to remain life-long friends.

In 1946 Newquay "took off" and the town was never to be the same again. The long term locals were staggered by the speed with which it happened. During the "Sutton" years before the war the family had never returned to Newquay to prepare for the season until Easter. The main booking period had been April and May and the season proper was from mid June to mid September, or even a little shorter, but from 1946 onwards it was to be a different ballgame — entirely different.

No one had had a proper holiday for five years and foreign travel was not yet available to the masses. There were no package holidays or cheap flights and many people simply did not know how to go abroad. For some years after the war there were currency controls so that legally one could only take £25 out of the country. Petrol was tightly rationed until the 1950s and so the English seaside resorts came into their own and traditional seaside holidays were the thing. Cornwall, and especially Newquay, was among the most popular destinations. The boom was on, there was to be no downturn in Newquay's fortunes as a holiday resort for the next thirty years. It was to continue to grow with ever more accommodation of all kinds on offer until the mid-seventies, when the post-war bonanza would tail off and the real battle would begin with the foreign package holidays, holiday camps and self-catering as serious competition.

After the war some locals soon realised there was an easy way of earning money with their spare rooms — "Bed and Breakfast", and before long a rash of Bed and Breakfast signs appeared on houses and cottages all over the county. They flourished for a year or two, but then the visitors realised that it was not a very economical way of holidaying, especially with a family. It meant buying, and often queuing, for every meal, and the most formidable landladies banned the guests from returning to their rooms until a certain time in the evening. Some became greedy and overcharged; before long many visitors sensibly refused to book the rooms unless an evening meal was provided. The Bed and Breakfast boom was over and landladies had to cook an evening meal for guests if they wished to fill their rooms. Bed and Breakfast then reverted to what it had always been — just a bed for people passing through on touring holidays.

There were as yet no holiday camps, and very few camp sites. Most offered no facilities, a pitch for a tent or caravan, perhaps a communal cold water tap and sanitary arrangements in the corner of the field. They were not very inviting except for the young, impecunious and the most rugged of holidaymakers but they were to have a lasting impact on the town.

From 1946 the quiet and elegant pre-war Newquay with its short seasons, high class shops and four theatres quickly became a bustling, traditional resort for middleclass families. In those wild and heady days immediately after the war one could have let a coal hole in Newquay if it had a bed in it. That year the licensing laws were radically overhauled and for the first time small hotels were granted

George and Charles Dutton (later Lord Sherborne) and Michael Ward, with Michael perched on his minute, illegal bar counter.

restricted licences. From the outset Michael had been determined to get a licence for the Edgcumbe and was quick off the mark about it. When the hotel opened in 1946 it was one of the first small establishments in Newquay to be licensed, but the restrictions imposed with the first licence were nonsensical. There was to be no bar or counter over which drinks could be served, and no-one, not even residents, was permitted to drink after 10.00 p.m. Imagine trying to tell a room full of partying guests that they cannot have another drink after 10.00 p.m. It was farcical, but such was the joyous feeling of euphoria that prevailed that season — it seemed not to matter. Whisky was only available on the black market — at a price, and the hotel had to charge accordingly. The breweries introduced a quota system for the beer. It was never enough, and when it ran out Michael had to somehow get hold of more. One memorable evening, having collected a firkin of beer (nine gallons) for the evening party, his little old car, a battered Morris 8, ran out of petrol and with no more available he abandoned it and the beer in a field at the bottom of Edgcumbe Avenue by the Viaduct. He came back to the hotel empty handed. Catastrophe! One burly chap — a fifteen pint-a-day man — volunteered to walk down and carry it back on his shoulder, and this he did, to the cheers of his drinking buddies and others. Another rip-roaring party was underway!

When Michael Armstrong decided to apply for a licence for Edgcumbe Hotel he really had no idea what he was taking on; or what a serious commitment it would be. Aged forty he had never tackled anything he could not walk away from and so when, at the height of that first hectic season, a wealthy friend from his ATA days invited him to fly down to Monte Carlo for the weekend in his Messenger he considered it. When he put it to Bettye she said "Yes, it would be fun but before you went you'd have to let the guests know when you would be back to open the bar again." Of course he didn't go and for the next ten years he ran the little bar single handed from May - September seven nights a week. It was all late nights and parties, but at the time both Armstrongs took it in their stride and enjoyed it. Occasionally in those heady days, if the party was going well — and Michael especially liked the guests, he and Bettye would invite them into the kitchen to carry on after the dreaded 10.00 p.m. deadline. Sometimes everyone ended up eating eggs and bacon at the kitchen table. Happy days! Thankfully the licensing laws were fairly soon amended and became more practical.

Immediately after the war the Cosy Nook, the New Theatre and the

Newquay Theatre sprang to life like the rest of Newquay, and for a few years they flourished. The large hotels made block bookings — and of course the Armstrongs copied them — and arranged weekly theatre parties for their guests, but change was in the air. Before long every other little joint in town was licensed and had a small bar, even if it was only in a cupboard under the stairs. The new licensees quickly realised that if there was a little "in-house" entertainment, perhaps just a chap strumming a guitar, and there were plenty of those around, the guests would stay in and keep the bar tills ringing merrily. That was to have a very far-reaching effect and certainly was partly the cause of the demise of the Newquay theatres.

Although amazingly successful, the 1946 season was not without enormous difficulties, and the greatest of these was the rationing; most of the necessities in life were in very short supply. Of course, standards were low compared with the present day but people seemed not to mind too much — they understood. Rationing was very strict, and it did make catering difficult — much ingenuity was needed! Kid was sometimes served as roast lamb, rabbit as itself and as chicken. Orange juice and blackcurrant puree, officially available only to children, made flavoursome puddings. Sausages contained 80-90% bread. There was plenty of dried egg which often tasted like scrambled cardboard, but which in skilled hands could be very useful. There were no bananas but banana flavouring was available and popular. Of course the black-market flourished. Michael and Bettye spent many afternoons driving around the countryside cajoling cream, eggs and poultry from friendly farmers. At the time it was illegal for farmers to make cream, but there was always a little to be had if one knew the right people and talked "pretty" to them.

The Armstrongs had a farmer friend, Bert Lutey[1], who Michael had met at the gliding club at Perranporth who offered them a little extra meat to help eke out the meagre ration of 1s 2d. (6p) weekly. They were delighted. He then asked if he might occasionally use The Edgcumbe kitchen table to cut up some meat late at night. That was all right, but after a while he really went too far. Bettye and Michael suddenly realised their kitchen was being used as the butchery for his entire black market operation which was supplying many of the hotels in Newquay. That was not acceptable. They had to put a stop to it smartly, but how helpful that extra meat was at the time. It was difficult to get anything extra, even tea towels had to be bought with coupons.

---

[1] Bert Lutey got into trouble over his 'black market' activities but to his credit he did not implicate his customers.

Bettye, dealing with the office and everything else, found it impossible to cope with the system which entailed collecting a ration book from every guest and cutting out a tiny tea coupon about the size of a little finger nail. Once a month the coupons had to be sent to the Food Office, together with a detailed tally of every meal and every light meal served to both guests and staff throughout that month. The hotel received its complete quota of rations for the next month on the number of tea coupons collected. Guests would rarely offer their ration books voluntarily, for if they managed to retain their tea coupons it would mean extra rations for them when they got home. Inevitably, there came the day when the coupons had to be sent in and Bettye had only collected about half the number she should have had. What to do? She knew she would be in for a battle royal at the Food Office. She decided that they would accept more easily the fact that she had no tea coupons at all, so she went in trepidation to the Food Office, saw the Chief Food Officer and told him they had all been thrown away by mistake. He accepted that happily and she got her full quota of rations for the next month. Not a very creditable story — but she came out with a smile on her face!

Food Enforcement Officers came around every so often to inspect the larder to make sure there was no black market food being used. In a barn near The Mill House, Down St Mary, Devon, where Michael's mother lived, a Danish "spiv" had a mountain of sultanas which had been condemned by the Ministry of Food because they had got wet. They found their way into many bakeries in the West Country and Michael managed to get a constant supply for the Edgcumbe. There was very little sugar to be had and they were an enormous help. At one stage Edgcumbe nearly got into trouble when a disgruntled chef reported to the Food Office that bananas were being served at the hotel. They were available but legally only for children. Bettye managed to talk her way out of that one! Rationing continued until the early fifties.

But with all this the reader can be assured the difficulties recounted here were in fact no worse than the restrictions hoteliers face today. Nothing changes really. Today it is not the Food Enforcement Officers, it is the Environmental Health and Safety inspectors who come round inspecting the cold rooms, searching for any food they fear might be contaminated — perhaps fish which has been in the same 'fridge as meat!! In these days Fire Inspections, Health and Hygiene, Entertainment Licences, Building Control, Planners, and all kinds of officials are telling business people what they may or may not do. In 1946 there really was far, far greater freedom than we now have; the rules and regulations are becoming ever tighter and sometimes they seem well over-the-top and not always even sensible.

In the early days Bettye walked a tightrope with the sleeping out arrangements — officially referred to as 'Annexe rooms'; of course they were nothing of the sort. In those days the demand for rooms far exceeded the supply. People were desperate to get in and would take anything, and Bettye had always found it difficult to say "No". During the high season when there were no rooms available, if someone would accept an 'annexe room' she would take the booking and then endeavour to find a room 'near-by' the hotel for them — and sometimes it was not so 'near by'; perhaps the far end of Edgcumbe Gardens, or Eliot Gardens. She was well versed in who had vacant rooms in the vicinity and who would or would not let them for sleepers. She paid two guineas (£2.10) per double room per week. All bookings were Saturday-Saturday. She spent many Saturday mornings knocking on doors searching for rooms for people to whom she had promised accommodation and who would be arriving in the afternoon.

Occasionally it blew up in her face when the rooms proved to be unacceptable, usually too far from the hotel, too seedy or no hot and cold water, and then there would be a little scene, but it usually worked quite well. In the main people were unfussy as long as they could get in. Gradually all that was to change as standards rose and guests became more discerning. Today with the trades description act, etc., one would be hung, drawn and quartered for such practices, but at the time it helped things along and everyone was happy — especially the Bank Manager!

In 1946 none of these difficulties seemed to matter — it was carnival time — the shortages, trials, and tribulations were there but they mattered not. Michael and Bettye and their team worked very, very hard, and everyone worked a seven day week. The chef had a half day off on Sunday when Bettye relieved him, sometimes with Mary, aged two, in a high chair beside her. At that time a day off during the season was unheard of, but they all had fun too. Occasionally Michael would close the bar when the dancing finished at midnight and join the guests on Tolcarne Beach for a midnight swim, and on returning to the Hotel he would re-open the bar and continue the party far into the night. There were inter-hotel cricket matches on the beach, fancy dress parties, the inevitable table tennis tournaments with a silver cup for the winner, and an ongoing festive atmosphere.

Bettye recalls one bright — but scatty — idea she had about this time. The Edgcumbe would have dinner dances every Saturday throughout the winter. Fired with impetuous enthusiasm she tore up the carpets in the dining room, had a proper strip oak floor laid, bought two large carpet squares that could be taken up for dancing and engaged a trio. The hotel was cold and draughty — there was no heating and there were NO full-time staff. Nobody came — it was a wash-out. Needless to say very soon the oak strip floor had to be covered up with a new fitted carpet. Bettye had wasted much money which they could ill afford and it was a painful lesson. How the young can get carried away when fired by enthusiasm!

Although in the ensuing years standards were to rise — they had to! The hotel became better organised and much more professional, never again was there to be quite the accord between proprietors, guests and staff. It was as though for one summer everyone united to celebrate the peace and all were prepared to suffer the shortages and deficiencies with good humour, knowing that they were inevitable. The Armstrongs closed the hotel on 25th September, after taking their last five guests to Summercourt Fair and having a final party with them afterwards. Whew! What a season, Michael and Bettye were very weary, but elated and well satisfied with their decision to take on the Edgcumbe.

When the season ended Olive Whittington was also delighted with the outcome. For the first time there was money in the bank and she was very generous to Michael and Bettye and shared it with them. There were still many bills to be paid, but the Armstrongs were able to buy their first house, a little bungalow at Holywell Bay, seven miles from Newquay, called "Sand Dunes", with a large garden. They bought it for £1,200 from a close friend, Lingard Duke, who was later to be John's godfather. They put down £500 cash and borrowed the rest from the Midland Bank, and for the first three years let the bungalow furnished in the summer to help pay off the mortgage. While it was let they had to tuck away in an "Ashby" attic and Mary slept with Grannie. The family were up to their necks in mortgages in those days; they had a mountain to climb.

Sand Dunes, the small bungalow with a large garden full of daffodils at Holywell Bay which the Armstrongs bought in 1946 – their first home.

MRS. O. E. B. WHITTINGTON

HOTEL REVENUE ACCOUNT for the year ended 31st. March, 1946

	£	s	d		£	s	d
To Provisions	281	8	-	By Rents receivable	363	2	6
" Wages & National Insurance	193	18	7	" Board Residence	821	10	1
" Rent	64	-	-	" Maintenance	55	10	-
" Rates	98	18	10				
" Lighting & Heating	46	17	5				
" Rooms Out	1	8	6				
" Repairs & Renewals	72	19	9				
" Telephone	12	15	11				
" Laundry	32	14	5				
" Postages, Stationery & Advertising	29	15	11				
" Sundry Expenses	50	11	10				
" Mortgage & Loan Interest	146	16	-				
" Depreciation:- Furniture, Fixtures & Fittings @ 5% p.a.	31	13	10				
" Net Profit	176	3	7				
	1240	2	7		1240	2	7

BALANCE SHEET as at 31st. March, 1946

LIABILITIES	£	s	d	£	s	d	ASSETS	£	s	d	£	s	d
Sundry Creditors				96	6	-	Property at Cost (Subject to Mortgage)				4322	3	9
Loans - Exors. of T. H. Farmer, dec'd	330	-	-				Furniture, Fixtures & Fittings at cost						
Mr. Whittington	250	-	-				Less Depreciation	572	8	8			
Mrs. Armstrong	50	-	-	630	-	-	Additions	61	9	-			
Mortgage				3340	-	-		633	17	8			
							Less: Depreciation @ 5% p.a.	31	13	10	602	3	10
Rehabilitation Payment from War Office	700	-	-										
Less: Expenditure	300	-	-	400	-	-	Linen, Cutlery etc.				280	1	11
Capital Account. Mrs. O. E. B. Whittington							Cash Deposits				22	19	2
Balance as at 1st. April, 1945	1579	3	11				Cash at Bank				100	19	4
Add: Net Profit for the year	176	3	7										
	1755	7	6										
Less: Drawings	893	5	6	862	2	-							
				5328	8	-					5328	8	-

1946 Balance Sheet. Profit for the year was £176. 3s. 7d. Michael and Bettye felt truly 'well-heeled'.

In the autumn of 1946 Michael was able to take Bettye, by train from Victoria, to Chantilly, twenty-five miles south of Paris, where his father had been the English Chaplain during the First World War, and where he had spent many happy years during his boyhood. He introduced her to his old family friends and haunts. They had a lovely and well deserved holiday. While they were away, Grannie looked after Mary, then two and a half years old, with a daily Nannie 'Margie'. Olive had moved into the annexe across the road for the winter, it being cosier than the hotel, and of course the improvements for the next season had to be tackled. Olive Whittington was a very dedicated Grandmother; she adored children and was always happy to be with them.[2] When Bettye and Michael returned from their holiday they moved back, with Mary, to Sand Dunes at Holywell for the winter and worked at Edgcumbe daily from there. They directed the builder and coped with all the bookings and paperwork themselves and in the evenings Bettye made the simple unlined curtains for the hotel bedrooms, while her mother lived in "Ashby" and arranged luncheons for them, and looked after Mary with a daily nursemaid.

Mary among the daffodils at Sand Dunes.

After the wildly successful 1946 season Michael and Bettye really felt they were on their way, but there were more problems ahead. Peter Whittington, Bettye's brother, had not yet returned from India, where he had been serving with the Royal Engineers. When he did come home in November 1946 he was much undecided which

Peter Whittington, John Murray and friend painting the outside of Edgcumbe in the spring of 1947.

[2] Many years later when Bettye's turn for "Grannying" came she reflected ruefully that she could not match her Mother's ability with the little ones. Although she delighted in their company when they were a little older – as she put it – when she could talk to them.

way his life should go, but he was determined he would not go back to his pre-war occupation as a Post Office Engineer. He was offered a very lucrative contract as a civil engineer in Argentina, but he turned it down and again, before he could really decide his future, fate took a hand.

The receptionist Bettye engaged in January 1947 was Barbara Bavistock. She was married and her husband was the manager of the Pavilion Cinema. Barbara was a very intelligent, well educated girl with a great love of opera and had studied medicine for several years before giving it up in order to marry. It was not long before she and Peter had fallen for each other. The family were much upset when Peter and Barbara fell in love; it caused a major family uproar. Remember, this was early in 1947 when these matters were viewed differently. Bettye sacked her, Peter's Mother was shocked and upset, and with a great rush Peter and Barbara departed for London amid a family furore.

About a year after departure Peter and Barbara, now married, returned to Newquay and temporarily took a furnished house in Ulalia Road, but still had no firm idea of exactly what they planned to do. They were very keen to try a spell in the hotel, and so it was arranged, for one season only, the Whittingtons and the Armstrongs would run the Edgcumbe together.

From the beginning Bettye and Michael were aggrieved. She felt she had been working hard with her Mother for several years to put the hotel on its feet and Michael, with great difficulty, had managed to get the licence. They felt it unfair that Peter and Barbara should be allowed to come back and push their way in. In spite of their protests, they came. Peter took charge of the kitchen and Barbara the office. Michael went on running the bar, Bettye did the general management and front of house. She also ran the entertainments, including M.C.-ing the dances, but it was disastrous; they simply could not, and would not, work together and it was a very troublesome season for everyone concerned.

The working arrangements were impossible. The hotel was too small, and the wise and peace loving Olive Whittington said "If you cannot work together you must separate". Then Peter and Barbara decided that if it was possible they would like to buy a farm. So it was that with many family conferences and much advice from the family solicitors, the Agreement was drawn up, by which Peter was to be given £5,000 capital to buy a farm. Bettye and Michael were to raise the money to pay him out — another mortgage! They were also to pay Bettye's mother an annual income of £400 and 'house and keep her in the way to which she had lived hitherto' (the family solicitor's phrasing). This seems very little in the twenty-first century but remember, immediately after the war the tariff at Edgcumbe was from 4 - 7 guineas per person per week for full board, including afternoon tea.

In the autumn of 1948 the Family Agreement was signed. Peter went for six months as a student farmer to the Davey's Farm, Tresillian Barton, at Kestle Mill, four miles from Newquay. The Davey family had farmed 400-500 acres there since 1926 and so were vastly experienced and well established. They were also very enterprising; for some thirty years later they were to diversify and open 'Dairyland' as a country attraction for families on some fifty acres of their land, but that is another story.

While Peter was learning he and Barbara remained in the furnished house in Ulalia Road. He bought many books on farming and they spent their evenings swatting up farming 'know how' and of course planning what they would do. Peter was also negotiating to buy Tregoose Farm at Colan — it was a busy winter for them.

During the winter Peter's car broke down and he had to catch a 7.30 a.m. bus to be at the farm by 8.00 a.m. Barbara thought that very hard and said so. Bettye replied "Yes, but aren't early mornings always a part of life on a farm?", "Oh yes," said Barbara, "but when we have our own farm it will be quite different. We will be able to milk the cows and go back to bed." For the next nine years they were up at 6.00 a.m. daily to catch the milk lorry — and there was no "going back to bed" — so little did they know!

Tregoose Farm 1948 – 1956

Peter and Barbara Whittington circa 1948.

Peter Whittington bought Tregoose Farm in the winter of 1948 with his £5,000 capital and that was the only capital he was ever to have, apart from the odd small loan from his mother. Tregoose was a one hundred and thirty-five acre farm at Colan four miles from Newquay. Peter paid £3,500 for the farm which left him with some £1,500 and whatever the bank would lend him to buy stock and machinery, which, since he had no track record, was very little. Not nearly enough money with which to get a farm going. However, they managed to shuffle in with their few bits and pieces in the spring of 1949.

Front of Tregoose Farmhouse.

Tregoose was an attractive four bedroom stone farm house on a south facing slope with a pleasant garden at the front, and a good stone barn and outbuildings at the back. There was a large yard between the house, the barn, and the building earmarked to be the milking parlour, which was a constant morass of mud and slurry.

6 a.m. - and no going back to bed!

Inside, the house was rugged to a degree. No heating, a large kitchen with a rough stone floor, a clome sink in one corner, and a black Cornish range with brass knobs which they could not manage; it kept going out. Peter soon threw that out and replaced it with an electric cooker. They set about their innumerable problems with gusto.

The Whittingtons had virtually no furniture — a bed, a table, two chairs, and two armchairs, with orange boxes as bed-side tables — but they always had books and classical records which were very important to both of them. Peter's mother soon became most concerned at their discomfort in the house and by the fact that they had no proper furniture and so at that time she made a will leaving Peter all her furniture. It was not the sort of furniture he would have wanted and most of it he would have sold or dumped, but that was beside the point!

After much consideration they decided to establish a herd of pedigree Guernseys. They started the herd, which they called The Bredon Herd, with just four cows and then a milking machine! Being an engineer Peter always had a great love of machinery. They joined the Guernsey Breeders' Association and they toiled early and late, seven days a week. The milk lorry from the Milk Marketing Board came to collect the milk churns at 7.00 a.m. every day and they had to be there, ready. There was no let up, and certainly no going back to bed! At that time it was still illegal to make cream from the milk as wartime rationing still prevailed.

After a while Peter and Barbara decided that the slimy mud in their yard was impossible and the yard, which was large, must be concreted. There was no spare money to pay builders to do it and so Peter bought a second hand concrete mixer and he and Barbara did it themselves. While they were concreting the yard Barbara had a nasty accident when the concrete mixer fell on her foot and crushed it and she was out of action for quite a long time, which made life even more difficult for them.

Part of the Tregoose Yard, very different from when the Whittingtons bought it in 1948 when this area was a constant morass of mud and slurry.

Their only car was a battered old blue Riley — really an old banger, but Peter had no taste for reliable little family saloons, they were not his style. He spent many happy hours under the car trying to keep it on the road, but there is no doubt they had a very hard time. Thirty years later he had a yellow Ferrari!

They eventually managed to employ one farmhand to help them. He was a nice young man, a German ex-prisoner of war called Wolf, who had remained in England to improve his English. He was their 'right hand man' and stayed with them for several years.

They tried poultry farming with free range hens, eventually one thousand of them, which they housed in one end of the barn at night. They sold the eggs to Newquay hotels, including Edgcumbe. Food rationing was still in force and only one egg per week was allowed. Poultry was not rationed but was, of course, very difficult to come by so that "poultry and eggs direct from the farm" became a much used phrase in adverts and hotel brochures. Once there was a farm in the family, Bettye and Michael at the Edgcumbe were very quick to make the most of it, and by 1950 were advertising "own poultry farm" which had enormous pulling power on paper, in those days of rationing.

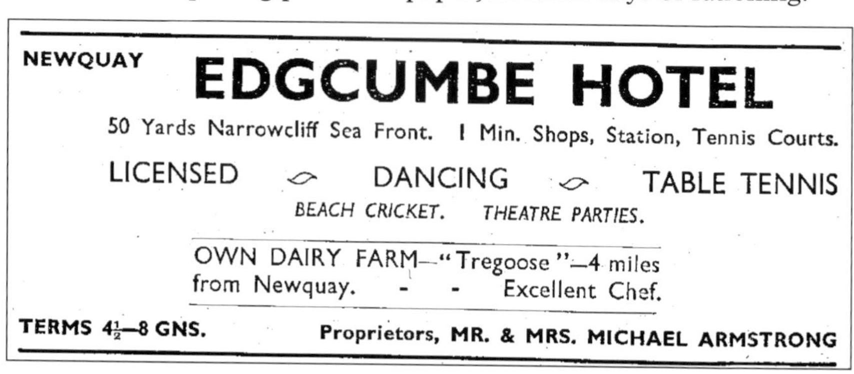

Holiday Haunts 1950 advert "Own Dairy Farm".

Peter later became somewhat aggrieved about that, especially when occasionally Edgcumbe guests asked to see the "family poultry farm" and had to be taken out to Tregoose for a conducted tour. He felt he and his farm were being exploited, and, looking back, perhaps to some extent they were! It certainly gave the Edgcumbe a big advantage at the time which, maybe, wasn't quite fair especially as the Whittingtons were having such a hard struggle.

In the early days at the farm Peter would sometimes say, Bettye thought rather smugly, "We are not really interested in worldly success. We enjoy our life on the farm with our books and our music". Possibly at the time that was true. Barbara was an intellectual, they were very much in tune and seemed to be very happy, but Peter's mother was much concerned. Life seemed such a struggle for them. They were getting nowhere.

In 1953, after a lapse of five years and when they had almost given up hope of having a family, their eldest daughter Maria was born and when two years later Sonia arrived, their views on life began to change. They thought about it long and hard; they both loved life on the farm but they wanted to educate their children properly and so with much courage and great sadness in 1956 they decided to sell the farm and go into the hotel business, which seemed to offer a great deal more comfortable life style. Also, Newquay was still very seasonal and hotel life at that time offered a three month holiday between October and Christmas, which appealed to them very much too.

When Barbara and Peter decided to sell the farm they set about it with typical Whittington thoroughness. Peter had spent the previous nine years buying ever more machinery. He had a passion for it, and his barn was full of discarded implements. Now they raked out all the old machinery and farm chattels from the barn and outhouses and worked hard for several months painting them, and generally tidying them up ready for sale. It proved to be time well spent for when their farm sale was held in November 1956 they and everyone else were astounded by the prices achieved. They also held a dispersal sale of their pedigree herd of thirty six Guernseys and they fetched extraordinarily high prices, although it must have been a great wrench to part with the cows, as they had become fond of them. When Peter telephoned his sister that evening to tell her about the sale, he wept!

The farm was sold privately, for £6,500, and their nine years of farming were over. They were now ready for the next stage in their lives. Later Peter was to say, "The farm wasn't big enough and I did not have enough capital." That was certainly true, but it was sad; they loved the life, apart from its incessant rigours, and they had worked so hard to make it successful. They had put their hearts and souls into it — not to mention their backs! They did in fact emerge from their farming days with much more money in the kitty than they had envisaged —they were going to need it. They had a most expensive project ahead!

While arranging the sale of the farm Peter and Barbara had been looking at hotels in Newquay and at the time they were offered two possible properties. After much deliberation and lengthy negotiations Peter and Barbara bought Knowle Links. They took it over in January 1957 and so began a new chapter in their lives. They were looking forward to their new project but with two small children, Maria was nearly four, and Sonia was soon to be two years old, they had several more years of struggle ahead.

Olive Whittington with Betty, Barbara and Peter.

Edgcumbe Hotel
1948-1957

Once the Family Agreement was signed Michael and Bettye at last felt settled. Every summer the hotel managed to accommodate a few more people. The planners had not yet got their grip and many lofts in the town sprouted illicit dormer windows which made extra bedrooms and many little flat roof projections were surreptitiously added to the back or sides of the buildings to make extra space. At the time everything was slightly haywire — one only had to tell the local surveyor what one intended to do and pass a bottle of whisky over and that was that! One got on. The only thing really under control was the rationing, which was rigid until the early 1950s. Soon, of course, as peacetime order was restored all that was to change and go on changing until today when all the businesses are completely swamped by bureaucratic rules and regulations which at times threaten their very existence. Surely many of the monstrosities that now disfigure Newquay and other towns were built after the planning department came into being. The main object in those early days was to get as many people in as possible and give them a cracking good holiday, and this the Armstrongs did very successfully at the Edgcumbe for many years.

In the early years the Edgcumbe took about sixty guests, thirty-two odd in the main hotel and about fourteen in "Ashby", the "annexe" opposite. The rest "slept out" in bedrooms up and down the road — although for the purpose of booking these were referred to as "annexe rooms". None of the rooms had views, so there was no complication about sea view or otherwise. The hotel and annexe rooms were charged the same, but the "sleeping out" ones were cheaper. Rooms without hot and cold water were still usually acceptable but increasingly the lack of basins caused difficulties. Very soon it was going to become impossible to let rooms without them, just as today it is difficult to persuade guests to take rooms without private baths or showers, even in quite lowly hotels.

After the 1948 season Bettye and Michael looked forward to a peaceful winter with Mary at "Sand Dunes", Holywell Bay, but another problem arose. Since they had taken on the Edgcumbe, with the rush of the hectic summer seasons at the hotel, Michael had not managed to visit his mother in Devon as often as he or she would have wished so in the summer of 1948 she made plans to move to Cornwall. She gave up her tenancy of The Mill House. The landlord paid her

£500 disturbance money which she gave to Michael and in October of that year she arrived at "Sand Dunes" with her most cherished possessions. Bettye was less than happy with the arrangement! Agatha Armstrong left most of her furnishings stored in a barn in Devon, and they were never seen again, but she brought far too much for the little house, including Michael's father's large Edwardian desk, which he treasured. Bettye had to put up with that desk for another thirty five years.

Agatha Armstrong, Michael's mother.

Heaven only knows how it would have worked out. It seems unlikely that Bettye and her mother-in-law would have settled down happily together in such a small house long term, but fate intervened. Three months later Michael's mother had a stroke and died within weeks at "Sand Dunes" on 20th February 1949, five months before her grandson, John Armstrong, was born. At least at the end she was with her beloved son. She was buried at Down St Mary beside Michael's father.

Bettye and Michael had soon realised that whatever the large hotels on Narrowcliff sea front could offer, they could also offer — but more reasonably, and that was the secret of their success. So very soon, their brochure and advertisements were offering a Full Programme of Entertainments, Resident Dance Band, Maple Floor Ballroom, Beach Cricket, Tennis Tournaments, and all fifty yards from the sea front to boot. No matter that it was a terrace house down a side road, they referred to it as being "fifty yards from Narrowcliff sea front" and on paper it all sounded similar to the sea front hotels[1] but, they were charging less and so were always full. Every room that would take an extra small bed was booked as a treble and the seasons soon extended from Easter to October. It was all very hectic and everyone worked exceedingly hard seven days a week.

The kitchen equipment at the Edgcumbe was much out of date. The Armstrongs were not technically minded and in Edgcumbe

[1] Today they would be contravening the Trades Description Act.

The outdated kitchen at Edgcumbe, with Beryl Luxon, cook.

Avenue they never had a dishwasher and certainly not a washing machine, but at that time all washing went to the laundry. There was a coal boiler in the kitchen for the hot water, which Michael had to stoke every night before he went to bed; if it went out there would be no hot water in the morning. Edgcumbe didn't have a refrigerator of any sort until the 1950s, and then it was a second hand one. There were no deep freezers or frozen vegetables. Everything was fresh. Meat, fish, vegetables, milk, cream, and ice cream were delivered daily — they had to be! The preparation of fresh vegetables meant much hard work for the kitchen staff who spent hours peeling spuds, slicing beans, shelling peas, etc. They hadn't even a machine for peeling potatoes. In the 1950s a little back street industry sprang up in the town providing prepared vegetables for hotels, and for several years it flourished. How thankful the hard pushed hoteliers were when peeled potatoes in buckets of water and other prepared vegetables were delivered to the back doors, ready for the pot. It was an expensive way to buy, of course, but oh! what labour it saved and how delighted the hoteliers were to use the service.

The Edgcumbe in Edgcumbe Avenue never had a porter. A schoolboy came on Saturdays to carry the luggage and lug the linen around. There are so many things we take for granted today which had to be attended to by the staff. For example, in the 1940s and 1950s there were no tea-making facilities in the bedrooms, morning tea trays had to be carried to the bedrooms by the chambermaids. Workers did not have cars in those days and many lived "in the clay" around Bugle and Stenalees, and travelled in daily by bus. Since there were no buses or trains on Sundays or Bank Holidays, for years Michael had to get up and do an early morning staff run to get the chambermaids in by 7.30 a.m. — often after a very late night in the bar. Bettye had to relieve the hotel chef for his Sunday half day off when a cold supper was served. It was heavy going in those early post-war days, but it was also a lot of fun.

Another problem was a permanent on-going battle with the neighbours about noise. Looking back, how awful it must have been for quiet elderly folk to have been living side by side with the rackety little Edgcumbe Hotel of the '40s and '50s when there was dancing and loud music several nights a week at least up to midnight.

Bettye's mother continued to be a tower of strength. Although she no longer wanted the responsibility of the hotel, she was very interested in it and more than happy to help it prosper in every way she could. She acted as housekeeper; in those days sheets and towels etc., were only changed once a week and all the guests came and went on Saturdays. Her role therefore mainly consisted of dealing with the laundry. She was also very happy to do an office "duty" on Friday evenings, when all the guests paid their weekly bills. Olive Whittington enjoyed the Edgcumbe's success and having her family around her: she was content.

1949 was an eventful year for the Armstrongs. They were expecting their second baby in July. All bookings were still being done by letter and Bettye and Michael were busy taking bookings in January when they received an enquiry for a family wanting two rooms for three weeks in August: one room for the parents and a six week old baby and another one for two youngsters. In those days people did not usually dash around with babies a few weeks old, and Bettye, pregnant herself, was convinced it was frivolous booking and when it came to it the family would not turn up. She booked the two smallest rooms in the hotel, and thought no more about it.

In mid July their son, John, was born amidst great drama. It had been arranged that Bettye would have a caesarean in Bath but the baby began to appear about ten days early in Newquay — panic! A 7.00 a.m. consultation with their GP, Dr O'Shea, and it was

The Fairchild in which John was nearly born!

decided that she'd better get to Bath quickly. Michael grabbed a plane, a four seater Fairchild, from St Mawgan airfield, pushed his wife into it in her dressing gown, and with great aplomb flew her, through a violent thunder storm, to Bath. They landed at a disused airfield where Michael's doctor aunt and an ambulance were waiting. They drove straight to Forbes Fraser Hospital where the gynaecologist was ready. John was born half an hour later. Michael then flew them home again thirteen days later where the recently engaged Nannie was waiting for her new charge.

Michael had not quite approved of Bettye's choice of Nannie at the time. She was a spinster of forty, barely five feet tall and she wore white ankle socks. He would have preferred someone a little more decorative! He said "How could you engage that funny little woman in white ankle socks?" but Nannie was a capable and experienced Children's Nurse and she was a character; she stayed with the Armstrong's for almost forty years. John was her last baby and he was always her blue-eyed boy.

John's Nannie – 1949

In August Bettye's so-called 'frivolous booking' turned up — in full force. They arrived in the largest car yet seen at the Edgcumbe, towing a trailer packed with everything but the kitchen sink. They had brought an ironing board,

Bettye's 'frivolous booking' turned up. The Charnaud's arrival, August 1949.

baby bath, electric kettle, crib, pushchair and all baby accoutrements, plus beach clobber for the family, surf boards, floats, large towels, picnic basket etc., etc. There wasn't room for it all in the hall — let alone in the small bedroom.

They were shown to their rooms, the double, Room 12, about 9ft x 11ft with a 2ft wide window and the wife sat on the bed and wept, saying she could not possibly stay in that small room for three weeks. The husband went to talk to the receptionist, and he, with an eye for a pretty girl, was beguiled by her. She told him the hotel was full, she could do nothing, but Mr and Mrs Armstrong would be back by about 6 p.m. and he could talk to them then.

When Michael and Bettye appeared and heard of the Charnaud's arrival they were horrified and alarmed — they could not afford to lose a three week booking for two rooms, but they had no other rooms to offer. However at 6.00 p.m. they all met in the hall and the Armstrongs listened to the complaint about the room sympathetically; they well knew it was fully justified. They turned on the charm: Michael said "Do come and have a drink." They all retired to the bar where he produced his special Pimms — always well laced! and Bettye explained that there was no other room available but she would see what she could do later in the stay, then they had another Pimms and by dinnertime they were all the best of friends. With great forbearance the Charnauds put up with that little room for the three weeks and after a bad start the holiday was a big success and whilst there they chose their room — the biggest and best — for the following year. They spent three weeks every August at Edgcumbe for the next seventeen years until they retired and bought a house in Feock, on Restronguet Creek, where Joy Charnaud still lives. She remains a firm family friend. Sadly, John Charnaud died in 2007 aged ninety-five.

At the end of the 1949 season, when the furnished lettings at "Sand Dunes" had finished, Michael and Bettye with Nannie and the children moved back to Holywell Bay and lived there until the end of the following season.

The Armstrongs had few proper holidays in those days, but Michael and Bettye did have a memorable one in the spring of 1950. They had been unable to get away after the 1949 season because of the baby and so in the following April, when John was nine months old, they left Nannie in charge and went off for a break before the season. They set off in their old battered Citroen, not really sure where they were going. They badly wanted to go to Chantilly, to see Michael's interesting family friends, but decided they really could not afford it, and so they headed for Newmarket where the five days Guineas Meeting was being held.

On arrival they booked in for the week at Bedford Lodge Hotel. It had just changed hands and was new and unknown. It was a shabby country house hotel where they negotiated terms of six guineas (£6.30) each for the week for dinner, bed and breakfast. Nowadays Bedford Lodge Hotel is fashionable, up-market and expensive. Like the Armstrongs' its standing has improved over the years! Every day they went to the races and every day they lost — they simply could not find a winner. Their fellow guests at Bedford Lodge were owners, trainers, jockeys, etc., and every evening they had a most convivial time. One chap said to Michael,

"How did you do today, Armstrong?"

"Not too well." replied Michael, "How did you do?"

"Oh, not badly." came the reply. "Yesterday I lost £16,000 and today I won £20,000." So deeply were they out of their depth financially, but they did have such fun!

Michael contacted some pre-war family friends connected with racing from Chantilly, and he and Bettye were invited to one or two big cocktail parties held by the successful trainers. At one, in the corner was a bunch of the jockeys 'talking shop'. "Can't think why Gordon Richards (the leading jockey of the day) hasn't got it" said one. "It doesn't really matter who is on its back." said another, "There is nothing that can beat it." Bettye and Michael, eavesdropping, hung on to every word and finally the horse's name emerged — Supertello.

They went on losing every day and on the fourth day were reduced to going in the 'silver ring' with hoi polloi; they could afford nothing else. They had carefully put aside their £12.12s. for the hotel bill, emptied their private bank accounts, drawn as much as they dared on the Edgcumbe account, and were scat. The last day of the meeting dawned, should they crawl away with their tails between their legs or raise some money and have a last fling? They decided on the latter course. So they drove into Cambridge, some thirteen miles, and pawned Bettye's diamond rings (engagement ring and one of her grandmother's, given to her on her twenty-first birthday). They then went to the races in style, back to Tattersalls and had a lovely time, but they backed a loser in every race!

The next morning, with just enough money left for petrol, they drove to their friend Eve Longmore's house in Epsom where the spring meeting was being held the following week. They went racing every day. Supertello was running on the second day. They put their shirts — and pants — on him and he won easily at 7-1. They were back in the black and had had a simply glorious, exciting holiday. They returned home and back to work happily: the rings were redeemed later.

For the summer of 1950 they remained at Holywell Bay and Olive Whittington joined them, but Michael and Bettye found the seven mile journey too much. They only had one car — an old banger at that, and they worked long and late hours. So they put the bungalow on the market that autumn and sold it for more than double what they had paid for it! That was a great help! Fortunately, at the same time they were able to buy Edgcumbe Lodge, the well-built seven bedroom house in Edgcumbe Gardens immediately behind Edgcumbe Hotel. They had to live, rather uncomfortably, in the hotel for that winter while the builders made alterations to the house. They moved in with great relief in the spring of 1951 and the whole family were to live there happily for the next fifteen years. Olive Whittington lived with them in her own quarters on the first floor. At last they all had a comfortable home, although for years the spare bedrooms in the house were used as annexe rooms for the guests during the season. Even Mary's room was sometimes used while she was away at school.

By the early 1950s most people were no longer bothering about garages, they just wanted parking, and free parking was becoming one of the important facilities to be offered, although it was still possible to park in most roads. The Armstrongs who always liked to be one jump ahead managed to make a small car park at the rear of the hotel and then they were able to offer the all important "Free Parking".

There is no doubt that life was a great struggle for the whole family from 1945 to the early 1950s but from then on, at least for the Armstrongs, it all became much more comfortable. The poor Whittingtons, still struggling to get going on the farm and sort themselves out, were distressingly impecunious.

"Ashby", the annexe opposite the Edgcumbe was still being rented for £1 per week and when the landlord died early in 1950, Michael and Bettye were offered the freehold cheaply as sitting tenants. They persuaded Western Counties Building Society, with whom they were on splendid terms, to put up the whole of the purchase price of £2,600, and they bought it — another mortgage! After the season they installed hot and cold water in some of the rooms and the spacious, but useless, attic rooms on the second floor were given dormer windows and converted into rooms for guests. Extra bedrooms — another bottle of whisky! The house then slept twenty guests.

For some years after the war foreign travel was impossible for the masses and difficult for everyone. At one time one was only allowed to take £25 out of the country legally. Of course, for those who knew how, or had contacts abroad, there were ways round it but there was an immense clamour for accommodation in Cornwall. One day early in 1950 Nigel Tangye rang up and said he had decided to open his family home, "Glendorgal" as an hotel and he and Marguerite would like to come and have a chat and look around. He had already had a 'chat' with Mrs Francis at the Hotel Bristol. They came and Bettye and Michael showed them round; the tiny bar contrived out of a passage where Michael held sway (really it was only a dispense with a 3ft bar counter) the small bedrooms into which Bettye had somehow squashed a 4ft double bed which she called 'small doubles' and the large front family rooms with children's beds in all possible corners. The old fashioned kitchen with two gas stoves and had no modern aids — not even a 'fridge at that time, just a cool larder with slate shelves. When Nigel opened Glendorgal as an hotel later that year he quickly put his individual stamp on it and it became arguably Cornwall's most stylish hotel and certainly Newquay's best. He speedily learnt how to use all available space, as the reader will hear.

By early 1951 the Armstrongs were more organised and had a seasonal receptionist for the Edgcumbe. They also had cards printed saying "The hotel is fully booked for the dates you require" and offering the first available dates. Those cards were sent out for the next twenty years, once the hotel was fully booked.

In those early days in Edgcumbe Avenue the front door was never locked from the beginning of the season to the end. When Michael was asked what time he locked the front door, he would say "the end of October". The guests loved it. How times have changed! Nowadays most hotels in Newquay not only lock their doors but have a night security man as well — and he is usually seriously necessary.

In the winter of 1952-1953 a new floor of eight bedrooms was built on the flat roof at the back of the hotel and Michael did the whole of the electric wiring; no electrician was employed. Edgcumbe then had twenty-eight bedrooms in the hotel and twelve in the annexe across the road, and of course all the 'sleeping out' which was still acceptable. Later it became absolutely impossible to let sleeping out rooms, guests simply would not take them, but that is another story.

One day a tidy little middle-aged couple, respectable and working class (she in a Terrylene dress and white court shoes and a frilly perm, and he in tan sand shoes and pale grey Terrylene trousers and jersey), arrived for their holiday. While there, they confided to Bettye that their little seventeen year old daughter would be coming to stay in a couple of weeks' time with her friend, who was the same age. They said the two girls had never been away from home on their own before and they were very shy, please would the Armstrongs keep an eye on them. Bettye said, "Of course." When the teenage girls arrived a few weeks later they turned out to be worldly-wise little minxes of seventeen going on thirty-five. The first night after dinner they ordered themselves a taxi to take them to the local bar, where the roughest and toughest of the Royal Air Force chaps could be found. They were naughty girls, and they knew the ropes. They had a wonderful holiday, but there was no way the Armstrongs could look after them and they both felt somewhat abashed when a few weeks later they had a letter from the parents thanking them for looking after the girls so well. The poor parents — little did they know!

Cars were still difficult to get, but in 1952 Bettye and Michael were able to buy their first new car on hire purchase, a Sunbeam Talbot 90 drop head coupe. They were inordinately proud of it. In those days decent cars still did not stand outside so they rented a garage for it just off Edgcumbe Avenue. Bettye joined Newquay Car Club and entered the car rallies with Pete Wilson as her navigator.

Bettye taking part in a night rally

All through the '50s the family were fortunate to have the use of a little flat in Bath for holidays. Michael's elderly Aunt, who had been a practising GP there for some fifty years, had a surgery on the ground floor at 35 The Paragon. One day she said to Michael "My first floor flat is becoming vacant and I would love you and Bettye to have it. The rent is £25 per year and I will furnish it for you." The Armstrongs were delighted and much enjoyed it and Bath for the next ten years.

The flat was extremely basic, it consisted of just two rooms and a primitive kitchen with a grey gas stove on legs, an old clome sink with wooden draining board in the corner and included the bath, also on legs, complete with geyser. There was curling lino on the floor. The bedroom was painted a hideous bright green with cream walls and had one double and two single beds in a row and led directly into the sitting room, which Aunt Vee furnished for them with antiques and a divan for the sitting room. The only heating was a small gas fire. The lavatory was on the next floor and shared. When Mary was at Cheltenham and John was at Wells House, Malvern, they used it for school visiting weekends. Everybody loved it and nobody minded that it was so rugged.

In the fifties there were no swimming pools in Newquay, and so the warm swimming pool in Bath was a great attraction to Mary and John. Sometimes Nannie put the dogs on the train to Bath and they travelled by themselves in the guard's van for half-terms. Everyone loved to have them there for walks in the park. Peter and Barbara Whittington borrowed the flat sometimes, and they also found it a splendid place to relax away from the trials and tribulations of farm life. In all, the little flat was a great success and everyone was sad when Aunt Vee, aged ninety, died in the early 1960s and it had to be given up.

In the early 1950s 'skiffle', popularised by Lonnie Donegan, became the rage. It was the impromptu music of the day — poor man's jazz. The instruments were a guitar, a tea chest with wooden broom handle set in it and a string which, when tweaked, went 'boom boom' and an old fashioned wooden washing board with a corrugated zinc front which was strummed with a thimble. Singing was an important part of skiffle and the groups sang old traditional American jazz songs. Hugh, the Head Waiter at Edgcumbe at the time, ran a skiffle group. One fine summer evening a barbecue party was planned for the guests after dinner in the big cave on Tolcarne Beach and Hugh promised to provide the music with his skiffle group. On the night his group let him down and none of them turned up. The poor little fellow was too afraid to face the guests the next day — he did a bunk and was

The Edgcumbe Dance Band – Ken Stratton on drums, Ted Watts on saxophone, and Ken Langmaid on piano.

The dances were jolly affairs with Ken Stratton in charge, 1950s.

never heard of again! The trouble was that he was the mainstay of the overcrowded dining room.

The dance band at the Edgcumbe — referred to in the brochure as "The Resident Orchestra" — consisted of a beguiling little trio of local chaps. The pay was thirty shillings (£1.50) per man per night from 8.30 - 12.00. Bettye was the MC and the dances were jolly affairs with everyone joining in. There were many novelty dances including free ranging congas around the houses! The trio consisted of Ken Langmaid, the pianist, Ted Watts, the saxophonist and Ken Stratton, the drummer, and they just played. Bettye did all the talking — some might say, "She would!" and Michael was behind the bar, it was all very "hands-on".

The highlight of these jollifications was the Wednesday Fancy Dress. The guests, always enthusiastic, spent hours and hours making their costumes. Charles Woolf, the local photographer, came and photographed them all and Wednesday night became Gala Night — a late night with much merrymaking, no doubt extremely irritating to the poor old neighbours next door.

The guests, in fancy dress, congregated upstairs on the landing and all paraded down the stairs together watched by an admiring crowd in the hall. One day in August 1954, Bettye had a heavy cold and was unable to deal with the fancy dress parade or the dance. The young drummer, Ken Stratton, offered to do it. When the guests realised she was not there, they backed up the stairs en masse and refused to come down. They felt their "big show" was being down-graded with only an unknown young drummer boy in charge. Eventually they appeared

A Wednesday Fancy Dress parade, led by Ken Stratton.

and Ken dealt with the whole thing brilliantly, and that was the first time his talent became apparent. Gradually, from then on he gained in stature and confidence and eventually he became the Bandleader, MC, Entertainer, Children's Party Host, in all the family hotels. He had the talent to turn a children's party into adult entertainment, and he was a great favourite with guests and staff alike. Regular guests would arrive and their first words would often be 'Is Ken here?' He was immensely popular.

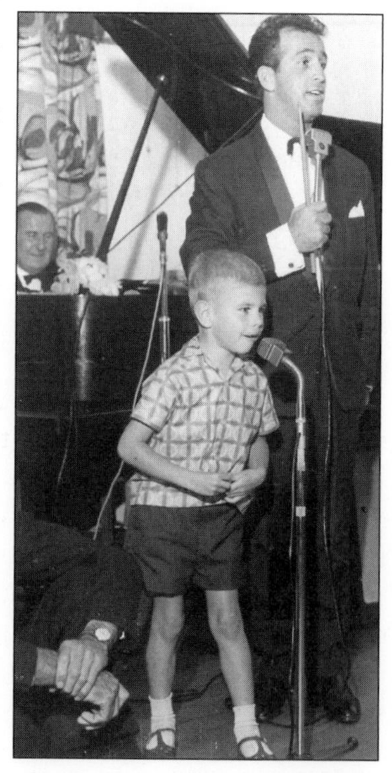

Ken Stratton, children's party host.

As the reader will have gathered, by 1954 Edgcumbe was a rackety, overcrowded little hotel and every now and again quite the wrong type of people would book rooms. When they arrived they hated it and would complain bitterly that the dancing kept them awake (half the rooms were over the ballroom) and it was all too noisy for them. As the demand for rooms was so heavy, Bettye felt they could afford to deter the people to whom the hotel would not appeal, and so from then on

EDGCUMBE HOTEL

A word to prospective guests . . .

We think it very important from your point of view and ours that you choose the right TYPE of Hotel for your Holiday, one where you will meet congenial people of your own kind. Before you book consider carefully what type of hotel will suit you. Do you want a quiet restful holiday, early nights and peaceful secluded Lounges for quiet reading or bridge? If so please do not choose "EDGCUMBE" because it will NOT suit you.

If on the other hand you want lots of fun, dancing, jolly parties and plenty going on in a friendly informal atmosphere with Entertainments of one sort or another almost every evening "EDGCUMBE" IS the Hotel FOR YOU.

If you DO decide to come to "EDGCUMBE" we can assure you that we will do our best to give you a really happy holiday.

NEWQUAY

The warning leaflet sent to prospective guests, 1954.

a leaflet was sent with every enquiry for a brochure. It worked like a dream, but looking back it must really have made the place even noisier because there were no quiet guests any more — the poor neighbours.

Although a comparatively small hotel, just a terrace house down a side road, during the fifties the Edgcumbe was faithfully following Uncle Graham Farmer's footsteps in leading the way, and introducing new ideas. Roger Davis, a general assistant who was very keen on cars, introduced weekly car rallies which were immensely popular on summer evenings, before the days of congested roads and when driving was still a pleasure. There were prizes for winning drivers and navigators, and from then on the hotel ran car rallies every week for many years and the guests loved them.

In talking of Edgcumbe Hotel in later years people were inclined to think Bettye was the architect of its success. That may be, but the reader can be assured the people who really knew how it was in those early days realised that, if anything, Michael worked harder than his wife. Remember, there was never an employed barman in all those busy summers in Edgcumbe Avenue. Michael did it all, early and late, seven days a week from April - October. Often in the afternoon he would take the guests flying, which he and they loved. He was also a skilled electrician and during those early winters he did all the electrical work that was needed, putting in bedside lights, etc. When in 1953 a new floor of eight bedrooms was added he did the whole of the wiring from scratch, while Bettye made all the curtains for them. There is no doubt that for years after the war they both worked very hard, and Michael, if anything, did more than his share.

Taking guests for an afternoon flight.

Michael also brought another invaluable asset to the business. In spite of his family background he had a high degree of the common touch, which meant he could easily mix with Tom, Dick and Harry and make them feel thoroughly at home; and they could call him "Mike". Sometimes the guests were rough. Boilermakers, factory workers, and the like. He could cope with them all. At the hotel they often felt he was their best friend, and for the week or the fortnight they were there, he probably was. They loved him!

During the whole of the 1950s certainly Michael and Bettye had very hard rackety six month seasons, working long hours, seven days a week relentlessly — but their winters at home for six months were extremely comfortable and well ordered. In the winter Beryl arrived at 8.00 a.m. every day and took morning tea to Bettye and Michael in bed. She then cooked and served a traditional breakfast which was on the table by 9.00 a.m. Life became quite civilized.

Olive Whittington, who enjoyed housekeeping and ordering the food, would telephone the butcher, fishmonger, and greengrocer, and order what was required for luncheon and it would be delivered to the house within the hour — every day. Beryl would then cook a proper lunch with hot pudding which she would serve at 1.00 p.m. precisely.

There was a bell on the dining table which was rung when the family were ready for the pudding, after which they had coffee in the drawing room. Olive would then retire to her sitting room for her afternoon siesta and everyone else went about their business. How civilized it seems now — over forty years later. In fact it was no more than a continuation of how things had been in Grandmother's house in Sutton; but it was so different from the scrappy snatched snacks that pass for luncheon for many people today. One can understand why Peter and Barbara, roughing it on the farm, began to feel they must change their course if they were ever to live comfortably.

Although the Armstrongs lived in extreme comfort out of season, Michael and Bettye still had busy winters after their autumn holiday. Through the 1950s only a seasonal receptionist was employed and 99% of the bookings were done by letter in January, February and March which meant up to one hundred letters daily had to be dealt with. These Bettye, Michael, and Olive Whittington dealt with between them. They sat at the dining table, Bettye did the typing, Michael checked and signed them, Olive Whittington put them in the envelopes and they could get through them all before the table had to be cleared for lunch.

By 1955 the Edgcumbe was taking one hundred and ten people in a space that would have accommodated sixty comfortably, and the summers were becoming increasingly stressful; it was far too crowded. One of the amenities often proudly advertised by small hotels was 'separate tables'. There was no such refinement at Edgcumbe. All the rectangular tables, arranged tea shop fashion, were for four. There was no question of a couple having a table for two. Occasionally there would be a major 'mis-match' which would cause amusement or consternation. It was all tricky, but in those rough and ready days Bettye and Michael and their team got away with it!

For several years the little cocktail bar had to be used as an overflow dining room. Breakfast, luncheon, and dinner for twenty-four people were served there every day. In the evenings the tables were stripped and it became the busy cocktail bar, often until the small hours. Every night, before retiring, Bettye and Michael had to make sure the room was clear of glasses, ashtrays, etc., and clean cloths were on the tables for breakfast. The tables were laid up in the morning. As can be imagined there was no room for error and it put great strain on the Armstrongs. The old coke boiler still had to be stoked last thing at night or there would have been no hot water in the morning — it was heavy going!

However, it was all still great fun and at night there were parties. From time to time there would be a spate of mid-night bathing, and sometimes it was the making of apple pie beds. Today's youngsters would no doubt pooh! pooh! these pursuits as juvenile, but fifty years ago there was a different code of behaviour — the world has changed! Occasionally things would go too far. Once, two personable young bachelors suffered the whole week from the apple pie beds their friends made them every night, and on the last night they were determined to have their revenge. They got hold of a large quantity of stinking fish from the harbour and filled their chief tormentors' room with it. The smell was so bad the occupants were found the next morning asleep wrapped in their blankets in the lounge downstairs. They had had to abandon their room! Well, that was all right but what was not all right was that the stench was so foul it could not be got rid of easily and Michael and Bettye were in dead trouble with the next people who arrived to occupy the room — it still smelled!

One of the 'midnight swims'.

One more recollection about the apple pie beds — in the late 1950s young John Armstrong, son of the house, was about nine and dying to join in with these nightly high jinks. He made friends with a boy a few years older than himself who was staying with his parents, and was determined to give the boy's room a 'going over'. He wrecked the room! He was very pleased with himself until the next morning when there was an outraged father at the office complaining bitterly "someone had wrecked his daughter's room" — John had 'done' the wrong one! There was a dreadful to-do and John was despatched to apologise to the father and explain himself. He was dared ever to touch a guest's room again, and he never did!

By 1955 the Armstrongs had managed to engage a general

assistant, Joan Eden[2]. She was personable and adaptable with a talent for people — a good all rounder — who was a great help to them and did everything and anything. Before long Joan was able to relieve Michael in the bar occasionally. Once she had settled, although there was not yet any spare money, Michael and Bettye began to yearn for a bolt hole, even if it was only a shack, away from the hubbub of the hotel and from people where they could escape for a few hours. They found a cottage at Feock, a short distance from "Greenbank", where they had had such happy times with Peter during the war.

Cherry Tree Cottage, Feock, bought at auction for £500 and named after the cherry tree the Armstrongs planted in the front garden.

The cottage was auctioned in 1956; Michael went to the sale and bought it for £500. It was a double fronted detached cottage, end on to the road and a few yards from the old Feock Post Office, sound but primitive. Bettye soon sorted that! Before long it had three bedrooms, bathroom, comfortable living room with windows to the south and west and a small front garden which they were able to screen from the road with wattle fencing. They planted a cherry tree and called the little house "Cherry Tree Cottage". It was let furnished for about eight weeks in July and August, like everything else at that time it had to earn its keep. Apart from those weeks the Armstrongs enjoyed it in short bursts. They would take Nannie and the children and dogs over, settle them down in the cottage, and scuttle to and fro from Newquay. Obviously the time Michael and Bettye could spend there during the

[2] Who later became Joan Brooker

season was limited, they only had one car, but they managed to have some idyllic little sojourns in "Cherry Tree Cottage".

All through the '50s at the Edgcumbe the Armstrongs were having trouble with the neighbours about the noise, and they were increasingly hampered by lack of space. They had tried repeatedly to buy the house next door, 3 Edgcumbe Avenue, but their neighbour, Miss Rickard, was adamant she would not sell to them. An additional factor was that Peter and Barbara had sold their farm and bought an hotel which was twice the size and had much more potential, while nothing further could be done at Edgcumbe. They had found being in a side road no drawback, but they just wanted sixty bedrooms; therefore, by the autumn of 1957 Michael and Bettye had made up their minds that they must have more room, and if that meant moving, so be it. Ironically, later owners of the hotel were able to buy the two adjoining houses. If the Armstrongs had managed to buy even one they would never have moved.

A precious afternoon away from the hotel. Bettye, Michael and John.

Bettye began the search for larger premises, and there were many discussions about it. Michael Armstrong and Olive Whittington were somewhat reluctant to move, but they were eventually carried along by Bettye's enthusiasm. There was one point on which they all agreed — if and when they moved, they were not going to sell the name "Edgcumbe". They would take it with them and re-name whatever they bought "Edgcumbe". They had a large following of regular guests and they felt they could not afford to lose them.

But we must break away and leave the Armstrongs with their problems for the moment — this is a Newquay story too!

The 1950s - 1970s was a rip roaring period in Newquay. After the deprivations of the Second World War the whole country was in party mood and those years were Newquay's heyday as a middle class family resort. The established hotels had managed to recover from the ravages of their war time occupation. New ones had opened: there were at that time over three hundred hotels in the town. Many were rugged and over-crowded to a degree and all were generally mediocre, but they flourished and the winters were a hustle and a bustle with making extra rooms and improvements for the following season. Looking back standards were deplorably low, but the guests were unfussy. The important thing in those years was that they managed to get in somewhere.

At the time there were just two hotels that were giants among the pygmies — and one that should have been, but wasn't. They were the Hotel Bristol on Narrowcliff, Glendorgal at Porth and the stately Headland, which, lamentably, seemed to have lost its way. These three outstanding hotels were nothing to do with the family.

The reader has already heard about the Hotel Bristol on Narrowcliff from 1927 when it was founded by Mr and Mrs Howard Young assisted by Mrs Young's widowed sister, Mrs Francis. They made a splendid team and worked well together. The hotel was hugely successful from the outset and by 1939 it had overtaken Tolcarne Hotel and had become Cornwall's largest and brightest holiday hotel.

Hotel Bristol, 1927.

During the Second World War, with canny foresight, the Youngs made a private arrangement with Benenden Girls' School from Kent, whereby the school took over the whole hotel for the duration and the Youngs catered for them. It was a most advantageous arrangement for it meant the furniture and fittings could remain in place and when the school departed for the holidays, four weeks at Christmas and Easter and eight weeks in the summer, the Bristol could revert briefly to being a hotel, if only in a much restricted way. They were also able to retain some of their older, experienced staff who were ineligible to be called up for war service. Therefore, in 1945, when hostilities ceased, the Hotel Bristol had a head and shoulders start and the Youngs made the most of it. They forged ahead and by the early 1950s they had one hundred and forty-seven bedrooms, including forty-two singles, but, interestingly, only about three private bathrooms, and thirty lock-up garages — in those days most people wanted a garage — cars did not 'stand out' as they do today. The garages were an important amenity and were proudly advertised.

Extension of Hotel Bristol 1931-1932.

Hotel Bristol 1932.

Due to the on-going currency restrictions only the privileged few could go abroad and the rich and famous flocked to the Hotel Bristol, which was, at that time, not only Newquay's, but Cornwall's largest and most glamorous hotel and it was lauded far and wide. There was nightly dancing in long dresses and black ties to Norman Nankervis and his five piece orchestra which also played in the dining room for luncheon and dinner, and in spite of the war time restrictions, which were not lifted for some five or six years, at the Hotel Bristol there was an air of luxury and, indeed, opulence which others could not match; it was in a league of its own.

The pre-war weekly programme of activities was resumed, with a picnic to Treyarnon Bay when the staff went too taking elaborate teas in large, wicker laundry baskets which they served. There were regular tennis tournaments on the tennis courts at Trenance, and fortnightly sports for the guests on Tolcarne Beach, when the pitch was properly marked out and lined with deck chairs for the spectators and again the hotel staff served tea in great style. Their Christmas programme was always booked solid with the same guests returning year after year. The Hotel Bristol also established an excellent winter function business: they offered consistently good food and service and in spite of serious competition over the years, to this day many of the county's most prestigious dinners are held there.

Mr and Mrs Young Senior retired in 1946 to their house, 'By the Sea', where Mary Young (Bernard's widow) still lives. Sadly, Mr Howard Young died in 1951 and their only son, Bernard, took over. Bernard had been in the Royal Navy during the war and his war service had left him with chest problems. In the early 1950s he developed TB and was a semi-invalid for the rest of his life. He died in 1971 aged fifty-seven. His eldest son, Stuart, a Chartered Accountant, had taken over in 1965. He was ably supported by Mrs Francis, affectionately known as Auntie Bill to generations of Hotel Bristol guests. To her, the Bristol was her home, her work and her life for nearly fifty years. She died in 1979 age eighty-six.

Stuart Young made two important additions to the Bristol. In the early 1960s he installed the modern indoor swimming pool; he did it well and it is extremely popular. He bought land in Hilgrove Road and made a large car park with easy access to the rear entrance of the hotel, and he also tackled the problem of all those single rooms, turning them into spacious doubles with private bathrooms; and many others were converted into service rooms: hairdresser, beautician, offices, laundry, sewing room, etc. Unlike many hotels, the Bristol never had to struggle to find space.

The Hotel Bristol has now been owned and run by the Young family for over eighty years and they still have a family team in charge. Stuart is the Chairman, his elder son, Howard (the fourth generation) is the Managing Director, and Stuart's second wife, Vera, controls the seventy-five bedrooms. Although the hotel has long lost the glamour it had in the giddy years after the Second World War, it has a gracious air and has remained steadfast to is own immaculate old-fashioned, traditional standards of quality and service: change has been resisted and today it remains one of Newquay's few enduring landmarks.

Now a little about the Headland Hotel, which for some forty years before the war had been Newquay's grandest and stuffiest hotel. Regrettably, after the war it fell into the hands of people who had little knowledge of the hotel business and it quickly lost its aura of grandeur. The new owners were misguidedly determined to modernise the interior with disastrous results. By the late 1950s internally the Headland had become an atrocious jumble of styles — it really had been vandalised. The standards and service had steeply declined, its reputation had slumped, and it was no longer Newquay's classiest hotel as it had long been. A sorry tale!

But in 1950 a new star appeared on the Newquay hotel scene when Nigel Tangye opened his family home, Glendorgal, Porth as an hotel. From the beginning Glendorgal had the 'wow' factor, largely generated by Nigel's personality and background. Here is the story of how he achieved it.

Nigel ran the hotel in an extremely hands-on way for some twenty-two years. He was very much the host and stamped it with his personal style. Nigel was a man of the world. He had gone to Dartmouth, aged fourteen, as was the custom in those days, and spent some years in the Royal Navy. He was an experienced aviator and during the war he transferred to the RAF and became a Spitfire pilot. A writer of distinction he had written several books, but as a writer he had never quite received the acclaim of his brother Derek[3]. Nigel had had a chequered career. He was widely travelled, spoke fluent French and German, and was a connoisseur of wines — in short a man of many parts who knew people in all walks of life and many were the doors open to him — perhaps above all he had style in spades. His first wife was Ann Todd, the film star, and they had a daughter, Francesca.

3 Nigel's brother, Derek, wrote the 'Minack Chronicles' about life on a flower farm in West Cornwall. There were the kind of books one gave to one's maiden aunt for Christmas, all about the birds and the bees without any sex, but they were amazingly popular.

Glendorgal House, circa 1875-1880. – *Courtesy Moira Tangye.*

Glendorgal was utterly unique and a far cry from the hundreds of other hotels in Newquay at the time. It really was in a class of its own and was a great success from the outset. Nigel wisely changed as little of the interior as possible and managed to preserve the country house atmosphere. The billiards room became the bar room, the hub of the hotel. It had a high canopied ceiling and a large circular alcove in one wall in which Nigel's interesting collection of modern pictures was hung. There was no bar, just a long antique mahogany table laden with the stylish accoutrements for mixing drinks, and at the back a glass fronted wall cupboard where the liquor was kept. The chairs and tables were a hotch-potch; some metal, some cane, some wooden, even plastic — all utterly dissimilar, but effectively grouped to create a casually elegant atmosphere without the stilted look of many hotel lounges with matching everything.

In a corner near the bay window was an upright piano and Nigel's second wife, Lady Marguerite, would often accompany the pianist by strumming on her guitar and singing in a deep husky ginny voice. The guests loved it, of course, and sometimes Nigel would join in playing his accordion often with a cigar in his mouth. French doors led to the terrace restaurant which had been glazed with modern zig zag windows designed by Sheila Tribe with built in tables so that every diner faced the sea, and sometimes the sunset — it was exceedingly popular and always well booked.

The dining room with warm red walls, lovely old original carpet, Louis XV dark marble fireplace and one wall dominated by a large flowery water colour by Jacob Epstein had polished mahogany tables gleaming with silver and candles and was completely traditional. The coffee was always served in silver coffee pots. The drawing room was

Glendorgal, showing the terrace restaurant with the zig-zag windows.
Courtesy Moira Tangye.

furnished with antiques and soft colours with family portraits on the walls. It looked as one would imagine it had always looked.

The entrance and hall remained virtually unchanged, essentially 'private house' with no sign of a reception desk or office, but there was a long narrow glass case full of family mementos, wartime relics and other items of interest. For some seventeen years Nigel had a most reliable aide — Mrs Freemantle — although not usually seen, she presided over the bookings etc. She was able to take charge when he had a day off and she never let him down.

A window table in the Terrace Restaurant. – *Courtesy Moira Tangye.*

When Nigel's mother died in 1954 she left Glendorgal to her three sons Colin, Nigel and Derek and so in 1955 Nigel had to buy his brothers out. That left him with limited resources, but it didn't cramp his style in the least. For years his only car was a pre-war cream and black R type Bentley and, as he explained, it was so much easier to tell the gas man he would have to wait for his bill to be paid with a Bentley standing outside the door. In the late 1950s he built six studio rooms in the grounds facing the sea. They were modern, stylish, and highly popular.

Nigel was masterly at side-stepping awkward issues with aplomb. He hated taking guests to the worst bedroom — all hotels have them. It was a north facing room with sloping ceiling and a high window, furnished largely with the original furniture. On the way to it he would tell them how nostalgic the room was for him and what fond memories he had of it because it had been his childhood nursery, etc., etc., ending with "do join me for a drink later". How difficult then for them to tell him they didn't like the room without seeming churlish. When a guest complained about the wine and said to Nigel "you call yourself an expert" Nigel replied "No, I don't call myself an expert, but I must say I haven't drunk water since 1946."

Every winter Nigel travelled to the continent in search of good staff for the following season. He always managed to arrange it and they certainly contributed to the slightly continental flavour of the hotel — it was also a jolly good reason for an annual business trip to Germany and France!

For hotels in Newquay the 1950s and 1960s was a sellers' market and people were begging for rooms and prepared to sleep anywhere just to get in. Glendorgal joined that bandwagon and Nigel arranged for extra rooms in the bungalows near the hotel for 'sleeping out' — they were referred to as annexe rooms, of course — and he even managed to convert what had been the coal cellar. He put in a small window, decorated the room and it made a splendid 'single' and was always well booked.

There was one party of guests who arrived at Glendorgal by chance. They were Cockney East End barrow boys with their women. They had booked at a small nearby hotel and when they turned up the proprietors refused to take them because they had an unexpected baby in a Moses basket but maybe that was just an excuse! Newquay was full to overflowing in those days and there was little hope of finding rooms. They were despondent, but someone wildly suggested, rather tongue in cheek, "try Glendorgal", which was nearby. At Glendorgal they were squashed in and they completely beguiled The Tangyes with their Cockney humour and natural charm. In the evenings they would join their hosts to make music — it was hilarious and they helped to create a wonderful atmosphere of spontaneous jollification. Everybody loved them because they didn't try to be 'posh', and they became regular guests every August for years.

Nigel adored his boat *Spray of Glendorgal*, a 30 ft Falmouth Pilot boat, ketch rigged, with two cabins. She was moored at Malpas. He was an experienced helmsman and he would sometimes take guests out for a day's sailing. It was done in style; the picnic was usually champagne, lobster sandwiches and strawberries and cream and there were many trips to Helford — or perhaps on rougher days just exploring the countless creeks on the south coast of Cornwall, and he, a true Cornishman, would regale his guests with sea stories.

In 1963 Nigel married Moira, his third wife, and that marriage endured. They had four children. While Nigel was at Glendorgal it remained the one hotel in Newquay that was so unlike the others and it had enormous appeal to discerning guests, but running it in such a 'hands on' way took its toll and by 1972 Nigel, aged sixty-three, was ready to retire and he sold it. He, Moira and their children moved into the Lodge and the charm of the hotel went with them. Sadly Glendorgal's glory days were over; before long it became just another dreary Newquay hotel but for twenty-two years the Newquay hotel scene had been enhanced by the chic and elegance and style of Nigel Tangye's 'Glendorgal'.

But now back to the family story.

Olive Whittington with her son, Peter and daughter, Bettye Armstrong, circa 1953.

Bredon Court Hotel

Knowle Links Hotel – which became Bredon Court

The house that was to become Knowle Links and then Bredon Court was built in the early 1900s as a private house in its own grounds. It was in a splendid position on the edge of Newquay Golf Course facing the sea and very near the Clubhouse and the first tee. In the early 1930s the house was bought by Mr and Mrs Walter Horler, who had been successfully running Knowle Hotel in Crantock Street for some years. When they moved they took the name with them and called their new hotel Knowle Links. The Knowle Hotel in Crantock Street then became Ashville, which it is today.

Knowle House – the original house that became Bredon Court Hotel.

Knowle Links, under Mr and Mrs Horler, was a highly successful upmarket hotel that catered for golfers. They added a new three storey wing of bedrooms to the hotel. Unfortunately at that time there was a public footpath by the side of the building and the wing was built on the far side of it, thus dividing the new wing from the hotel on the ground floor — the footpath virtually went through the middle of the building.

Mr and Mrs Horler were good hoteliers and under them Knowle Links flourished. They were much-respected members of the community and he was a leading light in the Newquay Hotels Association. After the war Mr Horler sold the hotel and the new owners were not so successful; the pre-war type of guests no longer came to Newquay. Knowle Links did not keep pace with the changing market, and so gradually it went down and finally floundered. When it was put on the market in 1956 for £20,000, it was an extremely low price for a sixty bedroom hotel at that time, but it was shabby, outdated and badly in need of modernising.

In 1956 Peter and Barbara were offered The Bolowthas at the entrance to the town — later renamed The Savoia, then a few years later to become The Riviera Hotel. The Bolowthas had about thirty bedrooms and the asking price was £20,000. For the same price they were offered Knowle Links Hotel with its sixty bedrooms but in a much less prominent position — what a choice! The Knowle had splendid space around it which they later were to put to good use, but its location was extremely odd. Facing the sea and virtually on the golf links by the first tee in the front, but being tucked in behind a dreary row of terrace houses in Tower Road it was sometimes difficult for guests to find. (Peter was later to overcome this difficulty by buying the corner house in Tower Road so that he could erect a large direction sign to the Hotel in the front garden).

After much deliberation and lengthy negotiations, despite its poor reputation and odd position, the Whittingtons offered £17,000 for Knowle Links which was accepted. They renamed it Bredon Court, after their herd of pedigree Guernseys.

Peter and Barbara Whittington took over in January 1957 and on the first Sunday morning after they had moved in Bettye went to have a look at their new acquisition. On the ground floor of the bedroom wing she suddenly said "But this corridor isn't the full length of the building. There must be more." On looking closer they found indeed there was more; another eight bedrooms, four on each side of the corridor, which had been cut off and given an outside entrance and used as staff rooms. What a find! Peter and Barbara were delighted. No mention of those rooms had been made in the agents' particulars, which says a great deal about the efficiency of the estate agents handling the sale!

The Whittingtons soon had the partition across the corridor down and turned the rooms back into accommodation for guests. To buy an hotel with sixty bedrooms and then discover there are sixty-eight is quite something! Thus Bredon Court opened in April 1957 with sixty-eight bedrooms. In those days in Newquay, as all hoteliers know, it was

Drawing room

Dining room

Lounge

Knowle Links Hotel as Peter Whittington bought it in 1957.

NEWQUAY

BREDON COURT HOTEL

FULLY LICENSED FOR RESIDENTS

Standing in own grounds overlooking Fistral Beach.
Adjoining Golf Club. Glorious Sea Views. 5 minutes from Shops

★ **DANCING THREE TIMES WEEKLY TO OUR OWN ORCHESTRA** ★
★ **OWN TENNIS AND SQUASH COURTS IN THE GROUNDS** ★
★ **70 BEDROOMS. SLUMBERLAND BEDS. H. & C.** ★
★ **NEW FULL-SIZE BILLIARD ROOM** ★
★ **FREE CAR PARK FOR RESIDENTS** ★
★ **COCKTAIL LOUNGE** ★
★ **NO RESTRICTIONS** ★

Entertainment Programme in full swing from May includes Billiards, Tennis, Squash, Table Tennis Tournaments, Midnight Barbacues, Beach Cricket, Own Skiffle Group

THE BEST VALUE IN CORNWALL

Tel : Newquay 2345 **Terms $6\frac{1}{2}$–$12\frac{1}{2}$ gns.** No Service Charge

UNDER SAME DIRECTION AS EDGCUMBE HOTEL

Peter's first advertisement for Bredon Court Hotel – "under the same direction as the Edgcumbe Hotel".

"bods in beds" that counted and they had unexpectedly found beds for another sixteen people. Today, when guests are much more discerning, it is said that it's no good having bedrooms if one cannot fill them, but when Bredon Court opened they were very happy with their sixty-eight bedrooms; the boom was still on and they knew they could fill them easily. They had decided to follow the Edgcumbe's proven successful formula offering cheery good value holidays for families and young people with plenty of activities and nightly entertainment.

During the winter they had managed to get out a reasonable brochure and an advertisement in the Town Guide, which in those days was absolutely essential. Barbara understood the bookings, having worked for a season at the Edgcumbe ten years before, and she made sure the hotel was well booked by the time they opened.

Peter and Barbara were really "as green as grass" for the first season — but they worked early and late all through the spring, and were up at 5.00 a.m. on the opening day. Unfortunately, the very first guests arrived at 8.00 a.m. to find the stair carpet being laid by Peter — and walked straight out again! It was mortifying. He always sailed close to the wind, but that was sheer bad luck, for those guests might not have arrived until the evening when all would have been ready. However, the next guests who arrived in the afternoon thought it was wonderful and were to return again and again. Bredon Court was under way and the Whittingtons soon got going with what was to be a very hectic — but successful — first season.

Olive Whittington had watched Peter and Barbara's ten years of struggle on the farm with great concern and when they took on Bredon Court she was determined to help them although she was then seventy years of age. Sonia and Maria were aged two and four years and Peter took a furnished bungalow in Eliot Gardens for that first summer and his mother moved into it with the children and a nursemaid. She took them off their parents' hands for the three busy months so that they could give their full attention to the hotel.

The Whittingtons were happy to run under the Edgcumbe banner for the first two or three seasons, and they advertised "under the same direction as the Edgcumbe Hotel". After that Peter was ready to put his own highly personal stamp on Bredon Court, and his subsequent hotels, which he did with marked success.

From the beginning Peter, always a 'back room chap,' spent much of his time in the kitchen. He was seriously interested in the food and how they were going to serve it; consequently his menus were more adventurous than those at the Edgcumbe, where traditional English cooking was offered. Peter and Barbara decided to serve continental cuisine and engage continental staff. They were indeed fortunate to find a first class German chef, Kurt, who returned to Bredon Court year after year. Later he brought his own German assistants back with him from Germany each year. Peter worked alongside Kurt in the kitchen and learnt much from him. The family remained in touch with him until his death in 1998.

When hotels change hands, the first years are invariably hard for the new owners. The hotels are usually run down and nobody knows what is there or where it is, and so it was at Bredon Court when the Whittingtons took over. The previous owners had only been catering for about eighty to ninety guests and Peter and Barbara, following the successful Edgcumbe formula of 'pack 'em in', immediately pushed the numbers up to one hundred and fifty with children's beds tucked into every corner. (In later years the numbers were to be even greater). Consequently, in 1957 there were shortages of everything. Peter spent several Saturday mornings during that first season in his workshop knocking up dining tables to be ready for the new guests arriving that afternoon, and they were constantly borrowing items from the Edgcumbe. From the beginning they were lucky to book Ken Stratton to run their three weekly dances and the children's party. He was a great help in getting the entertainments going, and it was an enormous relief to Peter and Barbara who had no wish to be mixed up with that side of the business, unlike the Armstrongs who at that time did it with gusto and loved it.

There was a massive amount of work planned for the following winter — far too much of course, but that was how Peter liked things. He felt ready to make up for lost time after the ten wasted years on the farm, and he was soon to put his own very individual stamp on the hotel. During that winter they managed to replace the former staff bedrooms with a staff block of eight single rooms further away from the hotel, a much more satisfactory arrangement. They gutted the public rooms on the ground floor completely, creating a new office and open plan lounges. It was an enormous improvement.

The first few seasons were exceptionally hard for Peter and Barbara. They already had two young children, Maria and Sonia, no home and sketchy help for the two girls, and in 1958 their third daughter, Sarah, was born. By this time, sadly, cracks were showing in the marriage. Peter yearned for a son and perhaps had he and Barbara ever produced one, this story might have had a different outcome, but it was not to be.

In those early summers the Whittingtons camped in a couple of attic rooms in the hotel. It was very cramped and uncomfortable with small children and it was a great relief when the seasons ended. Sonia recalls being tethered like a pony on the front lawn sometimes when

Lounge Ballroom.

Dining Room.

The Cocktail Lounge.

Bredon Court Hotel, 1958, after Peter Whittington's winter renovations.

The front lawn of Bredon Court where Sonia was tethered at desperate moments.

the nursemaid was off duty and for several years the Whittingtons were unable to take a holiday. There was no spare money and far too much to be tackled in the hotel during the winter. They really had a very hard time for a year or two.

Without doubt the early days at Bredon Court were also a great financial struggle. At that time Peter was "doing an Uncle Graham", constantly trying to raise money, and occasionally his mother helped him. When the Midland Bank, with whom his family had enjoyed an excellent relationship for some forty years, would advance him no more he was furious and he walked across the road in a rage to Lloyds Bank who immediately agreed to meet his financial requirements. His account was lost to Midland for ever and Lloyds Bank was to be his main bank from then on. He became a much-valued customer.

When Peter and Barbara sold the farm at Colan and bought Bredon Court it was quite clear that Peter would never conform to the accepted image of an hotel proprietor. He never wore a tie, he always wore dark grey flannel bags and black leather lace up shoes, in the summer without socks, and a navy blue pullover. When it was hot he would tie knots in the four corners of a large handkerchief and wear it on his head. He usually carried a tool box, so he looked like the maintenance man rather than the owner. He was a talented engineer and always did most of the maintenance himself. One day a rather pompous, well-dressed man arrived to see the owner. Peter was down a hole in the front garden at Bredon Court dealing with a drainage problem and the man had walked past him. When told that that was the owner of the hotel, the man replied "That cannot be the owner, he is not wearing socks!"

Unlike his sister, Bettye, Peter never actually enjoyed contact with the guests. He would always avoid them if possible and he never had anything to do with the reception office. He was essentially a 'back room boy' interested in the food, including the cooking, the wine, and all the technical problems of keeping the hotel running. Fortunately Barbara was very efficient at the office side of the business and enjoyed it. She trained the receptionists well, but neither she nor Peter ever liked the bar, or socialising with the guests. In those days they didn't really drink, except wine at dinner. They made a good team and loved the work, but never seemed to get the fun out of it that the Armstrongs had in the early days.

There was a spacious well-built detached house facing the golf course next to Bredon Court called Zabuloe and Peter managed to buy it and join it to the hotel. He and Barbara, with their three children, had a splendid ground floor flat and they made a very comfortable and stylish home there. The upper floor was completely cut off and became rooms for hotel guests. The new flat was greatly appreciated by the Whittington family as they had been 'tucking away' in the summer, and as everyone who has ever done so knows, with young children that is hideously uncomfortable and inconvenient.

At Bredon Court Peter was getting it all under control. Although he was always at one with his staff, as the Whittingtons are to this day, he could also be adamant about what was to happen. At one stage Peter felt that some of his staff were not really pulling their weight so he put up a large notice on the staff room board saying "Some members of staff are skiving, and I will not stand it. There is no room in Bredon Court for skivers." He immediately had a near riot on his hands and three of the staff actually walked out — that did not make life any easier!

Financially the decision to move from the farm had proved to be the right one, and soon the changes in Peter and Barbara's financial status and life style became apparent. The growing success of the hotel allowed them to take autumn holidays in the Mediterranean for a loll in the sun without the children, and of course they still occasionally used the Armstrongs' little flat in Bath. It was a great relief to the whole family that Peter was at last prospering.

When Peter Whittington had come out of the Army in November 1946 he had marked socialistic views and he was, at that time, very left wing. When he bought Bredon Court he was a rabid socialist and treated his staff accordingly. He allowed the staff and their buddies to use the main bar of the hotel when they came off duty and to join in the dances and to use all the facilities, including the swimming pool. This, of course, eventually caused difficulties. One can imagine that if staff and their friends are allowed to crowd into the bar in the evening there really will not be much room for guests — or the guests will be crowded out, and so it happened. Although there were many regular guests at Bredon Court who loved it, some guests did not wish to mix with the staff, and one complained bitterly that Bredon Court was a good hotel but it was run by the staff for the staff. Fortunately before long Peter got his sense of proportion more balanced and the staff were no longer allowed to join in the evening entertainment for the guests, or to use the hotel facilities. Michael and Bettye, who had much more conservative ideas, were somewhat relieved when what they considered to be 'that nonsense' ceased, because the Edgcumbe staff were aggrieved that they were not given the same privileges as the staff at Bredon Court. The Armstrongs had absolutely no intention of allowing it at the Edgcumbe! The truth is they always drew a fine line between the 'upper and lower decks' but to the Whittingtons there was only one deck and they were all on it together.

Soon it was Bredon Court's turn to lead the way as far as the family hotels were concerned. Whittington was the first person to build a squash court in Newquay and for a few years the court at Bredon Court was the only one in the town, and the Newquay Squash Club played there in the winter.[1] Peter made a hard tennis court and engaged a Pakistani professional coach who came every summer for years to instruct the guests in squash and tennis. He was very popular and that worked well. Peter also put in a large, kidney shaped swimming pool overlooking the golf links. In fact it was too large, too deep and costly to heat therefore too cold for guests' comfort, but it was a magnificent pool. It was one of the first in Newquay and certainly the largest.

In those halcyon days when beaches were free, when one could walk dogs, light fires, drink and play loud music, barbecues on the beaches were the order of the day. Several hotels arranged evening barbecues for their guests, usually on the nearest beach, but Peter Whittington, who always had to go one better, decided one evening to hold his weekly barbecue in the Banqueting Cavern at Porth. Michael and Bettye and their friends went along to see the fun.

---

[1] By the 1990s there were about nine squash courts in the area, four of which were in the family hotels.

It was riotous and chaotic; the approach to the cavern was so difficult. They all had to trudge along Porth Headland and then clamber down from the top carrying crates of beer and all the other barbecue paraphernalia, including two guitars. On the beach, in the dark, the guests sploshed through pools of water, some unsuitably dressed in frilly dresses and high-heeled white shoes, amidst shrieks of laughter — they loved it. Never had they had such a "way-out" party. But that evening there was nearly a ghastly accident. One chap carrying a crate of beer fell through the hole in the roof of the cavern. There is no doubt he would have gone right down onto the rocks below but he was wedged by his elbows because he was carrying the crate of beer and they saved him. His legs were swinging in space. His friends pulled him out and all was well, but it was a dicey moment. The evening was hilarious and memorable but even Peter decided it had been too much and he never did it again.

In the 1950s hotels were rated largely on the number of beds available for guests. So hotels like the Edgcumbe and Bredon Court, which put extra beds in every corner and made singles into small doubles, were at a great disadvantage when being rated. The rating officer would inspect the rooms, counting beds. A room with a single bed was a single, regardless of the size of room, and so therefore when an inspection was imminent all extra beds had to be removed. Twin bedded rooms became singles, family rooms became doubles. Peter used to store all the extra beds in the squash court for the rating officer's visit. Happily, a more practical system is now applied for rating hotels.

Peter was always tenacious. When he bought Bredon Court, as the reader has heard, the building was bisected in the centre by the public footpath, and there was no access from one building to the other on the ground floor. The bedroom wing was on one side of it and the main hotel on the other, and it was extremely tiresome. As many people have discovered, it is extremely difficult to get a public footpath moved. But Peter battled with the local authorities for a long time and eventually was successful in getting the path moved to around the end of the building so that the ground floor could be joined. That was no mean feat, but he was quite determined and in the end won his battle with the council — it was the first of many!

In the late 1950s the family were finding it difficult to buy the furnishings etc. for the hotels wholesale, and obviously it wasn't sensible to walk into local shops and pay retail prices. So in 1960 Peter opened a small shop called Scandia in Newquay selling well designed Scandinavian fabrics, furniture, china, glass, and jewellery, which were much in vogue at the time. In fact they are the 20th century classics and will be the antiques of the future. It was a splendid little shop and there is no shop in Newquay — or in Cornwall, today that sells such quality things. It did not really supply the family hotels, of course, because the goods Peter sold were much too high quality for hotel purposes, but it did give him the right to buy wholesale, and that was what he really wanted. Although the shop has now long gone, the wholesale accounts are still open, and the family now use them for buying stock for the boutiques in the hotels.

During the first season at Bredon Court, fate again took a hand. An up and coming young architect from Stockton-on-Tees, Tom Malcolm, arrived with his wife Doreen and their two young children, Susan aged five, and Nicholas aged three. They stayed for a fortnight and during that time the seeds of friendship were sown between Peter and Tom; they both shared the same interests and each recognised the other's talents. When the Malcolm family arrived again for a fortnight the following year a firm friendship was cemented and it was one which was to change the course of both families' lives for ever.

During the winter of 1958-1959, while Tom Malcolm was supervising the work on the extension to the Coniston, soon to become the new Edgcumbe, Peter Whittington was offered the derelict Bedruthan Steps Hotel at Mawgan Porth, six miles from Newquay. It had thirty bedrooms, the roof leaked like a sieve, the metal window frames were all warped, and many would not close. The building really needed demolishing but it was in an excellent position with five acres of land and it had a full licence. Included in the sale was a little jerry built three-bedroom house called "Bedruthan House" also in a very sorry state. All through the thirties and after the war there had been constant development of the Trenance Estate on which the hotel stood. By the time Peter Whittington and Tom Malcolm looked at it in 1959 Bedruthan Steps was surrounded by bungalows and houses, but it was still being offered with five acres of land — very valuable land, most of it in front of and below the hotel sloping down towards the sea. Whittington and Malcolm thought that very important, for if they bought it they had ambitious plans for the site.

Whilst Tom Malcolm spent much time that winter working on the Coniston project in Cornwall his wife, Doreen, stayed in Stockton-on Tees with her young children and initially, therefore, she was not really included in the family friendship that was developing. At that time Peter was very taken with his new friend, Tom, but was not much impressed with Doreen Malcolm; he thought her dull, dreary and a boring little 'Haus Frau'; as she laughingly today recalls, "he said I was a cabbage". How wrong he was about that!

Peter Whittington was full of enthusiasm for the property. He could see great potential there and finally became determined to buy it if he possibly could. He persuaded Tom Malcolm to go into partnership with him. They formed a company; The Bedruthan Steps Hotel Limited. Peter's wife, Barbara, became a director and he asked his sister, Bettye, to join the board, but she felt fully committed to what she was doing at the Edgcumbe, and apart from that she thought Bedruthan Steps was too far out of town and a dump. She would have nothing to do with it. Peter Whittington and Tom Malcolm then spent several months considering it, negotiating with the agents and discussing ways and means, their appetites whetted by the exciting Edgcumbe development which was proceeding apace. They finally agreed to buy Bedruthan Steps Hotel for £10,000 which was really no more than the value of the freehold site and the full liquor licence. But where was the money to come from? It was finally agreed that each couple would put up £5,000. The Malcolm's only asset was their four bedroom house in Thornton, outside Stockton-on-Tees, which Tom had designed and they had literally built themselves. In the process Tom's wife, Doreen, had worked extremely hard and became quite an expert. She had put the architraves around all the doors, laid all the upstairs floors, painted the whole of the outside, and landscaped the large garden. At the time she had two young children, and there was soon to be a third.

Tom and Doreen Malcolm put their house on the market and fairly quickly sold it for £5,000 which gave them the necessary capital, and which, incidentally, went straight into Bredon Court's coffers! Peter then had to raise £10,000 and of course he had no spare money, he was already deeply financially committed at Bredon Court. His mother, who always had a little put by for a rainy day, declined to help him; she would have preferred him to get on with the hotel he already had and felt he had no need to take on another one. However after three successful seasons at Bredon Court he had something of a track record and with the help of his friendly bank manager, Bill Collins, and good family friend, Mr Whetter, head of Western Counties Building Society, he managed to raise the money. And so in the winter of 1959-1960 the Bedruthan Hotel Company Limited bought Bedruthan Steps Hotel with five acres of land and a full licence for the agreed £10,000. It was arranged that Tom and Doreen Malcolm, who knew nothing about hotels, would manage it, and Peter, who was still at Bredon

Court, would work with them to guide and help them.

While on the farm Peter and Barbara had seemed to be completely happy and in tune, although he was later to say that was not so, but when they went into the hotel business, although they worked well together, the marriage began to crumble and their relationship deteriorated. It is well known that hotel life is not the easiest in which to nurture a marriage. The hours are long and anti-social, there can be many temptations along the way, and unless there is a very sound, stable relationship it can cause trouble. Sadly in their new lifestyle they seemed to lose their compatibility and they slowly drifted apart.

By then the Whittingtons had been married some fourteen years and the family had become very fond of Barbara. She and Peter had seemed so well suited in many ways. It was she who gave Peter his love of opera, classical music, and the arts. To some extent she educated him. Everyone, particularly Peter's mother, was upset when their marriage began to get into difficulties. His mother tried to dissuade him, especially because of the children, but Peter had made up his mind and eventually he and Barbara were divorced and it was arranged that Barbara would continue to run Bredon Court on her own.

Barbara Whittington 1965.

It was of course very sad for the children when their parents' marriage broke up, and the youngest, Sarah, was only a baby. Barbara had worked hard on the farm and alongside Peter in their struggle to establish the hotel. It says much for her good nature that she remained friends with everyone and on terms with Peter. In fact she loved him dearly for the rest of her life, and when later someone suggested to her that Peter had behaved badly she would have none of it and said "Oh no, it was my fault. You don't know how awful I was." She was a kindly, well educated woman, but she really was a free spirit and could be decidedly temperamental if things didn't go well.

From the time Whittington and

Malcolm had brought Bedruthan Steps Hotel in 1960 Peter had been spending most of his time there and when he and Barbara separated he moved out of the house and joined his new partners at Bedruthan Steps. By then all his interest and attention was concentrated on the new venture. Fortunately Bredon Court was doing well and for the next twenty years or so Barbara ran it more or less on her own, with directions from Peter, from time to time. She continued to live at Zabuloe with her three daughters. It was very hard on her.

The end of Edgcumbe Hotel, Edgcumbe Avenue 1958

In their search for more space in the summer of 1957 the Armstrongs decided to buy the sixty bedroom Grantham Hotel in Edgcumbe Gardens for £25,000. They knew it well; it had been the RAF Officers' Club during the war and under the previous owners, Mr and Mrs Drake, had been successful. By this time it was not doing so well and had a very poor reputation. The deposit was paid and the contract drawn up and about to be signed when the owner, a rather odd middle-aged spinster who had been a waitress there at one time, and subsequently inherited the hotel from her aged 'lover boy', heard that the Armstrongs intended to change the name to Edgcumbe. She was outraged and refused to sell it to them. She had heard about the change of name because Bettye (who has always had a capacity for speaking out of turn) interviewed the Grantham head chef whom they were intending to employ, and during the interview she unnecessarily told him that they would be re-naming the hotel "Edgcumbe". He related that news back to Miss Phillips, the owner, who immediately took umbrage and withdrew from the sale. She subsequently sold the Grantham to friends of the Armstrongs for a considerably lower price!

The Armstrongs were devastated, because while they were negotiating to buy the Grantham they had a buyer for the Edgcumbe (without its name). The prospective purchaser was a regular guest who had been interested in it for several years and a price had been agreed; £19,000 for the freehold, including furniture and fittings of course — less £1,000 because they were not selling the name. The annexe opposite was not included in the sale. That was to be sold later. When the Grantham sale fell through they were not at all sure they could find another suitable hotel and so they withdrew from the sale of the Edgcumbe and decided for the time being they must "stay put". Their resolve that when they moved the name "Edgcumbe" would move with them was not weakened, however. They had worked extremely hard for twelve years, and the Edgcumbe had a good reputation and a hard core of guests who returned year after year, whom they were also determined to take with them wherever they went!

In retrospect, of course, it was an ill wind when the Grantham deal collapsed.

It would not have been a wise move. Grantham Astor, as it now is, is not in a prime position, it was already fully developed and, biggest snag of all, it had virtually no car parking space, but at the time the Armstrongs were obsessed with having sixty bedrooms and were devastated when the deal fell through. They then set about looking at other hotels but there seemed to be nothing suitable on the market. They had just missed Beachcroft which had been sold to a friend of theirs a few months earlier and so, nursing their aspirations, they settled back into their comfortable winter routine; three months leisure, a family Christmas at home and back to the grind in January when the children had returned to school. It suited them well.

In the meanwhile the Whittingtons were busy knocking their hotel about and Bettye watched their activities with great interest and a certain amount of envy — all that lovely space!

In January 1958, out of the blue, the Armstrongs were offered the Coniston Hotel on Narrowcliff and after much consideration they decided to buy it, provided they could arrange the money to double its size to sixty bedrooms, but they realised they faced the possibility of having two hotels on their hands for the 1958 season — a daunting, indeed alarming prospect, but Bettye had got the bit between her teeth and was raring to go! Bettye's mother, although reluctant about the move at first, eventually gave the project her blessing, but she could never quite understand why they could not accommodate fewer people and remain in Edgcumbe Avenue. She was a contented woman, without her son and daughter's driving ambitions. She was later to say she had had many sleepless nights over the decision to buy the Coniston, but she was very supportive.

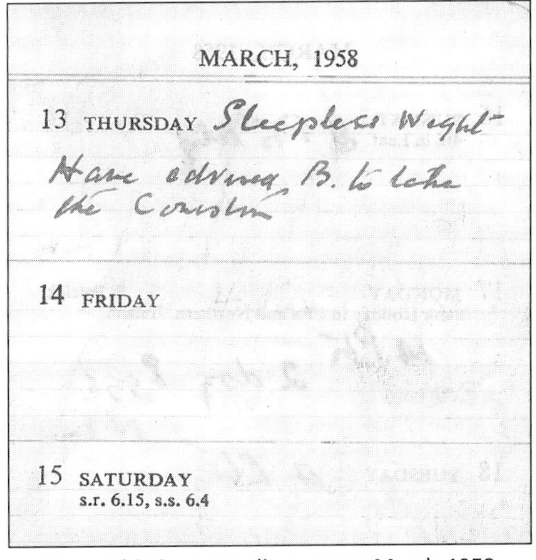
MARCH, 1958

13 THURSDAY Sleepless Night – Have advised B. to take the Coniston

14 FRIDAY

15 SATURDAY
s.r. 6.15, s.s. 6.4

Olive Whittington's diary entry, March 1958. Ironically, Michael and Bettye had already signed the contract to buy Coniston.

The Edgcumbe had been running most successfully for some twelve years and the Armstrongs were on excellent terms with their Bank Manager and with Mr Whetter, the Cornish Manager of the Western Counties Building Society based in Bude, who had arranged mortgages for them for every property they had bought so far. They enjoyed cordial relations with their builder, Arnold Pearce, who had been doing all the Edgcumbe alterations and building work every winter since 1946. He was a successful, well-heeled, builder who had inherited the business from his father, and he was also a very straight man and pleasant to deal with.

They called a meeting with all these people one afternoon at Edgcumbe Lodge to discuss various 'ways and means' of raising the purchase price of £30,000, plus the extra capital needed to increase the size of the hotel. The meeting was held in Olive Whittington's sitting room on the first floor at Edgcumbe Lodge. It was in full swing when there was a knock on the door and a scarlet faced Nannie put her head around the door and said "I'd like to speak to Mrs Armstrong please." Bettye was furious with her for interrupting but she left the room, and Nannie said to her outside the door "I do not know what is going on in there (she did, of course!) but I've got £400 in the Post Office and I'd be very happy for you to have that if it will help." Bettye declined the kind offer and returned to the meeting but that was the measure of the loyalty and devotion Nannie gave the family. The meeting was successful; the Bank and Western Counties Building Society were very helpful and it was arranged that the builder, Arnold Pearce, would have a second mortgage for the proposed work he was to carry out. It was to be a good investment for him, and he did all the building work for the whole family for the next fifteen years. They were all very sorry when he retired. Peter had recently met and become friends with a clever new architect, Tom Malcolm, whom he recommended to the Armstrongs, and he became their architect. Having been appointed for the Armstrongs' new project Tom Malcolm came to Newquay many times during the winter of 1958-1959 and made friends with them.

By mid-summer 1958 no buyer for the Edgcumbe had appeared and the family were getting very anxious, but in early September Mr and Mrs Butler, who had been running a ten bedroom hotel on Pentire, made an offer of £18,500 which was accepted. It was a great relief when the contract was signed in October and it was arranged the Butlers would take over on 1st January 1959. The little Edgcumbe would be no more! The new owners planned to rename it The Cavendish.

There's one rather interesting thing about the Butlers who bought the Edgcumbe. They only kept it for a couple of years because they couldn't cope with it. They had been running their previous hotel successfully, but twenty six bedrooms were too many for them. Why?

Because they were too pernickety and they felt they had to do it all themselves. Mrs Butler washed the tea towels every afternoon because she thought the staff did not wash them properly, and Mr Butler could not go to bed at night until all guests were in and the front door locked. If Michael and Bettye had felt the need to do that they would not have gone to bed at all during the summer since they never locked their front door! Some people in business never understand that if they concentrate on improving their turnover the rest of it will fall into place and petty economies are useless. If the tea towels aren't being washed properly send them to the laundry, buy more and go on the beach and have a rest. The Butlers were not alone in feeling they had to do everything themselves. Many people feel that and it makes life unnecessarily hard for them.

Usually, seasonal hotels are bought and sold in the summer so that the new owners can take possession in January with time to prepare for the coming season. But it was mid-January before Bettye and Michael even looked at the Coniston, by then they had lost their buyer for the Edgcumbe, who had bought another hotel. The Armstrongs and Olive Whittington were very busy dealing with the Edgcumbe bookings (about one hundred letters a day, there were virtually no telephone bookings then). They had no secretarial help, but they had a good system.

In reflecting on the post war years 1945-1960 it must be remembered that none of the family was taking family holidays as such — there was no time and no spare money. Certainly for several years the Armstrongs went to Nice for a month after the seasons, but it really was 'on a shoestring'. They went down to the South of France by train taking with them an enormous green canvas trunk full of food and rented a little flat with one bedroom on the fourth floor of a house in the Rue de la Buffa, just behind the Promenade des Anglais with NO lift. The rent was about £3.00 per week. They lazed on the beach all day and went to the casino every evening to play roulette. If they won they went out to dinner afterwards on the winnings and if they lost they went straight back to the flat for supper. They were simple holidays indeed; the only glamorous bit being that they were in the South of France. By 1957 Michael and Bettye were beginning to feel mean that they never took their children for holidays and so they promised Mary and John that they would take them to the little fourth floor flat in Nice during the 1958 Easter holidays. The Armstrongs left by train from Victoria at 2.30 p.m. and arrived in Nice at 9.00 a.m. the next day. As they arrived John, aged eight, heaved a sigh of relief and said "Well, at least I can tell the chaps at school I've been to Nice" and that, for him, was the highlight of the holiday. It simply did not work. John developed a heavy cold and had to be kept off the beach or at least out of the water, which was freezing. The weather was poor; it was cold and wet, and the children did not like the food. No wonder so many families come to Cornwall happily year after year for their summer holidays!

The timing of that holiday was awkward. It meant that they would be in France when the Coniston deal was completed and they gave up possession of Cherry Tree Cottage. The family solicitor was horrified, but they were adamant; they were not going to disappoint Mary and John. They felt Coniston's turn would come. Nannie was left in charge of the move from Cherry Tree Cottage and she was most conscientious about it. She was determined to leave nothing behind insisting that even the cherry tree from which the cottage took its name be removed and when the Armstrongs came back from Nice there was a fine old fuss with the new owners, who wanted the cherry tree back. The removal man said to Bettye, "That little woman you left in charge of the move would have rolled up the lawn and taken it with her if she could!"

The final staff party at the Edgcumbe in Edgcumbe Avenue. Standing 2nd from left is Beryl 'Head Chef'

They were hardworking, but happy days. The Edgcumbe Hotel in Edgcumbe Avenue had done the family well. It had housed and fed them in the lean years, provided the farm for Peter, given the Armstrongs and Olive Whittington a comfortable standard of living for the previous ten years and made it possible for Mary and John to go to good schools. The day it closed for the last time, Olive wept and Bettye and Michael felt very sad. It really was the end of an era.

Bettye and Michael Armstrong always danced the last waltz at the Edgcumbe in Edgcumbe Avenue.

The Coniston
1932 – 1958

The thirty bedroom, unlicensed Coniston, which the Armstrongs bought in April 1959.

CONISTON HOTEL

FACING ATLANTIC
BATHING AND SURFING DIRECT
PUTTING GREENS OPPOSITE
GOLF, BOWLING GREENS & TENNIS COURTS
WITHIN EASY DISTANCE
ENTERTAINMENTS WEEKLY
TERMS
3 - 6 GUINEAS INCLUSIVE
according to Season
Brochure and further particulars on Application
Under the Personal Supervision of
Mr. and Mrs. T. G. COTTIER, Resident Director.

MODERN HOTEL
LOUNGE BALLROOM
(ROCK-MAPLE FLOOR)
RECREATION ROOM
OWN LOCK-UP GARAGES
H. & C. RUNNING WATER
IN ALL BEDROOMS
Telephone
Telegrams } NEWQUAY 417

An impression of the glorious panorama obtained from "Coniston"

ON THE SEA FRONT

Pre-war Coniston advertisement when owned and run by Mr and Mrs Cottier.

The Coniston had been built as a hotel in 1932, and at that time had cost £4,000 — pre-war jerry building and not at its best! It stood gaunt like a square box in the middle of a rough, spacious site which even by 1957 had never been landscaped, cultivated, or even tarmacadamed, and at the rear were twelve garages which were leased to the hotel. Until the war Mr and Mrs Cottier, the original owners, had managed the Coniston in a quiet genteel sort of way, certainly without the flamboyance of the pre-war Tolcarne and Bristol hotels.

In 1940 the Coniston was requisitioned by the Ministry of Defence. An Initial Training Wing (ITW) was based there. Aircrew Cadets were given an eight week course on elementary navigation before being sent to Canada to complete their training as pilots. They drilled and held their parades on the large car park which then was at the side of the hotel[1].

In 1946 the Cottiers sold the Coniston Hotel to people from the north of England, to whom it was just an investment. The hotel was

[1] The car park later became a filling station until 2006 when it was closed. The site was redeveloped in 2007 as apartments and shops.

The slum-like area at the rear of The Coniston where Michael and Bettye later created the swimming pool.

managed for them for some twelve years by Clifford Grundy, who was much respected locally and who played his full part in local hotel affairs, but under him the hotel had not moved with the times, and by 1958 was completely out of touch with post-war Newquay and therefore ripe for development.

Now back to the Armstrongs and their determination in 1957 to buy a sixty bedroom hotel. The reader has heard how in January 1958, after they had given up hope of moving that year, they were unexpectedly offered the Coniston Hotel on Narrowcliff. It was a rather ugly building and a very dreary hotel with thirty bedrooms. At first the Armstrongs were reluctant to look at Coniston, because it only had thirty bedrooms, but when they eventually viewed it they quickly realised there were several advantages about the hotel. Firstly its location on the sea front at the entrance to the town, which in 1957 was considered splendid. Secondly it had been built as an hotel. Many of the large hotels in Newquay had been converted from terraced houses, or at least large private houses. That often meant the upstairs was like a rabbit warren, whereas the purpose built Coniston had straight wide corridors and a good staircase and large public rooms. But perhaps most important of all, it had acres of space. To Michael and Bettye, used to their cramped little premises in Edgcumbe Avenue, it seemed vast. Lastly it stood alone, with plenty of room all round it (by the time they sold it thirty years later there wouldn't be an inch to spare anywhere!).

In 1958 the hotel was unlicensed and virtually a temperance establishment, quiet and utterly uninspiring. There was no reception office; the accounts came from a cupboard under the stairs in the basement. The thirty rooms all had names instead of numbers; 'The Haven', 'Treetops', 'Dawn', 'Sunset', 'The Nook', are some that come to mind. On the lower ground floor were dreadful staff rooms that had never been properly completed; some had mud floors. In the main the furnishings were pre-war and old fashioned but of excellent quality — Maples' best![2] The Coniston really had been left behind in the post war Newquay rat race, it had stood still for twelve years, but it had obvious potential.

MR. & MRS. ARMSTRONG

STATEMENT

CONISTON HOTEL

Purchase Price		20,000. 0. 0.
Add Agents fees		375. 0. 0.
		20,375. 0. 0.
Add		
Mortgagees Solicitors' Costs (statement already supplied)	131. 10. 0.	
Spencer, Gibson & Son's Costs and disbursements	608. 0. 0.	
		739. 10. 0.
		21,114. 10. 0.
Less		
Advance from Mr. Pearce	10,000. 0. 0.	
Deposit already paid	2,000. 0 . 0.	
Bookings paid in advance	490. 0. 0.	
	£	12,490. 0. 0.
	Balance required	£ 8,624. 10. 0.
	less	275
		8349. 10

Completion Statement Coniston Hotel April 1958.

[2] In 2008 some of the silver is still in use at The Nare Hotel

The Amstrongs took over the Coniston in April 1958 while the family were on holiday in the South of France as the reader has heard, but one of the snags about the late completion was that they had missed the boat for the bookings for the coming season. In those days punters were still fighting to get in and the best hotels of all grades were well booked by the end of March. The Coniston was not properly booked and there was very little they could do about it. They just had to shuffle in and get on. With the Edgcumbe unsold they knew they had a very tiresome season in front of them coping with the two hotels, not a prospect that they relished at all and, oh my dear life, how trying that season was to be!

Fortunately the Edgcumbe was well-booked with good staff and was running smoothly. The kitchen was in the capable hands of Beryl, who had been 'head chef' for years and so it was arranged that Michael and Bettye's mother would remain at the Edgcumbe for the one season and Bettye would take on the Coniston with their long term permanent personal assistant, Joan Eden. Joan had been a tower of strength to the Armstrongs for several years. She had a pleasing personality, was very good at dealing with people, and was to be the Manageress of the new hotel. She had just married her long term fiancé, Peter Brooker, a civilian meteorologist who was attached to RAF St Mawgan.

The Coniston opened for the last time at the beginning of June, 1958 but it had been a most tremendous struggle. There had only been eight weeks between taking possession of the hotel and opening for the season, but in that short time Bettye had managed to get the wretched little rooms under the lounge/ballroom more or less shipshape and ready for letting. Floors were laid; H & C basins, fitted carpets, and brand new furniture were installed. The new rooms were well booked, but they were poor, very cramped and not up to standard. As can be imagined they caused a certain amount of trouble from time to time, but Bettye was insistent that they must be used. "All available space had to earn" she said. Of course, sometimes there were complaints about them, but people had not yet become fussy and for the first year or two they served their purpose. Joan Brooker and her new husband slept in one of them. The following year Bettye and Michael occupied the largest of them for a season until they were able to make a little flat for themselves and Mary and John in the hotel. A year or two later the rooms were scrapped and became useful service areas — laundry, beer cellar, wine store, etc., but that is another story.

The Armstrongs retained as many Coniston seasonal staff for the 1958 season as possible. There was no proper long term staff except one nice woman, Mrs Cooper, who looked after the bedrooms. The receptionist engaged for the season, Miss Gregory, a podgy "pink and white" girl, fair, with round blue eyes, who rather resembled 'Miss Piggy', never knew for certain which rooms were occupied or which were vacant. One afternoon Bettye arrived to find her on the telephone booking guests into the Riviera Hotel. Miss Gregory was unaware that there were empty rooms in the Coniston at the time. As

COLLINS' *Cathedral* SERIES
SALARIES BOOK, No. 313 (Copyright)

DATE THURS. 3rd. July 1958 13

CARD REF. No.	Dept., Sect. or No.	NAME	Age if under 21	Weekly or Monthly Salary £	s.	d.	National Insurance Employee s.	d.	Income Tax £	s.	Balance Payable £	s.	d.	National Insurance Employer s.	d.
35	Manageress	MRS. J. BROOKER.		12	0	0	-	5	1	7	10	12	7	6	7
57	Head Waiter	G. MARSHALL.		8	0	0	9	5	-	6	7	5	7	8	1
119	Head Chef	J. KOWAL		15	0	0	9	5	-	14	13	16	7	8	1
35	2nd chef	MRS. M. SZCZYPKA.		10	0	0	-	5	1	0	8	19	7	6	7
32	H's Keeper	MRS. E. COOPER.		6	0	0	-	5	—	—	5	19	7	6	7
55	Porter	G. REES.		6	10	0	9	5	-	2	5	18	7	8	1
27	Ch: Maid	MISS P. TUCKER		4	10	0	7	8	—	—	4	2	4	6	7
E	K.P.	W. COTTON.		7	0	0	9	5	-	11	5	19	7	8	1
26		MISS L. TALBOT		4	10	0	7	8	—	—	4	2	4	6	7
35	Receptionist	MISS J. GREGORY.		5	10	0	7	8	-	4	4	18	4	6	7
E 35	Ch' Maid	MRS. ANNIE MARSH £5-0-0		5	10	0	7	8	-	5	4	17	4	6	7
35	Ch' Maid	MISS DOROTHY POLE		5	10	0	7	8	-	3	4	19	4	6	7
35	Waiter	MR. PATRICK BOYD.		6	0	0	9	5	—	—	5	10	7	8	1
E	Waiter	MR. JOHN WILLIAM BRAY		6	0	0	9	5	-	7	5	3	7	8	1
122		GEORGE THOMSON. £6-10-0		6	10	0	-	-	—	—	6	10	0	-	-
35		MICHAEL SHERMAN £5-0-0.		3	6	8	5	3	—	—	3	1	5	4	9
	3-7-58	MRS. GAY £7-0-0													
	8-7-58	JAMES LOGAN. £7-0-0													
		MR. McINTOSH. £6-0-0													
	12-7-58	MISS ELIZABETH JONES £4-0-0.													
	"	MISS MARY CLAY. £5-0-0													
	15-7-58	MR. ANTHONY CORNISH. £5-0-0.													
				£111	16	8	101/4		£4	18	£101	17	4	105/11	

WAGES. £101-17-4
NAT. INS. 10-7-3
PETTY CASH 10-0-0

Coniston weekly wages in 1958.

can be imagined, a very jolly confrontation followed that little episode! Bettye was furious and made a frightful fuss.

The chef, who had spent the previous season at The Coniston, could cook well — when he chose — but he was inconsistent and played up the whole summer constantly threatening to walk out unless he had more money. There was one fuss about the menus when Bettye had to face a deputation of guests in the hall who complained bitterly about the food. They said there were too many made-up dishes and that it had no taste. Privately she didn't think it was up to scratch either, but hardly knew what she could do about it in the middle of the season with a difficult chef. She apologised and said she would see what could be done. What she did, in fact, was to instruct the chef to give the guests steaks and chops and dishes that did not rely so much on accomplished cooking. She also went to the cash and carry and bought Swiss Knorr seasoning and told the chef to flop it over everything. Most of the guests were satisfied and some were gracious enough later to thank her and say the food had improved greatly. Bettye was always more willing to placate her guests than was her brother, Peter.

The hotel had been taken over at very short notice and whatever bookings had been accepted for that season had to be honoured. One booking was for a coach party of fifty for one week in early July. The family have never needed or wanted to take coach parties, which are really doom and gloom to holiday hotels and they have never accepted them except as a last resort rather than be left with vacant rooms, but the Armstrongs were stuck with that coach booking.

The coach party from the north consisted mostly of frizzy grey haired biddies and a few old chaps and they had a lovely week. On their last night they wanted a 'knees up' and they asked for hot pasties to be available for them at 10.30 p.m. Having had an early dinner they thought they would be peckish after all those Valetta and barn dances! Joan Brooker completely forgot about the pasties and went out for the evening with her husband and some friends — very remiss since with fifty old folk frolicking and no one really in charge, there might well be something needed. There was no porter or barman on duty. Bettye Armstrong had returned to the Edgcumbe after dinner and was absolutely livid when at 10.30 p.m. there was a call from Coniston asking where "Were the pasties for the coach party?" "Where is Mrs Brooker?" asked Bettye. "Out with her husband and some friends" came the reply. Bettye returned to the Coniston immediately and faced members of the coach party who were very cross indeed. The next day she confronted Joan Brooker and told her she was not giving the hotel enough attention and it would not do. Joan and her new husband departed hurriedly[3]. They had other things on their minds and, to them, more important matters to attend to!

After that Bettye had to cope with the hotel on her own for the rest of the season. She would arrive every morning for breakfast and remain there all day with a little break in the afternoon. She would see the dinner through and then return to the Edgcumbe to join Michael for the evening, which was always lively. She found the Coniston deadly dull after dinner. There was only one large lounge furnished with beige Parker Knoll chairs with wooden arms and there a few people would sit, mostly in silence, perhaps reading. With no bar, porter or evening service, no evening entertainment, not even a TV to her it seemed like a morgue, used as she was to the cheerful hubbub at the Edgcumbe. Bettye found it incredibly boring, but she did nothing about it; as far as she was concerned it was just a question of getting through the season. The one bright spot was that Tom Malcolm, their architect, kept turning up with sketches, plans, and ideas for the new hotel and her head was full of it. But oh dear! How dreary the Coniston Hotel seemed that summer. The guests were dull, the members of staff were poor and disinterested, and to be honest, so was she. She was impatient for it to end, and so the Coniston's last season went on its weary way.

Tom did a large coloured sketch of the proposed new Hotel which was on display at the Edgcumbe in Edgcumbe Avenue. Of course all the summer there was much talk about the new project and the Edgcumbe guests trouped up to The Coniston in droves to look round. They could not believe that by the following year it could be transformed into anything resembling Tom's drawing. In fact the sketch proved to be remarkably accurate.

In 1958, to the Armstrongs, used to the cramped and overcrowded little Edgcumbe in Edgcumbe Avenue, the Coniston seemed enormously spacious. Olive Whittington, then aged about seventy, soon decided she preferred lunch there in the uncrowded dining room, with its large well spaced tables, to the scrambling hustle and bustle at the Edgcumbe. Most days she would walk up to Narrowcliff to join Bettye sitting in solitary state at her corner table and over lunch she would lend her sympathetic ear to the trials and tribulations of the day.

---

[3] It says much for the relationship between the Armstrongs and Joan Brooker that they never lost touch and although her season at the Coniston was not a success they remained on good terms and she came back into their lives some twenty years later.

The Armstrongs were impatient for the season to finish. They decided to close in mid September and they did so with a flourish. They held a special gala farewell dinner for all their guests on 14th September 1958. There were black edged menus headed "Coniston est Mort". Guests and staff all entered into the spirit of burying the Coniston and it was the cheeriest evening of the whole summer. The next day, with great relief they waved the guests off, thanked the staff and closed. The Coniston Hotel had gone for ever. The builders moved in immediately; 1959 was going to be a new and exciting beginning for Michael and Bettye Armstrong.

There was no thought of a holiday for the Armstrongs that year; their new project was much too exciting and what was more it needed their full attention. They had a very busy winter supervising the building, ordering furnishings and generally getting ready for the opening of the New Edgcumbe, on Narrowcliff in April 1959 — much more fun than a holiday!

The New Edgcumbe Hotel, Narrowcliff
1959 – 1964

New Edgcumbe Hotel on Narrowcliff in 1959, with sixty bedrooms and what, to the Armstrongs, seemed acres of space.

Oh my dear life! The builders moved into the Coniston in mid September 1958 and by the time the hotel opened in April 1959 it had a new third floor, a rear wing of sixteen bedrooms and wings thrown out in every direction, a new kitchen, was licensed and, most important of all, it had sixty bedrooms. Whew! What a winter! But the Edgcumbe Hotel was back on Narrowcliff.

It was one of the largest extensions that had been built in Newquay for a very long time and there were persistent rumours day by day in the town that the building was about to grind to a halt because the money was running out. Bettye and Michael knew better — they had made their financial arrangements soundly — and from January the bookings were pouring in. The Armstrongs were on the building site by 9.00 a.m. every day and there was no thought of a holiday that year, but the result was well worth it. That winter's efforts completely changed the family's fortunes.

In January 1959 Bettye advertised for a receptionist for the New Edgcumbe Hotel. There were many applicants, but she was interested in one girl of twenty four, who had been a wages clerk for Western National Bus Company for several years. She was earning more money there than was being offered at the Edgcumbe and Bettye explained that she would have to accept a lower wage while she learnt the job, but if it was found she could cope with it, there was great scope for promotion. The applicant was an intelligent grammar school girl and she promised to go away and consider it. In Bettye's mind there were two reservations. One, the girl lived in a caravan and it would hardly be sensible to employ someone in a capacity that would mean handling a great deal of money if they lived in a caravan! It seemed somewhat unstable! A sort of here today — and possibly gone

PHONE: NEWQUAY 2527

ARNOLD PEARCE (BUILDERS) LTD.

DIRECTORS: A. J. PEARCE A. E. PEARCE

Builders & Contractors

REGISTERED OFFICE:
47, EDGCUMBE AVE.
NEWQUAY

Mrs Armstrong,
Edgcumbe Lodge,
Edgcumbe Gardens,
Newquay.

Oct IIth 1958.

ACCOUNTS MONTHLY

INTEREST CHARGED ON OVERDUE ACCOUNTS

ESTIMATE.

for

Alterations etc at The Coniston Hotel,
Newquay.

Item	No	I.	Cocktail lounge etc	2065	0	0
"	"	2.	2 storey Bedroom wing	7700	0	0
"	"	3.	New front & Porch.	I050	0	0
"	"	4	Reception office & private quarters.	420	0	0
"	"	5	New Kitchen block	4970	0	0
"	"	6	Dining room.	I630	0	0
"	"	7	New top storey & stairs	6087	0	0
"	"	8	Terrace & front wall.	287		
"	"	9	Basement cloakrooms etc	273.	0	0
				24482	0	0

Estimate for alterations etc at The Coniston Hotel, Newquay 1958.
Less than £25,000 what splendid value it seems in 2008.

tomorrow. The other thing that bothered her was that although the girl lived in a caravan down a muddy lane, that January day she was wearing white shoes with stiletto heels. Bettye, who had always had a taste for thick woollen stockings and brogues, found that odd! However the girl came back, and said she would like to take the job. In further talk it emerged that she and her husband had bought the caravan to live in while they saved up to buy a house, and in Bettye's mind that put a different complexion on it! She engaged her.

That girl was Mrs Daphne Burt and Bettye feels to this day that was one of the wisest decisions she ever made in her life. (Hear hear! says grandson Toby Ashworth. Today she is his Financial Director and Company Secretary).

When Mrs Burt was finally engaged, Bettye explained to her that in the hotel she would have to be "Mrs Burt"; there was to be no "Daphne" about it, because if she were successful in the post she later might be giving orders to staff. If they were calling her "Daphne" it would undermine her authority. So Mrs Burt she was and has been for fifty years, and anyone who thought otherwise was soon brought to heel!

In January 1959 when Mrs Burt joined 'the firm' it was bitterly cold and The New Edgcumbe Hotel, under construction, was little more than a building site. There was no heating and it was freezing. She had to climb up a ladder and get through the window into her make-

Mrs Burt in her office, January 1959.

shift office on the first floor. Looking back it is amazing that she didn't take fright and scarper. A lesser girl would not have coped with it, but Mrs Burt loved the work from the beginning, although the first few weeks were hard going with about a hundred letters a day to be dealt with. If an enquirer asked "Have you a double room available for the first two weeks in August?" she would take it as a booking and cross the room off on the booking chart. She found it difficult to understand that the enquirer had probably written to a dozen hotels asking the same question. Bettye recalls that she almost sacked her after two or three weeks because they were not managing to get through the letters and an outside typist had to be called in. However, Mrs Burt soon mastered the system and became highly skilled.

At this time the family were still living a comfortable well ordered life at Edgcumbe Lodge, where they were to remain for the next seven years. Bettye's mother was 'in charge' with the help of Nannie and Beryl, who continued to cook a proper breakfast and hot luncheon every day in the winter. After a while Olive Whittington said "We cannot leave that poor girl in the freezing building on her own at lunchtime, she had better come down here for lunch." And so it was arranged that Mrs Burt went to Edgcumbe Lodge for lunch which, at first, was given to her on a tray in the sitting room by the fire. Eventually she joined the family in the dining room, and when she went back to the office Bettye's mother would press a bun or a few biscuits into her hand for her afternoon tea. And so were the seeds of friendship sown. The reader will hear more of Mrs Burt as this family story unfolds. In the evenings when Bettye and Michael returned home cold and weary there was always Olive Whittington with a good fire in her sitting room offering tea, sympathy, an ear, and, often, wisdom. The evenings were peaceful. The telephone had not yet become the menace it is today.

It is interesting to recall that although Tom Malcolm was a forward thinking, up-to-date architect, who was later to be highly acclaimed, in 1958 it did not occur to him to install private bathrooms at the New Edgcumbe on Narrowcliff. In fact he gave it just two, but really only as a gimmick because the space was there and no other use could be found for it. Four guineas (£4.20) extra per week was charged for them. In the 1950s it is doubtful if there were more than a dozen private bathrooms in the whole of Newquay. The new rear wing had eight bedrooms, one bath, and two WCs on each floor. That was the accepted ratio at the time. The clamour for en suite baths or showers did not set in until the 1980s. Until then people were quite content to shuffle along the corridor to the nearest WC or bathroom and eight bedrooms to one bathroom was quite usual.

Tom Malcolm didn't think of bathrooms but he did introduce cosy little cubby holes for children. He called them 'children's cabins' and there have been 'children's cabins' in all the family hotels ever since, although nowadays they are proper single rooms attached to parents' rooms. The original cabins were on the top floor of the Edgcumbe, six feet square, with no window, just a roof light, a double decker bunk bed and a small chest of drawers. They were immensely popular with middle class families for their children and they were booked year after year. What is more, the Edgcumbe charged for them properly! In those halcyon days there wasn't such a thing as a 'free child'.

As can be imagined, while the building was in progress there were many items of furniture, fittings, china, glass etc., to be ordered. Curtains for the new rooms and rolls and rolls of new carpets were needed. There was a great fuss about the new bedroom furniture. Peter Whittington had met Oliver Lebus somewhere. He was a large, national manufacturer of cheapish but smart modern bedroom furniture. At the time Peter was also refurnishing Bredon Court's seventy bedrooms and so he gave Oliver Lebus a large order for about one hundred and fifty bedroom suites. When the first pantechnicon from Lebus arrived at the Edgcumbe, it was seen by one of John Julian's Directors (John Julian had about six furniture shops in Cornwall and were Lebus' biggest customers in the county). They immediately threatened Lebus that if they supplied the family hotels direct, Julians would close their account. Consternation! A tremendous battle ensued. It looked as though Bredon Court and the Edgcumbe would not get their new bedroom furniture — but Peter finally won and Lebus agreed to honour the order they had accepted but said they would never supply the hotels again — and they never did! Incidentally, the smart light oak bedroom furniture was very, very cheap with dressing tables for about £7.00. In fact they were 'quality' compared with the modern junk produced today — they lasted for years, and were later passed on to the next hotels the family bought.

The building was finished on time — just! Quite an achievement, although the carpet layers did have to work all night before opening day, and when the first guests arrived at about noon, there were still dust sheets all over the floors. The stairs to the basement had not been put in and the hole where they were to go was blocked up with a sheet of beaver board. Below stairs was still a building site! Bettye grabbed the first guests, and talking nineteen-to-the-dozen, rushed them up to the new bar, which was looking splendid. She gave them a welcome drink while the dust sheets were removed. All was well: the Edgcumbe Hotel was open and back on Narrowcliff!

Tom Malcolm had had to show an adequate number of spaces for cars, although there were twelve lock up garages at the back of the Coniston when they bought it. In fact the Armstrongs soon found that no-one wanted garages — and they certainly were not prepared to pay for them. By 1958 everyone just needed free parking. At that time the streets were not yet plastered with double yellow lines and parking was not an issue; most families only had one car, if that. There were no traffic wardens on the prowl — the sport of hounding the motorist had not yet set in. Now of course one cannot get planning permission to extend an hotel unless one can prove there are enough parking spaces, perhaps a ratio of one car space for every two bedrooms — not always easy in the middle of a town!

The first season was, of course, wildly hectic and for several weeks the builders were all over the place and many corners were still being finished, but in a short time the New Edgcumbe was flourishing, and the extra space made running the hotel much more straightforward.

Almost overnight "Mike" in the bar became Mr Armstrong, the host, in a dinner jacket on Dance Nights.

Beryl Luxon, the 'Head Chef' from Edgcumbe Avenue, was in charge of the kitchen for the first few seasons and she did well. She continued to cook for the family in the winters, but when she married she found the ever busier Edgcumbe too much, and so a new chef was engaged. Beryl then took over in the pastry room for several more years until she started a family.

Although the Armstrongs had been dead keen to move from Edgcumbe Avenue they had no idea how much it would change their way of life — they had simply wanted more space, which they thought would just make running the hotel easier. In fact the move to Narrowcliff changed their lives completely. They had a permanent receptionist; therefore they did not have to deal with the bookings in January and February. Bettye no longer had to take on the office nor make the bedroom curtains. Michael never went behind the bar again. Almost overnight they became Mr and Mrs Armstrong to the guests — apart from those Michael called their 'boon companions', meaning drinking buddies. But for the first few years they were very much on the spot and in charge; Michael playing the host in a dinner jacket on dance nights, and managing the licensed side of the hotel. He continued to charm the guests and took some of them flying in the afternoons. Ken Stratton and his trio moved to Narrowcliff and the Monday, Wednesday and Friday dances were as jolly — in fact as hilarious — as they had been in Edgcumbe Avenue, sometimes with congas along Narrowcliff and round about. Bettye dealt with the general management, and from then on every winter was busy with enlarging and upgrading the hotel.

Olive Whittington and Bettye enjoying Ken's performance.

The post war boom still raged and from the outset the hotel was very busy and successful. There was a happy, informal holiday atmosphere, but never again was there to be quite the same friendly, cosy air that had prevailed in Edgcumbe Avenue, and it is doubtful whether Michael ever enjoyed it as much. But the Armstrongs had moved on — and up!

Mrs Burt and John Armstrong leading the Conga around the houses.

Generally the family never employ friends or friends of friends on principle, but in the early '60s Bettye and Michael made an exception to this rule and engaged a social acquaintance as a general assistant. That proved to be a great stroke of luck for them. Her name was Joan Johnson and while she was at the Edgcumbe just for the one season she said to Bettye, "You must cherish that receptionist you have in the office. She is so loyal to you, and the minute your back is turned she is determined that everything is going to be just as you wish it to be, and she will fight everybody about it." Her advice was taken seriously and heeded and it turned out to be exactly as she said. That receptionist was Mrs Burt, employed by Bettye in 1959, and from then on the Armstrongs made every effort to increase her status in the hotel. For fifty years she has worked loyally and unstintingly for the whole family, and today she is a close friend. Sometimes employers have an efficient, hardworking, loyal, honest member of staff whose qualities get overlooked, or go unrecognised in the general hubbub of busy business life and so their full talents are never developed. The Armstrongs considered that they were very fortunate that Joan Johnson brought Mrs Burt's talents and loyalty to their attention

Throughout the 1960s there were occasional trips to London, without the children, when they booked a bed sitting room just off the Bayswater Road, which at that time cost them five guineas for the week, and the Whittingtons did the same thing. In that way it was possible to have an inexpensive week in London. The bed sitting room had a gas fire and a gas ring — excellent for making toast, boiling eggs and heating soup, etc. The bathroom was shared, but the Armstrongs and Whittingtons could go to theatres, see their friends, and generally have a most agreeable time on very little money, and they loved it. It must be remembered the prices are relative. Guests at the Edgcumbe were paying less than £10 per week at the time for full board and much entertainment. In those days people dressed tidily for London and Bettye always had her 'London suit and matching hat' which were kept for the London visits. There were also occasional visits to stay with friends, but expensive family holidays there were not. The children usually stayed at home in the care of Grannie and Nannie and had glorious summer holidays mainly spent on Tolcarne Beach, and sometimes with ponies, pony club rallies, and camps. In the autumn of 1960 Bettye and Michael holidayed in the south of Spain. They took an apartment on a beach and there they discovered water-skiing. They were frightfully enthusiastic about it and returned to Cornwall determined to buy a boat for the Edgcumbe so that they could offer their guests water skiing. This they did and when the hotel opened in 1961 the Edgcumbe had a hotel ski boat and the Armstrongs were offering instruction, although they were really beginners themselves at the time! Michael had nowhere to keep the boat except in the car park. For a year or two many sunny afternoons were spent trailing the boat around and launching it wherever they could catch the tide.

Gradually the hotel went up-grade and became more expensive. Many of the old Edgcumbe Hotel guests returned year after year, but in those early days on Narrowcliff it was still 'pack 'em in'. There were still extra beds in every corner where space could be found. The cabins were always full and the whole operation became a rather more couth version of the old Edgcumbe Hotel. Before long the extra space in the basement was put to good use. Soon there was a children's play room, billiards room and, later, a heated indoor swimming pool, followed by a hair dressing salon, a boutique, and a disco which became a teenage clubroom where the youngsters could gather and deafen themselves with loud music; mercifully out of earshot of the rest of the building.

In January 1961 for the first time the Armstrongs were able to take a proper family holiday; they went to Château d'Oex, in Switzerland, with Mary and John and began skiing. From the beginning it was a great success and they absolutely loved it. Skiing became a major sport for the whole family. Almost every year since, with few exceptions, there have been family skiing holidays.

By the early 1960s with Mary and John both away at school Nannie really hadn't enough to do. She was becoming very tiresome in the house, and there was a constant battle between Bettye's mother and Nannie about, of all ridiculous things, the top of the milk. Olive Whittington had the lifelong habit of saving the cream for her morning tea, and Nannie wanted it for her breakfast cereal and her cat. She took to nipping down early in the morning and hiding it, usually on the floor under the boiler. Bettye would then play 'hunt the thimble' to give it to her mother. It was farcical!

Skiing in Chateau d'Oex in the early 1960s.

Nannie developed a passion for polishing the parquet floor in the hall with the electric polisher and she spent the afternoons doing it. One afternoon, Michael and Bettye, having had a very late night, went to their room on the ground floor for a rest. Nannie started up with the polisher outside their door and Michael got in such a rage he grabbed the polisher and threw it at the bedroom ceiling with such force that it made a dent like a deep saucer, which was still there when they sold the house ten years later. Also, apart from anything else, Nannie was not being kind or helpful to Olive Whittington, who was becoming less mobile. Eventually the Armstrongs could stand no more and Bettye sent her home to St Agnes where her mother lived. Three days later she put Nannie's cat in a sack and sent it after her. It was a beastly cat, nobody liked it and the dogs chased it — poor thing! Nannie's banishment only lasted about a couple of years while she looked after her ailing mother. Then she gradually came back to the family to help with grandchildren and dogs. She was very good with both and everyone had an affection for her and was glad of her help from time to time.

Schooldays photograph of Mary and John.

From the right Mary Armstrong, Olive Whittington, Maggie Dyer, with the Spaniel, Mr Wag, on her lap, and Mrs Burt.

With Nannie gone Bettye had been somewhat concerned that her mother would be alone in the house at night while they went on holiday. By chance they happened to meet Maggie Dyer, who once again was undecided about what she was doing next, and she was asked if she would like to stay at Edgcumbe Lodge with Bettye's mother while the family was away for a month. Maggie was delighted to do so, and it worked so well that she lived in great harmony with Livvy, as she called Olive, for the next seven years as her driver companion, and they became great friends. In fact she was to be under the family's wing for the rest of her life.

Every year since 1908 the Motorcycle Club (MCC) has run its London-Lands End Reliability Trial over Easter and it is still held annually, although these days it starts from various points all over the country. The course is long and hazardous with several spectacular hill climbs, one of which is at Blue Hills Mine at St Agnes. The drivers drive non-stop through the night and it has long been a popular day out on Easter Saturday for local car enthusiasts to go to Blue Hills with a picnic and watch the weary mud-spattered competitors tackle the specially designed tortuous ascent.

Looking back, of course, it was even more exciting for the spectators in the very early days when cars were all open and much less reliable than they are today. There is an enormous entry every year. Motorbikes go first — hundreds of them. The drivers are a very mixed bag ranging from elderly 'posh' enthusiasts in super old classic cars to equally enthusiastic young mechanics on their motor bikes. Sometimes the bikes have sidecars with wives or girlfriends frenziedly throwing themselves around in an effort to help balance the machine around the hairpin bends. At the end of this epic, 24-hour drive, they all get together at one of the Cornish hotels for an evening of jollification — a dinner and dance and, of course, much talk about it all over many pints.

Michael and Bettye had always been interested in cars and the MCC trial and in the early sixties thought it would be a good idea to hold the final celebration at the Edgcumbe, so for several years the Edgcumbe was the Host hotel. The Committee, all elderly and mostly couth and classy, came and stayed for the weekend and many of the competitors stayed for a night or two. The evening celebration, as can be imagined, was boozy and hilarious but great fun, and everyone enjoyed it. It was part of the 'Edgcumbe Easter Programme' (as was the party to the Fourburrow Hunt Point to Point on Easter Monday).

Unfortunately, after a year or two, difficulties arose with the MCC.

There was not an over abundant supply of hot water at the hotel in those days. All the mud spattered motor cyclists would arrive at the hotel first, have baths all the afternoon (even some who were not staying) and by the time the car drivers arrived, the hot water had run out[1]. Then the Committee and the older drivers discovered hotel Kilbirnie immediately next door where they could be quiet and comfortable, while the Edgcumbe could cope with the young rowdies and the hot water problem — and they would still be on the spot for the evening celebration. For the Armstrongs — as Ken Stratton would have said, that was "not on" and so when the MCC tried to book for the following Easter 'regretfully' the rooms were not available! and they moved to another hotel.

At the Edgcumbe Michael and Bettye had found their make-shift summer quarters noisy and uncomfortable but they still felt they had to sleep on the premises. In 1961 a small flat was made on the ground floor at the hotel for them, with two small bedrooms for Mary and John. They also had a little private walled garden laid out by Treseders[2].

One August in the mid-sixties at about 1.00 a.m., the night porter came to Michael and Bettye's room after they had gone to bed and asked Mr Armstrong to come as Mrs Smith in room 68 had lost her husband. She was quite hysterical and wanted the police called. That is the last thing the proprietors of any hotel will do in the middle of the night, so Michael got up, dressed, and tried to pacify the woman and help find the missing husband. He and the porter searched the building for an hour, remember it was very rambling, but they could not find the husband and the woman became more anguished.

Eventually, at about 2.00 a.m. Michael returned to the bedroom and asked Bettye to come as the woman was quite beside herself and they had not found the husband. Bettye grumpily joined the search party in her robe. After a further hour of searching and talking the husband had not been found but the woman was persuaded to go to bed with the promise that, if he had not turned up by the morning, the police would be alerted.

In the morning the husband was there and not a word was said. Later that day he sidled up to Michael and apologised for the fuss he had caused, explaining that after going to the WC, he had gone to an empty room by mistake and had gone to sleep. His apology was

---

[1] In 2007 a guest staying at The Nare recalled to Bettye that some forty-six years ago, in 1961, he was one of the guilty motor cyclists and they had a nostalgic ten minutes chat about those days and a good laugh!
[2] At one time Treseders of Truro was one of the great suppliers of exotic plants in the United Kingdom.

accepted gracefully. Michael discreetly refrained from telling him there was no empty room in the hotel that night. Several days later, when the couple had gone home, the barman said, "I knew where he was. I heard him making the date." Ha! Ha! There is never a dull moment in a holiday hotel and sometimes it can be very amusing.

In the '50s and '60s the family hotels all served dinner between 7.00 and 8.00 p.m. Thus most people ate at about 7.30 p.m. The evenings were usually hectic and late — early nights were unheard of and, as can be imagined, by 11.00 p.m. or 12 midnight guests were often peckish and in need of a snack, or perhaps tea or coffee. Late night refreshments were introduced between 10.00 p.m. and midnight when hot drinks, sandwiches and biscuits etc., were available. This was a very popular service (and jolly good business) until a hot dog stall set up every night at 10.00 p.m. on the car park by the side of the hotel. Then, every night guests who were peckish rushed out and bought hot dogs and brought them into the hotel to eat! This was absolutely unacceptable — but what to do? The Armstrongs could hardly tell their guests that hot dogs were banned. It was decided to offer hot Cornish pasties as well as sandwiches from the snack bar. At the time J Lyons & Co were selling packs of 20 frozen small Cornish pasties and these pasties were cooked fresh every night at about ten. They smelt delicious and they were, if eaten immediately! Everyone loved them, and the sale of hot dogs fell dramatically.

There was just one snag with the Lyons frozen pasties. They smelled and tasted delicious when hot and freshly cooked, but when cold the next day were like cardboard and almost inedible. Often when guests asked to buy them to take home they had to be refused. The Armstrongs felt they could not sell them. In fact they bore no relation to a proper Cornish pasty, they had pearl barley and other oddments in them, but they were a very tasty snack, and they outdid the hot dogs. For several years the Edgcumbe sold these little pasties and it was most tiresome when J Lyons & Co announced they would no longer be making them. Bettye, full of ideas, decided the Edgcumbe would go one better and offer the guests small, but proper Cornish pasties at night between 10 - 12 midnight. She ordered them to be delivered fresh straight from Matthews Bakery, the best in town, at seven every evening. A great improvement she thought. The guests thought otherwise — they rejected them completely and said they didn't hold a candle to the ones they'd been having for years. Sandwiches were on again. Fortunately by then the hot dog stand had been moved on.

The end of Stafferi's Ice Cream, circa 1970. – *Courtesy Mrs Stafferi.*

One cannot sell anything any time anywhere these days. Obviously there have to be controls, but at times they seem to be most unfair and also to have an adverse effect on the services available to the public. There was a large and very respectable Italian family who had lived in Newquay for several generations called Stafferi. They made proper ice cream in a dairy at the back of their little terrace house in Robartes Road, unlike some of the rubbish offered as ice cream today. The dairy was tiled to the ceiling and was absolutely spotless. Many locals would take their bowls to Stafferi's dairy to collect ice cream. As the Stafferi children grew up they all joined the business and went out with little carts, and later motor vans, to various pitches around the town selling the ice cream — just good plain vanilla ice cream. In the 1970s, after at least 50 years trading in the town, they were drummed off the road by increased charges, rules and regulations. They were replaced by hot dog stands, manufactured ice cream (often made of white fat, the author is informed), hot chestnuts and other such fare being offered by a motley, scruffy, often grubby, collection of vendors, mostly strangers to the town, who obviously paid too much for their pitches and never lasted for very long; but that was just one small cog in the wheel of change in Newquay — and not for the better. Many local people regretted the demise of Stafferi's business and today, years later, in Newquay one hears a good home-made ice cream praised with the phrase "This is very good — it is just like Stafferi's".

If the world is a stage then sometimes holiday hotels must provide the pantomimes or the tragi-comedies on the stage. One morning a man staying at the Edgcumbe did not feel very well, but he got up, stumbled into the dining room and had his breakfast. He then went back to his room, laid down on the bed and promptly died. His widow was distraught. The doctor came, the undertaker was called and the poor chap went out of the side door feet first and the grieving widow followed him. The Edgcumbe had an empty room in the middle of August — which was unheard of. The room was immediately prepared for new occupants. About an hour later a couple walked in. "Have you got a room?" "Certainly, Madame, come this way". The couple were shown the room, took it, and the wife said "We never book when we come on holiday. I always tell my husband we'll get in somewhere, someone will die or something." Little did they know that only an hour before the corpse had been laid out on the bed. That is hotels for you, never a dull moment!

As the reader has already heard, during the 1950s and 1960s the more go-ahead hotels held weekly barbecues on the beaches and they were very popular and great fun. The guests helped by gathering wood for the fires and carrying some of the clobber; everyone seemed happy to lend a hand but it was hard work. After dinner they'd all set off for the beach with wood and firelighters, beer, wine, and the food, sausages etc., which would have been at least half cooked in the hotel kitchen. There would be music, usually guitars, and much merriment, and one or two hardier souls would bathe, and a splendid time was had by all; but these jollifications petered out because of the vagaries of the English weather. There was a weekly entertainment programme, which could not be changed and one night was set aside for the barbecue. If the weather was bad it was cancelled — not postponed.

Summer barbecues – come rain or shine.

The Edgcumbe tried holding them around the swimming pool (much easier of course) with groups playing but again in the long term the weather defeated them and soon the idea was dropped, but they were great fun while they lasted although they never quite achieved the enchantment of the beaches and caves.

When Michael's Aunt Vee died in the early sixties, the Armstrongs had to give up the little flat in Bath. Bettye and Michael were soon able to replace it with one in London. They arranged to rent a little flat in Hammersmith, London, from Peggy Bird[3], on a twenty year lease for £150 per annum, including rates. It consisted of just two rooms on the first floor of a small Regency cottage adjoining the busy A4 road into London near St Peter's Church. It had to be converted. Bettye installed a very small spiral staircase which led straight into the sitting room off which there was a little kitchenette about four feet square. There was just one bedroom with a small bathroom, but it was compact, very attractive, and convenient and for the next twenty years the whole family used it. John Armstrong lived there while he was training at the Cadogan hotel. He called it "The Cornish Embassy" and put a brass plaque on the wall outside the front door. There were many 'informal receptions' held at "The Cornish Embassy" in Hammersmith in the '60s! and he always gave a Boat Race day luncheon party.

During a holiday to San Francisco in the mid sixties the Armstrongs discovered on arrival in their hotel room a little outfit for making tea and coffee. They were delighted and brought the idea back to Newquay. No more 7.30 early morning tea trays to be taken to the rooms by the chambermaids. Brilliant! Life was getting easier! Today almost every hotel in England offers this facility, but it was not always so.

In the '60s the Edgcumbe had been appointed a 2-star hotel and that had been quite straightforward and in 1965 the Armstrongs decided to apply for an AA 3-star appointment, and then awaited the incognito inspection. It proved more difficult! Mrs Burt is very astute in these matters and when the booking came for a double room for one night in September she quickly worked out it was most likely that this would be the AA inspection. She allocated a very tidy room, had it spring cleaned and redecorated, and did her utmost to make sure that everything was in order. The AA and RAC have very rigid rules for their appointments, and of course the more stars an hotel has the stricter they are about how things must be. One of their stipulations

---

[3] Peggy Bird was Bettye's life-long friend.

is that the double beds must be 4 ft 6 ins and single beds must all be 3 ft Now at the time many of the double beds in the Edgcumbe were only 4 ft because the rooms were small and there were slightly smaller double beds to fit them. Having applied for the 3 stars, the Armstrongs were determined to achieve it and they went to enormous lengths to get things right, which included borrowing 4ft 6ins double beds from Bedruthan Steps to replace the 4 ft ones in many of the Edgcumbe bedrooms! It involved a tremendous amount of work but practically every 4 ft bed was replaced with a 4 ft 6 ins bed for the benefit of that inspection.

One afternoon in September the inspector arrived. He was a huge man with a very large wife and he was duly shown the room that had been prepared for him with special 'spit and polish' and the staff "did handsprings" for him. To Mrs Burt's horror, two hours later he rang down to reception in a towering rage and said, "Has nobody ever heard of sound insulation in this building? There are elephants rampaging in the room above me, for goodness sake give me another room, I will not stay in this room another moment".

Mrs Burt panicked. The hotel was busy and she had little choice as to where she could put him, and in her agitation gave him one of the few rooms left with a small 4 ft double bed. Of course, the moment she had done so she realised her mistake. She was mortified, and felt sure the Edgcumbe would not be granted its 3-star appointment. However, there was nothing for it but get on and the staff performed impeccably and the rest of the visit went exceedingly well! In the morning, as these inspectors always do, he declared himself and asked to see the Manager. Mrs Burt showed him all over the hotel which seemed to please him and there was great relief when finally he announced that he would recommend the hotel for a 3-star appointment. He obviously had had a good night in that small bed!

When he had gone, the Armstrongs and Mrs Burt were so relieved that they had got through the ordeal regardless of the gaffe about the 4ft bed that they opened a bottle of champagne to celebrate. Mrs Burt, who had had nothing to eat for 24 hours and had stayed awake all night worrying, quickly became the worse for wear. Bettye and Michael decided the best thing to do would be to put her to bed to sleep it off. The hotel was very busy and all the afternoon people kept asking for rooms until after tea the only room left was the little room where Mrs Burt was recovering. Even then Bettye was not prepared to lose a booking because Mrs Burt was lying on the bed with a hangover in the only room available! So when it was needed, she and Michael hurriedly bundled her out of it, straightened it up and it was booked, and Mrs Burt had to finish her recovery sitting in a chair in a dark corner! At the time the Armstrongs and Mrs Burt took that all as great fun. They were delighted when the 3-star appointment was later confirmed.

From then on the Edgcumbe was a 3-star hotel for 25 years until the Armstrongs sold it in January 1989.

Watergate Bay Hotel 1969 – 2000

1904 – 1971

Watergate Bay Hotel at the turn of the nineteenth century, showing the tennis court and garden in front of the hotel and Watergate Cottages top right hand corner.
Cornish Studies Library

Watergate Bay Hotel was built in 1904 as an hotel for the gentry. It was designed by Edward Ennor, one of the leading architects in Cornwall at the time. There was a coach house at the rear with stabling for the horses, and accommodation above for the coachmen. There was a garden at the front with a bowling green and a tennis lawn and at the back was a kitchen garden where fresh vegetables, etc., were grown for the table. A year or two later two semi-detached houses, Watergate Villas, were built up the hill behind the hotel for staff. The hotel had sixty bedrooms; all the front ones were large with fireplaces, and the back ones were very small for the servants. The public rooms consisted of a drawing room, smoking room, billiards room and a spacious dining room. The hotel was fully licensed.

"Certified sanitation" was advertised. It consisted of a brick built cesspit on the sea side of the hotel with vaulted arches in which was a large wheel which could be turned to release the raw sewage directly into the sea at high tide. That arrangement was perfectly acceptable until after the Second World War. "Incandescent Gas Lighting throughout" was also proudly advertised.

"Where to Stay in the West Country."
COPYRIGHT. 1904

The Watergate Bay Hotel,

Near NEWQUAY, CORNWALL.

First-Class Family Hotel, furnished by MAPLE & CO., Ltd.
Facing the Atlantic, South Aspect, Sheltered Position.
Riviera Climate, Mild but Bracing. Grand Cliff and Inland Scenery.
Charming Drives. Good Stabling. Billiard Room.

THE Hotel is splendidly situated in the midst of the finest cliff scenery in Cornwall, and contiguous to the famous Tregurrian Beach (the finest sands on the North Coast), and within walking distance of the sylvan Vale of Lanherne (Mawgan), Bedruthan Steps, and the charming seaside resort Newquay.

Moderate Terms. Specially Reduced Prices for Winter Months.

Apply—
MANAGERESS, WATERGATE BAY HOTEL.

Postal and Telegraphic Address—
ST. COLUMB MINOR, R.S.O., CORNWALL.

Illustration of 1904.

NEWQUAY.

"Watergate Bay" Hotel

Telephone No. 25 Newquay. Telegrams "Sunshine," St. Columb Minor.

MODERN HIGH-CLASS FAMILY HOTEL.

ALWAYS OPEN. □ TERMS MODERATE.

60 Rooms. Incandescent Gas Lighting. Two and a half miles from Newquay Town. Absolutely quiet.

Royal Automobile Club (Officially Appointed). Garage for 15 Cars, mostly lock-up. Petrol Stored.

The Hotel, facing South, is open to the West and Atlantic Ocean, and is sheltered from the North and East winds by the high hill.

TENNIS COURT AND BOWLING GREEN.

The famous Newquay 18-hole Golf Course is about 3½ miles from the Hotel.
Hotel Private Motor Cars meet Trains by arrangement.

Watergate Bay Hotel is in one of the most charming positions in the Cornish Riviera, and within 20 yards of the Atlantic Ocean.

Magnificent views of Cliffs, Sands and Ocean from Hotel Grounds. Within easy walking distance of Newquay, St. Mawgan, Bedruthan Steps, the famous Vale of Lanherne, Carnanton Woods, and many other places of interest.

Fishing, Shooting. Two miles of firm sands for Bathing, Riding and Walking

The great charm of this Hotel is being situated on the West Coast. 90 per cent. of the winds are from the sea, and the average rainfall for 10 years was only 33 inches, one of the lowest in England. Open all the year and special attention given to heating Hotel and comfort of visitors during the Winter.

For terms, etc., write to the Watergate Bay Hotel, St. Columb Minor, R.S.O., Cornwall

The position of the Hotel can be clearly seen in the view of "Watergate Bay."

Advert including gas lighting circa 1922.

The hotel had its own beach with direct access, as it still has of course, but in those early days before cars and commercialisation the Watergate guests virtually had it to themselves and it really was a private beach.

Until the war the hotel was moderately successful in a gentlemanly, understated way, although by 1939 it was becoming somewhat old fashioned and was being overtaken by the rapid developments in the town. It was losing its appeal to visitors to Newquay. The post war holiday makers were to be an entirely different breed.

In 1941 the Air Ministry requisitioned Watergate Bay Hotel, and it became the Officers' Mess for Squadron No. 53 Coastal Command stationed at the nearby St Eval aerodrome. There were many hilarious war time parties held there when a favourite, well remembered game was surfing down the main stairs on a surf board. Great fun! The coach house at the rear became the Station Commander's residence.

When the Second World War was over the hotel was bought by the Ministry of Defence and converted into ten very rambling flats as married quarters for the Officers of Coastal Command based at St Eval. The ground floor of the coach house became garages and the garden in front of the hotel became a car park. The Squadron was engaged in flying Shackletons on eight-hour patrols over the Atlantic — four hours out and four hours back. Planes in those days were not

1926 Original entrance. This car had been purchased specially to bring this family to Cornwall for their holiday. Later the lady in the white dress was to return regularly with her own family. In her later years she was a resident at the hotel until she died.

as reliable as they are today and the Armstrongs lost several good friends on those hazardous Atlantic patrols.

In the '50s the Squadron moved to Scotland and the married quarters at Watergate Bay stood empty for several years. In 1966 the Ministry of Defence sold the building freehold at public auction as "ten flats in need of modernisation". It fetched £27,000 and was bought by Peter Prowting, a very successful developer, who intended, no doubt, to convert it into holiday flats. A very serious stumbling block was that 'certified sanitation' was by then no longer acceptable. At the time there was a complete embargo on any building work or conversions in that area until the mains drainage was installed and that was not going to happen for several years.

After eighteen months the developer put Watergate Bay Flats back on the market, but there were obvious problems with the property which no doubt put many potential buyers off. By then it had been unoccupied for years, had deteriorated badly, and become a dilapidated shell of a building in a very sorry state. It was draped in barbed wire, the lead from the balconies had been stolen, and there was a large notice saying "Keep Out — Dangerous Roof", but it was basically a well built stone building in a wonderful position with its own beach.

John and Mary Ashworth had already decided to return to Cornwall when John came out of the Navy in three years' time and were looking for a suitable project. Undeterred by the drawbacks, they were extremely interested in the Watergate Bay Flats and they asked Bettye to make enquiries on their behalf.

When Bettye first approached John Julian, the agents in Newquay, they were asking £35,000 for the flats which only the year before had been sold for £27,000 at public auction. There was no inflation in those days. "So why," asked Bettye, "would the flats be worth £8,000 more than they had fetched the previous year? Besides there was a further year's deterioration!" "Make me an offer" said the Agent. Bettye suggested £22,500. The agent drew himself up and said "Mrs Armstrong, I am never insulted by an offer" although he clearly thought little of that suggestion. However, he put the figure forward on John Ashworth's behalf and the reply from Peter Prowting was that he would like to see Mr Ashworth in London.

A meeting was arranged with Peter Prowting in London in November 1967. John, as he recalls, sheltering behind Bettye's formidable mink-coated figure, formally offered £22,500. After being assured that the Ashworths planned to turn the building back into an hotel — and not keep it as flats — Peter Prowting accepted his offer. The Ashworths were amazed when their low offer was immediately accepted, and thought it owed more to Harold Wilson's infamous bank lending freeze which was to come into force the following week-end than to John's embryonic business skills. The vendor was an astute business man and he, in fact, would have lost far more than £5,000 had he kept the building standing empty for a further three years until the embargo was lifted. The timing suited the Ashworths perfectly, they knew it would be three years before John retired from the Navy and they could return to Cornwall.

None of the family's projects has ever been tackled without a great deal of determination and, of course, many problems. Watergate was no exception. Mary and John did not lack courage, but they realised they were in for a very difficult few years.

At the time they owned two holiday cottages — mortgaged to the hilt, on Point Green at Feock. They had bought them when they married with John's limited capital, inherited from his father who had been killed while serving in the Navy during the war, and some money which Michael and Bettye had given them as a wedding present in 1965. They also had Barley Cottage, in Detling, near Maidstone, Kent in which they were living, as John was stationed at Chatham. But they had no other capital and to buy Watergate flats they had to sell everything they owned as quickly as possible. This they did, and although their son Toby — born in September 1967 — was only a few months old, they had to move out of their cottage into a very mundane little married quarter on a housing estate, rather like a council house, in Maidstone. Poor Mary. She said later that was one of her worst moments and it was certainly the beginning of several very uncomfortable years for the Ashworths. They found the married quarter neither comfortable nor convenient. The little house was very cramped, but there in July 1969 their second son, Henry, was born. Michael and Bettye, with Wag, their blue roan spaniel, sitting in the back of Michael's Beagle Airdale, flew up from Cornwall with Nannie to give a hand with the new baby. John Ashworth met them at Rochester Airport.

During the Autumn of 1968 whilst John Ashworth grappled with the problem of a Victorian cesspit leaking on to the beach, Mary set to work on a brochure, a booking chart and advertisements, including one for the Town Guide which was considered absolutely essential in those days. The first serious set back came when Newquay's Tourist Office refused to accept the advertisement and would not give a reason. It was a great shock. John and Mary were still in Kent at the time and so, since she was in Cornwall, they asked Bettye to try and find out why? She eventually discovered through a friendly councillor that the council had no intention of permitting the Watergate Flats to be occupied until the mains drainage came — some three years hence.

Calamity — what was to be done? Mary and John could not possibly afford to have the flats standing empty for three years. After many consultations and discussions it emerged that the only way the council would allow the flats to be used before the drainage came was if the Ashworths built a private septic tank and that would cost £8,000 — the equivalent of, say, £100,000 today (2008). It was devastating for them. Jeremy Thring, family friend and solicitor, then came up with a brilliant suggestion. Build the swimming pool that would eventually be needed for the hotel and use it as a temporary septic tank until the drainage came. And that is what happened. In the end, by the skin of their teeth, they just managed to raise the money. Mary's grandmother, eighty years old, gave Mary her last £1,000 towards the septic tank. To the end of her life Livvy Whittington was determined to help her family!

Having raised the money and solved the problem of the septic tank the Ashworths were 'scat'. Furnishing the flats ready for letting had to be done on a shoestring, and a very short shoestring at that! However, the vital advert was in the Newquay Town Guide and the flats just had to be ready and booked for the next season. The winter of 1968-1969 was hectic. Mary in Kent, with Toby aged about sixteen months, did all the bookings, advertisements, printing and ordering etc., while Bettye, in Cornwall, rushed about the sale rooms and junk shops in search of basic, sturdy furniture — which had to be very cheap!

The flats were rambling, with Ministry of Defence brown lino everywhere. In the kitchens were large clome sinks on wooden legs with wooden draining boards; ugly galvanised cylinders called UDBs, stood under the draining board in each flat, to provide hot water. All the taps had been stolen. The huge baths, also on legs, stood on brown lino. It was all very basic and ugly. There was brown lino up the stairs too and for the time being that was going to have to remain, as were the hideous white light fittings, the size of footballs, which hung from every ceiling on solid rods that were nearly three feet long. Miles of material was needed for curtaining; all the windows were very high. Mary solved that problem by buying rolls and rolls of natural coloured crash (a kind of very coarse linen/cotton mixture) which would eventually be used as linings for the proper curtains when the time came. She paid 8/- (40p) per yard for it!

One wall in each bedroom was slapped with emulsion paint in a bright colour, fashionable at the time — purple, lime green, orange and peacock blue were predominant, and the other walls were white. Second hand carpet squares were plonked on the brown lino, which curled at the

1969 advertisement for Watergate Bay flats.

Watergate Bay, with its miles of firm golden sands, is situated 3½ miles from Cornwall's most popular resort, NEWQUAY.

The WATERGATE BAY HOLIDAY FLATS, facing south with magnificent views across Newquay Bay to the harbour and Headland, have their own private steps to the adjoining beach, well known for its surfing. These flats are really roomy and will appeal to families who want a carefree holiday with 'elbow-room' to enjoy themselves.

: : :

★ Spacious self-contained flats, each with its share of the glorious views.

★ Choice of flats —

1 bedroom
(sleep 2-4) kitchen/dining room, bathroom w.c., large sitting room

2 bedrooms
(sleep 4-6) hall, kitchen, bathroom w.c., large sitting/dining room

3 bedrooms
(sleep 6-8) hall, kitchen, bathroom w.c., large sitting/dining room

★ Well furnished and fully equipped with everything for your use, except linen.

★ All electric, with fridge, cooker, kettle, immersion heater, fire and an iron : a separate slot meter to each flat. A vacuum cleaner is kept on each landing and there is a public telephone in the entrance hall.

★ For the evenings, a T.V. lounge.

★ A large recreation room with table tennis.

★ Children's play area in the garden with swings, a see-saw and paddling pool. For the very young an enclosed area with a sand pit.

★ Well behaved pets welcome.

★ Ample car parking space.

★ Cots are available at no extra charge.

: : :

Milk, eggs, butter and cream delivered daily. A local village shop makes deliveries and your order by post will await your arrival.

A deposit of 25% of the total rent confirms a booking — the key to the flat will be sent on receipt of the balance prior to the date of the holiday.

There is a simple inventory to each flat; tenants are liable for breakages and damage and are requested to notify the caretaker immediately.

No responsibility can be accepted by the owners for injury to tenants or loss or damage to their personal property.

Facilities on offer in 1969.

edges, but when furnished with Bettye's bargains and strong Government surplus furniture with cheap brightly coloured matching candlewick bedspreads, the flats looked fresh and cheerful. There was a communal recreation room on the ground floor with a table-tennis table. A vacuum cleaner was placed on each landing, which had to be shared. Mary booked the flats well and most of the families who spent their holidays there for the next three years felt the spaciousness and the marvellous position by the beach made up for the basic state of the building and furnishings. They did not mind the lack of style and elegance. 10 guineas to 38 guineas per week (£10.30 - £39.18) was charged for the flats from April - October. Mary managed to engage a woman to deal with the Saturday changeovers, and they had a good first season, but it was a great relief when they closed for the winter. They managed to struggle through the following seasons in much the same rough and ready fashion. It was fortunate that the Watergate project began in the late 1960s. There were not so many flats available in those days and standards were much lower. Today flats as basic would be quite unacceptable but they served their purpose at the time.

In November 1969 Mary moved back to Cornwall with Toby, aged two and a quarter years, Henry, five months and their two dogs, Mr Wagg and Shami, a cream Saluki. They occupied three rooms in the rear wing at the Edgcumbe Hotel. John finally retired from the Navy early in 1970 and joined them. They could not possibly keep those rooms for the summer for they were already fully booked — naturally, Mrs Burt had seen to that! The Ashworths then bought a small semi-detached house in Bonython Road, Newquay. They moved into it in April 1970 and lived there for the next eighteen months until they could move out to Watergate Bay. Mary found an old discarded staff bicycle in the garden at Edgcumbe Lodge, quickly tidied it up, and fixed a small wooden Mateus Rosé box on the back for Toby and that was his first school transport. She cycled him, aged three, to Miss Luke's little school "Dandre" in Hilgrove Road every day, which coincidentally had also been her first little school some 21 years before.

For the 1970 season John and Mary Ashworth worked as part of Mrs Burt's team at the Edgcumbe, learning the ropes. It was the first time John had come face to face with the relentless grind that running a busy seasonal holiday hotel entails. It was a far cry from life with the Navy — and a far cry too from the rather glamorous view outsiders sometimes imagine life in an hotel to be.

Eventually, after much lobbying from John Pardoe, the Liberal Member of Parliament for North Cornwall, the Council announced a date for the completion of the drainage scheme at Watergate Bay — Spring 1971. Hallelujah! It was eventually finished in the middle of the 1971 season and the Ashworths were able to empty their cesspit for the last time, take off the lid, scrub it out, disinfect it, paint it, finish off the surround and Voila! there was the swimming pool. The fire brigade then arrived to fill it. This they did with such gusto that the water gushed so fiercely that much gravel and muck came with it and one tenant (half Indian) complained bitterly that it looked like the Ganges! But the pool was open! 1971 was the last season for the flats and the really hard work was about to begin.

The Ashworths felt it was very important that they lived on the spot and so they sold the little house in Bonython Road in the autumn of 1971 and converted the first floor of the coach house behind the hotel into a comfortable family flat. They lived there with the children until they were able to sort themselves out with a proper home, which in fact, was to take another three years. Fortunately they had a very good long-term nanny, Sarah, with whom they are still in touch.

John and Mary had been working hard for months with their architect, John Crowther, on the plans for the new Watergate Bay Hotel which happily had already been passed, and so in the autumn of 1971 they were able to begin building immediately. Unfortunately Arnold Pearce, the builder who had been building for the Armstrongs for twenty years, had recently retired and handed over to his son Richard.

The works included a new bar and ballroom and eight new bedrooms were created on two floors where the billiards room had been. A new entrance, foyer and reception office were built. The whole building was re-plumbed and re-wired. Back bedrooms were enlarged by narrowing corridors. In fact the upper floors were virtually gutted and rearranged, giving some rooms private bathrooms. A large new kitchen was built enclosing what had been a backyard, the billiards room was re-sited, and a children's playroom created.

The builder, Richard Pearce, was by no means the man his father had been and he found the burden of the Watergate Bay building operation too heavy. He could not really cope with it and constantly went sick. Fortunately his father's long-term team were excellent workmen and managed, with a great deal of support from John Ashworth, to get the building finished on time. It had been a very hard winter, and John Ashworth bore the brunt of it. It was to everyone's credit that the hotel was ready for the opening date, and the Ashworths were well satisfied with their winter's work.

Mary had worked hard all the winter to ensure the hotel was well booked. In May 1972, after a lapse of more than thirty years, Watergate Bay Hotel was open again. Ironically, as the new Watergate Bay Hotel was opening in May 1972 Graham Farmer was being cremated in Exeter. He died there on 7th May 1972 aged eighty and it was fifty years since he had opened the Tolcarne Hotel on Narrowcliff in 1922. His great niece and her husband were fulfilling his vision.

NEW — for the 1972 SEASON

WATERGATE BAY HOTEL

This is our last season as Flats.

Once upon a time .... the Watergate Bay Hotel, with its superb position and handsome building, was justifiably famous.

Next winter there will be extensive reconstruction and new building and, in 1972, the Watergate Bay Hotel will open again in this perfect holiday spot — this time as the Holiday Hotel for the Seventies.

At Watergate there will be plenty of things going on:—

For everyone dancing, entertainments, film shows, billiards, table tennis, swimming in the heated pool, and a carefree atmosphere away from the Town crowds — right beside our own sandy beach.

For the Children, parties, film shows, swimming galas, indoor and outdoor play areas, with cots, high chairs and a launderette available — also, reduced terms for season (during early and late season one child per family free).

★ For the evenings, a T.V. lounge and large recreation room with table tennis.

★ Well behaved pets welcome. Ample car parking space.

★ Children's play area enclosed in the garden, with swings, a see-saw, paddling pool and a sand pit.

★ Children's playroom - wall bars, climbing frame, swings, etc.

★ Drying and airing room with electric airers.

★ Cots are available at no extra charge.

New Heated Swimming Pool for 1972 Season.

Milk, eggs, butter and cream delivered daily. A local village shop makes deliveries and your order by post will await your arrival.

A deposit of half the first week's rent confirms a booking — the key to the flat will be sent on receipt of the balance prior to the date of the holiday.

There is a simple inventory to each flat; tenants are liable for breakages and damage and are requested to notify the caretaker immediately.

No responsibility can be accepted by the owners for injury to tenants or loss or damager to their personal property.

Announcing the re-opening of Watergate Bay as an hotel after a lapse of 30 years.

The New Watergate Bay Hotel – 1972

John and Mary Ashworth with their staff at Watergate Bay Hotel, 1972.

The Midland Bank funded the Watergate Bay project in its entirety (apart from John's naval gratuity and the sale of the cottages). Their local Managers, in the early days, appreciated the "security" offered by the new hotel being a "chip off the old block" — a compliment to the Edgcumbe. And it is recorded that on opening day, the 13th May 1972, Jim Cornish, the Midland Bank Manager, sat in his car in the lay-by above Watergate, biting his nails until the doors opened, the first guests walked in — and didn't walk straight out again!

From the beginning Watergate Bay Hotel went well, but, of course, there were the usual teething problems. It really is difficult to get an hotel going from scratch. The Ashworths were fortunate that Jill Teague, a most experienced and accomplished Head Receptionist, joined their team. She was with them for over twenty-five years before she retired. She managed the bookings splendidly.

All through the 1970s and the 1980s the major improvements to the hotel continued. A squash court, coffee shop, laundry, and children's playroom were added. The indoor pool, designed by John Crowther, was given a vaulted dark timber ceiling and Cornish stone walls. Adjoining were the sauna and solarium. The pool was small but very warm and the children adored it. The private steps to the beach were landscaped, the beach terrace widened and little suntraps created. The children's outdoor playground with a trampoline became very popular.

The spectacular circular sea lounge, perched above the beach, was built in 1979 to provide a refuge for adults away from children, who very firmly were not allowed there. The lounge had a small circular maple dance floor in the middle, and a very interesting ceiling, also designed by John Crowther. It really was a lovely room. Its roof was astro-turfed to create a putting green on the sea side of the ballroom above.

In 1974 the Ashworths bought Trevenna Cottage in St Mawgan, and they added a wing to it. They had stables, a paddock, and a croquet lawn. At last, after five years, they had a proper home again. Things were beginning to look up. Mary and John's third son, William, was born in October of that year.

When they bought Trevenna Cottage the Watergate Bay coach house was converted into annexe accommodation and being only ten yards from the hotel, and of course cheaper, the rooms are very popular to this day. At that time the ground floor of the coach house was still staff rooms, which caused problems from time to time. In the mid eighties Mary and John were able to buy another staff house so the ground floor of the coach house was then converted into very superior family suites for guests, and they were much in demand and always well booked.

By 1974 Watergate Bay and the Ashworths were forging ahead. They bought Watergate Villas, a pair of semi detached houses up the road behind the hotel. They paid £110,000 for them. The villas had originally been built as staff houses for the hotel, but had long since been converted into three good self-catering units. Mary made one of the garages into a table-tennis room and the other into a communal laundry for the three flats.

About two acres of land on the cliff top between the houses and the hotel came with the villas and a skate bowl for skateboarders. It had been made by the previous owner, but he had been unable to get planning permission for it, so it had never been used. Mary and John installed an all weather tennis court, and a nine hole approach and putt golf course. Later they were able to buy a large adjoining bramble patch for just £1,000 and there they made an additional car park.

In 1998 John Ashworth recalled:

In 1981 the Squash Court and wing bedrooms were built and in 1985 the Beach Hotel staff house was purchased, releasing the whole Coach House for conversion to more annexe bedrooms and the Foyer entrance was extended. In 1989, following the purchase of land from the owners of the hotel opposite, the Sports Hall was built to provide badminton and other indoor sports and skittles alleys. Fortunately the programme of expansion was completed before the recession of the early 1990s when, like all prudent businesses, retrenchment and make-do-and-mend became the order of the day, whilst all efforts went into seeking new markets, and the drive for economy and efficiency was stepped up.

A punch-up[1] *with the Ministry of Defence over maritime cable-laying operations that severely disrupted Watergate's spring business in 1992 resulted in a not unwelcome cheque in out-of-court settlement (handled most ably by John Newey on the hotel's behalf). As the holiday market began to pick up, a lean and hungry Watergate was ready for the upturn; led by faithful old guests ready to forget about their negative equities and job insecurity with a carefree holiday they were delighted to find that the hotel had not suffered from change.*

In 1981 John and Mary bought at auction a Duchy farmhouse with 36 acres of land at Trevithick East, 1 mile east of St Columb. Toby, Henry and William subsequently completed their education at Radley, before Toby went on to an engineering career in the Navy, and Henry and William both attended Oxford Brookes to study for a degree in Hotel and Catering Management.

Watergate, of all the hotels in the family, has remained closest to the Edgcumbe 'formula', swaying but not changing with fashion. Despite recession, and competition from overseas packages, feedback from guests suggests the 'formula' still holds good, and indeed nationally there seems to be a resurgence of interest in UK holidays. One result is the steady stream of old guests from the 1970s and 1980s, including ex-Edgcumbe (and Old Edgcumbe!) returning with their grown-up families to Watergate, and that continues to this day.

For the future, an embryo project may result in a new wing of bedrooms overlooking the beach which will be of great benefit to Watergate, for in spite of its splendid position with direct access to its own beach, because the hotel stands end on to the sea there are very few rooms with good sea views, and

---

[1] What John Ashworth refers to as his 'punch up with the MoD' was caused by a very "hush-hush" Anglo/U.S. operation — the laying of ten high tech. laser cables under the sea which had to be connected to the MoD installation at the top of the hill above Watergate. There were problems about which route their cable should take in front of the hotel. As a result the MoD changed the route and the work was not finished on time. Consequently, when the hotel opened for the 1992 season there was noise, disruption, dust and the view from the front was of a building site, with large machinery and the like, and the visitors complained bitterly. After a very prolonged battle led by John Ashworth, Watergate Bay was paid what was, in effect, disturbance money for this aggravation. Talk about butter out of a dog's throat! Well done John!

there is still a great demand for them. Perhaps one of the three Ashworth brothers will come aboard to take the helm.

In the early eighties there was a very unpleasant happening at Watergate Bay. Mary and John suddenly realised that their wages were not balancing. They went through the wages book and discovered there were discrepancies on every page. £10.00 was added on here and there, and so every week when the wages cheque was drawn it was for a larger amount than it should have been. The wages clerk had discovered an easy way to fiddle the books and she had been doing it for more than a year. It turned out that £3,000 had been stolen in this way. The police were called, and the girl was caught red handed with extra money in her own pay packet. She was charged, found guilty, and went to jail. Another lesson learned. Never again would the same person calculate the wages and put them in the envelopes. Ever after, one girl would work out the wages, and a second girl would put them up. Today, computers have cut out all that and wages and salaries are paid straight into the bank.

Mary and John Ashworth were delighted when Stephen Swire and his wife took over the management of the Watergate Bay Hotel in 1983 and settled down happily. They ran the hotel most ably for the next six seasons. Stephen Swire introduced computers to the hotel and dealt with the new legislation about health and safety. He managed the staff well and during his reign the seasonal staff turnover was very low. Stephen and Becky Swire were both popular with the Watergate guests. They lived firstly in a cottage behind the hotel but after a year or two they bought a house in St Mawgan village and seemed very settled, and Mary and John were all set to relax a little.

At the beginning of October 1984 there was a fire in the sauna, which spread to the swimming pool and the vaulted timber ceiling got badly damaged. John Armstrong brought in his little band of builders from the Headland; they worked unstintingly and within a week the pool was re-opened. Luckily, Cornwall was enjoying an Indian summer at the time and the weather was so warm the guests could use the outdoor pool happily. They were very sympathetic and good humoured about it.

In 1985 Mary Ashworth decided to take up ballooning, which had become very popular within the family. She bought a rainbow hued balloon called *Bubbles* which took two passengers, from a young couple who had come to the Great Cornwall Balloon Festival organised by John Armstrong every May. She quickly got her licence and became a qualified balloon pilot, to which she later added a Commercial Balloon Pilot's licence. Guests were offered sightseeing flights, and for a time *Bubbles* was used for low flights advertising the hotel. Mary was a very good pilot and loved it but found it too time-consuming and *Bubbles* was sold.

Mary Ashworth flying '*Bubbles*' the Watergate Bay balloon.

When in 1985 the family at last managed to get rid of the Beach Hotel in Watergate Bay, which as the reader will hear, became very tiresome, the Ashworths bought Spring Valley, the squalid little staff house up the hill. It was dilapidated and really needed rebuilding. They paid the family £25,000 for it. Spring Valley had already been a staff house for several years and was in a state of unimaginable disrepair. As all hoteliers know, put seasonal staff in a house and it will quickly deteriorate. There will be graffiti, neglect, even

RIGHT BESIDE *OUR OWN* SANDY BEACH WITH *OUR OWN* HOT AIR BALLOON

Not many Hotels can offer THAT!

SQUASH & TENNIS COURTS, INDOOR & OUTDOOR SWIMMING POOLS, DANCING & ENTERTAINMENTS FOR ALL AGES AND PLENTY MORE FACILITIES FOR FAMILIES

WATERGATE BAY HOTEL

3½ miles from Newquay

Telephone 0637 870543

Watergate Bay Hotel advertisement for the Great Cornwall Balloon Festival, 1986.

vandalism and it will not be very clean — to put it mildly. There are exceptions of course, but they are rare and Spring Valley was no exception. It provided very poor accommodation and in 1988 that was to cause Stephen Swire serious problems with his seasonal staff.

In the mid eighties the Ashworths built a large wooden sports hall with a full height badminton court. And a modern ten pin bowling alley. Unisex had not yet arrived, and the 'powers that be' insisted that three separate WC facilities were installed at the hall; one for men, one for women and one for disabled people. Surely a bit over-the-top?

Stephen Swire's wife gradually became disenchanted with the hotel business and in the mid-eighties she took up golf and quickly became good — very good. In 1986 she decided to retire from the hotel so that she could give more time to her golf, and after that Stephen Swire was managing very much on his own. She was missed by the guests and, of course, by her husband, but Stephen continued to cope very well, and he gathered a good team around him — he was an excellent Manager.

1988 was a most difficult season. The Restaurant Manager resigned and there were serious staff problems aggravated to a great extent by the poor staff quarters. Stephen Swire was not at all well or happy. He was still managing the hotel on his own with no-one to help him and undoubtedly he "went through the mincer". It was very stressful for him, and at the end of the season he threw in the sponge and resigned. He and Becky decided to sell their house and return to their roots in

The Ashworth family enjoy a winter picnic on Watergate Bay beach, 1988.

the Midlands. He did later say that he had made a mistake in not going to The Headland as it would have offered him more scope for his ambitions. It was a great blow to the Ashworths when Stephen Swire decided to leave and it was to be many years before Watergate was able to get a good management team together again.

By 1995 as more staff arranged their own accommodation "Spring Valley", the staff house, was no longer needed, and Mary and John decided to rebuild it during the 1995-1996 winter and convert it properly into a holiday cottage for letting. A proper drive into the property was made, the gardens landscaped to include a south facing patio. Double glazed windows and heating were installed. It became a tidy little three bedroom holiday house, which has proved to be very popular, especially as the tenants staying there are offered the use of the facilities at Watergate Bay Hotel. It works well.

As John Ashworth commented in 1998, "Watergate remained closest to the Edgcumbe formula". It had not changed or progressed very much, apart from the modern amenities that had been added from time to time. There were two basic reasons for this; they had a hard core of satisfied guests, often country folk, somewhat old fashioned who loved it all just as it was and begged "don't change anything". This had made Mary and John feel, rightly or wrongly, that the modern 'go getters' and the high fliers could go to Bedruthan Steps, or elsewhere, where everything was much slicker and more "sophisticated" and they were disinclined to make changes.

Mary loved Watergate Bay, but John had never been as enamoured with the hotel business as are other members of the family. Nevertheless he had steadfastly and loyally backed Mary for over thirty years. He dealt with the accounts office, the hotel's finances, and the licensed side of the business well. He took a keen interest in wines and gave great attention to choosing the wines for the wine list, while Mary coped with the bookings, furnishings, and general administration — they made a good team! He has a talent for negotiation and great tenacity and has fought some very successful battles over the years for the hotel and sometimes for the family.

In the mid-nineties Watergate Bay Hotel stood at the cross roads much as Tolcarne and Edgcumbe Hotels had in 1945. It has one of the finest positions of all the family hotels and enormous potential. What other Cornish hotel actually owns the beach immediately below it? Think of the possibilities that offers! There was also planning permission for a new wing of bedrooms facing the sea and for an enlarged, revamped poolside coffee shop. The hotel was outdated and needed new ideas and new blood to take it into the 21st century. It was about to get both when Henry and William returned.

In the meantime Watergate Bay Hotel had a good team: they were Michael Culls, the Head Chef who had joined the Ashworths in 1976 and David Simmons, Bar Manager, who had been with the family hotels for more than twenty years and who transferred to Watergate after the Edgcumbe was sold. Mr Keith, the Restaurant Manager, had also been there for over twenty years. He referred to himself to the young guests as "The Fat Controller" (from Thomas the Tank Engine) and kept small red and green flags in the restaurant with which he called them to order.

Henry Ashworth and his French wife, Sophie, returned from South Africa in April 1998 and decided to look for a project in Cornwall, but in the meanwhile Henry took on the marketing and publicity of the hotel. In September when the BBC announced they wanted to make a programme about surfing in Newquay, Henry managed to lure them to Watergate Bay. He wined and dined them and entertained them flat out for four days. He took them surfing and kiting on the beach and canoeing on the River Camel. The weather was glorious and they all had a wonderful time. As a result, when the programme was shown Watergate Bay received an avalanche of enquiries, including the following letter.

... I have just seen the article on the 'Holiday' programme on BBC1 this evening and I felt I had to write to you. My new husband and I visited your hotel for our honeymoon at the beginning of September 1976 (and we have a photo taken in your dining room to prove it!) so we were amazed to hear the name of your hotel mentioned on the television. During the programme we saw some shots of the hotel which seems to have changed very much for the better.

When I last visited the Watergate Bay as a 20 year old bride it was a very different story from what we saw on the television!

On our arrival we were told that the Honeymoon Suite had been given to another couple and we were given a single room! The room only had 1 curtain, cracked windows and 1 cupboard door. The pipes rattled and gargled all night and — to top it all — the weather broke during our stay and the huge plate glass windows in the dining room blew in!!

It was a bitter disappointment and we always said that we would never go back. However, seeing on the TV how nice it looks now, we would be grateful if you would send us a leaflet or some information on the hotel that might persuade us to make a return visit — preferably at the 1976 tariff??!!......

Mary Ashworth thinks their memories are playing them false. Watergate Bay never had a honeymoon suite, and the plate glass windows in the dining room never blew in, but it is all very interesting, nevertheless! The extra business and work, drummed up by Henry's efforts, of course made the office even busier for Mary to cope with.

In 1998 Watergate Bay sprang to life, no doubt due to Henry's efforts, but it was to be a hard season for Mary. The new Manager needed 'running in' and the receptionist who Mary had spent much time training left and it was difficult to replace her. There is no doubt that Mary was the hardest working member of the family that summer; she ran the reservations office.

When William finished his studies in Hotel and Business Management at Oxford Brookes and came back to Cornwall in June 1998, he was twenty four and he, too, joined the hotel team for the season. Like his uncle, John Armstrong, some thirty years before, he was full of interest and enthusiasm for the hotel, but unlike Uncle John at the same age, he was not yet quite ready to settle down to it long term — a few wild oats to be sown first, perhaps! However, he began putting his stamp on the hotel and his interest and flair for décor and design quickly became apparent. His parents approved of his ideas and soon gave him his head. When the hotel closed in November he got going with his schemes for updating the décor. He redesigned the dining room and gave it interesting murals and produced an original scheme to give the indoor swimming pool a much needed face-lift. The rough stone wall was plastered and it was given a skilful trompe-l'oeil painted by a well known local artist, Janet Shearer. When the vaulted ceiling was removed it was revealed that the roof had been badly damaged by the fire some fifteen years before and major repairs were needed. True to form John Ashworth went in action and managed to convince the insurance company that the damage could only have been caused by the fire. Although the claim had been settled in full at the time, he managed to persuade them to pay up again. Masterly negotiating, John!

In early November 1998 members of Squadron No. 53 Association returned to Watergate Bay for their final reunion dinner at the hotel. It was a very nostalgic and enjoyable evening for them, but sadly only six of the original officers who had been stationed at St Eval over fifty years before managed to attend.

In January 1999 William took off for London to work for a company publishing financial magazines. Bettye is not quite sure exactly what he did for them, but no doubt he found it interesting and learnt a lot, and the experience stood him in good stead. Certainly, like Uncle John Armstrong, he made the most of his spell in London!

The Retirement Years at Feock
1962 – 1979

Spindrift, Trolver Croft, Feock.

By 1962 the Armstrongs hadn't looked from left or right in the summers for many years. Michael was nearing sixty and longing to ease off. The Edgcumbe had got into its stride and was bowling along merrily, always full. Mrs Burt had found her feet, fallen in love with the Edgcumbe and the hotel business, and she applied her keen intelligence to it. She was well capable of being left in charge for long spells.

Michael and Bettye had water ski fever and were tired of trailing their boat about in the afternoons and so their thoughts began to turn to finding a bolt hole on the south coast to where they could perhaps escape for a couple of nights a week and moor their boat. They found a tatty little house on Restronguet Creek, Feock, called Spindrift. It had originally been built in the 1920s for £375 but its position was perfect; at the end of a quiet lane with its own beach where they could keep their boat on an outhaul in front of the house. It also had a ramshackle boathouse. They bought it for £5,000 and put the builders in! It became a delightful waterside retreat — just what the Armstrongs needed. To begin with they spent two or three nights a week there. It was the first time since the war that they had managed to have more than a few hours leisure at a time in the summer and they loved it! Gradually they spent more and more time there, leaving Mrs

Burt in charge of the hotel. For the winter they returned to the comforts of Edgcumbe Lodge, and Beryl's cooking, for Spindrift was essentially a summer house, without cavity walls or central heating, and in cold weather it was freezing.

Mary had left Cheltenham in 1962 and after her gap year, during which, having failed to get into the Voluntary Service Overseas (VSO) she worked at the Edgcumbe under Mrs Burt, she joined several of her school friends at Exeter University in October 1963. After she had been there about six weeks there was a University Saturday night 'hop'. Mary and her buddies had no partners, but one of them had a brother at the Royal Naval Engineering College at Manadon, Plymouth. She was persuaded to ring her brother and ask him to come to the dance and bring some friends. One of the chaps who came that night was John Ashworth, a clever young naval engineer on the general list who had won a scholarship to Dartmouth, and that was how he and Mary met.[1] The following summer she often invited her university and naval friends back to Feock for weekends. They had glorious times water skiing, sailing, etc. 1964 was a happy summer! Mary's parents loved it too.

At the end of the 1963 season Michael, who had never really liked Newquay, was enjoying Feock so much he firmly made up his mind he would formally retire and make his share of the partnership over to Mary and John, which he did. Bettye felt he had earned his retirement and she was happy to supervise the hotel by remote control — she would say she had long preferred to do it that way! That apart, she had

From the left: John Armstrong, John Ashworth, Olive Whittington, Mary Armstrong, Michael and Maggie Dyer, at Spindrift, Feock, in the 1960s – bliss!

[1] This was the night J F Kennedy's assassination was announced, 22nd November 1963.

complete faith in Mrs Burt who was growing in stature as time went on. Spindrift and Feock offered the Amstrongs something they had never known in the summers: complete freedom without looking at the clock, or having to talk to people, or dealing with problems. It was bliss, and the whole family revelled in it.

Olive Whittington and Bettye in the garden of Spindrift.

Michael enjoyed his boating and flying while Bettye converted several cottages and stripped pine furniture. She also did patchwork, and for a brief spell they wallowed in an informal "country cottagey" way of life. They were both interested in racing and so from time to time they would fly to Bath, or perhaps Newbury, for a day's racing. Once they even managed to fly to Ascot for Ladies Day.

Soon they were reluctant to return to Newquay at all and Spindrift was adapted to "year round" living with central heating, a new kitchen, extra bathrooms and a study for Michael and his desk! They also built a terrace on the beach, with no talk about planning permission! In short Spindrift became the family home, although Olive Whittington and Maggie Dyer continued to live in Edgcumbe Lodge in Newquay, looked after by Gwen, Olive's long term capable help.

Bettye stripping pine furniture at Spindrift, Trolver Croft, Feock.

John Ashworth and Mary became engaged in January 1965 and were married from Spindrift at Feock Parish church on 5th June 1965, when she was twenty-one and he was twenty-six, eighteen months after they had first met. There was a reception afterwards for about one hundred people at Killiganoon at Playing Place, which then was a country house hotel and restaurant. They flew to Ibiza for their honeymoon where the Charnauds, family friends, lent them an apartment. Two weeks after the wedding, John Ashworth sailed on HMS Ark Royal for the Far East, leaving behind his tearful bride. For the next three months Mary helped at the hotel and in September she flew out to Singapore to join John. Michael and Bettye took her to Heathrow and saw her off. They were very happy for her, but saddened for themselves. They would miss her badly, she was a beloved only daughter, and they realised she had really left home for a new life. When she had gone Bettye wept. John was waiting for Mary in Singapore. HMS Ark Royal was on a goodwill trip to Australia. Mary followed him by ship to Perth where they spent Christmas and made life-long friends with the Hohnen family. They returned to the UK six months later. John was then stationed at Chatham and they set up home in Barley Cottage, Detling, Kent, which they converted well and where they put in a spiral staircase.

In the autumn of 1968 Michael and Bettye had a two month tour of south-east Asia. They flew to Singapore where they stayed for three days to get over the jet lag, then flew to Hong Kong for a week, staying at the Grand Hotel in Kowloon. Grand it was not! They vowed next time they would stay at the Peninsular Hotel; unfortunately 'next time' never came. They had hoped to meet up with Joe Hardwick, Bettye's cousin, the long term 'Pro' at the Royal Hong Kong Golf Club, but he was away playing in a tournament in Australia. Hong Kong was overwhelmingly hot and crowded, but they loved it. They did the sights, shopped and Michael had a suit made — in three days. They went by hydrofoil to Macau where they had a highly successful session

Sorting out 'the catch' in Tobago.

Bettye with the basket of orchids awaiting them at Pattaya Beach, 2½ hours drive from Bankok.

Michael on Pattaya Beach, from where they tried paragliding.

Market scene.

at the roulette tables. Incidentally, today, under capitalist China, Macau has become the biggest gambling centre in the world. In 2007 its turnover overtook that of Las Vegas.

Next stop was Bangkok full of colour and bustle, but the most intriguing thing was the river; yellow opaque water with little teak houses on stilts lining its banks. They saw women washing in it, boys swimming in it — and 'piddling' in it; in fact as their guide explained the river dwellers used it for everything. Even Bettye, not fussily hygienic, was shocked but they all seemed healthy enough. While in Bangkok they were duped. Michael chatted to an Egyptian airline pilot who told him of a high-born Thai lady who would be happy to show them Bangkok in her car. Bettye and Michael were delighted! When she arrived to pick them up the next day in a large car she had two 'cousins' with her. They certainly 'did' the sights and restaurants with Michael paying for five people everywhere and the same thing happened the next day. The following day the Armstrongs cried off and made other arrangements, but on their last day they were offered a visit to the local wholesale silk depot where all the locals bought their silk. Bettye couldn't resist that and she purchased many lengths of silk (which later turned out not to be what they were purported to be).

The next day they left for Pattaya Beach, a resort some two-and-a-half hours drive from Bangkok, where they planned to relax on the beach for a week. When they arrived at their hotel they found a basket of orchids in their room from the Thai woman and half an hour later she and her companions were all in the hall asking for the Armstrongs, having followed them from Bangkok. Michael resolutely refused to appear so Bettye had to go down and see them off. In Pattaya Michael had hoped to meet up with a flying friend, racing driver Prince Bira[2], who had a holiday house there. Unfortunately, they had missed him by a few days but after the hubbub of Hong Kong and Bangkok, Pattaya Beach was bliss and they spent a quiet week on the beach before flying to Indonesia. They 'did' Jakarta and Jojakarta which, of course, they found intriguing with their strong Dutch influence. Next stop was Bali. Bali in the 1960s had not really been developed and it certainly was not the tourist hotspot it is today. It was so hot the sand burnt one's feet. There, they followed the tourist trail but later felt they had not really discovered rural Bali which would have been much more interesting. The most fascinating spectacle was a Hindu cremation on the beach — a funeral pyre with a canopy over it, about five musicians standing knee deep in the water playing local instruments and a queue of beautiful Balinese girls in exotic colourful garb bearing gifts on their heads, silk, fruit, and other items to go on the pyre with the deceased. When the fire had gone out the old local women came and grovelled around amid the ashes searching for mementoes of the departed — teeth, etc.

In Bali the Armstrongs also picked up with a couple of Yanks who were seasoned travellers and who the following year arranged a beach house for them on Laguna Beach, California and with whom they spent a month touring the Hawaiian Islands.

The Armstrongs loved Penang where they stayed on the beach but, with dire warnings about sea snakes, didn't venture into the sea. While

---

[2] Prince Bira was the racing driver cousin of Prince Chula who lived at St Tudy in Cornwall.

there Michael's godson, Michael Oliver, the manager of a large rubber plantation in Kuala Lumpur about one hundred miles away, invited them to stay and sent his car and driver to fetch them. They had a very pleasant sojourn there before returning to Singapore for the last leg of their tour where they stayed at the Goodwood Hotel and were royally entertained by Charles Wilson[3], a well established General Practitioner in practice there. He lent them his car and driver with daughter, Rosie, as guide, took them to lunch at the Cricket Club and gave a dinner party for them. It really was a splendid trip.

All through the '60s Bettye and Michael continued to enjoy their retirement at Feock; they felt very settled. They made Spindrift comfortable and attractive, although it was still basically a rag-tag little house. A few years later, after they had sold it, the front wall fell out and their luckless successors had to rebuild it. However, in 1970 they were offered "Carrick Cottage", on Restronguet Point. It had had a major conversion at enormous cost including every door and window being replaced with solid teak, and it had carpets, curtains, and fittings of the finest quality all entirely to their taste. The house had a landscaped garden running down to the water, three deep water moorings, a slipway and electric winch which meant Michael could have the larger boat he yearned for. They couldn't resist it, and they moved.

Sadly in September 1970 their water skiing days ended tragically. All through the '60s the popularity of the hotel water skiing at Feock had never waned and by the end of the decade it really had become

Carrick Cottage, Restronguet Point, Feock.

[3] Dr Charles Wilson was the father of John Wilson, John Armstrong's friend from his days at Cheltenham.

quite a chore. The guests were constantly demanding it, and Bettye and Michael really felt less inclined to take beginners as the years went by. One day in September 1970 there was one man very keen to water ski and Bettye, for some reason, was not available to help, and so Michael offered to do it by himself. He gathered the man and took him to Turnaware, which by then was the specified water skiing area in Carrick Roads. (During the '60s the rules about water skiing were tightening all the time, and by 1970 skiing was restricted to only one area at Turnaware.) The man was a beginner, and kept falling off. Michael was alone in the boat and concerned that he might run over a small rowing boat bobbing about in front of him. Michael's new boat had an inboard engine, which meant that the propeller could not be seen. While his attention was on the rowing boat at the front, the water skier, who had again fallen off, pulled himself in, hand over hand on the rope, straight on to the propeller, which chopped off one of his testicles. It really was a ghastly accident and at first it was thought his injuries were even more severe, it was thought he had lost both. Poor Michael had to manage the boat alone, somehow pull the injured man out of the bloodied water, and then had to get him back to the shore, call an ambulance to get him, bleeding profusely, to the hospital as quickly as possible.

The next morning there was another shock for the Armstrongs; when the insurance company was contacted they said "But the boat insurance has not been renewed this year, and the boat is not insured!" Bettye and Michael were aghast! It turned out that renewing the insurance that year had been completely overlooked — no insurance! Fortunately, the whole family had been insured with the Royal Insurance Company for some fifty years, and they were respected customers. When John Ashworth, who was very supportive, went into action and talked to the insurance company, he was able to persuade them to agree that as the boat had been consistently insured for the previous ten years, it really had only been an oversight. The Royal accepted the claim, but it was very worrying at the time.

The trauma of the accident upset Michael for a very long time. He could not sleep for weeks. The man did recover but there was eventually a court case about it, and he was awarded £3,000 damages for the loss of one testicle, which the insurance company paid. How important it is to have a good, long term working relationship with one's insurance company! So the Armstrongs' water skiing days ended abruptly and tragically and Michael, at least, never water skied again.

By the '70s Mrs Burt had the Edgcumbe Hotel well under control and running very smoothly. She had surrounded herself with a team of loyal staff. The Armstrongs had complete confidence in her and therefore for the first time in many years they were able to enjoy a peaceful life at Feock away from the Hotel. They really had retired.

Life was indeed sweet for the Armstrongs at Carrick Cottage in the '70s. Their children were grown up and getting on with their lives sensibly and at last Bettye and Michael had the time and money to really enjoy their leisure, and they made the most of it. Lovely summers were spent in Cornwall. Bettye had good, long-term help with her entertaining and socialising — but it must be said, she did not manage to acquire any domestic skills! She was never a domestic goddess!

Michael was able to fully indulge his passion for flying. He had a Beagle Airdale, a high wing four seater monoplane which he kept in a hangar at Perranporth Airfield. In return he was the Tug Master for the Cornwall Gliding Club which still operates from there. It was an arrangement that suited him perfectly. He loved towing the gliders and it gave him many hours of local flying. Later, he had a small two seater French Emeraude, a low wing monoplane, which he also enjoyed, and in which he and Bettye had many interesting flying trips.

Michael's Beagle Airdale which he kept at Perranporth.

In the autumn there were frequent jaunts to London for shopping, theatres, etc. where they stayed in the little flat in Hammersmith. After a family Christmas in Cornwall Bettye would set the alterations and repairs for the hotel going, brief Mrs Burt fully as to exactly what was to be done and happily head off to Switzerland leaving her to cope, which she did most ably for many years. In Switzerland they took a chalet or apartment in Gstaad for one or two months. Bettye skied enthusiastically and Michael curled. He joined the Palace Curling club and the village curling club. He was very keen on the game and became a good player. They both made life-long friends in Gstaad and

Michael curling at the Palace in Gstaad.

there were joyous reunions every winter when they arrived.

Each spring the Armstrongs would return to Feock and Bettye would spend some time with Mrs Burt listening to the problems and planning what was needed for the forthcoming season at the Edgcumbe. The summers were spent boating, entertaining friends (often from Gstaad), and planning their autumn trips, of course.

In the July of 1974 they had an interesting visit to Canada, first staying with Henslow cousins in Mississauga, then a week on Big Lake Joseph — very picturesque, but with water colder than the Cornish sea!

All togged up to walk under Niagara Falls.

Stampede at Calgary.

followed by Quebec, Ottawa and Montreal, and then a train across Canada to Calgary to stay with friends for "stampede", when the cowboys come to town in force in their finery and Stetsons. It is a huge spectacle with enormous stands erected in the streets for thousands of spectators. They flew home from Edmonton to the devastating news that while they had been gallivanting poor John and Mary had been having a battle royal with the Fire Authorities about the fire precautions at the Beach Hotel, Watergate Bay which had ended with it being closed down for the season, as the reader will hear later.

The Armstrongs enjoyed a comfortable life of retirement in Feock. In March 1977 Michael, because he was over seventy, had a very stiff medical, including a cardiograph and a chest x-ray, for his pilot's licence — he sailed through and the doctor said "Good God, Mike, you have got the blood pressure of a man of fifty-five. We shall have to shoot you when you are one hundred and ten!" Six weeks later he had a major stroke from which he never fully recovered. He was very ill for several months and when he finally emerged he had lost the use of his left arm completely, his balance had gone and he was permanently disabled. Sadly his plane and boat had to be sold. He was never able to drive again. From then on life was a slippery slope for him. From time to time he had medical setbacks which landed him in hospital and although he survived for seven and a half years, life was a burden and social life and entertaining became at first difficult, and then impossible. The Armstrongs struggled with his rehabilitation, but after two years Bettye felt isolated and was anxious to move back to Newquay to be nearer the family and the hotel. Later, Bettye always felt thankful that she and Michael had enjoyed nearly twenty happy retired years in Feock before he was struck down.

Michael's 70th birthday photograph, taken in Gstaad, 19th February 1976.

Bedruthan Steps Hotel
1924 – 1979

Bedruthan Steps circa 1930 with the new wings.

Bedruthan Steps with its annexe was built in 1924 and was owned by Mr and Mrs Willans. It was a small hotel with about fifteen bedrooms but from the beginning it had a full licence. At that time it stood almost alone on the sloping land above Mawgan Porth Beach with much space around it. In 1925 the grounds were landscaped and terraced and a lawn tennis court and a putting green were added. Mr and Mrs Willans ran it very successfully throughout the twenties and in 1930 a new wing was built. It was a long flat roofed building, doubling the size of the hotel which then had thirty bedrooms, some with balconies. It also had a ballroom and a drawing room.

Mr and Mrs Willans owned the hotel from 1924 when it was built until 1945. Having a full licence, it was popular as an out of town drinking venue and was a favourite haunt of the Farmer brothers. In those days pub crawls by car were the thing and Graham and Tom Farmer were drinking buddies of Mr and Mrs Willans. Many were the convivial drinking sessions they all enjoyed, after which the Farmer brothers would weave their often less than steady way home along the single track winding coastal road back to Newquay by car. There were no drink and drive laws to curb such journeys, and the cars were not so lethal — happy days!

In 1939 Bedruthan Steps was requisitioned by the Air Ministry for the duration of the war and was occupied by No.53 Squadron of the RAF who were flying Blenheim twin engine bombers from the nearby St Eval airfield.

BEDRUTHAN STEPS HOTEL

R.A.C. *(FULLY LICENSED)* A.A.

MAWGAN PORTH, CORNWALL

The Hotel occupies a commanding position overlooking Mawgan Porth and adjacent to the famous Bedruthan Steps. The Beach affords ideal bathing for children, with the finest surf bathing on the coast. Hard Tennis Court and Putting Green. The Hotel is furnished and conducted on modern lines with comfort. H. & C. running water in all rooms.

Terms from 3 gns. to 6½ gns. per week according to month and room selected.

For Tariff apply to E. WILLANS.

Telegraphic Address: HEALTH ST. COLUMB.

CC. 471

Advert during time of Willans.

When the hotel was de-requisitioned in 1945 it had been very badly knocked about. Mr Willans had died and Mrs Willans had no wish to take it on again. She sold it to Mr Briggs. He did his best to restore and refurbish it, but the times were difficult. Everything was in short supply. There was strict petrol rationing in force until the 1950s which made life very difficult for out of town hotels and so the building and the business gradually deteriorated until the late 1950s when it was put

As it was when Peter Whittington bought it. Derelict and run down Bed Steps 1960.

Drawing room

Dining room

Bedruthan Steps Hotel 1960.

on the market again. By that time it was in a very dilapidated state, and when Peter Whittington and Tom Malcolm bought it, the building was virtually crumbling and in dire need of major repairs — in fact, rebuilding, but it was to be about thirteen years before that could be tackled.

When the Malcolms arrived in Cornwall in October 1960 with their three children, aged five, three and less than one they had nowhere to live and very little money. It was planned that they would move into Bedruthan House, which went with the hotel and stood in the hotel grounds. It wasn't really habitable, and there was the usual problem about accommodation for them while the house and hotel were in the hands of the builders.

At first Tom and Doreen and their children stayed at Zabuloe, the large house adjoining Bredon Court, the ground floor of which was Peter and Barbara's home, and they looked after the flat for them while the Whittingtons went on holiday, which suited everyone. Then they took 'Three Corners', a furnished house down by the sea at Mawgan Porth, for three months while Bedruthan House was being renovated — but even after it was finished it was a very basic little abode. They later enlarged it and made it a much more stylish and comfortable home. Much later, of course, as the hotel prospered the whole family were able to buy comfortable, spacious houses well away from the business, but there is no doubt that in the spring of 1961, with three young children and no home, the going was 'rough and tough' and the Malcolms had a hard time; there was very little money available for anything but the hotel. There was an enormous amount of work to be done and, for them, much to be learnt.

Peter Whittington and the Malcolms took over Bedruthan Steps in November 1960 and began preparing it for the coming season but they could do little more than patch it, give it a lick of paint, tidy it up, and put buckets under the leaks when it rained. With tremendous effort they managed to get the hotel open for Whitsun 1961. Fortunately they had a good chef from the beginning. Peter took with him Juliano, the talented Italian second chef from Bredon Court, and put him in charge of the kitchen. He was a splendid chef and he was in charge of Bedruthan Steps kitchen until he retired — nearly fourty years later. From the beginning Bredon Court spawned Bedruthan Steps Hotel.

As a business partnership, Tom Malcolm and Peter Whittington made a formidable team, and each learned much from the other. Tom was a first class architect who, unlike many architects, was expert at designing stylish buildings as cheaply as possible and was always concerned about the cost to his clients. He was also experienced at dealing with the authorities. Peter was a talented engineer, with an astute business brain and they worked well together but soon serious personal problems arose.

Peter and Mary Whittington.

Peter was heavily involved in Bedruthan Steps from the outset and he spent much of his time there helping the Malcolms put it together while Barbara remained in charge at Bredon Court. When he began working with them he soon changed his mind about Doreen. He realised that she had a keen intelligence and was very hardworking, and although she had had little formal education she had innate good taste, was quick to learn, and her enthusiasm and capacity for work matched his own. What was more; she had a marvellous figure and a good sense of humour. He fell for her hook, line and sinker. Again, his mother was much upset. She bristled with disapproval and wrote to him very sternly giving her views. She was much concerned about the welfare of Peter's three daughters and she had no wish to meet Mrs Malcolm. Peter, typically, ignored her advice! Some people at the time thought he had been high- jacked out of his marriage. That was not so. Anyone who really knew Peter Whittington would know that if there was any high-jacking to be done Peter would be the one doing it.

When Peter and Doreen Malcolm seriously got together he thought the name 'Doreen' did not become his new love and he decided he was going to call her by her second name, Mary. This he did, but it is a measure of his force of character that not only did he call her Mary, but in a short time everyone else was calling her Mary too, including her own family, and Mary she is to everyone to this day.

In 1961 Peter and Mary fled to Plymouth leaving Tom in charge of Bedruthan Steps and they left all their children behind with their respective spouses. Mary's two elder children, Susan and Nicholas, spent most of their time with their grandmother in Devon. Debbie, her youngest child, then only about two and a half years old, was actually brought up by Tom Malcolm and his new wife, Ann, who was a kindly stepmother. She lived with them in their farmhouse at Yelverton for several years: she was very happy there and has affection for Ann to this day.

Peter managed to rent a charming little 18th century Garden House on the Mount Edgcumbe estate, Plymouth, for £250 a year. It had an octagonal sitting room but only one bedroom. Fortunately there was a slate roofed lean-to store attached at the back and before long Whittington was putting in windows and converting the store into two extra bedrooms so that the children could visit them from time to time. The Garden House stood in the most beautiful grounds surrounded by camellias, rhododendrons etc., and nearby was the ornate orangery. It was a glorious and peaceful setting. While at the Garden House Peter and Mary, who both enjoyed having a project, opened a larger branch of his Newquay shop "Scandia" at the top end of Union Street, Plymouth. There, with more space, they were able to sell really choice Scandinavian furniture, glass, and jewellery, by the leading designers of the day. Even Bettye, whose taste is naturally more traditional, drooled over some of the beautiful things they sold, especially the jewellery and glass. In those days presents from Peter were always interesting! There is no doubt their Plymouth shop was at that time one of the most elegant up-market shops in the city. In this very successful shop they also had the first Elizabeth David Kitchen Shop in the south-west which sold really well designed, expensive kitchen gadgetry etc. In 1963 they opened another branch of Scandia in Mutley Plain, but, although successful, that did not last very long for things were sorting themselves out in Cornwall and soon they were to return to Bedruthan Steps.

Peter and Mary Whittington

During those years in Plymouth, there was much to-ing and fro-ing for Peter and Mary to Bedruthan Steps, as Peter worked with Tom Malcolm on the restoration of the hotel in the winters. The seasons were very successful, but by 1964 Tom Malcolm, who had married again, was ready to return to his architectural practice full time, and so

The Whittington and Malcolm children, circa 1965. From the left: Susan Malcolm, Sarah Whittington, behind her Sonia Whittington, Debbie Malcolm, Nicholas Malcolm and Maria Whittington.

it was arranged that Peter and Mary, who were married that year, would return to take over the reins at Bedruthan Steps. After that there was no time for, or interest in, having shops in Plymouth; there was too much to do in Cornwall. Peter and Mary had the Garden House for fourteen years, and after they returned to Cornwall in 1964 they kept it as a weekend retreat until the estate was sold in 1973 and they had to give it up. They were very sorry to lose it. It had been a wonderful 'bolt hole' where they could occasionally escape from Cornwall's madding summer crowds, and they loved it.

By the time Peter and Mary returned to Cornwall, married, his mother had, to some extent, got over her misgivings. She never really approved but she realised how well they worked together and what a help Mary was to him, and although Mary understood she would never really be "top of the pops" with her mother-in-law all went well and they were back in the fold. Today, laughingly, Mary recalls that Peter's mother usually gave her a pair of lisle

Peter and Mary Whittington in party mood.

stockings for Christmas! But Olive Whittington had a quiet tongue and they never openly crossed swords.

On their return to Cornwall, Peter and Mary lived in Bedruthan House. When their two daughters were born — Emma in 1966 and Rebecca in 1968, they had eight children between them, three each from their first marriages and two of their own. The house was too cramped when all the children were there, and they began to think about buying a larger house away from the hotel.

Peter returned from Plymouth determined to do some serious building at the hotel and he quickly gathered a good team of workmen together. He meant to work them hard and insisted that they be given a proper hot meal every day, so for the first winter Mary cooked a hot lunch for fourteen workmen daily, and fed them on a trestle table in her kitchen. She was completely supportive of Peter.

In the early days at Bedruthan Steps, being seriously interested in cooking, Peter worked alongside Juliano in the kitchen and learnt a great deal from him. He spent much of his time there, as indeed he had at Bredon Court. The Bedruthan Steps kitchens were always in the forefront with the latest up-to-date equipment and gadgetry, and before long there was a proper bakery and butchery.

Peter was convinced his food was good — and it was! If guests thought otherwise they were out of order and he would tell them so. Once when someone at Bedruthan Steps asked for tomato ketchup Peter stormed into the dining room from the kitchen in his white coat and told them he was not having his food spoilt with tomato ketchup and he would not allow them to have it. He also became enraged at one point because some guests were complaining the service at dinner was too slow. He then put a notice on the bottom of the menu saying "Will all guests who wish to be in and out of the dining room in twenty minutes please wear hats." The next day several hats appeared. The hatted ones were served immediately — with their three courses on a tray in one movement. Typical Whittington!

As has been described, Bedruthan Steps stands on a sloping site with the land running down from the hotel towards the sea. In the late 1960s Peter, who always wanted to run a superior kitchen, managed to build a splendid restaurant under the main dining room where more upmarket menus were offered. He created a private kitchen behind it for himself by excavating under the main hotel kitchen and there he spent many happy hours cooking without interruption

"The Three Seasons", as Peter named his new restaurant, opened in 1968 and throughout the late sixties and seventies was one of the finest in the county and very popular with locals. Unfortunately, as so often happens with restaurants, it was never quite the same when he, personally, no longer cooked for it and eventually the family gave it up. It is now put to good use for special barbecue nights for the guests, and in the high season it becomes an 'overflow' dining room for guests without children.

Peter in his kitchen.

Until the late 1960s hotels were able to sell their kitchen scraps as 'pig swill' to the pig farmers, and it worked very well. The pig farmers paid 'a little something' for it, and collected it several times weekly and the pigs were well fed — much better fed than the cattle later given processed food which was thought to cause BSE. From time to time items of hotel silver would be found among the swill and the hotels then made an arrangement with the pig farmers to buy back any knives, spoons or forks at about sixpence per piece: a very homely arrangement, but it worked.

Then the government, in their wisdom, decreed that, by law, pig swill could not be fed to pigs unless it had been boiled. This, of course, upset the whole arrangement because it would have been an impossible task for the farmers. So today, scraps from guests' plates have to go straight into the waste disposal unit which means, surely, the pigs are deprived of jolly good grub and much food is wasted. More bureaucratic nonsense! In Bettye's personal view some of the current hygiene rules are barmy — well over the top.

In the sixties, Juliano was offered a suckling pig as a gift in return for the pig swill. He planned to use it on a large buffet he was preparing, and he was delighted with it. He went to the pig farm to collect it and it was handed over, alive and squealing. Having not long arrived from Italy, and speaking very little English, he was utterly unfamiliar with British laws regarding killing animals which, of course, must be carried out in an abattoir. He therefore brought it back to the hotel kitchen, where he intended to slit its throat. The pig escaped and was chased all around the hotel, with the dogs joining in the chase — chaos reigned! Eventually it was caught and taken to the local abattoir to be dealt with. Juliano then produced the most splendid feast for the buffet.

With the full licence there had always been a public bar at Bedruthan Steps and to begin with the Whittingtons kept it. It was open to Tom, Dick, and Harry — campers, locals, staff — anybody, but by the late 1960s Peter and Mary were finding it tiresome. It was impossible to keep the riff-raff out of the hotel — they were all over the place. By then Peter had learnt the hard way that staff cannot be given the run of the hotel facilities because they will upset the guests, but with a public bar open to one and all it was impossible. They could not control it and so they surrendered their full licence and made a separate bar for the staff, which gave them a sort of club room where they could get together when they had finished working. Oddly, none of the family has ever had a desire to own or run a pub. Certainly Bettye and Peter saw too much of the misery caused by drink when they were children.

In the late 1960s Peter built a row of villa flats in front of and below the hotel. Each flat consisted of a very large bed-sitting room for parents, a bathroom, and small kitchen in the middle and a room for two or three children at the back. The roof was turfed so that the hotel looked onto a flat lawn. At first the flats had to be reached by going outside, which was a great drawback in bad weather, but that problem was to be overcome later, as the reader will hear.

From the outset Bedruthan Steps was a jerry built, dilapidated, leaking hulk of a building ready to be demolished and very early on in their partnership Peter and Tom decided that they would like to knock it down and rebuild it from scratch. With much patience and negotiating skill over several years, they managed to persuade the tax authorities that this was feasible. After an inspection by the tax inspectors before the re-building began, it was agreed that they could completely demolish the hotel and rebuild it, and the whole operation would be called 'a repair and renewal'; therefore it would not be tax liable as a capital improvement. Thus they were able to enjoy a tax holiday for several years — clever chaps! But Peter and Tom were both clever— very clever!

When the rebuilding began Peter was fortunate to have a first class foreman, Len Morgan, in charge. Len had been a foreman for Dudley Coles, a large national firm of contractors. With Len's building experience and Peter's engineering expertise they could tackle anything — and they did. For fifteen years, from 1969 - 1984, Len was in charge of all of Whittington's building operations. He converted the house in London, built the Garden House in St Mawgan and, of course, Bedruthan Steps and Trevelgue Hotels. He was devoted to Peter and always referred to him and called him "Mister". Len kept in touch with Peter until the end of his life — even when visiting him meant an hour's drive each way to do so.

The total rebuilding of Bedruthan Steps as a repair and renewal was to set the Whittingtons and the Malcolms well on the way to financial affluence for, of course, the new building they then erected during the winter of 1972/1973 was modern, up-to-date, well designed and bore little relation to the tumble down edifice they had demolished. They managed to get the hotel rebuilt over two winters so that they did not lose a season while doing it. John Crowther recalled on the day before Bedruthan Steps re-opened there was an 'up-country' Italian team of tilers working against the clock to finish tiling the kitchen floor. When they told Peter they were "sorry but we will not be able to finish the work today" Peter replied "You will finish because I shall lock you in until you have finished. You have a lavatory there!" and he did just that! That was one way of getting the job done — typical Whittington!

In the early 1970s for £3,000 Peter bought all the teak which was being taken out of Battersea Power Station, London, when it was demolished. He then purchased a derelict building in St Columb Major and set up a joinery workshop. There was a massive amount of wood out of which he made furniture, including dozens of two- seater settees for the hotels. They were of simple design, rather squarish, but very strong and they were upholstered in black and white check tweed. They were not exactly luxurious, but they looked quite smart and were the main furnishings in the lounges of Bedruthan Steps and Trevelgue Hotel for several years.

In the early 1970s the Whittingtons managed to arrange the larger house they had been seeking within striking distance of Bedruthan Steps. Peter bought a substantial stone house with a large garden in

St Mawgan Village. He immediately separated most of the garden from the house, got planning permission to build in a delightful position on a south facing slope and sold the original house with a small garden around it. Peter then had a lovely time designing, planning, and building the house of his dreams. It has six bedrooms each with a bathroom (the main bedroom has a sunken marble bath in the middle of it), and a large T-shaped living room facing south. There is a wide balcony around three sides in colonial style. When the house was finished, their architect, John Crowther, said it was the most interesting modern house in Cornwall at the time. There is also a kidney shaped outdoor pool and massive solar panels on the flat roof of the house to aid the heating. Even in those days Peter was well ahead of his time. It is now surrounded by a mature and beautiful garden created by Mary, who is a dedicated and talented gardener.

In the early '80s Peter acquired a large piece of land with road frontage adjoining their garden in St Mawgan and there he made a small market garden with a huge greenhouse and several polythene tunnels to grow vegetables for the hotels. They had a good gardener and it worked very well except that occasionally there would be a glut of one particular vegetable and Peter would then insist that all the hotels were to use it. At one time it was beetroots and battles were fought because Peter wanted beetroot served with almost every meal. Impossible! "What are we expected to do with all these beetroots? Make beetroot pie?" asked one Bredon Court chef! For a long time the market garden was successful, but after Peter became disabled and the experienced gardener left, Mary found it too much to cope with. She then got planning permission for two houses on the site. When it was sold she generously gave the large greenhouse to a friend, Wilfred Curgenven who for many years has run the very successful garden centre at Quintrell Downs, Newquay.

The building programme at Bedruthan Steps continued year after year. After Len Morgan settled down with Peter they spent the summers happily planning the following winter's work, and both were completely absorbed by it; there was no holding them and they went from strength to strength. They thought up some really amazing schemes, and that is how Bedruthan Steps came to be the extensive, modern building it is today. Len worked for Peter for some thirty years and no doubt, had Peter not been struck down in 1986 they would have gone on to create another monster.

In 1974 a large new extension was built which consisted of two squash courts, one hundred and fifty seat proper cinema with a sloping floor, and children's recreation rooms. Peter always had the capacity to 'think big' and whereas several hotels in the area built a squash court for their guests, at that time Whittington built two courts, and the cinema and recreational space for children. He never did things by halves; he just had to have things bigger and better than anyone else. It was a charming little cinema, but not very well patronised by the guests because most of the films were 'way out' Continental films to Peter's taste. He felt that if they wanted to see ordinary 'run of the mill' films they could see them at the local cinema. Later the cinema was adapted to become a children's large indoor adventure play area, called the jungle. It was a wonderful place for them, and of course much more fun than the usual dreary little play rooms in hotels because it was much bigger and with double height.

By the late '70s people were objecting to going outside to reach the villa flats and it was decided there would have to be a tunnel to link them to the main hotel. John Crowther was consulted; his verdict was that it would be very difficult and extremely expensive but Peter, not to be beaten, put on his "thinking cap". John Crowther recalls Whittington came up with a brilliant idea, saying "We will build a narrow swimming pool and put a lid on it, and that will be quite straightforward." That is exactly what he did — simple, really. The tunnel became a well lit, 6 ft wide and gently sloping corridor carpeted and hung with modern pictures, it works well, and the villa flats are now part of the hotel.

Showing Peter's ingenious tunnel to the villa flats.

When hydrotherapy spas became fashionable in the 1970s many hotels installed them and they were virtually little hot tubs in which two or three people could soak. Peter, again thinking big, installed a hydrotherapy spa at Bedruthan Steps which is really a small hot indoor swimming pool in a large warm separate room; it is much larger than some of the hotel swimming pools in Newquay and the guests love it. Peter was always one jump ahead and by the end of the '70s he was advertising in the Town Guide five swimming pools at Bedruthan Steps and they were all bigger and better than anybody else's! Uncle Graham Farmer would have been proud of him!

The ballroom at Bedruthan Steps is in the middle of the building, near the bar, and more or less open plan. In the days when there were nightly rowdy entertainments, noise was a problem, and so in the early '80s Peter employed a small firm to insulate the ceiling between the ballroom and the first floor bedrooms. It was a difficult job entailing putting a concrete false ceiling in place. The small firm was hesitant about it and doubtful whether it would be effective and they told him so. Peter over-rode their misgivings and told them to get on with it. They did so, it did not work, and then Peter refused to pay them the full amount. They sued him in court for the bill (several thousand pounds) and although Peter had engaged a London barrister to act for him the Judge found in the firm's favour. The Judge decided Whittington was too knowledgeable and dominant and he had over-ridden the firm's advice and it had been <u>his</u> decision to experiment, therefore he must pay. Peter did not really mind. He had thoroughly enjoyed the battle.

The noise problem was eventually resolved when a really exotic area, called the Grotto, was built under the cinema, well out of earshot, where dancing, discotheques and jazz provided late night entertainment. The Grotto was like a cave, walled and ceilinged with large boulders and had a pool with running water, and brilliant coloured lighting effects in the pool and under the dance floor. It was a magical setting, with its own bar, and many late night, sophisticated parties were held there. For a few years the Grotto was a great success. Many of the guests enjoyed the late night discos, but by the early 1990s they were becoming outdated. Practically every little guest house had its weekly disco but the more 'go-ahead' hotels moved on to other forms of entertainment.

As time went on The Grotto was used less and less, and then the family had a very bright idea. They opened it as a disco and bar for the staff, with the added proviso that should guests wish to join the staff disco they could do so. That kept everyone happy. It is well out of earshot so that guests who did not wish to join in were not involved and those that did had a lovely time — with the staff. It would not do at some hotels but it was a happy solution to the noise problem at Bedruthan Steps.

Throughout the 1960s, 1970s and 1980s Bredon Court and Bedruthan Steps prospered. Both hotels did well and gradually the Whittingtons became gently affluent and life became more agreeable for them. It was the just reward for twenty years of dedicated hard work. There were many exotic family holidays to far-flung places. The children all went to good schools; Millfield, Bedales, Dartington, and Badminton. Peter bought a freehold derelict three storey mews house just off the Bayswater Road, London, for £30,000. He was not prepared to pay London builders' prices and so sent his team of builders with Len Morgan in charge to London to convert it. He sent up camp beds, chairs, a table, and a cooker, pots and pans etc. — all the essentials for camping — and the team camped in the house while they did the conversion. They loved it, of course. Many Cornish chaps would jump at the chance of a week or two in London with accommodation provided — however rough! It worked well and they did a good job. It was a wise investment. It now belongs to Peter's two youngest daughters.

In the late 1970s Whittington embarked on another 'project'. In partnership with Dennis May he bought the Camel Estuary oyster beds and at first they were a great success, and it was 'oysters with everything' at Bedruthan Steps and Bredon Court, which of course was very popular with the guests. But soon problems arose with the distribution. The oyster beds were on the far side of the Camel Estuary off Rock — too far away. The two hotels could not use them all and although they could have sold them to other establishments they could not get them delivered fresh. Peter and his partner lost money over the oyster beds, but as they said ruefully, "Well one cannot win them all" and that was the end of that project. It was a brilliant idea but it didn't quite come off.

Peter worked hard and fought many battles — and usually won! He would never give in. If he thought someone was trying to do him down he would chase them to the ends of the earth. On the other hand he could be very generous to those he felt had served him well. He presented Len, his long-term foreman, with a brand new Volvo car when he retired — a handsome gesture, and he sometimes did very complicated engineering jobs for people without charge. Peter seemed to have no middle course — it was always all or nothing!

By 1979 all the family hotels, the Edgcumbe, Bedruthan Steps, Bredon Court, Watergate Bay, and The Beach, were going great guns and John Armstrong had just acquired The Headland. Barbara Whittington was still running Bredon Court and Mary Whittington was coping with Bedruthan Steps with Mr Proofer as Manager. Nicholas Malcolm, who had taken his degree in business management, had joined the team there. Peter Whittington began to be concerned about the tax implication for his family. He formed a new company, which he called Merrogwidden Limited. The shareholders were his and Mary's eight children, Maria, Sonia and Sarah Whittington, Susan, Nicholas and Debbie Malcolm and their two youngest, Emma and Rebecca Whittington. From then on various properties were bought for self-catering in the name of the new company. One such investment was a field with a large barn and two derelict cottages in St Mawgan. They converted the two cottages into three letting units known as Lanvean Cottages and used the barn as a store. They then applied for planning permission to demolish the barn and build four more cottages, but it was to be years before that scheme could come to fruition. Peter began to feel restless and was looking for a new challenge and when he heard the Trevelgue Hotel was on the market he could not resist.

The Edgcumbe Hotel 1964 – 1971

For the 1964 season an Entertainments Host/General Assistant was engaged as a front man, and then the Armstrongs really felt the hotel could get along well without them being constantly there. But because Michael had the hotel boat which was illustrated in the brochure and mentioned in the advertisements, the water skiing had to be available to the guests. The Entertainments Host would ring up every

Edgcumbe water skiing party. Michael is at the back, and John is crouching in the front.

reasonably fine day and tell the Armstrongs how many people wanted to water ski. It was extremely popular, and they spent many mornings or afternoons giving the hotel guests, most of whom were beginners, water skiing lessons. Bettye had to stand waist deep in the cold water (before the days of wet suits) helping them up, holding them, and generally instructing them, and that soon became quite a chore. However, they still enjoyed their private water skiing parties, and the whole family became proficient at it. John was at Cheltenham College and his friends also came and stayed in the summer holidays, and really the sixties were a very happy time for the whole Armstrong family.

Bettye suffering in the cold water.

Although by 1965 the Armstrongs were spending time in Feock the Edgcumbe was not forgotten or neglected. It was getting bigger and better all the time. Every winter there was an ambitious building programme of extra rooms, amenities and improvements, and of course, ever more bathrooms. Bettye set the builders going and then left it to Mrs Burt to deal with them. She soon became capable at that side of the business too. Before long she knew exactly what would go where, how much space was needed for this or that, where to buy and how to get the best discounts. Bettye was teaching her well and she was lapping it up. From then on Mrs Burt increasingly coped with the Edgcumbe on her own with less and less attention from Bettye. She was proud of the hotel, and did a most splendid job although she was still officially only the Head Receptionist.

In 1965 Mary was twenty-one, and her parents gave a twenty-first birthday party for her at the Edgcumbe. She and her friends were rather sophisticated young things and she would have liked a steel band for her party but they were unable to arrange it and so Bettye and Michael decided she would have to have Ken Stratton and his trio — the hotel band. Mary, disappointed, agreed, but said firmly "I don't want any of Ken's "carry on" — family speak for Ken's special brand of comedy back chat when he MC-ed dances. She thought it rather vulgar — to be honest, the whole family did too! Ken was told he must "just play with no chat". The dance began sedately and so it was until supper. After supper it really did not get going again and it became

"I think you had better 'whip it up' Ken." Mary's 21st Birthday Party.

clear that very soon the guests would be saying 'thank you' and leaving and the party would peter out much earlier than planned. Mary then asked Ken to "whip it up". In a very short time he had got everyone on the floor, mixing and doing quite absurd things and the young people loved all his exuberant nonsense. It is a fact that if people can be persuaded to "let their hair down" they invariably have a good time. From then on the dance was a roaring success and Ken was begging to be allowed to play the last waltz at 4.30 a.m. It was a very good party!

The Armstrongs felt quite settled at Feock and had no wish to return to the Newquay rat race, but once again fate intervened. About two months after Mary's marriage, all was going smoothly. Bettye and Michael were at Spindrift, when at 8.00 a.m. on 2nd August they had a telephone call. The caller told them Mrs Burt had been rushed to hospital. "What is it?" asked Bettye. "It is Maternity" the caller replied. Mrs Burt, out of the blue, with no-one suspecting, had given birth to a son, John. That shattered the Armstrongs' idyllic summer at Feock. They had to move straight back to the flat in the hotel and take charge. In the meanwhile John and his school friend, John Wilson, who was staying with them, both aged sixteen made a little 'hay while the sun shone' — they had the boat, the water skis and the house to themselves, what more could two chaps on holiday from school ask for? They had a lovely time while John's parents and Mary coped with the Edgcumbe. They missed Mrs Burt badly but Mary really was a tower of strength to her parents that summer. The Armstrongs were thankful that Mary was there to help and she gave them enormous support. There was one major difficulty, Bettye had to do the bankings, balance the books, and keep the money straight. To her that was an impossible task and she could not do it any better in the 1960s than she had been able to do it in the '30s and '40s! Many afternoons were spent, with Mary's help, at Edgcumbe Lodge, counting the money and trying to make it balance, without success. In the end they scooped all the money, several thousand pounds, into an orange canvas beach bag and walked about with it for days before finally 'dumping' the whole lot at the Bank. No further questions were ever asked. Now, forty years later, in the days of VAT and when everything is much more tightly controlled, there would no doubt have been questions asked and a big fuss made, but then they got away with it. The money was all there, it just didn't balance!

The Armstrongs had been very shaken by the loss of Mrs Burt — she had been doing so well and they had come to rely on her and were not at all sure she would be able, or even wish to return to the

Edgcumbe. They were delighted when she came to see them in October and said she would like to come back, but they felt strongly that she could not manage the hotel office properly unless she arranged for her baby son to be cared for full time. There was no question of her bringing him to the hotel. There had to be some very straight talking about how her baby would be looked after if she came back. Bettye told her she must engage a full time nannie.

Now Mrs Burt has always been very good at thinking out a problem and seeking the solution that will work long term and that is what she did. She arranged for a good friend of hers, Iris, whose children were older, to look after her baby every day from first thing in the morning until bedtime six days a week and she agreed to pay her properly for doing so. That arrangement worked perfectly for seventeen years and when Mrs Burt's second son, James, was born two and a half years later, her friend looked after him too. Today Iris is helping with the Burts' two young grandchildren.

Although Mrs Burt had been running the hotel she was still officially only the Head Receptionist. The Armstrongs felt they were taking advantage of her and, determined not to return to Newquay themselves, decided to appoint a professionally trained and experienced Manager to manage the Edgcumbe for them.

In the autumn of 1965 Bettye and Michael gave much time and attention to finding a suitable Manager. They advertised nationally in The Caterer and The Telegraph and interviewed applicants from all over the country. Finally they appointed Michael Bell-Turner who had worked for seven years under Michael Chapman, at the Imperial Hotel, Torquay. He had a good reference from the Manager of the Headland Hotel, Newquay, who told them that Bell-Turner's wife was a very efficient receptionist, which of course was a big asset. It was arranged that the Bell-Turners would take up duties on 1st April 1966 and during the winter a three bedroom flat was built for them at the back of the Edgcumbe. It was considered essential in those days that they lived on the premises.

On 1st January 1966 Mrs Burt resumed her duties in charge of the office bookings. Her son, John, was five months old. The Bell-Turners moved into the new flat at the end of March. As a Manager, Bell-Turner was hopeless. He simply could not do it; he needed someone to tell him what to do — he had no initiative at all and his wife, who had two young children, did not come near the hotel. From the point of view of the management the season was disastrous. During that year, Mrs Burt behaved impeccably. She put her head down, got on with her work, ran the office and the bookings and did not cross swords with Bell-Turner. As the season wore on it was quite clear that he could not cope and so at the end of the summer he was dismissed. There were two legacies from Bell Turner's year at the Edgcumbe. The hotel was left with vast quantities of inferior orange juice. He bought enough for thirty years — Bettye swears she was still drinking it in the 1990s! The other was even longer term. He introduced 'Horse Racing' from the Imperial Hotel, Torquay. Of course, at the Imperial it was done with much more style. There were trellis fences, wooden horses, top hat and morning coat for the presenter and a wooden banner over the 'Tote'. At first the Edgcumbe tried to copy it faithfully — but the trappings soon went out of the window and it was reduced to just a marked canvas on the floor and two large rubber dice, and that is how it is played today. It is a game families can play. The children are often the horses, fathers can have a flutter and the guests simply love it, although it is jolly hard work for the presenter. Some Newquay hotels still do it — they all copied it from the Edgcumbe but the family hotels have long given up weekly entertainment programmes.

All through the '60s a fortnightly Flora Dance was held which gaily danced through the town from end to end. Headed by the town band and led by local school children with the girls dressed in white dresses it was an exuberant affair. Crowds lined the streets and the more energetic holidaymakers joined in. The whole scene provided a little local Cornish colour and the visitors loved it. On those evenings dinner at the Edgcumbe was served a little earlier so that the guests could get out and join in the dance if they so wished.

Another seasonal spectacular was the annual carnival held in August every year. Many of the hotels and businesses in the town spent much time and money decorating their floats for the big parade, and the town band was out in full force. It was the modern equivalent of the old Lifeboat Day of long ago and a gala atmosphere prevailed. Sadly it had to be abandoned when the rules and regulations were tightened after a child fell from a float and insurance became obligatory. For the major businesses in the town it then became too expensive to enter.

By 1966 Bettye's mother was finding it difficult to walk and she wanted to be nearer the new Edgcumbe. When she was offered "Bushy", No. 4 Hilgrove Road, just behind the hotel she was very keen to move. "Bushy" was a detached house of nine bedrooms, but really not nearly as substantial as the well built one in Edgcumbe Gardens. Bettye and Michael bought "Bushy" for £7,500 and put it in Livvy's (as Olive Whittington was now known to her family and friends) name, to give her security should anything happen to them. After all, she had handed over all her assets to Bettye and Peter in 1947.

The ground floor of the house was converted into a comfortable and spacious two bedroom flat for Olive Whittington and Maggie Dyer, and their long term help, Gwen, who moved with them and looked after them there. The first and second floors were completely cut off and given a separate outside staircase. There were then nine bedrooms used as an annexe for guests, and at that time they still booked readily, so that the house was put to good use. In the 1960s Newquay's post-war boom was in full swing and people were still prepared to sleep out.

Having sacked Bell-Turner in the autumn of 1966 the Armstrongs again faced a management problem. They thought it over carefully and decided to promote Mrs Burt to be the Manageress. And so early in 1967 Mrs Burt, single-handedly, took on the general management of the Edgcumbe, and she and her family moved in to the manager's flat behind the hotel.

When Mrs Burt was appointed Manageress she was about thirty years old with a good figure, and as soon as mini skirts became fashionable she raised her skirts to, say, two inches above the knee.

Edgcumbe Hotel

NEWQUAY

Introducing our annexe – Edgcumbe Lodge – just across the public car park adjoining the hotel. It has eleven bedrooms, most with private bath or private shower and w.c., all with intercom to the hotel, baby listening and electric kettles for making hot drinks. The house has full central heating. There is a quiet, comfortable lounge with television available at all times and a log fire early and late season. Private car park immediately outside the door. The full facilities of the hotel will, of course, be available to guests staying in the annexe. Generally speaking the terms are approximately £6·00 per person per week less than comparable rooms in the main building.

SEA

Edgcumbe Lodge 'annexe'. Sounds wonderful, but in fact it was badly furnished, noisy and extremely uncomfortable.

Olive Whittington, without saying a word to anyone, called her on one side and said gently, "I think dear, it is not very becoming for the Manageress of a large hotel to wear skirts above the knee." Also without a word being said, Mrs Burt's skirts immediately went down about four inches! She managed the hotel on her own most successfully for the next twenty-three years, gathering around her a team of loyal and devoted staff, reflecting her talent as a staff manager.

In 1966 John Armstrong had left Cheltenham College where he had been since 1962. The school was going through a bad patch at the time; it had an ineffectual Headmaster, Mr Ashcroft, and John's parents were less than pleased with it. They therefore removed him and sent him to Le Rosey, a Swiss International school where he remained for the next two years. He did well, thoroughly enjoyed his time there, and today considers it the most important part of his education. Some of the pupils came from very wealthy backgrounds. In the summer of 1968 two separate parents approached the Headmaster to ask if it could be arranged for John Armstrong, aged nineteen, to tutor their sons, ages thirteen or fourteen on their yachts in the Mediterranean for the two month summer holiday. The Headmaster wrote to John's parents with the suggestion, and they were nonplussed. While they felt their son had worked hard and deserved a holiday they were afraid that he would get a taste for life on a yacht in the Mediterranean before he had done anything, and so they "sat on it", pondering. They need not have worried for before they could decide, John came up with his own answer. He would have none of it. He said "I'm not wasting my time on a yacht in the Mediterranean: I'm coming back to start work in the hotel" and he did.

He arrived home at the beginning of July and immediately began to work. There wasn't really a job for him, but he donned a blazer and grey flannel bags and became 'dogsbody' under Mrs Burt. Before he began he was bounced by his mother. "Remember the whole staff knows you have just left school. They know you know nothing. You have to ask them to help you and tell you what you need to know, and you have to earn their respect. And another thing, if the dishwasher breaks down you are the first one who takes off his jacket, rolls up his sleeves and leads the way to the sink". And that actually happened a couple of weeks later! So it was that on his nineteenth birthday, when he could have been on a yacht in the South of France, he was washing dishes in the Edgcumbe kitchen. (In fact, being the showman he is, he would have taken off his jacket, led the way to the sink, washed dishes for about ten minutes, then grabbed someone and set them going with it!) but it is a good story and illustrates his enthusiasm for hotels which has never wavered and there is no doubt it is that attitude which has put him where he is today, some forty years later.

John just finished the one season at the Edgcumbe and in October, 1968 decided he needed to go away to get experience in hotels. He was keen to go to London where he had a girlfriend, so wrote to the Manager of every hotel in London known to him — some thirty in all. He immediately received a telegram from the manager of the Cadogan Hotel in Sloane Street inviting him for an interview. He got the job as a trainee assistant manager, again the 'dogs body'. He wore pin stripe trousers and a black jacket and pranced about the front hall, greeting guests, dealing with queries and complaints. He also hired and fired the kitchen porters and put up and paid out the wages. At weekends the manager went home for forty-eight hours and young Armstrong was left in complete charge of the ninety bedroom hotel and was forbidden to leave it. He was badly exploited for almost two years, which did not matter in the least as he learnt a great deal which later was to stand him in good stead. He worked under a good manager and recently recalled one piece of very useful advice he was given — never employ a fat housekeeper — very wise!

His salary was £1,000 per annum live out. Nineteen year old John Armstrong, to use his own phrase, thought that was "brilliant" but the living out was to pose a problem. Next time his parents went to London he had joined some friends with a furnished house in Chelsea. His room was an old, unconverted garage with no window, cobbled floor and ill-fitting, rickety garage doors which had a two inch gap at the bottom so when it rained the water blew under the garage door and trickled to the middle where there was a more or less permanent puddle on the cobbles. When they saw it, his parents were aghast and told him he would have to find somewhere else to live.

The next time they went to London, John was excited. He and three other boys had found a furnished house just off the Kings Road. He took Michael and Bettye to see it. They were being asked to guarantee the tenancy, and they were even more horrified! The house was furnished with new, plain pale grey fitted carpets throughout. The furniture was all new, Peter Jones mahogany reproductions. There was to be a Schedule of Condition. All the china and glass, obviously the young owners' wedding presents, was being left and the agent had blithely told the boys it would be quite all right because all breakages could be replaced at Peter Jones! After that the Armstrongs prudently decided to allow John to live in their little flat at Hammersmith.

After John Armstrong had returned to Cornwall the next time his father appeared at the flat the doorman in the building opposite asked after him. He said "'Ee had a good time while 'Ee was here. 'Ee made a lot of hay while the sun shone." John had enjoyed London!

But back to Newquay. The Edgcumbe was a tall box of a building on five floors and the laundry was in the basement. Imagine how the corridors must have been littered with linen on Saturdays — it was awful. Soon a linen chute was made from the top to the bottom of the building with a trap door on each floor into which soiled linen could be pushed and it all came out in the laundry area in the basement — it was a great boon.

One Saturday morning in the middle of the season, the linen chute suddenly became blocked solid — through five floors! Nothing would go in. There were two hundred and twenty-five people leaving and arriving that day. Mrs Burt was called and she discovered that the woman in charge of the laundry had 'walked out' at the height of the action and the whole operation had ground to a halt. Chaos! Mrs Burt had to set to and cope with it, and Livvy Whittington, ever helpful, assisted her and somehow they managed. Then the kindly Mrs Whittington took Mrs Burt to the family flat and said "I think, my dear, we'd better have a little sherry to revive us." No glasses, so they drank it out of tea cups! In fact they were Bettye's decorative tea cups in an ornamental corner cupboard! Friendships are often formed by the many tiresome happenings in hotels.

A woman booked for a week in August for herself and four children aged about seven to twelve years old. They were given a large family room on the ground floor of the rear wing. She paid a deposit and duly arrived. They were an attractive family; she blonde, well dressed and personable and the children good looking, the youngest a snub nosed beaming boy who beguiled everyone. They soon ganged up with the other children in the hotel. Mother made her own friends and went out and about with them, leaving the children to their own devices and they joined in everything, which meant the swimming pools, play room, and disco room with Juke box, young children's entertainment programme, etc. The eldest boy won the cup for the children's swimming gala and a lovely time was had by all.

Come Saturday when they were leaving the four children had breakfast, while mother ostensibly packed. After breakfast they all disappeared leaving the suitcases in the bedroom. It was assumed they had gone for a last look at the sea. By lunchtime they had not reappeared and the staff, anxious to prepare the room for the next guests, decided to move the suitcases. The cases were lightweight and when opened were found to be full of bright purple towels — and nothing else. The family had scarpered. When Mrs Burt sent the account to the address from where the booking had been made the letter was returned "Not known at this address". They had all had a splendid free holiday — it does happen!

When the Armstrongs decided to stay in Feock obviously their little flat had to be put to use. It was converted into two large family suites facing south and with the benefit of the small walled garden laid out by Treseders they became the most popular rooms in the hotel.

From the late 1960s and all through the 1970s the major winter work was upgrading the bedrooms and getting en suite baths or showers into them. No easy task. Bettye soon became very adept at it and Mrs Burt too. They made a good team because Bettye at heart was an interior designer whose main concern was how it would look and Mrs Burt would keep a firm eye on the practicalities of Bettye's schemes — she still does! By the time the Edgcumbe was sold in December 1988 every bedroom had a bath or shower <u>and</u> a WC and they were particularly proud of the fact that they had managed it without losing one bedroom. The hotel was sold with ninety bedrooms all en suite.

For the 1968 season the Armstrongs had a good Head Waiter, John Cobley, who had previously been Head Waiter at the hotel Victoria. By then the Edgcumbe seasons were getting longer and the hotel was only closing from November to March. That year, full central heating had been installed and so it was decided to open for the whole year and run a Christmas programme for a trial period of three years. The first Christmas was a great success. Mary and John Ashworth were home on leave from the Navy and Lorna, Graham Farmer's daughter, and her husband Peter Bicknell and their three sons came to stay. Everyone joined in the activities, including the Fancy Dress with a

John and Tony Cobley, Headwaiters, who learned many 'hotel-ing' skills at the Edgcumbe.

naval theme. It was great fun. Livvy Whittington enjoyed having her young family around her.

In the spring of 1969 John Cobley left to help his wife run Surfstop, her small ten bedroom hotel on Mount Wise, and he suggested his younger brother, Tony, could replace him. So for that season the Edgcumbe had a new Head Waiter, Tony Cobley. He also only worked for the one season and then left to help his wife run 'Camelot', a nine bedroom little hotel in Henver Road. As Head Waiters the brothers were good and they remained in business in the town for some years, aping all they had learned at the Edgcumbe.

In July 1970 John returned from London in time for his twenty-first birthday, which was celebrated at Carrick Cottage, Feock with music by Ken Stratton, of course. He had finished his training at The Cadogan Hotel, Pont Street, SW1 and began working with Mrs Burt at the Edgcumbe. Two projects awaited John's arrival at the Edgcumbe. The first was to make all the arrangements for installing an in-house laundry. The laundry in hotels is extremely important. Before the 1970s all hotel washing had been sent out to the laundry and there was always a bother about whether it would be returned on time. There was much labour involved counting the sheets, pillowcases, towels etc., putting them in laundry baskets, entering them in the laundry book and checking them back on the shelves two or three days later. A lot of work!

In the late sixties there had been a revolution in the laundry world — nylon sheets arrived! A company called Brentford Nylons appeared with a large warehouse on the Great West Road, now the A4, West London. They were selling new nylon sheets and pillow cases which were thin, shiny and slippery — rather like the old fashioned Celanese petticoats. Bettye first encountered them when she borrowed a London flat from a friend, and he said "Will you please wash the sheets before you leave? You can hang them over the bath." Wash the sheets? She had never washed a sheet in her life — she was aghast! But she then discovered how easy they were to wash, and no ironing! Of course those new nylon sheets were as simple to wash as a nylon nightie. From then on Bettye was keen to set up an 'in house' laundry but Mrs Burt, always reluctant to change, was not keen on the idea — she feared she would end up having to do it herself! And so it was not until John Armstrong arrived on the scene for good that the laundry was installed.

John was put in charge of this venture and he put it together very well. First he had to find the space and the rough bedrooms under the ballroom were converted. Then he had to buy the equipment, £10,000 worth (£100,000 today) and finally the linen, which at that time consisted of the new slippery non-iron nylon sheets and pillow cases, and seersucker table cloths and napkins. This was no easy task, but by 1972 the laundry was in operation and all the washing was being dealt with at the hotel, saving in one move the laundry bills which had soared to about £6,000 per annum (£55,000 today). It was also much easier to stuff sheets, etc. in the washing machines than to count them into laundry baskets, and check them back. Of course, later it all became more sophisticated — the nylon sheets and seersucker cloths soon became unacceptable and polyester cotton came in and Brentford Nylons disappeared without trace. Non-iron cotton and polyester sheets, and polyester table clothes and napkins were then used but before long there was another problem. The hotels could not get away without ironing; otherwise the beds looked as though they had been slept in and the table linen looked less than fresh, so rotary irons were introduced. Today all the family hotels have their own well equipped laundries, and iron their linen properly. Standards have improved a great deal since the early days of nylon sheets!

John's second project was to design and put together a disco room. Under the dining room was a dead area without windows in the centre of the building; it was virtually sound-proof. Although so popular with the young, the loud repetitive drumming of disco music can be pure torment to the 'wrinklies' and Bettye and Michael were keen to get it out of earshot. John's disco was called "The Downunder". It had a sunken circular maple dance floor, a silver glittering ceiling and purple felt walls. There was a small adjoining bar and for many years it was a great success. The young congregated down there and played the juke box and on certain nights there were "Junior Discos" for the teeny boppers. At times it became like a teenage club room, but it kept the ground floor of the hotel comparatively quiet and peaceful.

In 1970 in an attempt to improve the winter function business Mr Miller, a very experienced Catering Manager, was engaged. Mr Miller had been at RAF St Eval for years and had catered for royalty and

Mr Miller measuring the waitress' mini skirt. He would only allow 2ins above the knee.

half the 'nobs' in the land. He was old fashioned and in his early '60s. Mini skirts were in and he made all the waitresses kneel on the floor, he then measured the length of their skirts with a tape measure. He would only allow them to be two inches above the knee, and he really thought that too short!

The whole family gathered at the hotel for Christmas, 1970 and there was a very jolly family party which everybody loved. The Edgcumbe Christmases had been hard work: highly successful and much enjoyed, but unfortunately the winter months either side proved impossible. In Bettye's view, the Edgcumbe had never handled functions very well and therefore they had few bookings for dinners, dances, weddings, etc., and so after the three trial years the hotel reverted to being seasonal. Fortunately the seasons were getting ever longer and eventually the Edgcumbe was open from mid-February to mid-November — a far cry from the early pre-War days when it was mid-June to mid-September.

Livvy Whittington had greatly enjoyed the 1970 Christmas with her children, grandchildren and two great grandsons, Toby and Henry aged three and one, around her. Sadly it was to be her last, for in January she developed a heavy cold and sat in her armchair by a roaring fire for three days nursing it, but it turned to viral pneumonia and she was rushed to Treliske Hospial by ambulance in the middle of the night, where she died three days later on 11th January 1971. She was aged eighty-four years. Her family were absolutely devastated by her sudden death. She had been the pillar of wisdom and the cornerstone of their lives and she was sadly missed for a long time.

Soon after she died the family put a heavy teak seat in her memory outside the front of the Edgcumbe where she had loved to sit. It had a brass plaque on the back which read:

In memory of the Founder
O.E.B. Whittington
1887 – 1971

During the following season the plaque was wrenched off the back of the seat and stolen. Just mindless vandalism! Surely the scourge of our towns and cities today?

Olive Whittington was quiet and unassuming, but she was extremely resourceful and had much inner strength. She was utterly devoted to her family and had always been there for them with tea, sympathy, a ready ear, and perhaps, more important, a wise head and a quiet tongue. When she retired in 1947 she had handed over the whole of her meagre assests to Bettye and Peter to help them get started. They receieved £5,000 each and thereafter, for the rest of her life, she gave them her wholehearted support, although she did not always approve of their doings.

O.B.E. Whittington.

The Cavendish, Edgcumbe Avenue
1972-1979

John did well and was very interested in the Edgcumbe Hotel, but before long he was telling his parents he was keen to have his own hotel. They, in turn, thought long and hard about it. On the one hand they felt that a young man who really knows what he wants to do in life must be encouraged, on the other hand John, up to then, had had no responsibility at all. Eventually they decided it would be good for him to be responsible for himself, take his coat off, get down to it and pay his own bills. They agreed to see what was available. There seemed to be two possible hotels: The Pentire with about sixty bedrooms being offered for £55,000 and The Cavendish (which had originally been the Edgcumbe in Edgcumbe Avenue) which they had sold in 1959 for £18,500 with twenty-eight bedrooms and which was back on the market for £40,000 with forty bedrooms. The vendor had earlier bought the two adjoining houses and added them to The Cavendish so that it then would take about a hundred guests comfortably. On the face of it the Pentire Hotel, with potential, was the better prospect, but the Armstrongs were afraid it would be too much for the young John to cope with, and it would have meant him borrowing even more money. After much consideration their own intimate knowledge of the Cavendish convinced them it would be the better project for John. With the help of the Bank and the Western Counties Building Society, some guarantees, a 'little something' from his parents, and a scrape around the bottom of the barrel John offered £38,000, which was

The Cavendish Hotel, circa 1972.

accepted. When the Cavendish Hotel opened for the 1972 season the proud proprietor was John Armstrong, aged twenty-two years.

His parents were somewhat taken aback when, only six weeks later, he advertised in the Daily Telegraph for a Manageress and engaged a capable and experienced woman, old enough to be his mother, to run it for him. That was not exactly what the Armstrongs had had in mind. They had been thinking more of a "roll up his sleeves and get down to it" type of ownership. However, they felt he must get on with it and be allowed to do it his own way, and at least he'd have to take the responsibility for it and pay the bills.

His Manageress, Mrs Edwards, was a formidable woman with black dyed hair who always wore black, but she was personable and hard

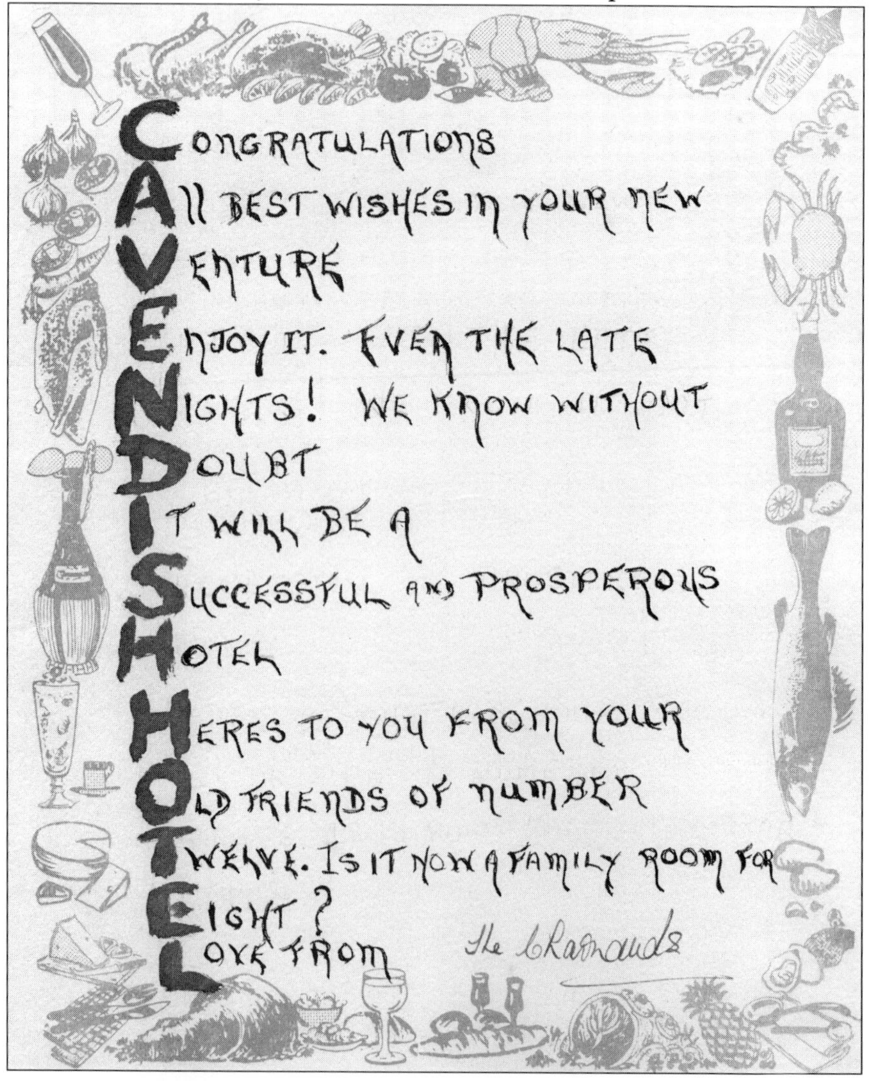

Good wishes to John Armstrong from the Charnaud family in 1972.

working, very experienced and well able to cope with the roughs and toughs who walk in and out of the Newquay hotels in the season. Mrs Edwards managed the Cavendish from the day John opened it to the day he sold it. She worked hard and what was more, she made the staff work hard with her. Her quarters were a comfortable ground floor room in Edgcumbe Lodge. She managed the hotel single handedly and without fuss and very rarely bothered John with the day to day problems associated with a busy hotel, and in those days it was always busy. John saw to that with his advertising — or marketing, as it is now called. Under Mrs Edwards it continued to be the cheery holiday hotel with a happy atmosphere it had been ever since the war — perhaps a little rougher around the edges!

In the summer of 1972 John met an attractive and intelligent girl of seventeen, Carol Harber, whose father was a dentist in Truro. She was at Truro High School where she had achieved good A-levels and she had been offered a place at University. John proposed to her and they

Special Announcement

The Cavendish Hotel has now Changed Hands

John Armstrong of the well known Edgcumbe Hotel, Newquay, has pleasure in announcing that he has recently acquired the Cavendish Hotel, adjoining Narrowcliff sea front and will be opening it for the 1972 season.

The new Cavendish will offer many of the facilities of a larger hotel, but without the prim and pompous atmosphere, and the terms will be very modest indeed — £12 to £22 including all entertainments and hotel facilities.

There will be a heated swimming pool, pool-side barbecues and swimming galas, a Sauna bath, a launderette, a disco evening, and, of course, dancing to our own band three times a week.

There will not be porters opening doors and staff seeking tips at every turn, but a friendly, casual atmosphere of a modern hotel. The menus and cooking will be the best English food, simply served, and of course, there will be plenty of Cornish Cream.

For the children there are very special arrangements :—

Cots and high chairs will be available, supper trays sent up to the bedrooms for the under sixes, a launderette for Mum to do the washing, baby listening in the evenings, film shows, a special party with fancy dress parade and prizes, swimming galas with a silver cup for the champion swimmer, and above all, the help and courtesy of all the staff.

The New Cavendish is certainly the Hotel for everyone who wants a gay, carefree holiday with plenty of entertainment and none of the stuffiness often found in larger hotels.

John Armstrong's proud announcement in 1972.

became engaged in August 1973, when she turned down the place at University. They decided to have a six month engagement, and that winter Carol went to London where she did a secretarial course. They set about house hunting and in the autumn of 1973 John bought an attractive three bedroom cottage with a secluded garden at Higher Tolcarne, St Mawgan in Pydar. "Tolcarne Cottage" was their first home, and they lived there for five years. He paid £17,500 for it and worked hard all the winter getting it ready. John and Carol were married on 16th March 1974 in St Feock Parish Church. The reception for about one hundred and fifty guests was held at The Royal Cornwall Yacht Club in Falmouth. Their honeymoon was spent at the Imperial Hotel, Torquay, still owned and run by Michael Chapman and not yet turned into the stereotype corporate hotel without character it has become today.

The Armstrongs had sold Edgcumbe Lodge behind The Cavendish in 1966 and the new owners of the hotel had a lease on it. The whole of what had been the Edgcumbe garden had been turned into a car park and when John bought The Cavendish he also took on the lease of Edgcumbe Lodge — it was back to the family — jolly useful — ten letting bedrooms and a car park!

It was arranged that for the 1974 season John's bride, Carol Armstrong, who had only left school the previous July, would help Mary and John Ashworth at Watergate to get an insight into the hotel business. John, officially working with Mrs Burt at the Edgcumbe Hotel, coped with the administration of the Cavendish. The family had recently bought Rosemere Hotel at Watergate Bay and re-named it The Beach Hotel, and so in 1974 John was also involved in helping the newly appointed Managers, Peggy and Dickie Bird, with the endless problems there. The Beach was to have a very traumatic season in 1974, as the reader will hear.

One evening in August 1974 John and Carol were dining with her parents at Feock when he received a 'phone call from Mrs Edwards.

"Mr Armstrong, have you taken the week's takings out of the safe?"

"No, I have not", said John.

"Well, they have gone!"

Poor John, he was devastated. The entire week's takings, some £4,000 (about £40,000 today) mostly in cash, had been put in the safe on Saturday ready for banking on Monday morning, but by Sunday evening they had disappeared. The police were called, they interviewed everyone. The money was never found, and eventually the insurance paid out the full amount. John was learning the pit falls of seasonal hotel keeping. The money was never left in the safe over the weekend again.

Although young Armstrong never took on the day to day management of the Cavendish, he did have the overall responsibility for it. Every winter when Mrs Edwards went away to stay with her daughter John and the builders took over and he worked very hard at the renovations and improvements for the following season. The long-term receptionist, who came from a much respected local family, came in daily to deal with the bookings. Mrs Edwards came back every year, full of energy, to spring clean and prepare the hotel for the opening. It was an admirable arrangement and it worked for seven years.

Mrs Edwards and her staff. She successfully ran the Cavendish for John for seven years until he sold it.

The previous owners, Mr and Mrs Bailey, had done well. They had bought the two adjoining houses and doubled the size of the dining room so it then seated one hundred-plus comfortably, and the rest of the rooms in the two houses provided twelve extra bedrooms. In 1972 it was a well balanced little outfit. John went on improving it. He squared up the roof at the front and gave all those rooms baths or showers — minute bathrooms — about 5ft x 4ft 6ins, but in those days size mattered not as long as they were there! In all, he installed baths or showers in twelve rooms. The irony is that had his parents managed to buy even one of the adjoining houses in the '50s they would never have sold the hotel in the first place.

The next four years were very busy for the young Armstrongs. One of John's triumphs at The Cavendish was the installation of the outdoor swimming pool. By the 1970s swimming pools had become very important and he felt there should be one at Cavendish but there really was no room. At the rear of the hotel was a fair size car park —

not really big enough of course — part of which had been the back garden of the two adjoining houses bought by the previous owner. John knew there was no way he would get planning permission for a swimming pool if it meant losing parking spaces. He called in John Battensby, an old family friend who was a landscape gardener and together they roughed up the garden area. Fortunately tarmac had not been laid although it had been used as a car park. They erected an old tumble-down wooden shed and littered the space with old timber, doors, windows, etc., and created what looked like a derelict area so that by the time the planners arrived to inspect the site it looked squalid to a degree. The planners had no hesitation in deciding that a swimming pool would be a big improvement, and the plans sailed through.

Apart from the swimming pool, which was installed for the 1974 season, John made major internal alterations to the building. The two adjoining houses had never been properly linked to the hotel upstairs so he put that right by constructing a corridor through the first floor bedrooms. He made new bedrooms under the eaves in the attics at the back. He moved and enlarged the bar and created a children's playroom. The Cavendish was still faithfully following the successful family formula, catering for families and young people.

Carol was still only twenty years old, but after the 1974 season the Birds retired and she and John agreed to manage the Beach Hotel for the family. The Cavendish continued to flourish under Mrs Edwards, and she kept it going very well for its young owner although John, of course, still had the full responsibility for it.

One day in 1975 John Armstrong was working at the Edgcumbe Hotel with Mrs Burt, when he received a telephone call from an irate guest demanding to see him to complain about something. The man came to the Edgcumbe and John sat him down comfortably and listened to his list of complaints — which was long and detailed. The food was poor, entertainments were all wrong, etc. After a while John could not quite tie up various things the man was saying and the penny dropped. It was all about Bedruthan Steps Hotel. The man had discovered the family connection and the fact that John was at the Edgcumbe and had tracked him down there. John heaved a sigh of relief, listened sympathetically and promised to pass the man's complaints to the right ear. It must be said, however, that sometimes he also had to listen to complaints about his own hotel. It was a rough little joint by the present day standards of the family hotels, but in those days it was still very successful. Newquay's post-war boom had not yet abated.

By the summer of 1978 John and Carol felt they had served their apprenticeship at the Beach Hotel and their thoughts were turning to bigger and better things. They decided they wanted to sell The Cavendish and take on something with more potential. When John's

HEATED SWIMMING POOL
★
CHILDREN'S PLAYROOM
★
DANCING 4 NIGHTS
★
SEPARATE COLOUR TV LOUNGE
★
CAR PARK

COCKTAIL BAR ★ LAUNDERETTE ★ FINEST ENGLISH FARE
52 BEDROOMS ALL WITH KETTLE, RADIO AND INTERCOM
MANY ROOMS WITH PRIVATE BATHROOM ★ BALLROOM

ENTERTAINMENT IN FULL SWING
FROM APRIL TILL OCTOBER

DANCING ★ DISCO ★ BEACH SPORTS ★ FISHING PARTIES
TABLE TENNIS TOURNAMENTS

FOR THE CHILDREN ★ COTS ★ HIGH CHAIRS ★ PARTIES
BABY-LISTENING ★ FILM SHOWS ★ MAGIC SHOW
SWIMMING GALA—SILVER CUP FOR THE WINNER

FREE COLOUR BROCHURE FROM T. ARMSTRONG

Terms: £35·00–£75·00 including all meals (+V.A.T.)
Free offer for Children May and September

1978 advertisement for the Cavendish in the Town Guide.

parents heard they were thinking of trying to buy the Headland, Michael and Bettye felt the young couple were setting their sights too high. But ambition and enthusiasm in the young must be encouraged and so, having made sure that Carol was of the same mind, they gave the project their blessing. The wheels were slowly set in motion to help them on their way and that meant quietly putting The Cavendish on the market, which John did immediately.

There was an element of luck about the timing because by then Mrs Edwards had had enough. Her relationship with John was wearing thin. She had been managing The Cavendish for seven years but when she went for her winter holiday that year, she disappeared and was never heard of again! She was not to know John was in the process of selling the hotel and there might have been another position for her, but on reflection perhaps she did know! She was a most capable Manageress and she had served him well.

It was not expected that The Cavendish Hotel would be easy to sell, but John Armstrong was again extremely fortunate. His next door neighbour, Derek Hayman, who owned the Eliot Hotel, had a burning ambition to own the largest hotel in Newquay. Therefore he was very keen to buy The Cavendish which had fifty-two bedrooms, a swimming pool and parking space to add to his hotel with forty bedrooms, but there was a mighty stumbling block. He had no spare money and was not creditworthy. He owned a block of flats on Pentire and the Eliot Hotel, no doubt both mortgaged to the hilt. He planned to sell the flats and buy The Cavendish. He had great difficulty in selling them and he was unable to arrange a bridging loan.

Meanwhile, John's negotiations about their next venture, the Headland, were going ahead in great secrecy and as the spring came he and Carol began to feel increasingly nervous about the possibility of having to face the season with the two hotels on their hands. Carol had been very busy all the winter taking bookings for the coming season. The Cavendish simply had to open early in April to honour those bookings, regardless of who owned it. It was a nerve-racking time for them!

Eventually in desperation John took a gamble — and it really was a gamble. He gave Hayman possession of The Cavendish while he was still desperately trying to raise the last of the money. John gave him an interest free loan for the balance which was to be repaid by three post dated cheques payable in July, August, and September — really very rash! Fortunately, Hayman managed to sell his flats during that summer and the post dated cheques were met. It was a great relief to John and Carol. He had achieved an excellent price for The

Cavendish. It fetched £225,000.

Hayman then made his biggest mistake. He bought the last terrace house in the block, a double fronted house called Ascot Hotel with nine bedrooms, which gave him an hotel with one hundred and twenty bedrooms, a swimming pool and a car park; he had indeed achieved his ambition to own the largest hotel in Newquay, but he had over-reached himself and he did not manage to keep it for very long. The post-war boom was over and in the mid-eighties Hayman went bankrupt. He disappeared, owing money to the tradesmen in the town who were never paid, and the Eliot Cavendish, as the sprawling monster was by then called, stood empty and derelict for several years until it was acquired by another ambitious 'man of straw'. The next sighting of Derek Hayman was at an exclusive flying club in the Midlands and he apparently had his own plane and a Rolls Royce or Bentley outside. Hearsay had it that his son was still in Newquay, being assisted by Social Security. It makes one think!

The next owner of the Eliot Cavendish was John Cobley, one time head waiter at the Edgcumbe, who picked it up for a song. It was by then in a very poor state and to give Cobley his due he put it together well. He linked The Cavendish and the Eliot properly, refurbished it and proudly invited Bettye to see his improvements. They were splendid. A year or two later he sold the hotel and his other business interests in the town and disappeared overnight without trace. The daily women workers on the next morning bus apparently heard Cobley's young daughter telling everyone "The police came looking for my daddy last night but they didn't find him, he was hiding in the wardrobe." As far as Bettye is aware, he has never been seen again.

The little Edgcumbe/Cavendish in Edgcumbe Avenue stood three generations of the family in good stead for nearly sixty years, and finally it had put John Armstrong on his feet. He had bought the hotel with forty bedrooms and by the time he sold it in 1979 it had fifty-two bedrooms, twelve with baths or showers, a much increased turnover, and most important, the swimming pool.

There was one bonus for John when he moved. When he sold the lease of Edcumbe Lodge behind the hotel, he managed to rescue some of the family treasures his parents had left behind in the house in 1966; pine bookcases, fireplaces, interesting fittings and many other bits and pieces. After all, they had no part in an hotel annexe and in fact wardrobes had been built in front of some of the fireplaces. The treasures were soon put to good use at the Headland.

It saddens Bettye to see the Eliot Cavendish today; it is an overgrown, rambling, hotch-potch of buildings, really too big for its site. It now belongs to a leisure company, which has about a dozen hotels in various resorts and offers package holidays by coach. The original Edgcumbe ground floor has been completely gutted. The hotel now has some seventy-nine bedrooms, most with baths or showers and a lift, and of course John Armstrong's little swimming pool. Considering its size and position it seems, once again, to have found its level but it is a far cry from the row of terrace houses, 1-5 Colchester Villas, built nearly one hundred years ago. Big is not always beautiful and in 2008 one wonders, what next? The lane that once ran behind the hotel parallel to Edgcumbe Avenue now has no right of way — it is blocked off — and there is also a large car park at the rear of the property. With the decline in the coach holidays to Newquay it seems probable that one day that site will be re-developed.

The Eliot Hotel, 2008, formerly The Ascot, Edgcumbe/Cavendish and Eliot Hotels.

The Beach Hotel, Watergate Bay 1974 – 1985 formerly Rosemere

Looking back over the last eighty years the family has not made too many major mistakes — business-wise — but in 1973-1974 the Armstrong clan made one which cost them dearly.

They bought the Rosemere Hotel in Watergate Bay early in 1974. The Cornish tourist boom looked like going on for ever, which everyone now knows did not happen. The family hotels, the Edgcumbe, Watergate Bay, Bedruthan Steps, Bredon Court and The Cavendish were all constantly full and doing very well. Mary and John Ashworth were living in the Coach House at Watergate Bay so it seemed a simple matter to take on a little hotel with twenty six bedrooms in a wonderful position with the beach just nearby. The family plan was that it would run for the 1974 season as it was, and the following winter would be spent putting it together properly. They paid about £60,000 for it.

Rosemere Hotel and tearooms, circa late 1930s. – *Courtesy Cornwall Studies Library*

The Rosemere was badly in need of attention and ripe for development. It stood on a difficult site, steeply sloping at the back and had limited potential, but it had a super position with an easy approach to one of Cornwall's finest beaches and had its own car park, which was very important. As John Ashworth said at the time, he and Mary would be "able to keep an eye on it", as they were living at Watergate Bay. It was also thought that it would slot in well for people who could not get into, or could not afford, Watergate Bay Hotel.

ROSEMERE HOUSE,
WATERGATE, ST. COLUMB MINOR.
Furnished Apartments, modern house, facing sea, close to bathing beach. Picnic parties accommodated. Teas and light refreshments provided. Moderate charges. Apply :—Mrs. BICE.
Mr. T. V. BICE,
Auctioneer and Estate Agent.

Early advert for furnished apartments.

Rosemere had originally been an apartment house at the beginning of the century and had become an hotel in the early 1930s. During the war it was requisitioned by the government, and used as a photographic reconnaissance interpretation unit with a highly hush-hush teleprinter line direct to Whitehall.

After the war it had been run very successfully, in a rather old fashioned comfortable way, by Mrs Nimb. She was a good cook who came from a farming background in Somerset and therefore knew all about good plain country fare. Mrs Nimb's catering, plus the proximity of Watergate beach was a successful formula, but she had sold the hotel years before and by the time the Armstrongs and Ashworths bought it in 1974 it was in a poor state. The widowed vendor, Mrs Lees, had long wearied of it, and was ready to retire. Rosemere needed someone with enthusiasm, vigour and up-to-date ideas to pick it up, shake it up, and modernise it, and that was just what the new owners planned to do with it.

Advert 1950s

The place really was a shambles and with hindsight one must wonder why the family took it on. Nothing, but nothing had been done for years. Doors and even corridors had been blocked up, the floor levels were higgledy-piggledy; it was like a rabbit warren. There were twenty-six small bedrooms and just three public bathrooms. A rickety sun room, badly in need of demolishing, ran the entire length of the front of the building. The only lounge, apart from the sun room, had no windows at all. There was nowhere for staff, and no access at the back. What a place to take on — but at the time the family were full of enthusiasm for it.

The Beach Hotel

The family took Rosemere over in April 1974 and planned to tidy it up as best they could, get through the first season and then do a major restoration job on it the following winter. But first they planned to change its name. It was decided to call it "The Beach Hotel, Watergate Bay" to emphasise the nearby beach. Little did they realise what troubles would beset the new Beach Hotel during its first season.

The first decision about the newly acquired hotel was who was to run it for 1974. At the time some old family friends, Basil and Peggy Bird were living in Cornwall and were wondering what to do next, and they offered to manage the hotel for that season. It was arranged that their assistant would be Tammy Davis, a pleasant, personable girl long known to the whole family. She was charming and did not mind what she did, but like many of that ilk she could not really do anything properly and certainly not paper work. She was to be the receptionist/general assistant and it was felt she would fit in well, be an asset to the hotel and a great help to the Birds who had also known her for many years, and with whom she was on Christian name terms.

Of course, as usual, the first weeks were tiresome to a degree, full of discoveries, both good and bad — at the Beach, mostly bad! A small flat was made for the Birds above the kitchen (which they were to find frightfully airless, hot and noisy). After about six weeks of feverish activity and much surface prettying with pictures, lamps, cushions, rugs, etc., and plenty of fresh flowers, they managed to open, as planned, for the Whitsun holiday at the end of May, 1974. Bettye joined them for the opening dinner, and they cracked a bottle of champagne — the new Beach Hotel was open! So far so good!

Since there was no accommodation for staff, for the first season the Beach staff shared the Watergate staff house up the hill at Tregurrian. That caused a certain amount of friction between the two camps, as can be imagined, but that first season just had to be endured by everyone concerned. It did eventually settle down and the hotel was going well, but in the middle of July it ran into trouble — serious trouble.

In early July a fireman came to stay. He did not like the hotel, nor was he enjoying his holiday, and the weather was bad. He spent his entire time checking on the fire precautions — which were nonexistent! He reported the matter to the local fire authority and the fire officers descended on the hotel. After they had inspected the place — in the middle of July —all hell was let loose. They were absolutely adamant that the hotel was a death-trap and that it must be closed down immediately. Disaster! The place was fully booked for the rest of the season, as was everywhere else in those days.

The family consulted the experts and fought tooth and nail to prevent the closure. They pleaded to be allowed to get through that one season, to no avail. In the middle of July they were taken to court and given 48 hours to get all the guests out and close the place down. The consternation it caused can be imagined. It really was very bad luck that the fireman, unhappy with his holiday, complained to the fire authority. In 1974 there were no inspections or fire certificates as there are today; the rule was the fire authority took no action unless there was a complaint, and then they had to act. Apart from the one disgruntled guest, the hotel would have got through its season and the planned alterations, including the fire precautions, would have been dealt with the following winter, and all would have been well.

As it was, alternative accommodation had to be found for all the guests at the height of the season, and remember this was in the days when all the hotels were constantly full to overflowing. It was devastating! To add to the confusion Tammy Davis had muddled all the bookings. She did not know which bookings were confirmed and which were not — nor who had paid deposits. It was utter chaos! Of course, if it had been one young couple trying to get going with limited capital they would have gone bust then and there, but the Armstrongs and Ashworths had other resources and were therefore able to weather the storm financially. It was all very unpleasant at the time, especially for Peggy Bird and her husband who had to deal with the outraged guests.

While their family coped with this extreme trauma Bettye and Michael were on holiday in Canada. When they returned they were absolutely horrified to hear what troubles their family had been facing. Bettye enraged everyone by saying, "If I had been at home I would not have allowed it to happen!" which was nonsense, of course, because once the hotel had been reported to the fire authorities no-one could have prevented it being closed. Its deficient fire precautions were far too serious. That was the end of the Beach Hotel for that year.

After the débâcle of the 1974 season the Birds retired and John and Carol Armstrong pluckily offered to take on the Beach Hotel, put it right during the winter, and run it for the following season. The arrangement was that Mrs Edwards would continue to manage the

J W A ARMSTRONG, MRS B O ARMSTRONG, MR & MRS J R H ASHWORTH — Page 5
BEACH HOTEL

TRADING AND PROFIT AND LOSS ACCOUNT
YEAR ENDED 31 DECEMBER 1975 — DRAFT

	Page	12 months to 31.12.75 £	11 months to 31.12.74 £
INCOME			
Residential		46,356	)
Bar takings		6,421	)5,174
Sundry		2,587	)
		55,364	5,174
EXPENSES			
Salaries and wages		13,843	3,807
Provisions		11,845	1,769
Wines, spirits and cigarettes		2,635	227
Rent and rates		1,105	315
Insurance		439	316
Lighting and heating		1,395	237
Repairs to property		6,000	408
Repairs and renewal of equipment		3,252	2,673
Cleaning and laundry		578	120
Postage, printing, stationery and advertising		2,431	1,076
Telephone		627	223
Entertainments		1,596	209
Motor expenses		315	4
Bank charges and interest		2,681	7,257
Bank loan interest		4,959	-
Depreciation		2,834	1,645
Professional fees		498	250
Sundry equipment rental		1,397	36
Suspense accounts		881	-
		59,311	20,572
Net loss	4	(3,947)	(15,398)

Trading and Profit and Loss Account year ended 31 December 1975.

Cavendish for John while he and Carol ran the Beach, and that is how it was to be for the next four seasons.

The young Armstrongs then had a very busy winter. The ramshackle sun room which sprawled across the front of the hotel was demolished and replaced by an up to date facade with saw shaped windows designed by John Crowther. A swimming pool was installed at the back and extra land bought from the Young-Jamiesons to make a crazy golf course behind the swimming pool — not a great success! The site was really too exposed and too steep. The kitchens were gutted, a recreation room with a bar and a small dance floor were made on the lower ground floor, bedrooms improved; some showers and baths installed — without losing rooms and that was another mistake because they were all too small.

A badly sited troublesome swimming pool at roof level behind the hotel.

But most difficult of all was the swimming pool; that really was a long term disaster. To begin with the site was technically almost impossible. A massive and hugely expensive retaining wall had to be built to provide the level site required. The pool was at second floor level behind the hotel with the filter house ten feet below the level of the water! There was a sea view across the hotel roof! Not ideal. The cheapest possible D.I.Y. pool kit with a flimsy liner was bought for £1,000 and that caused constant trouble. The whole undertaking was a nightmare, but the family were trying to do it on a shoestring, yet another big mistake!

It was decided to fill the pool from a hose pipe attached to a tap in the kitchen, 20 feet below it, which had to be left running all day and all night for several days. In the middle of one night the hose came off the tap and the water flowed back into the kitchen, which by morning was awash, as was the dining room with its new carpet! Oh that pool did cause trouble! It just shows 'penny pinching' does not work in hotels; everything gets such a trouncing, equipment must be robust.

Another problem which had to be tackled for the 1975 season was 'staff rooms'. Sharing the Watergate staff house hadn't worked at all. Fortunately, there was a run-down chalet type of house for sale half-way up the hill to Trevarrian, called "Spring Valley", and was just near enough to the hotel and, what was equally important, just far enough away! (Staff houses are notoriously noisy!) It was a ramshackle little house hardly fit for human habitation. It cost £20,000 and partitions

The first advertisement for the new Beach Hotel. Note the Fire Certificate number.

were hurriedly erected and one or two basins installed to adapt it for the staff. The little house had three advantages — it was quiet, sunny, and well situated. It provided five rather cramped staff rooms and was used until the hotel was sold ten years later when the Ashworths bought it for the Watergate staff.

Early in 1975 the family bought the house next door to the Beach Hotel, for £25,000. The owners left £10,000 on second mortgage and for that season the Armstrongs managed to use the rooms as guest bedrooms and the two garages became temporary extra staff rooms — the roughest of staff rooms without windows or proper floors, but the kitchen porters loved them; they were adjoining the pub next door!

By that time John and Carol Armstrong really had got into their stride. The Beach was doing well, notwithstanding the difficulties, and the Armstrongs were full of ideas for joining the new house to the hotel. John got to work with John Crowther, and they had another busy winter 1975-1976. The furniture and fittings from the Beach Hotel were moved to the Watergate Bay hotel when it closed at the end of the season, and work began, with John Armstrong in charge of the building operations. The house had been built with garages at ground floor level with two floors above. John dug out the whole of the ground floor under the house and virtually made it into a three storey building, which gave the Beach valuable extra bedrooms, all with bathrooms, but some of them were still small. John later recalled that it cost him a whole night's sleep agonising over whether every room in the new wing should have a bath or shower. He decided they should and in the morning instructed his foreman accordingly. That was a wise decision. They made a children's playroom, and a laundry and by the time the Beach Hotel opened for the 1976 season it had fifty bedrooms, many with baths or showers — and although most were too small the hotel was much improved. It had been a very hard winter for John who had been on the building site every morning at 8.00 a.m., and for Carol, busy with the bookings. They had worked hard and they worked well together, but there was one little hiccup to be dealt with before the season began.

The rooms John had been building were not what Carol had been booking! She didn't know which were doubles or twin-beds nor which were big enough to take a child's bed extra. "How could that happen?" asked John's mother when it came out. "Well", said John, "Carol (then only twenty years old) is very shy, and she couldn't get to the bedrooms being built without climbing up a ladder. If she went up the ladder she would get wolf whistles from the builders, so she didn't see the rooms until it was too late, and they were already booked". The pillow talk must have been about something else!

Beach Hotel building site, winter 1975. John Armstrong was on the site at 8.00 a.m. each day.

However, they got over that and the 1976 season went amazingly well, although it was still very much hands on for the young Armstrongs. Carol had to relieve the barman and the receptionist at times, John had to do the weekly dining room plan and stoke up the coal-fired boiler every night to make sure the water would be hot in the morning. It was heavy going, but it was a good training ground for them. The guests were happy and they managed to get reasonably good staff and keep them, but there was to be a nasty little hitch at the end of that season.

It had been a very hard year. The hotel closed on Saturday 29th September and Carol and John had a pressing date with friends up country. So they waved their last guests off on the Saturday morning, worked all day feverishly putting things away and locking everything up, and went off for a well earned holiday. There were about half a dozen staff who had asked if they might stay on until the following morning when they would go their various ways. "Certainly." said the Armstrongs. That night the staff who had stayed broke into the cocktail bar, had an all night party, drank everything in sight and then disappeared, never, of course, to be heard of again. That was the last time the Armstrongs would leave their hotel at the end of the season without seeing all staff off the premises, and the hotel firmly locked up first — another lesson learned the hard way!

HONEYMOONS AT THE BEACH

The Beach is not a 5 Star, de-luxe hotel — we have no bridal suite. However, we do have wonderful cliff scenery, miles of golden sand, a pleasant informal atmosphere, and, should you feel so inclined, dancing and entertainment.

We invite you to accept with our compliments a bottle of wine, and in May, and from mid-September, we offer specially reduced terms.

'Snazzy' advertisement to lure honeymooners.

Then all went well with the Beach Hotel for the next three years when another problem arose. One day in the summer of 1978 after John and Carol had been running the hotel for some five years, whilst walking the dogs with his mother on Watergate beach John suddenly said "Carol and I hear The Headland is on the market and we would like to buy it." Bettye was astounded and in an effort to put on the brake said "Firstly, you would need all the money you could raise, and secondly there is no-way you could run The Headland unless you lived on the premises. You would have to sell your house in St Mawgan and move into The Headland." "Yes, we know that", said John. But there was no doubt he and Carol had already firmly made up their minds. Carol was only twenty-three at the time and John's parents thought they were too young, but buy it they did as the reader will hear, and then the big question of life was who was going to run the Beach?

In the spring of 1979 advertisements were placed in the *Caterer* and a manager was appointed. There were many applications for the position but only one couple was interviewed, Stephen Swire and his wife Becky, who travelled down from Worcester. The family was so convinced that the young man was right they decided not to interview anyone else, and no references were taken up. What faith the family collectively had in their own judgement and it proved to be sound! But what was not realised at the time was that Stephen and Becky Swire were virtually on their honeymoon when they took on the management of The Beach Hotel. Poor Becky. She had had no experience of hotels — some honeymoon! The Beach was to prove a hard initiation — no wonder she decided later that hotels were not for her.

When the hotel opened for the 1979 season with Stephen Swire in charge the first guest to arrive, who happened to have a heart condition, was shown to his room on the top floor. He attempted to open the warped iron frame window which badly needed replacing and the whole frame came adrift in his hand — the hinges had rusted out! Fortunately, he clung to it bravely until help arrived, for had it fallen it would have crashed through the glass roof into the kitchen below. The trouble was ALL the old windows were in much the same state — there was still a great deal of work to be done, but it had to wait. Happily most of the windows were replaced for the following season.

In the smaller, lesser hotels it is always difficult to find — and keep — a good chef, and that was an on-going problem at the Beach. Stephen Swire caught one of his chefs with a van fully loaded with food stolen from the hotel ready for his winter trip to the Canaries. The foolish fellow wrote to his mother detailing all the food he was stealing and then left the letter lying around! Swire promptly sacked him.

As is well known pilfering is rife in hotels and it is not always easy to catch the culprits. The Swires, conscientious as they were, spent hours trying to catch out thieving staff, such as the waitress known to be stealing bottles from the bar who successfully evaded detection. Sometimes they were more successful and then of course the thief had to be dealt with which often created more difficulties. Stephen Swire also recalls:

The second week into our exciting new job, Saturday changeover, quite a fullish house expected and Becky was faced with raw sewage coming down the corridor by the TV lounge and children's playroom, to meet her in a tidal wave, and you can guess her reaction! The system had packed up somewhere. What a mess! New young manager with newish young bride had words about this 'get away from it all' opportunity in Cornwall.

Another incident which comes to mind was when our receptionist, Eileen Green who had a particularly dry sense of humour telephoned me in our 'flat' upstairs to say that she had one of our elderly residents standing at the reception desk and she was "looking a little damp". Did I think I could come down? I arrived in Reception to find a grandmother of about 85 years standing at the desk shivering, absolutely soaked. She had turned on the cold water tap in her room and it had come off in her hand. "Yes, it is still spraying water all over my room." We went to her room to find it calf deep in water, and her nightie, lace underclothes, and other personal effects were floating around the room. It was lucky the poor woman had not suffered a heart attack. I remember a very nasty interview with her son who was much displeased!

Stephen remembers, wryly, the "company car" provided for his use — a fifteen year old Mini! "He has let his imagination run away with him there", says Bettye. In fact it was the little automatic Mini, about three years old, which had been bought in the hope that Michael Armstrong would be able to drive after he had had his stroke in 1977. Sadly, Michael never did drive again.

Stephen Swire was a very good manager. He was properly trained, personable, honest, and full of integrity and enthusiasm. His wife did the flowers, charmed the guests, and arranged the entertainments. She was also an expert horsewoman and she kindly gave young Toby Ashworth riding lessons. The Swires both worked hard at the Beach Hotel and of course it was helpful to them to have Mary and John Ashworth nearby for advice and support in the early days.

The Beach was never the easiest hotel to run. There were not enough private bathrooms or showers and many of the rooms were too small. It really took too many guests, with children's beds tucked in the corners in many rooms. The Swires settled down and managed the hotel for the next four seasons, until the end of 1982, by which time they also had aspirations and felt ready and able to take on something a bit more up-market.

It is interesting how a chance remark can trigger a whole string of events and alter the course in a quite dramatic way. In about 1982, an estate agent rang Bettye and said The Nare hotel at Veryan would be coming on the market and were the family interested? The family descended en masse on The Nare for lunch one day to have an unofficial look around, and they decided yes, they were interested. Very interested! They were thinking of selling The Beach Hotel, buying The Nare and installing the Swires as managers, and Bettye sounded Stephen Swire out as to whether, if the family bought The Nare, he would be prepared to manage it. In the event The Nare did not come on to the market at that time — the owners withdrew it. However Stephen Swire had become unsettled and was very keen to take on a 3-star hotel. The family was anxious not to lose him and they offered him the management of either the Headland or the Watergate. The Armstrongs and the Ashworths both wanted him, but John Ashworth was more persuasive and persistent, and Stephen Swire, preferring to stay in the country, chose to go to Watergate Bay. Mary and John were delighted as by that time they had a house in St Mawgan village and three young sons aged fifteen, thirteen and eight years needing their attention and they were ready to distance themselves from the day to day running of the hotel. They had long wished to delegate some of their responsibilities so that they would be freer to give more time to their boys, and to their other interests. For the 1983 season the Ashworths appointed the Swires Managers of Watergate Bay Hotel and the Swires moved across the road to take up their appointment and that was when the difficulties with the Beach Hotel really became apparent.

Under the Armstrongs and the Swires the Beach Hotel ran smoothly and the guests were happy, because they all worked very hard making them so — although it was not really very profitable. Being only of two star standard and with a short season it really was not big enough to warrant a manager's salary, but that was not the Swires' fault and they did a very good job.

When the Swires decided to move to Watergate Bay Hotel in April 1983 the family was immediately in difficulty about the management of the Beach. The truth was by then no one in the family was really interested in it and it became a bothersome irritation in the corner. After many discussions it was decided to put it on the market, but still there was the ongoing problem of how it was to be managed until a buyer could be found.

Everyone was delighted when Graham Farmer's daughter, Lorna, and her husband, Peter Bicknell, to whom she had been happily married for nearly 30 years, accepted Bettye's offer to come to Cornwall and manage The Beach Hotel until it was sold. They were both just retiring from British Airways after many years service and were wondering "What next?" Lorna and Peter were well qualified. Lorna, Bettye's cousin, was an ex BOAC stewardess with previous hotel experience and her husband, Peter, was very experienced in air line cabin management and dealing with people world wide. He had retired from British Airways as Director of Cabin Services. They looked upon it as a challenge and a challenge it was to be! The Bicknells arrived in January, 1983 from their home in Surrey with a van load of clobber and two dogs.

Lorna's and Peter's Recollections

After a family Christmas at our Surrey home, we set off, complete with three boys, two dogs, and selected belongings in a hired van and the two family cars, on 4th January 1983. It was about 4.30 p.m. when we pulled up outside The Beach Hotel and unlocked the main doors. As we walked in the reception telephone was ringing. "Hello, Beach Hotel?" a northern voice said, "Can you do us a double room in the middle of June?" I opened the booking chart which was lying on the desk and entered the reservation with a flourish. The season had begun!

In the following dark, cold windy days a tour of the 'new baby' revealed some of the features which made it a daunting task for the new "Have a Go" management. In three bedrooms were discovered dozens of black plastic bags full of linen, blankets, bed covers of all colours and sizes and pillows galore. How and where to sort these was a nightmare, but good luck prevailed. An ex-housekeeper from the Watergate hotel was more than happy to take on this difficult task. A bit of a battle-axe, but she sorted every bedroom with its correct eiderdowns etc., and they all looked most presentable. What a blessing she was; she enabled us to get on with other tasks.

A tour of the kitchens and store rooms was even less encouraging as water penetration had occurred and a great deal of work would be required to put them in proper working order. Water penetration had also happened in the dining room and the carpet was soaking (both kitchen and dining room being blessed with a flat roof). The Beach Hotel operated throughout the season with this hazard. Patching up was done from time to time but in wet weather the guests sat among basins and buckets catching the drips while they took their meals. Fortunately in mid summer it was hot and dry most of the time.

A serious difficulty was that the swimming pool could not be made ready in time for the opening. It was found to have a leaking plastic lining and there was some concern about a subsidence crack in the supporting wall. The pool was built in the centre of the terrace behind and above the hotel. There were visions of this wall collapsing in mid-season and water sweeping into the reception and the kitchen, which backed on to it! A Surveyor gave assurance that such a calamity was a long time away. A new plastic liner was ordered, but this did not arrive until the hotel had already opened. John Armstrong, Peter Bicknell and 'Jimbo', the maintenance man fitted it. There was much shoving, pushing, sliding in bare feet on the bottom and sides as the pool was filling. At last success and a relief to all as the visitors expected a swimming pool as per brochure! Lorna was able to start the children's Swimming Gala, which was so popular every Wednesday morning, with a prize-giving at the end of a noisy and hilarious session.

From the beginning to the end recruiting of staff proved to be difficult. It was not easy to find the right people to work in this family hotel which provided full board and welcomed children and dogs. There was some form of entertainment every night and beach sports, swimming galas, and competitions such as car rallies on most days. Finding a Chef to suit the full board requirement was an enormous problem. None of them wanted to cook lunch, but we thought we had solved it when we saw an applicant who had worked on The Canberra to the Falkland Islands. He wanted to settle in Cornwall and work his way into the holiday hotel business and we engaged him. The kitchen was attacked with a ship's chef's enthusiasm, after some essential repairs had been completed, and all the equipment cleaned and put in working order. Menus were arranged, food ordered, the kitchen brigade recruited and there was every reason to suppose that a good choice had been made. His cooking skills were, however, never to be tried.

As the weeks went by and bookings came in, it was decided the Beach Hotel should not open until Whitsun. This gave more time to find the right staff, and finish essential decorations and repairs. Whitsun came quickly enough and on the opening day the hotel looked splendid with fresh flowers everywhere and it was pleasing to see the guests arriving — some 36 in number — children, babies and dogs included and all seemingly happy with their accommodation.

On the morning of opening day, news from the kitchen was, however, alarming. Chef was nowhere to be found. All the food was in, the menu decided, kitchen in good order, but Chef missing! The second chef, an ex-army corporal from the Catering Corp. took over and produced a perfectly good dinner. Cousin Bettye was invited to the opening cocktail party to greet the guests and to dinner. There, whilst entertaining, we could see two Police officers going to the reception desk and Peter had to go with them to the chef's quarters. His belongings were found all in order, including passport and address book. It was known he had taken the previous day off and the Police started the "missing persons" procedure. It was not until the following day that the chef was found 25 miles away, soaked to the waist, and wandering in a daze. It seemed he had had a nervous breakdown, brought on by the prospect of running a full board kitchen, six days a week, in a 50 bedroom hotel. Life on the Canberra must have been too comfortable! The second chef was then promoted and he proved capable and willing but unfortunately at the end of July he gave notice and moved to an hotel in Newquay where he could earn more money. He would not have to produce luncheon and what was more, he could enjoy the lovely Newquay night life. We could not compete against that — so we lost him! As can be imagined this was very worrying at the height of the season and we could find no one locally. Eventually, we engaged a chef from Newcastle and he stayed for the rest of the season, but not without causing problems. Having established himself, with some success, he started a campaign to pressure the management into increasing the wages for all the kitchen and dining room staff. This did not work entirely in his favour, due to his unpopularity in the dining room. He was a "Gazza" type whose brash manner was not appreciated by the waiting staff. Some re-arrangement of the work rota and a change of full lunch to a self service buffet overcame the situation but in mid-season it was all very difficult and we could have done without it.

There was no doubt the staff worked very hard, and mostly in harmony. During one week there were 135 adults plus 17 infants in high chairs in the dining room. Breakfast was what Winnie Farmer would describe as "hell up" with toddlers screaming and scrambled egg everywhere. Thankfully children's suppers at 5.30 p.m. were more peaceful.

Another problem was that the only tradesmen's entrance was at the front of the hotel in full view of the guests — in fact under the dining room windows, and everything had to come in and out that way. The dustbins stood there in a little house built for them — very difficult to keep it all tidy and sweet smelling during the heat of the summer!

There was a kitchen porter we had been persuaded to take on by the Job Centre — a young man who had lost one eye in an accident and had a dreadfully scarred face as a result. He was an excellent worker and we felt as long as he kept to the kitchen and avoided the front of the hotel his grotesque appearance mattered not. But sometimes he would appear sitting in the front, in the sun outside the kitchen while off duty in the afternoons. The children found the look of him very frightening. Poor chap! We had not the heart to tell him to hide himself. When he left, his replacement was better looking, but not nearly such a good worker.

The visitors enjoyed the entertainment provided every night, especially as there was an excellent baby-sitting service. There was a children's fancy dress party organised by the popular Ken Stratton, early on Wednesday night, followed by the adults' fancy dress, which proved enormous fun for all. Dance night on Friday was usually slow to start and we invariably took to the floor to get things going! With a bit of mingling and with Ken's encouragement and whipping it up most guests were strutting on the floor and often this led to a Conga, which wended its way out of the hotel and across the road to the Watergate ballroom! This they thought was great fun although we never had the pleasure of a return Conga from the Watergate — wonder why??

Fortunately, the weather remained hot and sunny for the rest of the season. Despite repeated staff problems (one evening a waiter — from Liverpool — stormed out of the hotel in the middle of dinner, throwing his jacket and bow tie on the floor, shouting abuse at the management) the season ended on a cheerful note, and we felt that it had been successful. We were very pleased when later in the year John Ashworth told us the turnover for the year was up on the previous years, and the expenses were down. In the main we had enjoyed it.

It was a truly rewarding experience to say goodbye to guests returning home after one or two weeks with us, having really enjoyed their holiday and, of course, the exceptionally hot and sunny weather, and many were booking for 1984. So the Bicknells survived their 'ordeal by fire', but decided not to return to the Beach Hotel for another season — Surrey was calling!

Bettye asked what had been the most tiresome aspects of the season. We had to admit that it would have been a great deal easier staff wise if we could have cut out lunches and just offered guests dinner, bed and breakfast as most small hotels were doing at that time. Also, if we are honest, we would have preferred to have had a freer hand and been left to solve the many problems in our own way, but it had been a most interesting season and we would not have missed it for anything. Bettye was of the opinion that we did not have enough backing from the family, but it must be said we never felt that, and Stephen and Becky Swire, from whom we had taken over and who by then were Managers at Watergate Bay, were very staunch supporters..

Lorna's and Peter's account of the 1983 season at the Beach sums it up very well. It was a great disappointment to the Armstrongs and Ashworths when they decided to return to Surrey. It had been a very tiresome season and they had coped magnificently. Everyone hoped they would settle down in Cornwall, but sadly it was not to be. Peter Bicknell soon found another appointment and one which suited him perfectly. He became the flats manager at Dolphin Square, London, where he remained until he finally retired twelve years later and, as an appreciation of his work there, had a "golden handshake".

With the departure of Lorna and Peter Bicknell the family decided it was even more important to sell the hotel and get it off their hands.

That was not so easy — it was on the market all the winter but proved impossible to sell, and with the 1984 summer looming it obviously had to be run for the season. By January 1984 no buyer had been found and there was no one to run it, and for the family the place had just become a damned nuisance.

Eventually a manager was appointed — in desperation — in the hope that he would cope until the hotel was sold. He was a young man called Harris who had worked at the Edgcumbe as a barman and waiter. He came from a decent background, had been to a good school, and the family knew him. Before long he asked if his girl friend could join the staff to help him manage the hotel and that was arranged but was utterly disastrous, and the Ashworths had no peace that summer. They were constantly being called to The Beach to deal with problems and complaints from guests.

One day the Beach Hotel guests were all assembled on the Watergate beach ready for the children's weekly sand-building competition and the manager's girlfriend, whose job it was to run it, was missing. Eventually she was found in bed — sleeping it off. She and her boyfriend had been partying half the night — some management!

In the middle of the season a stock take of the liquor was taken and clearly there was something amiss. The figures were wrong and obviously stock was missing. There was a huge fuss. John Armstrong arrived and sent Harris to his bedroom and told him to stay there while stocks were checked and it turned out that Harris and his girlfriend had been 'living the life of Riley' at the hotel's expense. Harris handed over a gold ring in lieu of part of the deficiency and also forfeited his wages and was packed off home. Before long his father, who was a solicitor, was threatening John with prosecution for wrongful imprisonment by sending the young man to his room, and claiming that the gold ring the boy had handed over was rightfully his. What a to-do! Soon, the father came down to see John at The Headland Hotel. The figures were checked and re-checked and it turned out that there had been no actual stealing — just the two of them and their friends partying and drinking the profits! The gold ring was handed back to the father, the young man forfeited his salary and bonus to cover the deficiency and that was the end of the matter — and it was the end of the Beach too as far as the Armstrongs and Ashworths were concerned. Fortunately it was almost the end of the season and the hotel very soon closed for good. It was a great relief all round, but the family had had enough and were ready to give the place away.

They were so desperate to get rid of the Beach by the end of that season they tried to sell it at auction. It was offered at the Molesworth Arms at Wadebridge in October of that year, but failed to reach its reserve of £245,000. Finally the sale came about because of a chance conversation in St Mawgan Village shop when Mr and Mrs Wharry, who ran it, told the Ashworths they were looking for a small hotel. In the spring, 1985 they bought the Beach for £197,000 — with some money left behind on second mortgage which, happily, was soon paid off. The family were thankful to get it off their hands although they had lost some £100,000. They had learned their lesson the hard way — never again would they take on an hotel unless one member of the family was prepared to move into it and be fully responsible for it, and later they were to turn down a very good proposition for that one reason: when they sat around a table to decide who would be responsible for it, there was no one willing and able to take it on. Some members of the family were not available and others simply said they had no stomach for it, and so they decided not to proceed.

On the plus side, John and Carol had 'served their apprenticeship' and gained much experience that would stand them in good stead at The Headland. To run a smallish down-market hotel is very hard for the Owner/Managers because they must be 'Jacks of all trades' able to relieve anywhere at any time, but there is no better way of learning the business. The day-to-day problems in an hotel are the same regardless of standard or size. Guests and staff have to be 'managed'. The 'tricks of the trade' cannot be learned on paper at a college. Owner/Managers have to relieve the barman for meals and his day off, at times deal with the laundry and the reception office and arrange the dining room seating plan, which if there are no spare tables can be very tricky. The wife must do the housekeeping and oversee the bedrooms. They must personally see the place locked up at night and constantly be on call, whereas in the larger, more up-market establishments, staff cover all these duties. Some owners do it very happily and, it must be said, in the early days the Armstrongs and Whittingtons did just that. The family has long progressed beyond DIY hotel keeping and today all the family hotels are larger and manned by properly trained professional staff. Thank goodness! For the whole family, from Graham Farmer down, the most exciting aspect of the hotel business has always been "What can we do next?" and The Beach simply did not offer enough scope — but it had served its purpose as a training ground and much had been learnt.

In retrospect the sad saga of The Beach Hotel was caused by two major errors of judgement. At the outset there was no one person taking full responsibility for it, also the family were slow to realise how rapidly hotel standards were rising by the 1970s. Had it been converted into a thirty-six bedroom hotel with larger rooms, more bathrooms and to a higher standard, it would have been easier to fill with guests and more straight-forward to manage. Peter Whittington, ahead of his time, was much more farsighted when he rebuilt Bedruthan Steps in the 1970s and Trevelgue in the 1980s. He built enormous rooms, thought at the time to be overlarge, but by the 1990s just right. His ability to think big stood him in good stead.

The second mistake at The Beach was a family reluctance to change. For some sixty years seaside holiday hotels had offered full board terms which meant all meals including lunch but by the mid 1970s most hotels had cut out luncheon. Not so this family. For a long time the Whittingtons, Armstrongs, and Ashworths insisted on including lunch in their terms and that made life difficult for the managers to get and keep good staff. There were plenty of jobs going where only breakfast and dinner were served and the day could be spent on the beach. Today lunch is never included.

Finally, as far as the family was concerned, after the Swires had moved to Watergate Bay Hotel the greatest difficulty of all was to find a responsible Manager; they didn't suceed in doing so but a valuable lesson had been learned.

Rosemere once again

When the new owners, Mr and Mrs Wherry, bought the Beach Hotel in 1985 they immediately changed its name back to Rosemere. They reduced the bedrooms to 40 — a very wise move. The swimming pool was put right by lining it with concrete.

They ran it in a very personal 'hands-on' way and lived on the premises staying open all the year catering mainly for coach parties and Rosemere reverted to what it had been many years before in Mrs Nimb's time; a quietly successful hotel, which was much more appropriate than what the Armstrongs had tried to do with it.

The Headland Hotel, Newquay 1979 – 2008

Brief history of The Headland

The Headland Hotel Company was formed in 1897 with the express intention of building the finest hotel in the South West. The architect was Silvanus Trevail. When work began there was much opposition from the locals, who claimed the hotel was being built on common land. Feelings ran high and local workmen were intimidated into stopping work. One night a group came up from the town and pulled down the foundation walls, burned the scaffolding and threw the foreman's hut into the sea. The Newquay Riots, as they were known, resulted in all work grinding to a halt. Two hundred unemployed miners from Redruth were recruited because the locals were unwilling to return to the site. As the new workers arrived in Newquay, traction engines equipped with steam hoses were used to keep the resentful locals at bay. The whole town was ablaze with contention.

The hotel was finished in 1900 to the highest modern standards of the day. It was the first hotel in Newquay to have electric light which was provided by its own DC generator installed in a remote underground chamber. The Headland was converted to the mains in 1921 when many hotels were still boasting incandescent gas lighting. It was most up to date! There were two bathrooms for gentlemen and two for ladies on each floor; and hot baths were 1/6d extra (7?p). Every bedroom had a fireplace, hot and cold running water, electric light, and an electric service bell. The third floor bedrooms, intended

Playing quoits on the lawn circa 1920.

Newquay 5

NEWQUAY, CORNWALL.

HEADLAND HOTEL

THE LARGEST and MOST PALATIAL HOTEL in the West of England.

EVERY LUXURY, combined with MODERATE CHARGES.

Situated in the VERY BEST POSITION on the unrivalled Coast of North Cornwall.

ELECTRIC LIGHT. ELECTRIC LIFTS.

OCEAN VIEW FROM EVERY WINDOW.

SPLENDID BATHING BEACHES on shore off the Hotel Grounds, which comprise OVER 5 ACRES.

The Golf Links adjoin.

Corridor Express Trains from Paddington, G.W.R.

Apply to the MANAGER.

1902 Advert.

for guests' servants, were furnished for 30/6d. each (£1.52), those on the second floor for 45/- (£2.25), whilst the furnishings for the finest rooms on the first floor cost £5 per room. The Headland opened in June 1900. The first manager was dismissed after six months for unexplained stock deficiencies — nothing really changes!

King Edward VII and Queen Alexandra stayed at the hotel on several occasions in the first decade of the century. In 1911 the Prince of Wales, later Edward VIII, came to The Headland to convalesce. His younger brother Prince Albert, later King George VI, joined him for company. The two princes occupied Rooms 102, 103 and 104 as a suite on the first floor. During this stay they visited friends in the county and had tea with the Tangye family at Glendorgal.

HM King Edward VII and Queen Alexandra on the steps of The Headland Hotel.
Cornish Studies Library

Between the wars the hotel was very stylish. The famous Black and Silver Ballroom with sprung floor was created in the early thirties from what had previously been a drawing room and a writing room. It was

The Black and Silver Ballroom 1930.

Drawing room

Writing room

Headland Hotel 1930.

spectacular. Fashionable London dance orchestras were booked for the summer seasons and the BBC broadcast Palm Court music from there regularly. The maple ballroom floor is very finely sprung and is certainly the finest in the county. In its pre-war hey-days the hotel was managed most ably long-term by Major and Mrs Polglase. They were much respected figures in the town, and there is no doubt that until 1939 The Headland was the most exclusive hotel in the south west.

Headland Hotel Hall and Bar 1930.

During the Second World War the hotel was requisitioned and became an RAF hospital for the duration; many of the casualties at Dunkirk were brought to The Headland in June, 1940. Numerous local girls became nurses and worked there as VADs throughout the war. Everyone had to take on war work of some kind.

When The Headland was de-requisitioned in 1946 it had been badly knocked about. The building was vandalised over the next few years, and an attempt was made to 'modernise' it, which was utterly inappropriate. Every fireplace on the ground floor was pulled out and replaced with low modern tiled ones. The marble pillars at the foot of the staircase were boxed in with plywood; some were thrown out completely and replaced with a modern utility glass screen. Original tiled floors were ripped up and replaced with lino. All the fireplaces were ripped out of the bedrooms, never to be replaced. Fine panelled doors were replaced with flimsy plain ones made of plywood or hardboard.

The work at The Headland was undertaken by a local builder, A F Luxon. The major post-war repairs needed at The Headland were exorbitantly expensive, went on for years, and at times were shoddy[1] and Mr Luxon sometimes agreed to accept shares in the company in lieu of payment. In this way he gradually became a major shareholder and in 1952, with a cash adjustment, he was able to buy out the other shareholders and so became the owner of The Headland Hotel. After the war The Headland went into a slow decline which lasted some thirty-three years until John Armstrong took it over in 1979.

The original approach to Mr Luxon was made by John's parents on his behalf. It was felt that if he wrote it would not be taken seriously — he was still in his twenties. When the first approach was made to the owner of The Headland Hotel in September 1978, they were told "Yes, the hotel is on the market, but an offer has been accepted and contracts are being drawn up." So the hotel was virtually sold and there seemed no point in discussing it further at that stage.

John and Carol Armstrong were very disappointed — they thought they had missed it. However, they were not without hope, as John knew that the prospective buyer was Tony Cobley, who had been Head Waiter at the Edgcumbe only a few years before. He therefore thought it possible that the deal might not be quite straightforward, and as it turned out it wasn't!

There was nothing to be done but wait and see what happened — a very nerve-racking wait for the Armstrongs, but nevertheless they went ahead with their preparations. Within three months their house, Tolcarne Cottage in St Mawgan, had been tidied up ready for selling

---

[1] A recent Nare guest recalled to Bettye staying at The Headland in the early 1930s with his parents. He said "it was all chintzy, lovely, and very much first class". In the early 1950s he returned for the first time and was shocked to the core. He said it was all rexine and linoleum. He asked the long-term concierge "What has happened?" The concierge replied "Well you see Sir; people like you don't stay here any more." Bettye suggested he would be amazed if he saw it now – perhaps he'll return one day!

and was on the market. They sold it for £34,500 in December 1978 and gave possession in January 1979. The young Armstrongs were then virtually homeless but at that time it was still by no means certain that they would manage to buy The Headland. As it happened John's parents had bought a bungalow in Newquay that year into which they planned to move, and John and Carol were able to camp there, amongst the builders, while they waited anxiously to hear the outcome of the deal with Cobley. Eventually Mr Luxon contacted John and said the sale of The Headland seemed not to be progressing and therefore he asked John to make an offer. John had already made his arrangements with the bank and was confident that he would be able to sell the Cavendish. He offered Mr Luxon £420,000, which was accepted. The negotiations for The Headland were cloaked in secrecy; the Armstrongs even had to view the hotel after dark in case they were seen there. No agents were involved and amazingly they managed to do the deal without a local leak. Tony Cobley said later he was shocked to the core when he heard John Armstrong had actually bought The Headland.

All through that winter John was also negotiating the sale of The Cavendish and Carol was doing the bookings for it as it was very uncertain which hotel — or both — they would have on their hands for the 1979 season, and it was important the bookings were done properly. After further protracted negotiations, with great difficulty, the contract for the sale of The Cavendish was finally arranged. They completed the purchase of The Headland in March 1979 and three days later they heaved a sigh of relief when the contract for the sale of The Cavendish was signed. Phew! What timing! The Cavendish fetched £225,000. John was twenty-nine at the time, and Carol was twenty-three. They had had a very difficult, uncomfortable winter but they were well pleased with the outcome and they were ready to climb the mountain facing them.

The Armstrongs at The Headland

When John Armstrong took over The Headland in April 1979 it was dilapidated to a degree. It had been slowly declining for the previous thirty-three years while in Mr Luxon's hands and it had only retained its 4-star rating from the AA because Mr Luxon had agreed not to use the third floor bedrooms, which increased the ratio of private bathrooms to the number of bedrooms.

MR. and MRS. JOHN ARMSTRONG, whose family have been running hotels in Newquay for over fifty years, are delighted to announce that they have acquired the renowned, four-star Headland Hotel. They plan to combine the service and standard of a first-class, luxury hotel with the relaxed, informal atmosphere of a family-holiday hotel.

There will be plenty going on for all the family from April to October. In the evenings there will be dancing, backgammon tournaments and the Headland races. In the grounds there is a large heated swimming pool and a separate smaller pool for children, three tennis courts, 9-hole pitch and putt course and a putting green.

In the hotel there is a full size billiards table, hairdressing salon, lift to all floors, lock-up garages, central heating and log fires in the public rooms, early and late season.

For the children there is a full range of activities—fancy dress party, swimming gala with a silver cup for the "Champ", family sand-building competition, Punch and Judy show and magic show by David John. For families there is a fully-equipped launderette and baby preparation room. The family suites with interconnecting rooms are very popular.

All the well-appointed bedrooms have sea views, G.P.O. telephone, radio and baby-listening; most have private bathroom and television is available.

We think the Headland Hotel will appeal to people who want a good family-holiday with a higher standard than is usually found at resort hotels.

BARGAIN HOLIDAYS

A holiday at the Headland Hotel in 1979 is obviously a fantastic bargain—Why? The reason is simple—having acquired the hotel only six weeks before the beginning of the summer season, with practically no bookings and minimal advertising we have now to set about attracting guests. The most obvious way of doing so is to offer an unbeatable bargain—this we are doing.

John and Carol Armstrong get their courage up and take on a mighty project.

When John and Carol moved into the hotel they had no proper home and had several arduous years in front of them. It was essential that they lived on the premises during the season and, true to family tradition, they had to "tuck away" somewhere. They were able to do it with a little more style than the older members of the family had

TARIFF 1979

RATES QUOTED ARE PER PERSON, PER DAY AND ARE EXCLUSIVE OF V.A.T.

	EN PENSION MINIMUM 3 DAYS	**DEMI PENSION MINIMUM 2 DAYS**	**APARTMENT AND BREAKFAST**
ECONOMY TIME			
May and October	£13–£15	£11–£13	£9–£11
LOW SEASON			
June and September	£15–£19	£12–£16	£10–£14
HIGH SEASON			
July and August	£18–£22	£14–£18	£11–£15

WEEKLY TERMS
A DISCOUNT OF 15% OF THE DAILY RATE IS ALLOWED FOR STAYS OF 7 DAYS OR MORE.

EN PENSION TERMS INCLUDE: English breakfast, table d'hôte luncheon, afternoon tea and table d'hôte dinner.

DEMI PENSION TERMS INCLUDE: English breakfast and table d'hôte luncheon or table d'hôte dinner.

APARTMENT AND BREAKFAST TERMS include an English breakfast.

THERE IS NO SERVICE CHARGE.

Bookings are accepted for any period and starting on any day.

Private bathroom or shower and w.c. *en suite* £1.00 per person, per day.

The offer of any room is subject to the room being available on receipt of the acceptance and a 10% deposit,which will be credited against the account. No allowance can be made for meals not taken or rooms not occupied for the full period of the booking. The facilities and entertainment programme may be amended as circumstances dictate.

Terms and arrangements for children overleaf.

The Armstrong's first tariff, 1979.

managed many years before. In the centre at the top of The Headland are two towers approached by separate little curving staircases. They were just disused attic lumber rooms full of junk. For the first season the Armstrongs converted one of the towers into a little studio apartment for themselves, with a bathroom tucked under the eaves —

really no more than a 'bed sit', but it was attractive. Fortunately they had no children or dogs at the time! The following year they converted the other tower into a more spacious affair for themselves. Today both towers are considered prime guest accommodation and they are most popular. For those two winters they had to move back to John's bachelor flat in "Edgcumbe Lodge" in Hilgrove Road, where Maggie Dyer was still living.

Very soon after taking over, John was in dispute with Mr Luxon because The Headland had been sold with good quality silver for two hundred and fifty persons. In fact, when checked there was only silver for one hundred and fifty persons — silver for one hundred persons had disappeared! Five members of staff had remained at the hotel, and of course they were more than willing to tell the Armstrongs what other items had been removed. Apparently, apart from the silver and small articles, a lorry load of furniture had gone. When asked about the missing items Mr Luxon replied that he had only been removing junk! Certainly most of what was left was junk, but the silver was important. The dispute almost ended in court but eventually a settlement was reached by the solicitors, and Mr Luxon repaid the Armstrongs £14,000 for the missing items, including the silver.

The five members of staff who remained included the barman, who gave in his notice after forty-eight hours when he heard there was to be a weekly stock take! The Head Chef lasted a month and then gave notice on the grounds of ill health — but not before a case of frozen chickens had been found in an odd place — ready to walk. The Head Waiter lasted a week; he was not prepared to move chairs around the restaurant! The maintenance man worked for the whole of the first season, was a great help to the new owners and then retired honourably, aged sixty-five, at the end of 1979. The housekeeper, Mrs Harris, was first class and managed the bedrooms for the next five years.

The first season was, of course, difficult and uncomfortable. The furniture was mostly old and shabby; much of it ended up on the skip. Some items such as chromium standard lamps and Lloyd Loom chairs, not yet back in vogue, were sold to the junk man in Truro for £1 each. On a later visit to the same junk shop, John saw a silver tea pot badged "Headland Hotel" and obviously stolen. John picked it up and said "This is mine. I am taking it." "You cannot do that," said the assistant, "I shall call the police." "Fine," said John, "I will wait here until they come." A policeman arrived — there was a little general argy-bargy and John went off happily with his recovered teapot.

Bettye spent the whole of that first season scouring the sale rooms for chairs and bedroom furniture to temporarily replace the rubbish in the bedrooms with slightly tidier rubbish. Every Saturday morning she arrived at the hotel with the week's haul and directed the porters where to put it. It was all eventually replaced by one order with a reputable manufacturer, but it was to be several years before that happened.

In April 1979 when the first liquor stock-take was carried out at The Headland there were many unexplained cases of duty-free liquor in the cellar. Later in the year the Armstrongs discovered how they came to be there. Every November for many years the U.S. Marine Corps had held their Birthday Ball, known as the Saturday Ball, at the hotel. It was their one big annual celebration and they brought their own 12-piece band resplendent in their scarlet uniforms. The local girls were invited, and it was a much sought after invitation among the local dolly-birds.

The arrangement was that the Marines brought their own liquor, which was duty free, and The Headland would charge them corkage on what was consumed. Apparently, the year before the Armstrongs took over, the drink had run out, and so for the November 1979 Ball they brought twenty cases of assorted hard spirits, two hundred and forty bottles for two hundred guests. The U.S. Marines are a tough, hard drinking band of men, but even so, when the ball was over there were fifteen cases of spirits left which were duly returned to the camp. The Quarter Master was amazed — they had never had any duty free liquor returned before. This is, perhaps, the explanation for the large quantity of duty free liquor found in the cellar when the Armstrongs took over.

Having survived its first season at the end of November 1979 the hotel closed and the serious work began. For some thirty years, ever since being de-requisitioned at the end of the war, the building had been vandalised by shoddy building works and at the Armstrongs' first AA inspection the hotel was relegated to 3-star AA and RAC. In fact at the time it was not really even that. It was to be many years before The Headland would be able to stand proudly again as Newquay's only 4-star hotel. In 1979 John and Carol were young and both looked even younger. In fact, age wise, Carol might have been the junior receptionist; she looked about eighteen. From time to time in the early years the guests would ask to see the owner and when John appeared would say "I wish to see your father", and Carol would get "I wish to see Mrs Armstrong!" At first it exasperated them, but later they found it wryly amusing.

Having shuffled into The Headland the young Armstrongs were left with very little money for refurbishment or alterations. First of all the hall had to be sorted out: the Reception Office and Porters Box were re-sited. In those days there was a great vogue for putting carpet on the walls of hotel public rooms and all the family hotels had some walls carpeted. The Armstrongs took over a flashy blue and gold carpet in the hall and corridors on the ground floor at The Headland which was not to their taste. They decided the easiest way to improve the appearance of the hall would be to put inexpensive plain dark blue carpet on the walls. This they did. The carpet cost £5,000 and the walls looked splendid, but there was trouble ahead. The fire authority objected to the carpet, insisting it was a fire hazard. After a prolonged argument between John, his experts and the fire authority, the matter ended up in court and John was given seven days to remove the carpet. It was replaced with wall paper of the same dark blue, which was effective, but of course not nearly as opulent looking as the dark blue carpet had been. The irony was that there was exactly the same carpet in different colours on several walls at the Edgcumbe hotel, including one narrow corridor, and the fire authorities were quite happy with it. In fact, as far as is known that carpet is still on some hotel walls in Newquay today and it seemed very hard on the young Armstrongs that it was not acceptable on the ground floor of The Headland, which has wide corridors and many exits. The fire authorities have enormous powers, but also great discretion to turn a blind eye if they feel so inclined.

Then John created a makeshift chandelier for the foyer from a bunch of little light fittings which had recently been thrown out from the Edgcumbe. His makeshift chandelier graced the hall for twenty years, which surely says something for its unobtrusive design — but improvisation was the order of the day!

That winter many private bathrooms were installed, new boilers were commissioned, an area of the basement was gutted, and a large sound-proof disco room was made with its own bar, but the major work was the installation of an indoor swimming pool which the Armstrongs considered essential. John Crowther, their architect, obtained planning permission and an estimate from E.H. Thomas of Falmouth. It was £314,000 and young Armstrong was horrified. John Crowther recalls him saying "That is much too much; we'll have to do it ourselves!" Fortunately at the time he had a little building team with a capable foreman in charge, Ivan Dover, and they set to with a will.

First they dug away the bank from outside the building to gain access and knocked a hole through into the basement; then a local firm of builders put in three RSJs to support the sprung ballroom floor above. John was on site at 7.30 every morning in his boiler suit. He hired two little digger dumpers and every chap on site, including the wine waiter and the porter, set to digging and dumping — fortunately all chaps love driving those little machines! The soil and rubble was used to form a level lawn on the south west corner of the property. At one stage Ivan Dover drove a dumper into one of the drainage trenches and ended up in hospital for three days. It was all hands to the pump! John Crowther was very helpful and kept his professional eye on what was going on. He was a good friend.

A concrete staircase had to be made from the hall to gain access to the new lower ground floor. The cement had to be laid immediately, and left for the weekend to set. It had to be wheel-barrowed through the front door and across the hall; the team worked all night to get it laid before it 'went off'. Banisters were the next problem. John made replicas of the existing cast iron ones in fibre glass. He did this work himself. "Very impressive", thought Mum! Today John's fibre glass banisters are indistinguishable from the original cast iron ones, which go right up through the building.

From the beginning John and Carol's one idea had been to restore the hotel to its former glory and for the next twenty years they were striving to do just that. Fortunately they found some of the original fireplaces and other fittings in the basement and they were able to reinstate them. The marble pillars at the foot of the staircase which had been covered with block board were restored and two others were found abandoned in the grounds. They were repolished and replaced in their original position outside the restaurant. After nearly twenty years of working to "undo" the ghastly modernisation that was inflicted on the building during the late '40s, '50s and '60s there was still much they intended to restore. Fifty years later there is a trend towards replacing original fixtures and fittings, but they are now extremely hard to find, and expensive.

Apart from the normal and expected restoring, redecorating and refurbishment, over the years the Armstrongs have had to cope with major repairs to the fabric of the building. The lift was condemned and the insurance company refused to insure it. The roof needed renewing — a massive undertaking. John decided to spend £5,000 a year on these repairs and it took about five years to complete. The whole of the third floor was derelict — it had not been used for years.

The kitchens were a shambles and within a few years £150,000 (£500,000 today) had to be spent to bring them up to a satisfactory standard to placate the health inspectors. The bedrooms were far below even three star standards but gradually all these difficulties have been overcome and over the years The Headland has regained most of the refinements and amenities one would expect in such an hotel, but it wasn't easy.

In the early 1980s the Armstrongs at The Headland faced a severe financial crisis. The post war boom in tourism began to wane and a ferocious price war had set in. John's bank manager was seriously concerned and, as John recounted recently, threatened to take away his Headland cheque book. He said to John's mother, "what are we going to do about John and The Headland? Fortunately his parents were able to help him out financially having just sold their house in Feock. But for that The Headland story might well have had a very different ending.

As it was the young Armstrongs persevered, worked unceasingly, and drew in their horns. There were no holidays for them but by 1983 after four hard seasons they were able to shuffle into an old farmhouse, Carevick, three miles from The Headland. They had been virtually homeless for some four years and it had been a hard struggle, but happily after that they never looked back. They went from strength to strength.

Carevick at Cubert was potentially a lovely house but at the beginning they could do little more than camp in it. There was much work to do to make it habitable in the first place and it took years to make it the comfortable home it is today. Their first daughter, Veryan, was born in December, 1983, to be followed by Morwenna in November, 1985 and George in May, 1987.

When the Armstrongs took over the hotel in 1979 it had, of course, a full licence and a public bar. There are some folk who consider a public bar the fast road to riches second only to gaming machines. Not so John and Carol. They are hoteliers and they were determined that The Headland was not going to be overrun with beer swilling yobbos from the beach. It is very difficult to segregate public bar customers and hotel guests unless the two operations, including the cloakrooms, can be separated. They just do not mix. After a few years the Armstrongs closed the public bar and created their Fistral suite which is now used for functions of all kinds. The Headland was not the first quality hotel in Newquay to do so and they have never regretted the decision.

Theft is always a problem in hotels and has to be dealt with as it comes. Here are a couple of examples. At a rather down-market dinner one evening it was reported to John that someone had just picked up a large oriental rug from the floor in the hall and had gone through the front door with it rolled up under his arm. John went to investigate and discovered the rug in a coach which was just about to leave. He reclaimed it. Not a word was said! Sadly these days incidents like this are all too frequent. After one RAF winter dinner, a friend and fellow hotelier called Armstrong aside and told him that some of the diners had been pocketing the table silver — knives, forks, etc. It turned out that silver for twenty three people had been stolen. John Armstrong contacted the Comanding Officer at RAF St Mawgan and the culprits were caught, dealt with by the Service, and the silver returned. It is quite extraordinary how normally honest folk think that hotel items are fair game. (One season at the Edgcumbe, one hundred and forty-four mugs disappeared from the coffee shop. No doubt that year the hotel was providing mugs for a local café!)

In 1985 a couple booked a week's holiday at The Headland in August. They came from Birmingham. They were in their fifties and she was a large blonde with a loud voice. They wined and dined on champagne and lobsters etc., and in the first few days ran up a huge bill of extras. They were completely 'over the top' and John became suspicious — their bill was mounting alarmingly. He made discreet enquiries and discovered that if a cheque was offered in settlement of their account it would not be met by the bank. John called the chap into his office and told him that he would require the account to be settled in cash. The guest jovially assured him that there would be no difficulty about that, "My dear chap", as he was "just off to the bank". Ho! Ho! Ho! John was not convinced, he still felt sure the couple would try to do a 'moonlight flit'. On their last night he arranged for a young man to spend the night in a car watching the couple's car with instructions that if they attempted to leave during the night the Night Manager must be told immediately. He would in turn alert the police. Sure enough at 4.00 a.m. the couple came down and got into their car. The police apprehended them on the Goss Moor and they were taken to Newquay police station. It turned out that she was his "floozie" and they had got together when he put an advertisement in a Birmingham Paper saying "Please come on holiday with me and I will give you a lovely time" — some lovely time! They both spent the weekend in the cells in Newquay police station but, sad to relate, John did not get his money.

One summer in the early 1980s a firm asked if it would be possible for them to tether their hot air balloon in The Headland grounds and what the charge would be. They wished to attend a jamboree being

John Armstrong's first balloon.

held on Fistral Beach. John gave them permission and said the charge would be a flight in a hot air balloon for him personally. The firm gave him a flight eventually — although he had to travel to Bristol for it. He was so enthralled by that first flight that he immediately resolved to take up hot air ballooning. He bought a 'Cameron 700' which would take four passengers, and obtained his licence to fly. The Headland Hotel had its own hot air balloon! He then qualified for his commercial pilot's licence which would allow him to charge the guests for flights. Hot air balloons are very heavy on fuel and therefore costs are high. Approximately £100 per hour per passenger was charged and John spent many hours flying Headland guests — with champagne on landing. He found it enjoyable and lucrative. He now has a second, larger balloon which will take six people. For many years, in early May, John organised the great Cornwall Balloon Festival. It was publicity for the town, but unfortunately too often the balloonists were

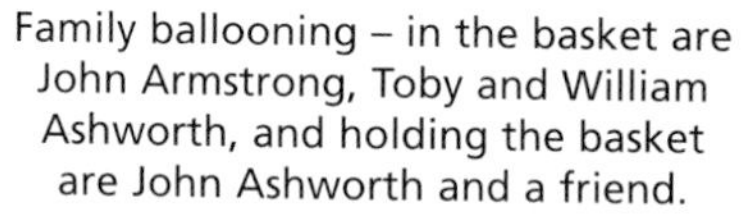

Family ballooning – in the basket are John Armstrong, Toby and William Ashworth, and holding the basket are John Ashworth and a friend.

Bettye and friends having a go at the balloon festival at Longleat, Wiltshire.

frustrated by high winds and poor weather and the Festival fizzled out.

John has since become an expert balloonist and belongs to the Balloon Explorers' Club. For several years he has taken his balloon and crew to the International Balloon Festival held every January in Château d'Oex, Switzerland. In 2006 and 2007 he scooped the board and won the three major events held during the week. He also uses the balloon for sales and marketing trips abroad. His co-pilot is his old school friend John Wilson, who is a General Practitioner in Bideford. The Headland is now well known as the centre of the ballooning in Cornwall. The continental trips have proved very successful in attracting visitors to the hotel.

When the Armstrongs bought The Headland there was a collection of tumbledown wooden sheds used as staff rooms, which they quickly demolished. On one corner of their land there was also an enormous ramshackle tin roofed building, known as the Billets, which had been built in the twenties as a huge garage for some fifty or sixty cars. The building had later been converted into very rough staff rooms with flimsy seven foot high partitions which did not reach the high galvanised corrugated roof. They were really only cubicles, and draughty and damp at that. The Armstrongs quickly decided that the quarters were unacceptable even to the roughest seasonal staff, and they bought two proper staff houses in Tower Road, which were used for some years until they proved to be too noisy, tiresome and unruly.

Today all staff have to arrange their own accommodation.

The Billets stood derelict for several years, and was a blot on the landscape. In the 1980s John announced that he was applying for planning permission to demolish it and build fifty cottages. "Fifty cottages?" said Bettye, when told of the plan. "You couldn't possibly get fifty cottages on that site." "No", said John, "but if I put in for fifty I shall be allowed twenty-five and that is what I want." After a prolonged and expensive battle, which John Crowther and a Planning QC from London fought brilliantly, permission for thirty-six cottages was finally granted on appeal when, at the suggestion of the QC, the application was put forward as an extension to The Headland Hotel. Unfortunately, before John could start building, the recession set in and there was so much work still to be done to the hotel that the cottages had to be set on one side for the time being. However, the footings were put in and the foundation stone was laid by the Mayor of Newquay, Olive Irons, in the autumn of 1990.

In 1987 HRH the Prince of Wales came to The Headland for a conference, "Cornwall, the Way Ahead". Its purpose was to boost Cornwall's Tourist Industry. No doubt it helped do so — but it must be said that that conference, which was a great success, also put The Headland on the map as far as conferences are concerned. This market has now broadened considerably and the hotel hosts many of the most prestigious events in the county — it does them well.

When in 1987 the building was listed Grade II as being of architectural interest, the Armstrongs had mixed feelings about it as of course that meant that in future it would be difficult to make any changes to the fabric of the building. How fortunate they had put so much effort into renovations during the previous eight years!

John Betjeman is said to have considered The Headland the ugliest building in Cornwall — and he loved old buildings, but beauty is in the eye of the beholder. To many people The Headland has a dignified splendour about it, which is sadly lacking in so many of the flat roofed box-like buildings that were built immediately after the war. In fact in 2004 one journalist called it "Newquay's grandest hotel and best looking building" in a travel article in the Daily Telegraph. How opinions differ!

The Headland, in common with all businesses, had a difficult time during the recession and Bettye, not to mention the bank manager, became very concerned for John and Carol. They were in level competition with much lesser places able, on paper, to offer the same facilities more reasonably. Of course it wouldn't work, for if they met their competitors' tariffs they would be losing money, their overheads

Garages (billets) etc., later to be the site of the Headland Village.

were so much higher. The Headland, like a Rolls Royce or a Bentley, is an expensive beast to run! Maintenance and refurbishing alone cost £150,000 per annum, and sometimes more.

In 1989, with great courage, John and Carol decided they would not and could not compete with the general run of Newquay hotels. In one year they raised their tariff 15% right across the board and did their utmost to raise their standards accordingly. That was their turning point. It was a bold move, but it paid off, for from that time they have gained ground. There has been a constant programme of upgrading every winter; they continue to improve the hotel and its facilities. Today their guests are largely people interested in surfing, who want more space and service and are prepared to pay for it.

When "Investors in People" was introduced in the early 1990s, the Armstrongs at The Headland were leaders in the field and embraced it wholeheartedly. Carol, especially, worked hard and received national recognition and awards for her efforts. The Headland was the first business in Cornwall (and one of the first hundred in the whole country) to achieve this Government flagship award, even ahead of Cornwall County Council and other formal companies. The Armstrongs were justly proud of their achievements. In 1993 The Headland Hotel was the holder of Cornwall's only National Training Award. The hotel was also awarded the Silver "England for Excellence" Tourism Training Award and they became part of Les Routiers Corps d'Elite for the presentation, range, and value of their wine list for five years, from 1993. Bettye could never come to terms with "Investors in People". "What is it all about?" she asked! To her it seemed utter nonsense and a complete waste of time; all meetings, statistics, graphs and paper-work. What has that got to do with running an hotel? Surely the staff's working hours would be better spent looking after the guests? "The chef at The Headland can take a booking on the 'phone." she was told. Is that really an advantage? Would he not be better getting on in his kitchen? And where is the receptionist while he is taking the booking — is she in the kitchen cooking? "Decisions are made in consultation with the staff." she was told, but surely serious business decisions must be made by the bosses! Apart from that, good business practice has always meant management working together with the staff. It is really an old, well tried formula in a new guise, but to the older generation it seems to be all "meetings and paperwork" rather than getting on with the job of looking after the guests. Apparently some hotels, including Bedruthan Steps, have now realised Investors in People makes for a great deal of extra paperwork and have dropped it.

One of her family recently suggested to Bettye that she would benefit from an hotel managers' course. She laughed; she felt it was a bit late after more than sixty years in the business! In fact, she realises technology has progressed so fast that older people cannot really cope today. It is a young person's business world and the older generations have to step back. Bettye is doing her best to do so! She does not find it easy! In her view trained managers walking about with eyes in the back of their heads are more important to hotels than backroom boys in offices pushing papers around and fiddling with statistics.

In the winter of 1996 the Armstrongs made major alterations to the ground floor at The Headland; they converted the conservatory into a modern south facing restaurant called The Garden Room overlooking Fistral Beach, and built a new kitchen under it which cost £30,000 to equip. It became, probably, the most popular hotel in Newquay for luncheon, and the Garden Room was open for meals in the summer from 10.00 a.m.-10.00 p.m.

During the winter of 1997-1998 restoration and upgrading continued. The goods lift which had been condemned and out of use ever since the Armstrongs bought the hotel in 1979 had to be replaced. An estimate of £26,000 had been accepted and a deposit paid. Before long Otis, the lift manufacturer, came up with "We cannot do the work. The lift shaft is four inches out of true." The deposit was returned. With six floors, a laundry and cellars in the basement, life at The Headland was very difficult without a goods lift. It was replaced for the 1999 season, four inches smaller, and hopefully there will be no more luggage up the front stairs! But as John remarked "Some of the luggage arriving these days is in plastic carrier bags" — not quite up to the old Headland style — just modern Newquay.

Writing about the goods lift brings to mind a pre-war story. One Saturday in July, 1937, there was a private champagne supper party booked for about thirty people in Room 103 — the Sitting Room of the Royal Suite. After supper the guests were to join in the dancing in the Black and Silver Ballroom.

The party hosts ran a small hotel in Newquay. They took about fifty guests, only had a small staff and had to do much of the work themselves; they ran a very 'hands on' little affair. In those days all bookings were from Saturday to Saturday, and so before the hosts could get away they had to see their new arrivals settled in and dinner served. They were late. By the time they arrived at The Headland some of their guests were already there and had taken themselves to the bar.

New Garden Room 1996.

The original conservatory.

John Armstrong's major alteration in the winter of 1996.

Upstairs in Room 103 the drinks were laid out on a sideboard with a waiter in charge. The party got going, the champagne flowed, and the buffet supper was sumptuous. All went well until the waiter was called away, then one of the wilder young guests leapt into action. He mixed a lethal concoction from the bottles on the sideboard and with enormous charm passed it around as a cocktail. It tasted delicious. Almost everyone drank it, including one or two older guests, and very soon they were all "well lit". The celebration moved into a higher gear and was a riot of fun. By the time the party ended regrettably some of the guests had to depart in a rather undignified manner — in the goods lift! It was a never-to-be-forgotten party, still talked about over seventy years later. It was Bettye's twenty-first birthday party!

Family at the Camel Estuary, 1997.

But on to 1998. Just before Easter a middle aged couple arrived with their little teenage student daughter who had been engaged to work in the Garden Room restaurant for the season. They fussed. They asked to see her room, father carried her case and mother helped her unpack. The following morning Mrs Blacklock, the Manageress, measured her for her uniform, including a smart fitted plaid waistcoat. The next day the poor girl was rushed by ambulance to Treliske Hospital in Truro with suspected appendicitis. The baby was born half an hour later! As John Armstrong commented, "The Newquay season was under way!"

In the late 1990s a farcical situation arose in Newquay about the swimming pools. Two small children drowned in murky hotel pools and proprietors were prosecuted and one of them blamed Restormel saying "This pool has not been inspected for five years". Restormel were severely rapped over the knuckles about it. They then overreacted with a raft of new regulations; some completely dotty and even The Headland got caught up in it. A closure order was slapped on their sparklingly clean and fenced pool because there was no lock on the gate leading to it. The Council decreed that all pools should be reduced to a depth of five feet. Some proprietors struggled to comply, but when it got to Sands Resort (formerly Trevelgue Hotel), Nicholas Malcolm firmly refused to do so unless the council indemnified him in

Headland Village under construction in March 2000.

writing against being sued by someone diving into too shallow water, and then the whole thing fizzled out. It seems parents no longer take the responsibility for their own children. With over one hundred pools in Newquay how could Restormel monitor them all?

The first ten cottages of The Headland 'holiday village' in the grounds were ready for the 2000 season and Carol Armstrong had a busy winter dealing with enquiries and bookings for them. John's mother was doubtful about the wisdom of such an expensive up-market development and voiced her fears to the Armstrongs. However, they were quite confident that the demand for cottages at The Headland was there and they were right; certainly self-catering is the modern trend and no doubt the village is a great asset to the hotel. The cottages are of an extremely high standard with terracotta floors, wood burning stoves and furnished in a simple, but elegant style. Every bedroom has its own en-suite bathroom and each "cottage" has a secluded patio or balcony for privacy and, of course, all have sea views. The front doors are four inches thick and the kitchens and bathrooms are equipped with the finest quality designer fittings — £38,000 of granite was ordered from China. The cottages are monitored by a computer in the hotel office. At the touch of a button locks, lights, hot water, heating etc., are activated immediately — wonderful modern technology! and the cottages are tremendously popular.

Headland Village.

In 2002 Carol Armstrong said, "I'm busy writing a letter to the guests regarding standards of dress in the restaurant in the evenings. Last night several teenagers tried to come in for dinner on roller blades, and we will not have it." Tee-shirts, jeans, and trainers were then banned in The Headland restaurant in the evenings. Guests who did not wish to conform were served dinner in their bedrooms and charged room service. The Armstrongs were determined to keep their standards up and their more couth guests greatly appreciated it.

The Garden Room was completely redesigned again in 2002 and it was renamed the Sands Brasserie. It has wooden floors, modern furnishings and rugs, Terry Frost paintings and coloured glass items in alcoves. The menus have been brought up to date to match, and it well suits the trendy folk who use it, and perhaps most important it overlooks Fistral Beach where many of the major surfing festivals are held. John and Carol have also created a terrace outside the Brasserie with a toughened glass screen all around which provides shelter from the sometimes ferocious breezes off the Atlantic, and therefore it can be used for much of the year.

Ivan Curtis, Manager, appointed in 2003.

In 2003 the Armstrongs appointed Ivan Curtis as General Manager of the hotel. He had been at the Island Hotel, Tresco, for some ten years and is most capable. He quickly took charge of the entire set up — including the cottages and today he is constantly upgrading The Headland and improving the standard.

For some years John had had an efficient, enthusiastic, blonde Personal Assistant called Val. Utterly devoted to John and The Headland she bustled about the place and seemed to know everything. In 2004 while John and Carol were having their annual sojourn in Switzerland Val instigated a secret party to celebrate their twenty-five years at the hotel. She sent out formal invitations to whoever had contributed in any way to the success of The Headland — professionals, master tradesmen, suppliers, PR people and long term old friends. It was a black tie affair, and the Armstrongs knew nothing about it. Over one hundred people came and Val, looking resplendent in a long black dress with a specially bought white fur jacket over it (she must have been far, far too hot — but no matter) was very much in charge. It really was a splendid evening. A short while after Bettye admired her new 'hair-do' — blonde, short, and straight and it really suited her. She accepted the compliment gracefully — only later was it explained to Bettye that she had lost all her hair. Val just slapped on a wig and carried on to the end. Mercifully, she died soon afterwards — a sad story.

On 10th December, 2004, just as her grandmother had celebrated her own twenty-first at The Headland nearly seventy years earlier, there was another family party for John and Carol's elder daughter, Veryan's, twenty-first birthday, although this dinner and dance was a very much grander affair than her grandmother's with about one hundred and fifty guests. It was a super party!

Interior of one of the luxury cottages in Headland Village.

By 2005 the Armstrongs felt they had successfully completed their rather ambitious project; the forty cottages were completed and well booked. They had a brainwave at the last moment when they managed to turn what would have been the worst cottage — almost without sea views — into the best by getting planning permission to make it four storeys. The ground floor and first floor each have a double bedroom and bathroom, the third floor has a kitchen/dining room and the sitting room is on the top floor with panoramic views. Now, of course, it is the favourite and everybody wants it! The architects, David Judson & Co. and the Armstrongs were delighted when 'the village' won a national design award in 2004. The three adjoining hard tennis courts were re-aligned and extra parking space was also provided.

In 2005 John and Carol felt their efforts and hard work were finally rewarded when The Headland was upgraded to the 4-star AA rating which it had held for some eighty years until it was downgraded in 1979. It had taken twenty-five years hard work and effort to restore it to its former status and traditional atmosphere of understated luxury and Newquay's leading hotel. Bettye, of course, rejoiced in her son's success. He has been one of the most successful family members of his generation. The Armstrongs have big plans for the future; they aim to upgrade The Headland even further, doubtless the building itself warrants it. Their next planned major scheme is a first class conference suite which will incorporate all the latest technology. They have plenty of space for it. These days The Headland has several enormous advantages location-wise. Firstly, it can be reached without going through Newquay's bustling town, secondly it offers superb views of the happenings on Fistral Beach and above all it has space around it — ten acres of space, and so guests really can avoid

Newquay's crowds if they so wish. One day, no doubt, The Headland will have five stars.

For Carol's fiftieth birthday in 2005 John bought her a 45 ft Southerly with a retractable keel appropriately called *Cinquant.* It was also a 'thank you' for thirty years support and cooperation. *Cinquant* has three double cabins with showers en suite; she is beautiful and they manage to spend much time on her, often with family or friends.

Theft really is a major problem in hotels which is why so many good hotels do not have valuable decorative items about. In a lounge at The Headland the Armstrongs had a magnificent bronze race-horse and rider about 2 ft x 3 ft. It stood at the end of the room on a side table against a pale yellow wall and looked splendid. During the winter of 2006-2007 it was stolen — it was heavy and would have had to be carried out through the front door — the audacity of the theft is amazing! The Headland, ever striving to improve standards, put white towelling robes into the bedrooms for the guests. In the first season over a hundred robes were stolen, even though it was made quite clear they could be bought from Reception.

Like Bedruthan Steps, but in a different way, The Headland is a monster to deal with. There are so many conferences, seminars, functions, corporate dinners and also many private guests on holiday all at the same time — no easy task. The Headland has become a thriving all year round business well capable of coping fluently with whatever comes its way. The hotel is now open for the whole year, except three days at Christmas, and it is, once again, Newquay's grandest hotel. It is certainly Newquay's most expensive, as it should be. The winters are busy with dinner dances, trade shows, meetings, and many other social and business functions. It also has a wedding licence and the many wedding ceremonies held there are done with great style.

John Armstrong has had three great assets in his business life. Firstly he knew exactly what he wanted to do in life from the age of eight when he became beguiled by hotels. Secondly he had helpful and supportive parents who were able to help him from time to time, and thirdly his wife shares his enthusiasm for hotels and has worked tirelessly with him for more than thirty years. Indeed she is now a recognised authority on tourism in the county. They make a good team.

By 2006 with school fees behind him, The Headland restored to its rightful position as Newquay's leading and only 4-star hotel and running smoothly in the capable hands of Ivan Curtis, and the village of forty cottages completed and letting like hot cakes, John felt ready to step back and think of other things. He was fifty-seven. For him

The Headland has been his life's work but for Carol it has been her whole life and she did not find it so easy to let go. She felt it was part of her. However, they had so enjoyed their sabbatical on their new boat that they spent many happy hours during the following winter planning their next jaunt for the summer of 2007 in *Cinquant*. They had discovered a way of life that suited them — gently sailing down the French coast exploring small creeks and harbours while living a simple life on the boat. It was a far cry from hotel life and they both adored it. Clearly by 2007 they had entered another phase in their lives. In the autumn they announced that in 2008 they planned to spend five months on the boat. It had been well earned.

The improvements continue: the 2007-2008 winter programme at The Headland included replacing the guest lift and extending it directly down to the indoor swimming pool which meant that guests no longer had to walk through the front hall in their white towelling robes to reach it.

A seven year development plan has been submitted to the planning authority. The scheme includes: an infinity edge swimming pool on the site of the tennis courts; an underground car park for one hundred cars opposite the front doors; a four hundred seat conference centre, complete with its own kitchen, where the old swimming pool sits; and the health and beauty treatment facilities in the basement will be greatly improved.

John and Carol were particularly pleased that the effort, thought and expense that went into the design resulted in not one single objection from all the interested parties and the general public whose views were canvassed as part of the planning process.

Coutts Bank give annual prizes for the best UK family owned and run businesses, and in 2008 The Headland won the regional prize, which covered southern England and Wales. John and Carol, with Veryan, Morwenna and George, went to Goodwood House, Sussex to a reception when the winners were announced. They had won! and of course were elated and returned to Cornwall, triumphant. In June the national finals were held at Coutts Bank in the Strand. Veryan and Morwenna went and it was a splendid evening, but sadly The Headland faced fierce competition in its class and were not successful — perhaps next year.

In September 2008 John and his family went to the AA Centenary dinner in the Great Room at Grosvenor House, Park Lane — incidentally, the largest banqueting room in London. The Annual Awards were being presented — regrettably The Headland didn't win,

Family at the AA Centenary Award Ceremony, Grosvenor House Hotel, Park Lane.

but Rick Stein was given a Lifetime Achievement Award for "*...a lifetime commitment to the highest quality of service and standards, a track record of constant improvement and an unswerving dedication to customer care*". Well merited too, for he has been an enormous asset to Cornwall for many years. He was negotiating for Fistral Blue in the spring of 2008 and the deal fell through, but his interest in opening a restaurant in Newquay remains. It would be a great boost for the town.

Veryan and Morwenna with Bettye at the Coutts National Family Business Award ceremony, at Coutts Bank in the Strand, London.

And what of the younger generation of Armstrongs? Veryan graduated from Exeter University in 2005 and is now in her second year as a trainee manager at The Goring Hotel in London where she is progressing up the ranks fast. Morwenna has just left Bristol University with a degree in Social Studies and is at present enjoying her gap year (between spells of well paid cooking to fund it) and George opted out of Loughborough University in his second year having firmly decided to go into the hotel business and keen to get on with it. He is at present at Goodwood Park Hotel, Sussex, as trainee assistant manager. He is doing well and he loves it. They seem to be firmly set on their paths through life.

Bettye is inordinately proud of John and Carol's achievements at The Headland. They took on a shabby, run down, out-dated monster some thirty years ago and have turned it into Newquay's — indeed, Cornwall's most gracious hotel, and their children will no doubt soon be ready to 'join the firm'.

Trevelgue Hotel, Porth, Newquay 1980 – 2008 (re-named Sands in 2000)

Trevelgue was built as a guest house in the mid 1930s. Architecturally designed with more style than most hotels in Newquay, it had eighteen bedrooms with a large garage attached at the side. There was a tennis court, private putting green and plenty of space around the house. In the early days it was called Trevelgue Guest House and was owned and run by Mr and Mrs Forrester-Smith. It was also one of the more expensive establishments in Newquay; the low season terms at one time were higher than those at the Hotel Bristol. It was well run, quiet, and elegant and Mr Forrester-Smith was a very active member of the Hotels Association.

During the Second World War Trevelgue was requisitioned by the Air Ministry. It was an Officers' Mess for the Photographic Reconnaissance Unit stationed at St Eval. The main base was at Benson, Oxfordshire and there were two flights, one at St Eval, and another at Wick. In 1942-43 the Cominding Officer was young Flt Lt Neil Wheeler — today he is Air Chief Marshal Sir Neil Wheeler GCB, CBE, DSO, DFC, AFC. During a visit to The Nare Hotel Sir Neil recalled that the Photographic Interpretation Section was based at Rosemere, Watergate Bay, but at the time, of course, it was all very "hush-hush".

Immediately after the war Mr and Mrs Forrester-Smith sold Trevelgue to some successful business people from Liverpool and they very quickly changed its image. Mrs Chapman, the wife of one of them, ran it. It soon became the rendezvous for the many RAF officers stationed at St Mawgan and St Eval and, as can be imagined, it quickly gained a reputation as one of Newquay's liveliest hotels where life was one long party. In those heady post-war days, the young were enjoying their new-found freedom but not quite the freedom that was to come in the 1960s! After all, they were carefree, released from the rigours of war, and not yet into the serious business of civilian life, and at Trevelgue in the late 1940s they made the most of it — anything went — it really was a wild establishment. The hotel was sold in the early 1950s and became once again a sedate little hotel. The next owners bought it in 1960 and improved it considerably and by the time they sold it in 1965 it had twenty seven bedrooms and comfortable owners' flat, but the tennis lawn and putting green were no longer there.

Where every Prospect Pleases!

Telephone
and
Telegrams:
NEWQUAY
564

LICENSED

From
4½ Gns.
per week

BLUE SEAS · GOLDEN SANDS
GLORIOUS SCENERY

A really modern Guest House with everything for your comfort. Overlooking sea.

Own Tennis Court and Putting Green.

Away from crowds, but near to everything to make your Holiday perfect.

MR. & MRS. FORRESTER-SMITH

Advertisement, 1937 when Trevelgue was as expensive as the Hotel Bristol.

1946 advertisement, when life at Trevelgue was one long party.

From 1965 it was owned by Ken Stratton in partnership with his close friends, Ronnie and Dorothy Pleydell. Dorothy, who was experienced and most capable, ran the hotel while Ronnie and Ken pursued their professional careers as musicians. Both had very good

1975 advertisement when owned by Ken Stratton and his partners.

local connections and were much in demand. They all lived comfortably in the flat in a ménage à trois for many years with Ken making his 'own arrangements' from time to time. Trevelgue flourished under Dorothy and they installed an attractive outdoor swimming pool and greatly improved the interior. Ken Stratton, who had originally been a carpenter by trade, worked hard in the winters upgrading the fixtures and fittings and it was a tidy well run little hotel. By the end of the 1978 season, with Ken by then married and living at St Columb, Dorothy and Ronnie felt ready to retire from the hotel business and so they put the Trevelgue on the market.

Trevelgue 1979

On behalf of Merrogwidden Limited, the company Peter Whittington had set up for his five daughters and three step-children, Peter began negotiating to buy Trevelgue Hotel from Ken Stratton and his partners. The negotiations were prolonged and drawn out because Peter wanted more land. The whole deal was done in the strictest secrecy, as these deals usually are, but Peter had thus managed to acquire the hotel with twenty seven bedrooms and grounds plus extra acres. He then bought a further few acres from his friend, Denis May. The space was all- important to Whittington and it was later to be put to good use. It is south facing and sheltered by the buildings from the worst of the north coast gales. He paid £190,000 for the hotel and land and immediately set about turning Trevelgue into a sixty bedroom hotel with all the latest modern amenities.

From the beginning, Peter planned to repeat his successful Bedruthan Steps formula — large, modern, with super facilities and arrangements for families. With his architect and friend, John Crowther, he spent most of 1979 planning it and in the autumn the builders moved in.

They enclosed the outdoor swimming pool and built two floors of bedrooms above it, all with bathrooms. All the new rooms were family suites with a very large bedroom for parents at the front and a small bedroom at the back for children, with a bathroom and wardrobe in the middle. Unusually, each bedroom had its own hot water cylinder with immersion heater, which would only be turned on when the suite was occupied, and that proved to be very successful. They also enlarged the dining room, bar and kitchen, and added a squash court. Even with two swimming pools, squash and tennis courts, and acres of ground for children, including a football pitch, adventure playground and pets corner, there was still space for anything else the family could think up.

As always with these new projects, one struggles to finish on time and of course the building costs escalate, and Trevelgue was no different. All the family hotels without exception have faced the same problems; a battle against time, and mounting costs. Again there were the usual hold ups; weather, late deliveries etc., and in the spring of 1980 very reluctantly Peter decided that the building simply could not be ready for that season. So the hotel did not open as planned and the building work continued all that summer and all the following winter. That was only possible because Bedruthan Steps and Bredon Court were doing so well.

Peter Whittington and John Crowther were firm friends with mutual respect for each other's talents, and they worked well together. John designed it and Peter applied himself to the engineering and technical problems. When the building was almost finished, John Crowther recalls he and Peter were sitting in the dining room gazing out of the window. Suddenly Peter said "We've got it wrong John. That floor is three feet too low — if it were three feet higher the view would be enormously improved." John Crowther said "I think you are

Peter Whittington in a serious mood.

right, but it is too late to do anything about it now." "No!" said Peter, "We must raise it." And with the utmost difficulty, and although it caused a long delay, raise it they did! Such was Whittington's determination and tenacity.

For months there had been many family discussions about who was to run the new hotel. It was offered firstly to Sonia, Peter and Barbara's second daughter. She turned it down because she thought her father would not allow her to make decisions and she was afraid he would want to control every detail. If she took it on, she insisted, she would want it entirely on her own. Then Nicholas Malcolm, Tom and Doreen Malcolm's son said he would "like to have a go at it", and so it was arranged. The new, enlarged Trevelgue Hotel with sixty bedrooms opened with a flourish in May 1981, with Nicholas Malcolm in charge. He was about thirty at the time and he had married Linda Rowsell, in Hawaii, in December 1979. They had two children, Rosie, born in 1982 and Tom, in 1985.

True to family tradition Trevelgue was at first put together with furnishings being handed down from Bedruthan Steps and Bredon Court, and the furniture Peter had made years before with the teak from Battersea Power Station. The whole family has had long experience at putting hotels together without spending too much money in the first place; plushier replacements come when the hotel has found its feet.

For the first season, of course, there were many unfinished corners and the furnishings were utilitarian to say the least. The bedrooms were sparsely furnished; in fact Bettye, with her traditional ideas, thought the furnishings rather odd. Not really conventional bedroom furniture, she thought. In fact it was all there, built in, and so very little was needed, but most of the rooms were huge and there was so much space to fill. However, when the guests arrived, in the main they thought them splendid; although one disgruntled guest did tell Nicholas he thought the bedroom furnishings were more suitable for a university campus! In fact they were later to be upgraded.

There were the usual difficulties about staff rooms but the following year Peter managed to buy Sea Croft, the little hotel next door to Trevelgue, with fourteen bedrooms. He paid £70,000 for it and with it came another large parcel of land at the back, which was soon put to good use. Sea Croft today is comfortable staff quarters. It has eighteen bedrooms, many with sea view! In Sea Croft there was a large cream four oven Aga — and Peter, who had not discovered the joy of an Aga, threw it out and sold it to his nephew, John Armstrong, for £50. John was delighted: surely the bargain of the century!

Trevelgue, after Peter Whittington got his hands on it.

In the early days Nicholas had a very tiresome time with his stepfather, Peter. It is not easy to create something and then turn one's back on it and hand it over and in the early 1980s Peter and Mary Whittington found it very hard to let go. They had over twenty years experience behind them and Nicholas had had little experience and no serious responsibility before, but he was "in the hot seat" coping with the problems and he wanted to be left alone to do it in his own way. Many times Bettye lent him a sympathetic ear! It is doubtful whether he would have survived at Trevelgue had fate not intervened in the mid 1980s as the reader will hear.

Nicholas very quickly identified his main source of business — catering for families, and he set about it with enthusiasm. It must have been the most family orientated hotel in Cornwall, and Nicholas makes no bones about it. The hotel was described in the brochure as

"...the UK's first family only hotel. We only take customers who have children, so at Trevelgue you will find that there is no compromise in the running of the hotel which is done exclusively with families in mind.

We have swept away the formality of the traditional British hotel and replaced it with an atmosphere where children are truly made welcome and parents can relax..."

He installed every amenity he could think of to keep children entertained and happy and the parents were not forgotten. There is a gymnasium where aerobic classes are held, and hairdressing and beauty salons with three treatment rooms where mothers can sit back and be pampered. For a while Trevelgue only took people with children, and that proved to be a great success, as the children could be taken completely off their parents' hands. It was a very bold move on Nicholas' part, but it paid off. All this sounds as though the hotel is over-run with children — certainly there are sometimes one hundred and thirty youngsters staying with their parents, but they are so well segregated and organised that peace usually reigns.

Nicholas still organises clubs for each age group, which today are: "Nippers (ratio 1:3) 1 year and under. Pirates (ratio 1:4) 2 & 3 years. Adventure Club (ratio 1:8) 4 to 7 years. O-Zone Club (organised activities) 8 to 12 years which is run only in school holidays. There is also a club for 13 years and older". At times Trevelgue employs as many as twenty helpers, in shifts, to run the clubs and look after the children. But most of the guests are 'well heeled' and are used to paying for their children to be taken off their hands. It gives them a peaceful holiday and the children have a wonderful time.

Nicholas has inherited a strong flair for design from his father, and in the main, didn't go in for the "Wattiez bargains" the rest of the family bought. He is, first and foremost, a designer and he designed many of the decorative items and then set up a small workshop in the winter and used local labour to put his designs together. He also designed much of the furniture and built it in where possible. As he said, "If you "build in" a bed you do not have to carpet under it". He is full of bright ideas and the hotel looks splendid.

Sadly Linda and Nicholas split up in 1989 and in 1993 Nicholas married Sarah Hunter, a probation officer, and their son, Jack, was born in March 1996. Unfortunately Sarah does not find hotels beguiling or interesting. When asked if she sometimes went to Trevelgue she replied "No, not really. It is just somewhere where Nicholas works". But he loves it and it is greatly to his credit that single-handedly he coped so competently for many years. It is brilliantly successful.

In 1994 Trevelgue was given Egon Ronay's Family Hotel of the Year award, and Nicholas was immensely pleased when, in 1995 the BBC Television programme "That's Life", presented by Esther Rantzen, decided that Trevelgue was the most parent friendly hotel in Britain.

Nicholas is a talented organiser, and he has succeeded in putting his personal stamp on the hotel today, which very much reflects his personal taste and ideas. He employs many young staff from the colonies. They come in the summer for the surfing and he often designs their uniforms, which can be very individual; sometimes 'way out'. Today Trevelgue has a young, vibrant atmosphere about it, which is refreshing and different, but its standards have remained constant.

When Nicholas decided he had got Trevelgue running smoothly he turned his attention to courting the journalists who write about hotels. He invited them down, accommodated them, wined and dined them and, as a result, several of them wrote glowing articles which appeared in national papers and magazines. Clever indeed! For it is more productive to entertain journalists than to advertise in the national press. In the 1990s Trevelgue spent little money on advertising and it was always bustling for a long season. Well done, Nicholas! As he put it "To be successful in a holiday hotel one has to decide who one is catering for and then do it better than anyone else." That is a highly successful formula, as the family have proved.

In 1996, Sarah Whittington, Peter and Barbara's third daughter, an artist and potter, by then married to her second husband and living in Devon, decided that she wished to have her money out of Trevelgue. Although the family tried hard to persuade her that she would be much wiser to leave it in the family business and draw a steady income from it, she insisted. At the end of the year she was paid out £200,000 for her share, which left Trevelgue owned by six of Peter and Mary Whittington's children. Sonia, Peter and Barbara's second daughter, had already taken her money out in 1992 to buy Polmaily House Hotel, in Scotland. Today the only one of Peter's first family who has retained her interest in the hotel is Maria.

Nicholas has a Merrogwidden shareholders' meeting with his sisters once a year at Trevelgue, when sparks sometimes fly, but he has made a huge success of the hotel, and nowadays the whole family acknowledges the fact and wisely leaves the running of it to him. He does it well. What is more he works very hard in the winters on improvements and additions and designing decorative fittings. The hotel has gone from strength to strength but like all Newquay hotels it went through a difficult patch at the end of the twentieth century.

In 1995-1996 the dining room was enlarged to seat an extra sixty guests comfortably and the following year fifteen extra suites were built, each accommodating a family of four. The new rooms faced south and overlooked the large, kidney shaped outdoor swimming pool. When full the hotel then catered for two hundred and eighty people of which more than one hundred were usually children. Imagine the dining room at breakfast — at times it must have been bedlam!! But they don't have any nonsense with children in the evening. They are still very firm about not having under-sevens in the dining room during dinner. The baby listeners and children's clubs look after them while their parents dine. Unfortunately Nicholas found that some parents resolutely refused to be separated from their "little darlings" even at dinner and that did cause problems. He later dealt with that by creating a separate dining room where families all eat together. There are forty high-chairs available for babies.

In the 1997-1998 winter the whole ground floor front of the hotel was thrown forward 15 ft. to make extra bar and lounge space which includes a small dance floor, and there is a long bar with decorations and decor that give it a 'beach bar' atmosphere. It is called Beachcombers Bar and the decor has a strong Caribbean flavour with colourful modern stained glass windows, and light fittings made of bottles and lifebelts, all designed by Nicholas and made in his workshop. The carpet with a sea shell motif was especially woven to Nicholas' design.

In 1998 football coaching was offered to the youngsters during the school holidays. A Football Association coach was booked to run five-day training sessions. Unfortunately that didn't work very well owing to the fickle weather. If it was a brilliantly sunny day the boys were off to the beach and didn't turn up for the football training and the coach was left cooling his costly heels.

In the winter of 1998-1999 Trevelgue remained open and for the first time catered for functions of all kind. They had one rather interesting booking in November. "Neilsons Ski", a firm specialising in chalet ski holidays, booked the hotel for a week for a training course for their chalet girls and boys. One hundred and sixty youngsters were on the course and they had to make their own beds, serve at table, and do much of the cooking. Neilsons paid £39.00 a night per head for them. Every evening there were activities laid on: lectures, quizzes, etc., and the girls and boys had a marvellous week. They spent about £1,000 nightly in the bar! For Trevelgue it meant a great deal of organisation and of course much clearing up afterwards, but the course was a big success and Neilsons later wrote to Nicholas and said it was the best course they had ever run. He was delighted, and immediately pencilled in the date for the November 1999 course, which again proved most successful.

The hotel is now licensed as a venue for weddings and Nicholas has designed a splendid setting for them, rather like an exotic Caribbean beach hut. He would only need to sprinkle a few buckets of sand in front of it and the bridal couples, with soaring imaginations, would feel they were getting married in the Caribbean. It is extremely popular with Newquay's young people and several very colourful weddings have been held there. A lively imagination is a marvellous thing when one is young and in love!

In the autumn of 1998 after eighteen busy seasons Nicholas felt some serious refurbishment was needed, especially in the bathrooms, and so, ever resourceful, he shipped a load of marble over from Spain for them. They became very stylish.

For the 1999 season a new large hydrotherapy spa, which takes ten people, with a sauna beside it was installed by the indoor swimming pool. The spa was one of the first and was highly successful with, eventually, six treatment rooms and operators kept busy — but as happens soon every hotel copied him; today many have spas and therefore it has declined somewhat. It didn't help when the head beautician left and her local clients followed her. Behind the hotel a new nine hole par three approach golf course was built. That has been very popular. Apart from all that the kitchens were "tidied up" — the new floor alone cost £10,000. "So boring," says Nicholas, "but it does look better."

By 1999 Nicholas, who is forward thinking, had been running Trevelgue for some twenty years, but he felt there were too many hotels in Newquay chasing the same market. On paper, they all sounded the same. There were at least a dozen offering the "best". Best position, views, facilities and food, but in fact they varied enormously, and there were good, bad, and indifferent ones. Some took children free throughout the season, which in Bettye's view was plain barmy. It must be so difficult for visitors to decide which hotel will suit them.

Nicholas is courageous and he firmly decided to change the name and image of Trevelgue to Sands Resort, which he did in November 1999. It specialises in "quality parent time" with the full range of health-farm facilities for adults and an energetic programme of sporting activities for children. There are also capable child carers for the little ones. In fact it is a completely new concept, and is certainly quite different from anything that is being offered in Newquay at the moment — very much a one off! It is in a league of its own for families with young children.

Sands Family Resort 2000

One might ask — "If Trevelgue was so successful why change the name? It was a very expensive operation to do so." Here's why!

In the valley behind the hotel is Trevelgue Holiday Park, also offering all the latest amenities and facilities for young people. It is massive and noisy and can accommodate ten thousand, mostly youngsters. Over the years there was confusion between the two establishments. Guests, letters, and sometimes even bills arrive at the wrong place. Also Trevelgue is not an easy name for strangers to pronounce or remember and there are at least half a dozen hotels in Newquay with the prefix TRE- this that or the other, whereas Sands Family Resort is distinctive and immediately lifts the establishment into another category. It certainly has become a small resort in its own right and surely deserves the title?

Below is the text of the letter Nicholas sent out in autumn 1999 with the new Sands Family Resort brochure.

" Hi

Welcome to our 2000 millennium brochure, which not only heralds a new century for us, but also a raft of exciting new developments that we hope will strengthen our ties with our existing valued customers and extend to new guests an enhanced "Family Holiday" experience.

For the past 20 years I have worked with my staff to establish the hotel as a "children's Paradise", where parents could relax knowing that their children were happy, occupied and contented. As a result of these efforts we have earned many awards, commendation from the travel press and, most importantly, the trust that so many of you place in us, year after year, in making your family holiday a good one.

Since starting work in my parents' hotel in 1963, I have seen tremendous change in the requirements of families on holiday. In order to ensure that we maintain a leading position in family holiday provision, I have spent the last year listening to our customers' views about their ideal holiday and this brochure, along with the new name and philosophy, is the result of this process.

Our new "Resort philosophy" is designed to ensure that not only do we carry on making sure that children still get their "Paradise", but that we also focus more on the needs of parents and provide quality time of their own.

The "Quality Parents' Time" might be dinner without your children, a relaxing massage, a chance to sit and read a book, finding a partner for a casual game of golf or tennis, or just the opportunity to walk on the cliff and watch the sun set — but knowing that your children are safe and happy.

At "Sands Family Resort" we are investing in the facilities and staff training to ensure that we can offer the sporting, relaxation and childcare, facilities and services, to facilitate your own personal "Quality moments".

Holidays with my own children Rosie, Tom and Jack, have demonstrated to me the need for truly "family friendly" hotels. I hope that my staff and I can welcome you to "Sands Family Resort" this year and prove to you that we have become one of these rare destinations. "

That letter and the change of name proved to be highly successful.

The exciting adventure playground at Sands.

For more than twenty years Nicholas Malcolm ran the hotel on his own, but happily in 2005 his daughter, Rosie, joined him and she ran the bar with much aplomb, but after a couple of years she returned to her first, and greatest, passion, horses . In 2006 his elder son, Tom, joined the team. He soon learned the ropes and today he is duty manager. He is full of enthusiasm and is good at it, and gives Nicholas much needed support.

Sands must be the most child friendly hotel in the south west. Most hotels take children, many hotels tolerate them, some hotels suffer them, but at Sands they are welcomed with open arms. At times they have one hundred and forty children and about the same number of adults — but it all goes smoothly because the main aim at Sands is to give families with their children good holidays, and they do it superbly. Everybody is catered for, even babies.

Sands Family Resort had a busy winter 2007-2008 converting the squash court into two conference rooms, equipped with all the latest technology, each for forty people. As Newquay grows in stature with its new image more and more firms are bringing their conferences to the town and it is a lucrative side of the business. Nicholas also refurbished some thirty rooms, which was a major undertaking as all the walls had to be re-plastered to get rid of the rough stippling: a boring and expensive job, but the rooms are much improved, and they are a far cry from the original simple, pine furnished rooms which were more suitable for a students' hostel. The ground floor has also been

Porth Suite at Sands – a conference room, equipped with all the latest technology.

Sands refurbished bedrooms – a far cry from the sparsely furnished Trevelgue bedrooms.

re-arranged and refurbished. It was always stylish, Nicholas would see to that, but it is now much 'plushier' with comfortable sofas etc. More appropriate for a good 3-star hotel, which Sands now is.

The reader has heard some amusing tales of life in hotels. Nicholas tells one. In 2007 a man booked in at Sands Resort for six weeks while his divorce was going through. He paid up fully in advance. At 11.00 a.m. on the first morning he appeared in a dress and earrings, which caused something of a stir. However, things went from bad to worse as, although he swore he didn't drink, his room was full of empty vodka bottles. Clearly they had an alcoholic transvestite on their hands — for six weeks! He was foul mouthed and abusive and so they decided to return his money and eject him. He became even more abusive; it caused a frightful fuss, but eventually they threw him out. An hour later he was back rather shame-faced – he'd lost one of his earrings!

Looking back, how wise Peter Whittington was to insist on buying all the extra land behind the hotel. Some has been put to good use and it is possible that in the future some will be used for development. It has certainly made a difference to what Nicholas has been able to do at Sands Resort. Sadly, Peter was never aware how successful his last project had become. It set his second family up well and to their credit they have carried on the family tradition for the last twenty two years most successfully.

Nicholas Malcolm and his sons Tom and Jack (centre).

Edgcumbe Hotel
1971 – 1988

When their grandmother died in January 1971 John Armstrong and Mary Ashworth inherited her house in Hilgrove Road, Newquay, but it was leased to the hotel and so the upper floors continued to be used for sleepers in conjunction with the Edgcumbe. On John's return he took over the ground floor and refurbished it completely to his taste, including giving his bedroom an elaborate bathroom with a terrazzo sunken bath, etc., and a huge built-in wardrobe. His parents insisted he paid for these alterations himself. They seemed somewhat over-the-top, but by the time he had finished the flat was much improved and he lived there, with Maggie Dyer who at that time was in charge of the Housekeeping at the Edgcumbe, until he married in 1974.

Staff accommodation is always a problem. It must be provided because the working hours are unsocial and the staff must be on hand, but staff quarters can be, and usually are, noisy, untidy and collectively an eyesore. Of course there are exceptions — tidy, quiet people who need a corner by themselves, but they are in the minority. Usually hotel staff are young, gregarious, often ready for a party when they have finished work — late! All the hotels in turn have provided staff rooms on the premises only to realise that it is more satisfactory to accommodate them in separate houses nearby — but out of sight and earshot! And that is how they are usually housed today.

The Edgcumbe had three separate staff houses in nearby roads. One for the chaps, one for the girls, and one for the quieter staff. It usually worked, but it was not very popular with the people living in neighbouring houses! The young hotel staff usually have no homes nearby and they like to decorate their rooms, put up their posters, and play their music. Imagine what a purple ceiling and black walls covered in posters can do to a room, and that, and similar colour schemes, were often found in rooms at the end of a season.

And the NOISE! Noise has always been another problem in the staff houses; the young love loud music. Once, while Bettye and John were having dinner at the Edgcumbe, the receptionist came twice to tell them the neighbours next to a staff house in Ulalia Road had telephoned to complain about the noise coming from the house. As it was only early evening the Armstrongs decided to ignore it. The receptionist came a third time; the neighbours had called the police. Bettye and John thought they had better go and see what was going on. They arrived at the house with the police close behind them. The noise was deafening and coming from the ground floor front room.

They burst into the room, which was crammed with about forty young people. There was a stunned silence. “What is going on here, and whose room is this?” fiercely from John Armstrong. A little voice came from the back of the crowd.

“This is my room. It’s my 21st birthday, we’re having a party. I didn’t ask all these people, they just came!”

“Of course you want a party on your 21st birthday, but you cannot have it in a little room like this. Why don’t you have it on Tolcarne Beach?” asked Bettye.

“Can’t do that M’am, they would put the dogs on us.” And the sad truth is, they would! Gone were the days when a party could be held on the beach in the evening. The young guests melted away and the party was over — bad luck, Birthday Boy!

At the Edgcumbe the original staff rooms beneath the kitchen had always been very poor. Most of them eventually became a cold store, butchery, bakery, vegetable room etc. One evening at about 10.30 p.m. there was a commotion outside the hotel. Someone rushed in and said “Call an ambulance. A man has collapsed on the pavement.” The porter went out to investigate and came back unperturbed. “It’s quite all right” he said, “it’s just Dennis coming home after his day off”. Dennis, the long-term pot man, would spend his entire day off and his week’s pay in the pub 100 yards from the hotel and then crawl back to his “hole” under the kitchen. The next morning he would be back in his pot room at 7.30 a.m., and work right through to his next day off — it was his way of life and there are many kitchen porters like him.

Dennis amid his ‘pots’ after his day off.

Ken Stratton, who had moved with the Armstrongs to Narrowcliff in 1959, continued to entertain and delight the guests young and old. He was very popular and during all those years he played for every private party the family gave. How could a party be flat with Ken in charge? They never were.

The Armstrongs had complete confidence in Mrs Burt and therefore for the first time in many years they were able to enjoy a peaceful life at Feock away from the hotel. Mrs Burt kept the Edgcumbe running very successfully, she could not have given the hotel more attention had it been her own. Bettye would set up the winter programme of improvements and refurbishments and leave them to Mrs Burt to deal with. The finishing touches were left until the Armstrongs returned from their winter holidays in Gstaad. Every year there were more bathrooms and showers. To Bettye that was a game of ingenuity for, as the reader has heard, they had to be put in without loss of beds — it was still 'bods in beds' that earned the money. Bettye made sure they were not lost while Mrs Burt ensured they were filled. She was well able to supervise the alterations and watched the expenditure as though every penny was coming out of her own pocket. Under her management the Edgcumbe was probably the most successful hotel in Newquay at the time.

At the hotels people often ask "How do you buy your furnishings?" A good question, for how does one furnish hotels with good quality, stylish furnishings with an antique flavour which must be constantly replaced without the resources of an Arab with an oil well? In the late 1970s an advertisement appeared in the Hotel and Caterer offering second hand five star hotel furnishings. This was to prove a very useful source for all the family. A beguiling little rogue called Nick Wattiez had built up a thriving business. When Arabs and others were completely stripping and refurbishing their grand London hotels, he had the contract for clearing them, even down to the door knobs. He then sent out lists of what he would be buying, or thought he would be buying, and of course, there was a clamour from his customers for the more attractive furnishings. Sometimes Nick would sell, and be paid for, not only the items he had, but the ones he hoped would come his way. Then, of course, if he didn't manage to get them he was in trouble and he had several long 'holidays' at Her Majesty's expense — but he was resilient and when he was released he always bounced back. Fortunately for him he had a well developed sense of humour which never seemed to desert him.

The difficulty was that the descriptions of available articles were often wildly inaccurate. Nick was colour blind for a start, so colour, size, quality and condition had all to be carefully checked. Nothing would be paid for until it was over the door step and had been thoroughly inspected, and everyone understood that. His delivery system was erratic, to say the least. Wild looking, exhausted chaps (the most regular of these bearing the name "Haddock") would arrive at any hour in the biggest pantechnicons ever seen, often with their floozie on board, having driven all through the night. They then disgorged a motley collection of goods on to the car park which soon resembled a large flea market or car boot sale. Everyone raked through the goods and with much bargaining on the 'phone with Nick by the end of the day the hotel generally had some pleasing new furnishings — although it was known for the whole load to be refused and sent back, much to Wattiez's fury! However, all that came to an abrupt end in about 1999 when he was sent to prison for ten years. He is a likeable rogue, but a fool, he could have had (in fact, he had) a very successful business but he simply could not play the game straight. In 2006 he was still inside and trading from there. He was on the telephone offering this and that — he is nothing if not a survivor.

In the mid '70s the wind of change began to blow strongly around the Newquay tourist scene; the bureaucratic lion began to roar with an ever louder voice and life became increasingly difficult for hotels. They began to be strangled by rules and regulations but the Armstrongs, happily ensconced in Feock, were hardly aware of it — Mrs Burt was still managing to keep the Edgcumbe fully booked. For thirty years Newquay had enjoyed enormous prosperity but the boom was over! The decline began gently, but by the late1970s it was not so easy to fill the hotels as it had been for thirty years, packed to overflowing. No longer were they booked solid for the summer by the end of January. Bookings had to be worked at; the holiday-makers had much choice and could bargain about terms. A price war set in and the battle about free children began. Business-wise that was lunacy but it did not make life any easier for the hotels who refused because they felt they could not afford to give such discounts, and it all became very cut-throat and difficult.

At first the family hotels did not really feel the pinch. They were just aware that they had to increase their efforts to fill the rooms. Guests were becoming more discerning and would no longer sleep out or accept rooms without baths or showers. Standards were creeping up; no longer would "anything go" the hotels had to pull their socks up. It was becoming a buyer's market and there was strong competition growing from other quarters; camp sites and package holidays were coming into their own.

The Armstrongs' Return to Newquay

Having decided to return to Newquay Bettye, more than ten years younger than Michael, resourceful and not one to buckle down under adversity, set about it. She found a large secluded bungalow facing Trenance Gardens in Newquay which they moved into in 1980, and there slowly picked up the threads of their life again.

Bettye needed people around her to make her tick and so she surrounded herself with them — in fact she set up a 'household' of helpers. First there was Joan Brooker[1], weeping on the phone because her husband had left her. Bettye invited her to join them in Gstaad for a month. She did some of the driving, sat with Michael while Bettye skied and was generally helpful. It worked well.

Soon they were joined by another bereaved old friend, Roddy Roch, who had an estate in Spain. Roddy, like Michael, was essentially a flying man who had been in ATA, and had long been the Armstrongs' favourite house guest in Feock. In 1980 his German wife died. Roddy, as English as John Bull, felt isolated in Spain and he arrived on the Armstrongs' door step and virtually lived with them until he died in 1984, twelve weeks before Michael. Roddy fitted in well, doing some of the driving and acting as an aide, helping Michael with his personal needs. He was congenial company for both of them; he and Michael would 'open the hangar doors' and talk flying for hours. He eased their path and with his and Joan Booker's help they were able to limp along. The truth was that they were all having a difficult time and they supported each other.

Michael Armstrong in Switzerland after his stroke, with Joan Brooker, who became a helper.

As can be imagined Michael's stroke had really turned the Armstrong's life upside down and further adjustments had to be made

---

[1] Manageress of the Coniston in 1958. She stayed with the Armstrongs for some time in the 1980s until her divorce was settled and she bought a cottage in Cubert which Bettye converted for her.

if they were to do anything other than sit in a heap. The homely little one bedroom flat in Hammersmith which the whole family had used happily as a pied-à-terre for some twenty years no longer fitted the bill; they needed a second bedroom, Michael found the tiny spiral staircase frightfully difficult and the flat was too far out of town. So one spring morning in 1981 John and Bettye Armstrong took the early Newquay to London flight to meet an estate agent. Their specification was: two bedrooms on the ground floor in the Kensington area. The agent showed them about six flats and by lunchtime they had chosen one in Duchess of Bedford Walk, adjoining Holland Park in Camden Hill, just north of Kensington. It cost £70,000. It had two double bedrooms, a large reception room and was on the ground floor. Bettye and John caught the afternoon flight back to Cornwall well satisfied with their day's work. The flat was in a deplorable state but Bettye soon arranged for it to be smartened up and given an extra bathroom. It proved to be a sound investment and a great boon for the many business trips the family have always had to make to London. It is still in the family today.

In 1982 poor Michael faced another serious set-back. A drunken motorist slewed across Henver Road and hit their car head on. Fortunately at the time they were only doing twenty-five miles an hour but Michael sustained injuries to his back which gave him severe pain for the rest of his life, and from then on for him it was an even steeper downward path; he deteriorated slowly and life became ever more difficult. For the last six months of his life he felt he had come to the end of the road; he had constant pain in his back. Michael had a deep and abiding faith, and he was ready to go. Every night when the nurse came to put him to bed and give him his pills he would say, "The only pill I'm waiting for is the last one" and he really meant it. When he died in August, 1984 it was a happy release and the family's grief was mitigated to some extent by the fact that his suffering was over.

When Michael died Bettye felt bereft, aimless and hopeless. They had been married forty-one years and suddenly she felt she had no purpose in life and, as she put it, she was "not ready to sit down and pick up her knitting or her tapestry". She was still on the sunny side of seventy, for heavens sake! Her ever loyal Nannie came to her rescue and moved in and although then in her late seventies Nannie made herself useful feeding the dogs, making tea, answering the phone and above all being there — she really was a comfort.

With no object in life and back in Newquay after being away for almost twenty years, Bettye explored the town with fresh eyes. She hardly recognized it, it had changed so much and not for the better.

Gone were the traditional high class shops; they had been replaced by surf shops, betting shops, amusement arcades, fast food outlets and the like, and she was shocked. It was no longer the Newquay she knew, there was a different atmosphere and the visitors were different, too.

A few evenings later Bettye went for dinner to a smallish hotel out of Newquay where they offered no more than reasonable food in pleasant surroundings — and no entertainment at all. She discovered they were charging exactly double what the Newquay hotels were charging and with no free children and that brought home to her the drawback of having an hotel in Newquay. At that time the Edgcumbe was spending £700.00 per week (£2,000 today) on entertainment. There is no doubt the seed of movement was sown in Bettye's mind by that dinner and her walk around the town.

From then on she began to feel restless; she and Mrs Burt put their heads together and seriously considered moving out of Newquay. By the mid-eighties the Edgcumbe really was fully developed. All the bedrooms had a bath or shower, and Bettye was proud of the fact that the only beds they had lost were extra children's beds tucked into the corners of the rooms — and they had not lost many of those. There were still ninety bedrooms. The hotel had every amenity it could be given: two swimming pools, coffee shop, boutique, hairdressing salon, two dance floors, two bars, sauna and solarium, billiards room, etc. There was no more space to do anything. Bettye and Mrs Burt felt it had nowhere to go, but down.

The post war boom was well and truly over and Newquay was no longer a resort for middle class families. It was slowly becoming a leading surfing Mecca in Europe. No doubt that was good business for the town but the Edgcumbe never could offer what the new breed of holiday maker

Edgcumbe has long been known as a holiday hotel with a happy, casual, 'unstuffy' atmosphere and we cherish that reputation for it is just that.
But, there is one thing . . . .

Wear what you please but at dinner in the evening we like it to be casually elegant — most of our guests prefer this too ! Please — no jeans or tee-shirts in the evening.

We hope you will have a splendid holiday and if you come to Edgcumbe we shall do our best to see that it is so.

Mrs Burt's dress code for the Edgcumbe guests.

wanted and it all began to get rather tiresome. There was one middle class family who had stayed every August for some years. Father was a jacket and tie man in the evenings. After their last visit in the early '80s he wrote and complained bitterly and explained that he would not be bringing his family again. They had been severely offended by the garb and language of guests at adjoining tables. Mrs Burt was most upset. She had tried hard to enforce standards of dress in the evenings and it had proved difficult, in fact almost impossible. Sometimes guests would say they only had jeans, and often they would take umbrage at being told what to wear!

Bettye felt that Newquay was going down-market, the surfing fraternity were taking over; even the famous cavern on the headland, given to the local council many years before by Colonel Tangye of Glendorgal was deemed unsafe and in 1987 it was decided to demolish it in the name of safety. It took three and a half tonnes of dynamite sunk into fifty-six holes which had been drilled into the headland to blow it up. It vanished in a cloud of smoke, much to the regret of the long-term locals and the concert goers, and that was the end of the concerts. The middle class families which had been the backbone of Newquay's and the Edgcumbe's prosperity for so long were no longer coming and it was time to move on. The 94 dollar question was where? Bettye visited many hotels around the county, but none

Blowing up the 'concert' cavern, Porth, in 1998.

seemed to fit the bill. When Budock Vean Hotel at Mawnan Smith came on the market in 1985 and was offered to the family Bettye was very keen to sell the Edgcumbe and buy it. She took Mrs Burt to see it; she was also of the opinion that if a move out of Newquay could be arranged it would be beneficial to the family and she promised that if they bought Budock Vean she would move there and take charge of it. A price was virtually agreed, there was a potential buyer for the Edgcumbe so they seemed 'all set'.

However, John Armstrong and Mary Ashworth thought otherwise and one day John rang his mother and said that he and Mary would like to speak to her. She went to John's house to see them and they said "We think Budock Vean is too big for you to take on and it is too far away from us." Bettye who was still emotionally fragile from the trauma of 1984 burst into tears and gave in. She was very disappointed, but did not feel strong enough to battle with Mary and John at that time. Budock Vean was quickly sold to others, and life went on as before with Mrs Burt in charge at the Edgcumbe and Bettye wondering 'what next'.

Bettye thought she might take up Bridge. She planned to stay in the London flat and take a course of lessons at the London Bridge School and was in contact with them when in November 1985 she was invited to a lunch party at Cubert and there she met Tommie Gray, a widower of long standing, who lived at Ladock. They struck up an immediate rapport. He was obviously very doggy, which appealed to her. When he invited her out to dinner (incidentally to The Nare which was his favourite hotel) she soon realised he was different and she was intrigued. All her life she had been surrounded by people striving for something: socially, financially, professionally or whatever, and here was a man who had little, wanted nothing and felt he had more than enough for his worldly needs. As a Master Brewer and senior executive with a national brewery he had been successful in life but had turned his back on a substantial pension and escaped to Cornwall in search of peace. Now, fifteen years later when they met, Tommie was utterly content to be in Cornwall with his garden and his dog and that to Bettye was like a breath of fresh air. She was completely beguiled by him and their engagement was announced the following July at Bettye's seventieth birthday party, a dance given by John and Carol at "Carevick", Cubert, which had already been arranged.

One person who was not pleased at this turn of events was Nannie. She had been with the family for nearly forty years and since Michael

Armstrong's death had been company for Bettye, but there was a price to be paid. Whenever Bettye went out in the evening Nannie always waited up for her, however late. She would then make tea and would want to hear all about it, not very exciting, mostly supper with the family or close friends, but it seemed churlish to deny her that small pleasure. However, when Tommie Gray arrived on the scene it was a different matter. Nannie took umbrage and would not speak to him, not even to say good morning, and there was no more waiting up — just as well; it was sometimes very late! She had to be removed to a cottage of John's where she lived until she died in 1994 aged eighty-four.

Nannie - devoted for forty years

Bettye and Tommie were married in Cubert Parish Church in September 1986 followed by a reception for about twenty-eight people at "Carevick". Happily the whole family accepted Tommie Gray and were most supportive. After a honeymoon spent touring in North Wales they lived in Tommie's house at Ladock — it was most important to him that he provided the marital home, and they lived there quietly for the next two years. Bettye had found her new path in life and all thoughts of hotels went out of her head, as did the plans about Bridge. Tommie hated the game; he felt his childhood home life had been marred by his mother's Bridge parties and so considered it a ghastly game.

Tommy and Bettye's wedding, September 1986.

Out of the blue in the summer of 1988 an estate agent rang the Grays and said "The Nare Hotel is on the market. Would you be interested?" Bettye was out at the time and Tommie, who answered the 'phone said, "Yes, perhaps we might". Bettye was amazed at his reply because it had not even crossed their minds that they might take on another hotel. Since marrying Tommie she had thought no more about them. However, always ready for the next thing, she was delighted by his reaction and before long they were both very keen on the idea.

So they set about selling the Edgcumbe and buying The Nare. Considering their ages, seventy-seven and seventy-two years at the time, it was, perhaps, a bold move which they would not have contemplated for one moment unless Mrs Burt had agreed to move with them lock, stock and barrel and manage it for them. Fortunately, she was of the same mind and was also ready to tackle a new venture. For Tommie and Bettye it was a stimulating retirement project and they were filled with enthusiasm for it.

Although there had been much idle talk about moving from the Edgcumbe for some time it came as something of a shock to the younger members of the family when they realised the "Edgcumbe Team" were seriously bent on buying The Nare; they did not approve of the scheme and there followed many heated discussions. The Edgcumbe had a strong following of regular guests who returned year after year and business was still flourishing — so why sell? This time with Tommie's support Bettye was determined. She felt sure the Edgcumbe had run its course and time was to prove her right.

Bettye, married for two years and living out of Newquay as she had for most of the previous twenty years, felt strongly that the hotel could only go into decline. It could not be enlarged or upgraded as there was no space left and therefore it had no further potential; she felt nothing further could be done with it, and she wanted OUT! In this she was supported by Tommie and Mrs Burt. In spite of all this it is unlikely that the move would have happened if they had not been offered The Nare Hotel which the family had already looked at years before and decided had great possibilities, and so in 1988 Bettye carried her point and the Edgcumbe was put on the market.

It was a momentous decision to sell the Edgcumbe. It had been the cornerstone of the family fortunes for more than sixty years and had spawned all the other family hotels, including Bredon Court. At the time it was arguably the most successful hotel in Newquay. Mrs Burt had been a very able Manager for over twenty years and had been constantly improving the standard as the hotel grew. By the time the Edgcumbe was put on the market in 1988 it was a good, ninety bedroom 3-star AA hotel.

Then, as can be imagined, there were many consultations with John and Mary, both of whom were very much against the move. Tommie and Bettye could never understand "why?" It was obviously such a sound business deal for the family. However to John's credit, reluctant as he was, he offered to negotiate the sale of the Edgcumbe, which he did brilliantly. Fortunately there were two local businessmen who really wanted it and could afford to buy it and he eventually sold it at a very good price. By the time the small staff houses belonging to the Edgcumbe had been sold separately the Grays were able to buy The Nare for approximately £1,000,000 and also have capital with which to upgrade it and put it into good order. The Grays were well satisfied. The timing was immaculate too. The Edgcumbe was handed over and the move to The Nare completed within three days of each other. Now Bettye and Tommie had something to get to grips with.

The family gave a farewell luncheon party at Hotel Bristol in December 1988 for the permanent staff who, under the terms of the sale contract, had to be left behind. The whole family were there including the younger Ashworths. There were about seven members of staff who had been at the Edgcumbe nearly twenty years and two who had been there for nearly thirty years. Mrs Burt was very sorry to leave them and made a splendid speech thanking them for their loyal support over the years. Bettye found it all very emotional but the die was cast and on 3rd January 1989 the new owner, Mr Christopheros, who already owned the Barrowfield Hotel in Hilgrove Road, took over the Edgcumbe Hotel on Narrowcliff and its excellent staff.

The family and Mrs Burt were sad at severing the ties with the Edgcumbe, especially about leaving their loyal long-term staff. The truth was that the regular middle class guests, who were the backbone of the business, were no longer coming to Newquay and the new guests were of a different age, class and type. The Grays and Mrs Burt, old fashioned and traditional, didn't find them acceptable, and what was more, couldn't cope with them and they were determined they were not going to have all those "free" and often badly behaved children! They had outgrown Newquay, or perhaps Newquay had outgrown them: it was time to move on. They had new fields to conquer.

The family had owned the Edgcumbe Hotel, Newquay for sixty-three years, from 1926-1989, and they were sad to part with it, but there is no doubt it had reached its full potential and had had its day.

From 1989 it steadily declined; it soon lost its 3-star AA rating. The dining room was enlarged and could then seat over three hundred people on long canteen style tables. In the autumn it catered for what are known as 'Turkey and Tinsel' parties; and the staff Christmas parties for small, local firms.

Troublesome Years for Peter and his Family

Although it had been arranged that Barbara would run Bredon Court after she and Peter divorced Peter had been unable to let go of it completely, and this caused problems. In 1968 Barbara had married Donald Carlton, a retired mining engineer who had spent his working life in South Africa. They bought "Jennings", a charming cottage with a few acres and a large wooded garden near Goonhavern, where they lived with Maria, Sonia, and Sarah for many years. Donald loved gardening and worked hard in his vegetable garden and grew many of the vegetables for Bredon Court. He also made a large trout pond, so they always had a supply of fresh trout. Donald was very easy going and they all got on well, and as they grew up the girls helped their mother in the hotel from time to time, but Sonia was the only one who really liked it.

Barbara was a hard worker, experienced and well able to cope with Bredon Court, but before long it was clear that Peter and her new husband did not see eye to eye, which was not surprising. Donald was basically peaceful, and all he wanted to do was garden. Apart from anything else, Peter really only ever admired and got on with people who had achieved something or who were prepared to have a go. Therefore he and Donald Carlton, who had a pension from his mining days, and was now content to sit with a drink and watch the world go by, had little in common. This caused dissension and Peter, forceful as ever and still the owner and very much in command at Bredon Court, decreed that Donald was to have no drinks from the hotel bar. This made life very difficult for Barbara because, of course, Donald then did not wish to go into the hotel at all and she could no longer put in the hours which were needed, and which she felt were really necessary.

Sonia, Peter and Barbara's second daughter, had always been keenly interested in the hotel and when she left Bedales she did a hotel management course and then joined her mother permanently at Bredon Court. In 1978, aged twenty-three, she married Felix Phillips, a farmer's son from Penzance, and for a couple of seasons they both worked in the hotel with Barbara. They worked well together, but soon there were difficulties with Peter. Felix left and he and Sonia were divorced. Despite the agreement that Barbara and Sonia would run Bredon Court, Peter still wanted to control it. He could not turn his back on it. Long after he had moved to Bedruthan Steps, and made it probably the largest and most successful hotel in Cornwall he insisted on dictating what should happen at Bredon Court. He wanted to set

BREDON COURT

LICENSED

Open April to October

Telephone: Newquay 2345

FACING FISTRAL BEACH OVERLOOKING GOLF COURSE

FOR 1979 NEW JAKUSI THERMAL HOT WHIRLPOOLS, WITH SAUNAS, SOLARIUM AND WINE BAR, AND MAGNIFICENT INDOOR POOL (84°F)

WHATEVER THE WEATHER, YOU STILL HAVE A GOOD HOLIDAY AT BREDON COURT

Squash and Tennis Courts with our own professional Coach, Golf Tournaments, Indoor and outdoor heated Swimming Pools, Dancing, Discos, Hairdressing, Launderette, Boutique, 75 bedrooms.

ALL BEDROOMS AND FAMILY SUITES HAVE PRIVATE BATHROOMS

Everything for the children, including PONY CARTING AND PICNIC BARBECUES, Children's Hostess, weekly party, teas and suppers in their own dining room.

Our reputation for food has been created over eleven years by our Swiss Chef, Jurg Hedinger, and our wine prices won't spoil your appetite!

TARIFF: (Full Board, including Lunch) £45·00–£88·00 (+V.A.T.)

ALL ENTERTAINMENTS AND FACILITIES AVAILABLE APRIL TO OCTOBER ONE CHILD PER FAMILY FREE EARLY AND LATE SEASON

OWNED BY THE SAME FAMILY SINCE 1957
(The second generation, Sonia and Felix, will be here in 1979)

1978 advertisement – note the arrival of the 'second generation'.

up a central office at Bedruthan Steps with all accounts, bookings, and administration for both hotels — and, in due course, Trevelgue — dealt with from there. He also set up a central bakery at Bedruthan Steps and for a while all sweets were made there and delivered to the other hotels. All this was sound business practice but it was not acceptable to Barbara and Sonia who had been used to making their own arrangements. Barbara might have gone along with it but Sonia simply wouldn't stand for it and so she left. Then poor Barbara had years of coping with Bredon Court on her own, fighting Peter because all his attention, enthusiasm and whatever money he could lay hands on was concentrated on Bedruthan Steps while at the same time he still wanted to dictate what should happen at Bredon Court. He would not leave them alone and he would not agree to any money being spent on it, which of course upset Barbara. As far as he was concerned it was only Bedruthan Steps that mattered. Barbara felt that was very unfair because Bredon Court had already financed Bedruthan Steps from the beginning, apart from the Malcolm's £5,000 input. No other money was available — it all had to come from Bredon Court and it did. After a prolonged battle with Peter about the cost, Barbara did manage to install a very fine indoor pool, spa, and leisure centre at Bredon Court.

In 1984 Barbara became ill and there were again major problems about who was to run Bredon Court. Sonia was persuaded by Peter to return to help her mother, but there is no doubt she still found it impossible to work with him. The final straw came when he brought in Mrs Prufer, the German Manageress, and gave her the higher authority. One reason for his doing this was that Mrs Prufer would do exactly what she was told while Sonia, who had quite a lot of her father in her, would contend with him on every point. So Sonia once again left and went off to start her own outside catering business. In this she was helped, financially, from time to time by Peter. He could be very generous and sometimes he bought her the expensive equipment she badly needed and for a time Whittington's Catering Co. could be seen all around Devon and Cornwall at the smartest events.

After that the ongoing problem about who should run Bredon Court became more serious. Sonia had left, Barbara was ailing and so it was arranged for the 1985 season that Debbie Wakefield, the Malcolms' younger daughter, should go there and work with Mrs Prufer. Debbie is a highly trained and talented cook. She trained at Prue Leith's and afterwards cooked at Langhams Brasserie and for the Roux brothers. She had married Richard Wakefield the year before and he had joined Bedruthan Steps as trainee Maintenance Manager under the direction of Peter, who taught him a great deal, and naturally Debbie was keen to return to Bedruthan Steps to be with her husband. She did not find Mrs Prufer easy to work with and so she was only at Bredon Court for the one season, and thereafter Mrs Prufer managed on her own most ably. But it was the beginning of the end for Bredon Court for there was no-one in the family to be there and these family holiday hotels do need a family presence to jolly them along. Peter's second family were all involved with Bedruthan Steps and Trevelgue, which was the latest exciting project and much more interesting! Bredon Court had served the family well for nearly thirty years, but sadly its time had come and it was put on the market.

By 1985 Trevelgue was well established, and with Bredon Court and Bedruthan Steps booming Peter was again getting restless, and he began looking around for another project. He set his sights on Dinas Hotel at Padstow. It was small, but in a choice position with plenty of space around it for development and he was determined to buy it. However, Mary felt very strongly that they had worked extremely hard for some twenty-five years and it was time for a little leisure and relaxation. She was adamant that she would have nothing to do with it. As can be imagined this was causing a certain amount of friction and there was deadlock between them. Mary had already arranged a cottage to which she intended to move if Peter persisted in taking on the Padstow property — but fate stepped in.

On 17th November, 1986, Peter and Mary left for London en route for Barbados where they planned to stay for three weeks at the Colony Club. The night before they were due to fly out they stayed at Fulton Mews and gave a party at le Gavroche Restaurant for Peter's sixty-seventh birthday. It was a great party, but the next morning he did not wake up and they could not rouse him. He was rushed to St Mary's Hospital, Paddington where it was discovered that he had had a subarachnoid cerebral haemorrhage in the night and was not expected to survive. For six months he was in hospital desperately ill and when he finally emerged he was seriously disabled physically and mentally and the long struggle was about to begin; it was to last twenty years.

All through those years Mary struggled endlessly to give him some quality of life; she never gave up. He was seen by the finest doctors, had every treatment available and all the latest aids were installed at the Garden House, in St Mawgan village, including an indoor swimming pool — all to no avail except, perhaps, to ensure that he was as comfortable as was possible. He was pampered and given every attention but his wife, who has a marked preference for having her house to herself (unlike Bettye who always needs people around her to make her tick) chose not to have a nurse living in and she looked after him devotedly for some twenty years with minimal help. Her tenacity about it was much admired. Peter never seemed to realize his situation. He had his favourite foods and wines and, most important, his classical music and although at times he could be demanding in the main he had no pain and he just accepted things as they were — really it was Mary who went through the mincer, but she persevered to the end. During those difficult years she found solace in travel. She discovered a good nursing home at Trebetherick, booked a room permanently there for Peter and he then spent part of every month there while she travelled. He was not neglected; every morning his private nurse attended to him for several hours, gave him breakfast, exercised and massaged him. He seemed content and comfortable and there was nothing more that could have been done for him. Meanwhile Mary travelled widely to New Zealand, Canada, The Gambia, USA, the Caribbean and all over Europe. She would return refreshed and ready to resume her arduous nursing duties; she was indeed stoic.

To add to the difficulties, Barbara's husband, Donald Carlton, died suddenly of a heart attack in 1986, aged sixty-seven. Shortly afterwards she retired and continued to live at Goonhavern, but she was to be a very lonely woman for the rest of her life.

It is very difficult to create something as Peter had created Bredon Court and then leave it to others to cope with. Peter could not run both hotels and Barbara and Sonia would have got along very well if he could have left them alone. It is a sad fact that Sonia and Peter were too much alike. If her father could only have 'let go' when he went to Bedruthan Steps, Sonia would have taken it on and coped with it and Bredon Court might still be in the family, but Sonia had gone. The stability of their home life went out of the window when Peter left Maria, Sonia, and Sarah, aged seven, five, and two. After that all Peter's attention was focused on Bedruthan Steps and his new family. Barbara, not naturally maternal, was busy running Bredon Court and she soon remarried but their home life was patchy, to say the least. Good schools yes — the very best and sometimes exotic holidays with their step-siblings. Peter occasionally put his hand in his pocket to help them get started with this or that but in the main they lacked a wise guiding hand during their formative years and they were left largely to fend for themselves.

Bredon Court, with its eighty bedrooms, tennis and squash courts, and two large swimming pools was sold in 1988 to Mecca Leisure for just £750,000. It seemed a poor price at the time, but it had reached its full potential and it was time to move on.

After the outstanding bills and expenses had been paid Peter and Barbara received just £267,000 each for their half-share. It had, of course, been heavily mortgaged to fund Bedruthan Steps and Trevelgue but it seemed a poor return for Peter and Barbara's thirty years hard work. Peter and Barbara's three daughters were saddened when the hotel was sold; their parents had created Bredon Court which produced the money to get Bedruthan Steps and later the Trevelgue Hotel going, and there is no doubt the sisters were the losers. In 1989 Barbara became terminally ill and was eventually persuaded to go and live with her daughter, Sonia, in Chagford, Devon, where she died in December, 1991 aged seventy. She was very lonely during her last years. She never stopped loving Peter.

Bedruthan Steps goes from strength to strength

When it was clear that Peter was permanently disabled his money had to be controlled under the rules of the Court of Protection. They are most tiresome to deal with because they assume that the disabled one is surrounded by crooks after the money and they demand yearly accounts with receipts for everything spent down to the last penny. Under these rules Peter's income could only be spent on him or his business. His wife chose to look after him at home with minimum help so that there were ample funds available to upgrade and refine the hotel. Consequently much money was lavished on it during those years and it shows. It has been refurbished from top to bottom and today is surely the most elegant hotel in Cornwall.

Peter Whittington, circa 1988

Fortunately in 1986 Peter Whittington's wife and daughters were ready to take on the hotel. It continued to flourish, even through the recession of the early '90s. Bedruthan Steps specialises in family holidays but makes big efforts to keep the families apart from those guests without children. The dining room is cleverly partitioned so that families all eat together and an 'Adults Only' room for guests without children provides a haven from the torment of other people's children while dining. Also strict rules are rigorously applied as to where and when children are allowed, all very necessary if there are hordes of them — and there are! The hotel runs on oiled wheels. There is no compromise about the children's arrangements; the guests must conform to the house rules. Some mothers can be very demanding about their little darlings! Occasionally it is "How can darling Samantha possibly wait until 5.30 for her supper, if she usually has it at 5.15?" At Bedruthan Steps she will have to conform. They run children's clubs for the various age groups and that works well by keeping the children occupied and out of the way. In 1997 and 1998 several new apartments were added; they were converted from newly acquired bungalows around the hotel grounds and are very popular with families.

1996 saw much change in the Whittington clan. In March, Nicholas and Sarah Malcolm had a son, Jack, and in May Emma and Colin Stratton's first son Dominic was born. In November Colin became financial director of St Austell Brewery, and he and Emma, and the Wakefields, (Emma's half-sister and her husband, Richard) bought Glynn House, a beautiful forty-roomed mansion in the Glynn valley. They had a wing each and with good canny business sense Bedruthan Steps joined in and bought part of it, which gave the hotel four large flats for letting. They all had many plans for the house and were determined to restore it to its former glory, but quickly found themselves tied in knots by the demands of English Heritage and the

Glynn House which the Whittingtons bought in 1996.

Georgian Society — such are the difficulties of this country today. Those battles continued through 1997 but they eventually succeeded in converting it sympathetically and they each had a comfortable apartment, and Bedruthan Steps Hotel had some splendid self-catering units to let.

Sadly in the long term Glynn did not work out as well as they had hoped and Debbie and her family moved out in 2004. She and Richard bought an old house with a large walled garden at Lerryn, near Fowey on the south coast. Emma and Colin were undecided about where to live for sometime, but in 2006 they bought a spacious modern house with magnificent views at Portloe on the Roseland Peninsula and Glynn was sold. It had been an interesting project, but they felt it was time to move on.

It is now nearly fifty years since Peter Whittington and Tom Malcolm bought the crumbling Bedruthan Steps hotel for £10,000. It has been turned into one of the most successful holiday hotels in Cornwall. It is already taking bookings for the 2009 season. In fact, of course, it really is more than a hotel and also caters for conferences in the new conference suite. The whole complex with its five swimming pools, magnificent luxury spa with three treatment rooms and six operators is almost a holiday resort in its own right. It takes three hundred and sixty guests, with sometimes as many as one hundred children. It has many self-catering units around it, and when it comes to facilities it has them all — bigger and better than most. How Uncle Graham Farmer would have approved.

In September 1999 there was a big party for about eighty people at Bedruthan Steps for Mary Whittington's seventieth birthday. It was shared with a long term friend, Ron Hampton, who was also seventy. The Four Seasons restaurant was beautifully decorated by Mary's daughter, Debbie. There was a five course gourmet dinner with dancing afterwards to a splendid five-piece band arranged by Ron Hampton. Peter was there, and all Mary's family had come from far and wide. The youngest guest was their latest grandson, Joshua South, Rebecca's son, just nine days old. Nicholas Malcolm made a very witty and amusing speech lauding his mother and her contribution to the hotel and saying how fortunate the whole family had been to have had such an advantageous start in life — quite right! But Bettye, with Peter sitting beside her in a wheelchair, reflected sadly that the memories of Peter's and Tom Malcolm's early struggles and achievements had already faded in the mists of time — how relentlessly life rolls on.

Peter died on 4th April 2006 aged eighty-six: it really was a happy release. He was a committed life-long atheist, the outcome of five years at Truro Cathedral School in the 1930s with church three times on Sundays. After he left school he never willingly went into church again, not even to family weddings. His family gave him a most appropriate send off. The wake, held in the new Conference Suite at Bedruthan Steps, was well attended. It was completely non-religious but was arranged with decorum and sensitivity. A large flat screen was installed in the vestibule where a continuous film of Peter in his hey day was shown. It was very nostalgic and moving. Afterwards Peter was cremated at Bodmin crematorium with dignity but without religion and with just close family there. That day there was just one jarring note. While the family were at the crematorium and everyone was leaving the hotel two men in overalls arrived in a white van to dismantle the huge screen; they had difficulty in getting it off the wall and asked the staff to help them, which they did. It was put in the van and the men drove off — they were thieves and had succeeded in stealing a £2,000 flat screen: surely a sad reflection on our country today. No fuss was made about it.

In Peter's Will, made in 1983, after two small bequests he left everything to Mary, his wife, unconditionally. It was well merited; she had been a loyal wife for forty years. His three daughters from his first marriage were greatly hurt and upset that they were not even mentioned in their father's Will, but they had had little contact with him after he and their mother were divorced and he had taken his second family deeply to his heart. Life has not been easy or kind to Peter's first family. There is a striking difference between the life style of Peter's first and second families. Today Sarah has a five-bedroom 'Bed & Breakfast' which she runs in Totnes. Maria has left her husband and has a job as a social worker in Newcastle. She is the only one who has retained her interest in the Merrogwidden Company Peter set up. In 2008 Maria's son, Andrew Simpson, Peter's eldest grandson, achieved a first in History from Edinburgh University. How proud Peter would have been. Sonia is still in Scotland married to her third husband, a plumber. In 2007, her elder daughter, Natalie, had a daughter called Alana and in 2008 she had another daughter called Virginia, Peter's first great-grandchildren. There is no doubt the instability of their early life has had a marked effect on their lives.

Peter Whittington was a highly talented 'oddball', deeply thinking and a man ahead of his time. His behaviour at times, socially and in business, was outrageous. He cared nothing for social niceties and hated 'small talk' but at times he could be most amusing and entertaining and a generous host. He was essentially his own man and there is little doubt he would have made a big success of whatever he decided to tackle in life. A leading solicitor once said of him "He would have made a first class Barrister." Certainly he was impressive in debate. He would not abide by the rules but with a battle looming — and there were many — he would always mug up the facts with the aid of a serious book on the subject and would often be more au fait about them than his adversary — and above all he loved a battle. There were two major disappointments in Peter's life which never left him. One was that he was only about 5 ft 7 ins tall and he really minded that; at one time he would have the heels of his shoes built up. The other frustration was that he never had a son. He had always longed for a boy. The nursery rhyme "When he was good he was very, very good, but when he was bad, he was horrid" sums up Peter Whittington perfectly.

Certainly Peter's death was the end of an era; we shall not see his like again. For his sister, Bettye, he was the last remaining link with her childhood and to the end she had been able to talk to him because he remembered their early days and although speechless, he understood and would smile and chuckle. She was left with a keen sense of loss when he died.

After Peter Whittington had died and his affairs had been settled his widow, Mary, donned the mantle of Matriarch of the Whittington and Malcolm clans. She made a determined effort to keep them together and in touch. In the autumn of 2006, some six months after Peter's death, she invited them all to a family gathering at Center Parc, Longleat, Lord Bath's estate in Wiltshire. It is in a forest area of some four hundred acres. Run by an American company and rather like an upmarket "Butlins" it offers absolutely everything — indoor football area and tennis courts, ice skating, six restaurants, nightclubs, bars, swimming pools and can accommodate three or four thousand people. Mary booked seven lodges for three days — one for each family and succeeded in getting them all there with the exception of three or four grandchildren who were otherwise engaged. They were a family party of twenty-seven. They all got on splendidly and had a marvellous time. Mary also paid for the air fares for the Whittington girls and their families who had to travel down from the north. That get-together was a great credit to her; no doubt it helped with family unity, which is fragile to say the least. How could it be otherwise?

Bedruthan Steps Hotel today

Given the complexity of Peter's family set-up it seems that his second family have managed to sort out his affairs rather well. In 2007 the owners of Bedruthan Steps are: Emma Stratton, née Whittington, Rebecca South née Whittington and their half sister Debbie Wakefield née Malcolm. Debbie is the Managing Director and is in charge of the catering. She is a highly qualified chef seriously interested in food, having trained under Prue Leith, and the food at the hotel is extremely good. Her husband, Richard, is the Maintenance Manager and computer expert and they both work very hard. Emma and Rebecca direct the hotel part-time. They deal with the administration, publicity, and environmental sustainability for which they have great enthusiasm. Rebecca, who lives in Bradford-on-Avon, comes down for a day or two every week or so. They don't always see eye to eye, but what family does?

Emma has set-up a 'Green Team' at Bedruthan Steps whose task is to come up with as many environmentally friendly practices as possible and they have been highly successful at it; certainly today the hotel is 'greener' than grass! In 2005 Bedruthan Steps Hotel swept the

Emma leading her 'green team'

board at the Cornwall Tourist Board's Awards. They won Cornwall Tourist Board's Hotel of the Year, Sustainable Tourist Champions, and also Winner of Winner's Trophy. The next year Emma and her Green Team won the Southwest Tourism Gold Award for Large Hotel of the Year and Silver for Tourism Sustainability and also the Business Tourism Award. In 2008 at the Cornwall Tourism Award Ceremony held at The Headland Hotel, Bedruthan Steps won the Cornwall's Gold Large Hotel of the Year Award, the Gold Sustainable Award and Silver for the Website of the Year. None of the other family hotels entered this year. Peter would have been very proud of his second family's achievements.

They have also been winning other national awards for their various 'green' activities and no doubt more are in the pipeline.

Emma accepts the Gold, Large Hotel of the Year 2008 award.

Today at Bedruthan Steps the younger generation have got the bit between their teeth, they are thoroughly fired up, and there will be no holding them. As Bettye felt at the Edgcumbe in the 1980s they feel the hotel has reached its full potential. It is in tip-top condition, has every facility it can be given and it would not be improved if made bigger, and so they plan to create a small, luxury hotel. The new project is already underway. They have bought The Tredragon Hotel, below Bedruthan Steps at Mawgan Porth, which they have demolished. With the hotel came one-and-a-half acres of land with a path direct to the beach. They were triumphant when in October 2007, after a major battle with the planners and strong objections from The National Trust, the Whittingtons were finally given planning consent to build a luxury thirty-six bedroom hotel on the site. It will be called Scarlet, and will surely be the most modern, stylish, up-to-

Tredragon Hotel circa 1990s

Construction of Scarlet, the new hotel, in progress September 2008.

Artist's impression of Scarlet, opening in 2009/10

date hotel in the county, and they will certainly do it well. They have announced that they intend to give The Tresanton Hotel in St Mawes, and The Nare a run for their money, and no doubt they will. Well done, girls! Their mother has been extremely generous to them; they will not be hamstrung by lack of cash as the earlier generations of the family were when trying to get going and they are indeed most successfully carrying on where Peter left off.

Health & Safety bureaucracy 2008.

Maria

Emma

Nicolas

Sonia

Mary Whittington

Rebecca

Debbie

Peter's family members at Bettye's 90th birthday party.

Tom Malcolm

What happened to Tom Malcolm? By 1964 when Peter and Mary came back from their spell in Plymouth, Tom Malcolm was ready to move on. He had married again and bought and converted a very attractive stone farm house near Yelverton, on the edge of the moors, where he and his second wife, Ann, brought up their two children Peter and Kate, and also Debbie, his younger daughter by Doreen. His architectural practice flourished and he was highly successful but he still owned a half share of Bedruthan Steps. Peter and Mary were keen to buy him out, but they had great difficulty in agreeing a price with him. There was an uncomfortable deadlock for some time and inevitably relations became somewhat strained. Eventually, in 1986 a price was agreed with Peter Whittington when Tom's half share was valued at £500,000. It was bought by Merrogwidden Limited, the company owned by his and Peter's eight children.

By 1987 he had been divorced from his second wife and had been living in London for some time on his own. That year, aged fifty nine years, he retired and emigrated to Australia where he had an old girlfriend. He arrived in early October and married her within a few weeks. Tragically, a month later he was diagnosed with cancer and given only a few weeks to live. He phoned Nicholas and gave him the news in late November. All his five children from both marriages managed to get out there to see him before he died in January 1988. Everyone was saddened by his death. He had contributed greatly to Bedruthan Steps. He left half his money to his new wife and the other half to his children. He was a gentle man with a huge talent.

Tom Malcolm – 1928 – 1988, the architect of the Edgcumbe Hotel on Narrowcliff and Bedruthan Steps Hotel.

The Fun Factory, St. George's Road, Newquay 1988 – 2002

In 1988 with Trevelgue running smoothly and teeming with happy children all the summer Nicholas Malcolm came up with a brilliant but very simple idea. An indoor adventure playground in the middle of Newquay, open to the public, to be equipped with all the exciting climbing paraphernalia, holes and tunnels, so dear to children's hearts. In the autumn of 1988 he and his two sisters, in partnership with his friend Geoffrey Warmington, bought George Bullnore's premises, the old established Seed Merchants and Farm Implements, etc., at the bottom of St George's Road.

It was a solid stone-built rambling building on two floors. The inside had to be gutted and the space re-arranged. Planning permission for change of use had to be obtained; this was granted, with the restrictions that there were to be no gaming machines, and that fire regulations must be complied with, and of course "building regs." had to have their say! Much imagination was needed, but with Nicholas' flair for design this was comparatively simple and he had a busy, happy winter thinking up ideas and designing apparatus to delight the children.

The fun factory opened for the 1989 season with Geoffrey Warmington in charge. It was a completely new idea in Cornwall and it "hit the jackpot" and from the beginning on dull days the children fought to get in. The size of the children allowed entry was controlled — or they would have had fathers joining in! There was a wooden painted monkey standing outside with its arm out — at about 4 ft 9 ins high. If the child could not walk under the monkey's arm when standing straight, the child was too big to be admitted. That worked quite well.

On arrival the children had to take off their shoes and their anoraks and put them in the pigeon holes provided and then they were free to rampage for an hour to their hearts' content. The charge was £3.50 per session or they could join the club for £7.50 which gave them, in effect, a season ticket and they could come and go as they wished.

The ground floor of the Fun Factory was carpeted with bright orange carpet from Wattiez's "emporium" and the whole area was filled with tunnels, swings, "wobbly" bridges, bouncers and a huge pool of balls, all highly coloured. The walls were padded with coloured panels of pvc. It really was a children's paradise.

On the first floor was a splendid grand prix circuit with little racing cars for the smaller children to drive. They were a mini version of the dodgems of long ago. There was a barrier in the middle and the children tore around the course with excited cries of brmm, brmm. The cars were well built and sturdy: they cost £1,500 each. Adjoining was the Temple of Doom, an adventure maze based on Indiana Jones. It was dark and eerie with murals of animals and jungle with exotic lighting effects. There were tunnels to crawl through, caves, ladders, a fireman's pole and a huge boulder to push up hill. It was a thrilling and hazardous course for the over sixes with symbols and clues to follow on the walls. The children were given a clue sheet to be filled in and there was a £20 prize for the winner. Nicholas must have had a lot of fun thinking it all up. The Grand Prix and the Temple of Doom were both charged 50p extra a go and the children loved them — really the parents hadn't a chance!

Also upstairs on the first floor there was Greedy Gussy's Ice Cream Parlour and tea room where parents could read the paper and have a drink while their little darlings let off steam. When they finished they could cool them off with ice creams — some very exotic ones with wonderful names, and in the corner of Greedy Gussy's was the Candy Shop, full of the tempting, lurid sweet confections so beloved by children. Birthday parties were held in the tea room. Modern Mums no longer spend the morning making jellies, cakes, and sausage rolls preparing for a birthday party which will nearly wreck the house and leave them exhausted. These days they just book a party somewhere. The charge at the Fun Factory was £5.95 per child and the minimum number for a party was five. There was also an extra special birthday party which was £7.95 and the children were then given a party bag each and party blowers and balloons.

Unaccompanied children were not allowed in and parents were not permitted to dump them and leave them there. One day a boy of about five or six walked in on his own and said "My Mum is just coming, she is finishing the shopping." The girl on the door let him in and he happily joined the mob of climbing, bouncing, screaming children. After about an hour and a half they realised "Mum" hadn't appeared and they thought they had better do something about it. The boy didn't know his address but he thought he knew where he lived. A member of staff was despatched to take him home. When they reached Tower Road they found pandemonium, with two police cars with flashing lights and the helicopter hovering overhead. Mum was hysterical and beside herself with worry. She had missed her son ten minutes after he had left the house and had alerted the police, and they had been searching for him for nearly two hours! That boy will go far!

In the early days the Fun Factory opened at 10.00 a.m. and by 10.30, if it was not beach weather, there would be a queue round the block which lasted all day — alas no more! Times change and as Nicholas says ruefully, "If you get a good idea, everyone will soon copy it." And that was what happened. The premises were sold in 2002, with much difficulty, and the Fun Factory was gone. It was fun while it lasted but it had had its day. Today the building still stands empty.

The Fun Factory, St. George's Road, Newquay.

The Nare Hotel, Veryan 1989 – 2008

The Nare Hotel in 1930 – already it has a tennis court.

A brief history

The Nare was built in 1929 as a thirty-six bedroom hotel. A group of local businessmen financed it and formed The Nare Hotel Company Limited. Mrs Hodgson, who still lives in Veryan, remembers that her husband was the first person to <u>book</u> a room at The Nare in the spring of 1930, shortly before it opened. The tariff was five guineas per week (£5.25) full board, including morning tea and newspapers — expensive at the time! All the bedrooms were small and the back ones, even smaller, were for guests' servants. In the early days the hotel had nineteen lock-up garages across the

Tariff . . .

Inclusive terms (including Light, Attendance, Baths and Afternoon Teas).

July 1st to Sep. 30th	...	6 to 9 gns. per week	For not less than 3 days.
October	...	$3\frac{1}{2}$ to $5\frac{1}{2}$ gns. per week	
Nov. 1st to Easter	...	$3\frac{1}{2}$ to $4\frac{1}{2}$ gns. per week	
Easter to June 30th	...	5 to 6 gns. per week	

(No deduction is made in case of absence.)

Breakfast :—Table d'hote, 3/6.
Lunch :—Table d'hote, Cold, 3/6. Hot, 4/-.
Dinner :—Table d'hote, 6/-.

Governesses taking Table d'hote meals in the Dining Room will be charged full rates.

Early morning Tea 6d. extra. Meals served in Bedrooms 1/- extra.

Garage 1/6. Lock-up 2/-.
There are 19 Garages.

Under no circumstances can reservations for August and September be cancelled.

Visitors wishing to be placed on En Pension terms, if staying over three days, are requested to give notice on arrival otherwise they will be charged according to Tariff.

Visitors leaving their rooms must give notice before noon, or the day of departure will be charged.

•

THE NARE HOTEL
VERYAN S. CORNWALL

The tariff from the first Nare Hotel brochure 1930.

Sketch from the first Nare Hotel brochure pointing out the garages across the road.

road which were later converted into annexe rooms for guests; and when 'sleeping out' became no longer acceptable they were converted to staff quarters. There was a garden at the rear where vegetables for the hotel were grown; a tennis court was sited lower down on the road

The Nare Hotel. Note vegetable garden behind the hotel.

side, where the swimming pool now is. The Nare was always a somewhat exclusive little hotel in a glorious position above Carne Beach and by 1939 the terms were seven guineas per week (£7.14), which was more than the best hotels in Newquay were charging. But the hotel has had many ups and downs in the last seventy years as the reader will hear.

St Peter's School, Seaford, Sussex, evacuated to The Nare in 1941.

At the beginning of the Second World War for the summer term of 1940 The Nare was taken over by St Peter's Preparatory School for Boys from Seaford, Essex. Some of the boys slept in the annexe across the road and the main building was used as classrooms. The boys did their PT on the beach at low tide. After the one term the school moved to Barnstaple, where it spent the rest of the war.

In 1941 the hotel was requisitioned by the Ministry of Defence and occupied by the Army on lookout duties, guarding the coast in case of invasion. A round concrete observation post was built in the garden and is still there to this day. A recent guest to the hotel recalls being billeted at The Nare in 1942 and 1943. He was serving with the Green Howards at the time. It must really have been a very agreeable billet for the soldiers who were posted to Veryan — how peaceful it must have been — and how isolated with the petrol rationing! The house opposite, with its own tennis court, was the Commanding Officer's residence, and an octagonal concrete observation post was also built in the garden there.

When the hotel was de-requisitioned in 1945 Mr E C Stringer was appointed Manager. He had previously been Catering Controller to the House of Lords and he knew what he was about. He ran The Nare in a very 'hands on' way, playing the host, serving the drinks from a small bar in the hall tucked under the stairs. A recent guest recalled staying with his parents in the early 1960s. He was a student, and while there Mr Stringer asked him if he'd like to stay on for a few

The Nare circa 1960. Note the drive around the front of the hotel and through the building.

Lounge – the same fireplace is there today.

Dining room – now the bar.

weeks and run the bar. He was delighted; he moved into the annexe across the road, and had a blissful August in Cornwall while manning the little bar under the stairs. Mr Stringer also carved the joints in the dining room himself, from a silver carving trolley he had brought with him from the House of Lords; sometimes in the summer just wearing a long white coat thrown over his beach shorts. He was a big chap with a personality to match and was hugely popular with the guests and under him the hotel flourished.

From 1952 he had an accomplished local woman cook, Mrs Harris, in charge of the kitchen where she ruled from 1952-1970. Her husband was the Head Waiter. Their quarters were on the first floor of the cottage across the road which at the time had an outside staircase. The hotel laundry was on the ground floor of the cottage. By then the garages opposite had long been converted into annexe rooms for guests which gave the hotel fifty bedrooms. In those days "sleeping out" was still acceptable, even at The Nare! The hotel then took eighty guests and was highly successful. In the late 1950s Mr Stringer formed his own company and became the tenant of The Nare Hotel Co. Ltd., and he ran the hotel most successfully until he retired in 1963. He lived in a round house in the village.

When E C Stringer retired in 1963 the hotel was taken over by a Birmingham based company with John Stringer, his son, as one of the directors. The new company had ambitious plans for it; they intended to have a full licence and build an extra twenty-four bedrooms. They did not manage to get the licence nor to build the bedrooms, but they carried out some of their plans, and did them well. They redesigned the ground floor, refurbished and decorated much of the interior of the hotel "brown", which was the fashionable colour in the 1960s. They built the new dining room, moved the outdoor tennis court to its present position, and built the outdoor swimming pool. They spent a great deal of money, but unfortunately their funds did not match their

Artist's impression of what the owners hoped to do with The Nare in the early 1970s.

The revenge of the local builder who hadn't been paid for the swimming pool.

ideas, the cash ran out and they went bust. One of the local tradesmen became so enraged at not being paid that he deliberately drove an old lorry into the new swimming pool full of water, saying "They haven't paid me and they are not going to use it!" History does not record how the lorry was removed, but that little episode is still talked about in the village to this day.

During the 1970s The Nare was put on the market and proved not easy to sell. Financially it was a difficult time. Inflation was raging under the Wilson Government and the property market was very unstable. Eventually the hotel was bought by Mr Hall, a retired wholesale Smithfield butcher, recently widowed and with three bachelor sons. None of them had any experience in the hotel business, they just thought it would provide them with a home, which it did for nine years!

The Halls took over The Nare in 1979. After they had been there about a year they had a little family difficulty among themselves when one of the brothers became involved in a long-term relationship with a waitress and the hotel was briefly put back on the market. As the reader has heard, at that time the estate agents contacted the Armstrongs and said it was likely The Nare would be up for sale again and would the family be interested? They all went to look at the hotel, incognito, and decided they would be interested — very interested, but then the Halls managed to sort themselves out and it was withdrawn from the market. Two of the brothers, John and Martin Hall, took it on and kept it going in a comfortable, if rather homely, way for the next nine years but they ignored the major underlying problems of the cliff erosion and the drainage which were potentially serious.

The Hall brothers did little to the hotel during those years. They made no improvements, did minimal maintenance and under them it was just "make do and mend". When the lounge fire smoked they simply decided not to light it and stood an electric fire in front of it. When the Grays arrived they were told the fire had not been lit for five years, even at Christmas. The Halls made no effort to cope with the constantly rising standards and so gradually the whole place became outdated, run-down and shabby. Some of the forty bedrooms were virtually unusable. By 1988 the hotel had lost its 4-star AA rating and was in dire need of attention to bring it up to scratch, and as a project that appealed to the Grays enormously. They felt The Nare's perfect location justified whatever they might manage to do with it.

The Halls did, however, tackle one major project at The Nare. The annexe across the road had long been used as staff rooms but the buildings were crumbling and dilapidated. The brothers completely re-built one of them and they did it extremely well, converting it into a good, modern block of staff rooms each with its own entrance, central heating, shower, and WC In fact when the Grays bought The Nare the new staff rooms across the road were larger and more comfortable than some of the cramped little guest rooms with small windows in the hotel!

Martin Hall is a good cook and sometimes he was the breakfast chef. He was quite capable of taking over from the chef if necessary, and at times he did so. The brothers installed a butcher's shop, bought all the cheapest cuts of meat, and did the butchering themselves. They also bought a lot of produce locally and were popular in the village but they never really understood the hotel business.

John Hall's personality made up for much and guests returned year after year. The Nare remained an agreeable place for a quiet holiday away from the madding crowd, above a glorious beach with swimming pool and tennis court; people accepted it — providing they were unfussy about their rooms! Greatly to John Hall's credit the hotel did not lose its homely, cheerful, holiday atmosphere. He was a congenial host, popular with the guests. When the barman went home at night he would take over behind the bar, and of course the guests loved that. The brothers had had no hotel experience but they ran The Nare very much in their own style; they made many friends and to this day old Nare guests occasionally ask after them.

The summer of 1988 was an extremely difficult one for the Halls at The Nare. The Manager and Restaurant Manager had both left and it had proved impossible to replace them. There was a serious shortage of seasonal staff and the strain became too much for John Hall. The hotel only managed to shuffle through that season with the support of the small band of loyal, local staff led by the Head Chef, Malcolm Sparks, and twenty two year old receptionist, Julie Couch, who had already been there seven years. She managed the office and the front of house. Julie recalls that she came in at 7.00 a.m. every morning. She had a couple hours off in the afternoons, and in the evenings she returned and did the duties of the Restaurant Manager. The Halls relied on her, Malcolm Sparks, the chef and Ken Cracknell, the barman, completely. The permanent staff did their best and coped well, but that season was the last straw. John was ill; his doctor was urgently advising him to retire and threatening dire consequences if he did not do so. They decided to sell up and put the hotel, with planning permission for extra bedrooms, on the market and retire to their house nearby at the end of the 1988 season. Martin still lives there but, sadly, John Hall died in 2003.

The Grays take over The Nare

When the Agent contacted the Grays in 1988 and the question about buying The Nare and selling the Edgcumbe came up again, Tommie and Bettye were dead keen but John Armstrong and Mary Ashworth were very doubtful about it. They thought the hotel needed too much doing to it to get it up to standard. "What can you do with all those awful little bedrooms?" they asked. Bettye had every intention of showing them! In fact John and Mary were concerned for their mother; they thought she and Tommie were too old and it would be too much for them, but they were not allowing for the Grays' enthusiasm and determination and, coupled with the fact that Mrs Burt was ready to move with them and manage it for them. It did not help matters at all when Bettye told them firmly, with her usual tact, that she and Tommie had no intention of running the hotel with directions from Newquay. The freedom to create an hotel without interference is the most enjoyable part of the operation, and the Grays wanted the fun of doing it. There was a mighty family huff and John and Mary both declined to be directors of the new Nare Hotel Company Limited. In fact John's huff lasted about two years! Of course, that made the "Nare Team" even more determined to take it on and strive to create the best hotel in Cornwall. They were full of ideas and gradually as the hotel improved and gathered momentum the whole family became happy to be associated with it. It is a splendid place for entertaining one's friends!!

Bettye and Tommie Gray took possession of The Nare Hotel on 6th January 1989. On the front door at the time was a large, bold notice saying "NO DOGS ALLOWED". As they entered the hotel, Tommie tore that notice down; both were very 'doggy' and were determined to take dogs. Immediately they sent out a circular letter to past Nare guests announcing their arrival and informing them, among other things, that in future dogs would be welcome. Most people were delighted — but one man wrote "I am sorry to hear you are proposing to ruin that delightful hotel by accepting dogs. I shall not be coming again".

So dogs were in but the Grays were not so sure about children. One of the reasons for leaving Newquay had been to escape the hordes of children — often very badly behaved — and the Newquay hotels' battle about taking them free. They certainly had no intention of having The Nare over-run with children. Prudently they decided to get through one season before making a firm decision to ban the under-eights and they were very glad they did so. During that first summer in 1989 they realised what a wide divide there is between the Roseland peninsula and Newquay. Situated on one of the least crowded, safest sandy beaches in Cornwall The Nare is different, the guests are different and happily the children are different and many charming families come year after year — but to the end of his life if Tommie heard a squeak from a child in the dining room at breakfast he would murmur to Bettye "Children double and dogs free". He simply adored dogs!

In January 1989 Mrs Burt and her husband, Michael, moved into the three-bedroom flat across the road provided by the hotel, but the Grays themselves were to have several years of house problems. Their house at Ladock proved to be too far away, so they bought a round house in the village but could not get planning permission to enlarge it as they wished. They then let it furnished for a year or two as a holiday house until they were able to sell it. Eventually they managed to buy The White House just across the road from the hotel, which had been the Commanding Officer's quarters during the Second World War, and where Bettye still lives. Incidentally, later she was to have a happy day with her grandchildren making the war time observation post in the garden into a shell house with shells she had collected on the beach — great fun!

When the Grays took over the hotel there was a vast amount of work to be tackled and there were just ten weeks before the opening date in mid-March. They called in two firms of builders, one from

Bettye and Mary with Veryan, Morwenna and George Armstrong making the shell house in the garden of the White House.

Newquay and one "cowboy" firm from God knows where and set one team going at each end of the building. Bettye had to forgo her paid-for skiing trip to Gstaad — which hurt, but she was so engrossed with the new project, she had no time to think about it. The Nare was much more exciting and it was something quite new for her. For some fifty years she had been making extra bedrooms out of nooks and crannies and stuffing beds in corners, and was very good at it; now she was making twelve small rooms into six large ones. Certainly all available space still had to 'earn' and the three room manager's flat in the hotel was quickly converted into guest bedrooms, but suddenly the "stuff 'em in" regime had gone firmly out of the window. As far as Bettye was concerned this was a completely new approach; now it was to be all about space, quality, standards and service — a very different ball game and, to her, much more interesting and stimulating.

Oh, what a scramble it was! Several teams of curtain makers and upholsterers were kept busy. Rolls and rolls of new carpet were ordered, but the real problem was the furniture. Much of it had to be chucked out, so they put it all in what was then the Concord Room, later to be renamed the Gwendra Room (Gwendra being the original name for Carne Beach), advertised it in the local paper and held a sale. Then it had to be replaced — and quickly! Bettye and Tommie paid a flying visit to Nick Wattiez's rambling depot in a hangar-like building outside Peterborough. There they found good furniture and many choice decorative items which suited The Nare well. They went in a

Refurbished dining room.

large car and returned with it packed with mirrors, lamps, pictures and other useful items and Wattiez's huge pantechnicon followed a few days later with the furniture. Bettye also scoured the family attics, cottages, the junk shops, and sale rooms — not forgetting the flea markets. She donated some of her life-long treasures to the hotel. Luckily, she had always been a magpie! The cricketing prints on the stairs came to light in a rather interesting way. Michael Armstrong, Bettye's late husband, had inherited a large Edwardian desk from his father, who had died in 1934. To Bettye it was an oversized monstrosity and she hated it, but Michael would not be parted from it and so for forty years space had had to be found for it everywhere they lived. When Michael died in 1984 she gave the desk to John and he was happy to have it for his study, where it is to this day. Before handing it over, Bettye went through the many drawers and discovered to her amazement that most of them had been left completely untouched for some fifty years. She unearthed many interesting family 'bits' including the cricketing prints which were rolled up in a scroll of discoloured tissue paper. Bettye was delighted; she had them mounted, framed, and hung on The Nare stairs. They are much admired!

For ten weeks at the beginning of 1989 there was feverish activity in every corner of the building. Extra bathrooms and a laundry were installed, the hall and lounge were gutted, and the whole place was redecorated. Much of the 1960s "brown" had to be replaced; it was at

Aerial view of Nare showing how Tommie's garden was developing.

least twenty years out of date[1]. Carpets, curtains, and furnishings were renewed, new sofas, armchairs and beds were ordered. Modern pictures were hung and by the time The Nare re-opened in March the public rooms and most bedrooms had been transformed. Log fires burned brightly in the drawing room and in the lounge — the hotel had begun to take on the country house look for which the Grays were striving.

The garden had not been forgotten; Tommie tackled it with enthusiasm. When the Grays took over much of the land around the hotel had not been cultivated and it was just rough ground. Tommy, who was a keen and knowledgeable gardener, and a Vice-President of the Cornwall Garden Society, was determined to put that right and he set about it with a will. He had it landscaped and planted. The terrace was widened, and a new luncheon terrace was laid outside the Gwendra Room. The tennis court was re-surfaced by En tout cas. Many shrubs, hydrangeas, and agapanthus were planted. The Government Experimental Gardens at Rosewarne, Camborne were being closed at the time and Tommies' friend, who was in charge telephoned him and said "We are selling a whole field of agapanthus. Would you like some?" Tommie was delighted. He hired a lorry and went down there with a Nare cheque book and left Bettye pleading "Please buy fifty". When he came back with just five large clumps in the lorry she was disappointed. "Why didn't you buy more?" she asked. "I didn't want to be greedy", said Tommie. That was Tommie! But the truth was he was a plantsman and really preferred to grow them from seed.

---

[1] In 2005 the 'gents' cloakroom was still tiled in 1960s brown!

Mrs Burt struggled for the first year or two, and it is greatly to her credit that she stuck it. Firstly the business itself was so different from the Edgcumbe which she had been running almost single-handedly for some twenty-five years. There, all bookings were weekly, mostly from Saturday to Saturday, and although sometimes there had been as many as two hundred guests leaving in the morning and two hundred new ones arriving in the afternoon it was a highly organised affair and therefore very straightforward; many of the Edgcumbe guests came regularly and most were easily pleased. At The Nare it was far more complicated. Guests arrived, came and went as they wished, and were much more discerning. All children were charged half price if in their parents' rooms and the under sevens were not allowed in the dining room for dinner. It worked well, but of course most of the guests were of an entirely different ilk.

From the beginning the Grays and Mrs Burt had one aim — to make The Nare the best hotel in Cornwall but they had a long way to go and they gave it their all. Tommie designed and made the garden. He was also a talented wordsmith and he worked hard on the brochure and advertisements. Bettye gathered furnishings and generally put the interior together. She constantly came up with ideas for improving the service and pampering the guests, while Mrs Burt worked long hours making sure the hotel routine ran smoothly and, most importantly, ensuring it was well booked. They made a good team.

When they had been at The Nare for a few weeks John Armstrong brought his family to Sunday luncheon. There was taped music playing in the dining room although they had planned that there would be no 'canned music'. Bettye said, "Oh dear, the staff will turn that music on (it was piped throughout the ground floor) — it is difficult to stop them, they love it." Without saying a word John left the table, went to the office, said to the girl, "Have you a pair of scissors?" He cut the wires from the machine and there has been no piped music at The Nare since. That was one way of dealing with it! Nine years later Toby Ashworth was redesigning and rewiring the office when the music machine was found, still playing, with the wires severed. No one had thought to turn it off!

Fortunately because of the advantageous deal which John had negotiated for the sale of the Edgcumbe, the Grays arrived at The Nare with capital to spend. My goodness, how it was needed! For the next few years the winters were to be very busy and improvements continued apace. The six large de luxe bedrooms, for which there was planning permission, were built and the poorest rooms were scrapped. Two of them were converted into the billiards room. Great care was taken to achieve the all-important country house atmosphere.

Tommie supervising cutting the footings for the West Wing.

At first Mrs Burt was seriously out of her depth; she met stiff resistance from some quarters. The Nare staff were good, they had served the previous owners well, but the hotel had been run in a very slap-happy way. They were not used to having a manager; they did much as they wished and often made their own arrangements. It was all very lax, nothing, but nothing was ever locked up and at first some of the staff did not take kindly to the firmer control that Mrs Burt enforced. In fact, the Grays were told in the village that The Nare was known as the 'rest home'. They were never quite sure whether it was a rest home for the staff or guests — perhaps both! In fact the weekend relief receptionist always brought her book to read with her! But very soon all that was to change — at least, as far as the staff were concerned! From Mrs Burt's point of view it was another world and a great challenge for her. She grappled with it enthusiastically; before long she was coping and taking it all in her stride, but she was to say later she had found it a darned sight more difficult than Bettye had promised her it would be — "a quiet little thirty six bedroom Hotel" she had been told!

During that first season Mrs Burt was very glad to have Julie to help her find her feet. Mrs Burt's arrival must have been immensely difficult for her too, but to the credit of both they soon managed to settle down and before long were working together in harmony. Julie was Mrs Burt's number one for ten years. Married to Clive Johns, and with two children, she is still giving stalwart support, although only able to work part time these days. Julie has great flair for dealing with people and is very popular with the guests. She has been at The Nare for over twenty-five years and now she and Toby Ashworth have a sound working relationship.

Mrs Burt at The Nare.

When they took over the Grays were extremely fortunate in one respect. They inherited a talented Head Chef, Malcolm Sparks, who had been trained in a five star hotel. He had already been in charge of The Nare kitchen for several years. Malcolm is a real professional, full of integrity, and was most co-operative from the outset. He was seriously interested in producing good food. The previous owners had kept him on a low tight budget. They did their own butchering and they were too tight fisted about what was spent at the fishmongers! insisting on keeping the catering costs down. Chef was delighted when the Grays told him the menus were to be upgraded. Then he was able to introduce oysters, lobsters and all the fresh sea foods which are so important to visitors to Cornwall. He soon set about improving the standard of the catering.

The Halls certainly had not tackled the major problems of the drainage and cliff erosion in front of the hotel, nor the crumbling second staff block across the road. It was referred to by the long-term staff as "the condemned building"! Bettye and Tommie didn't like the sound of that, and thought it wiser not to enquire too closely as to whether it actually had been condemned or whether it was just talk. It certainly was not really habitable but it had to be used temporarily in the summer for seasonal staff. They tidied it up as best they could and got on with it; rebuilding it had to wait, there were more urgent matters to attend to.

That first year the Newquay Team had a mountain to climb. Mrs Burt's own experience was only that of the Edgcumbe, and Bettye, who had very firm ideas about what was to be done, was impulsive, impatient, and demanding; she wanted everything done yesterday.

There is no doubt that in the summer of 1989 they went through the mincer together! All this, of course, was behind the baize door. From the guests' point of view the hotel rapidly improved, and gradually the staff accepted the new regime. About five seasonal members of the Edgcumbe staff eventually followed Mrs Burt from Newquay and they, of course, were solidly behind her. They and the nine Nare staff who remained — some of whom are still there today, slowly grew into an harmonious team, but it did not happen overnight — it took time!

Before the Grays arrived children had been accommodated free if they were in their parents' room and had been charged for whatever meals they had taken. During the first winter a woman rang and asked for a room for herself and her three children for a fortnight. She understood there would be no charge for the children. When the receptionist explained that they would now be half price, but there would be little difference because, although the previous owners had accommodated the children free, a charge had always been made for their food, the woman said, "Oh but my children will not want any food." "How will they be fed?" asked the receptionist. "I shall feed them in the bedroom out of tins" came the reply. That was one booking that was not accepted.

When the Edgcumbe was sold in late 1988 a clause in the contract banned the whole family from employing permanent Edgcumbe Hotel staff for the next twelve months. A porter called Eric, who had been employed there for some fifteen years, was determined to follow the Grays, or perhaps more accurately, Mrs Burt. He did not see eye to eye with his new employer and so set about getting himself sacked. After a couple of months he was dismissed for insubordination; he then promptly applied to The Nare and was taken on. There was a furore. Solicitors' threatening letters flew; the Grays were breaking their contract. When Eric began muttering loudly about unfair dismissal, the matter was dropped! One wonders how far he might have gone had he been able to read and write! — shades of Maugham's "The Verger". Eric was Cornish, had common-sense and natural old-fashioned courtesy. He was an extremely popular porter at The Nare for the next seven years, until he retired in 1996. Guests still ask for him. It is always difficult to get settled with extra seasonal staff; they are often young drifters. A young waiter was engaged and was doing very well. One day in July, in the middle of luncheon, the police came for him and carted him off. It turned out that he was wanted for a bank robbery up-country. He was never seen again!

At first The Grays did not do very well in dealing with the locals. The freemasons had been using the Gwendra Room for their meetings in the winters for several years; they wanted the room completely cleared of furniture once a month and paid very little for it. The Grays honoured the booking until the end of the first winter. They then politely gave the freemasons notice in writing that they would not be able to have the room the following winter, explaining it was planned to use it as a Luncheon Room and it would not be possible to remove the furniture. The matter was handled in a strictly business-like way, but it ruffled feathers locally.

Bettye had been in business in Newquay where commerce is king for more than sixty years, where there was no Parish Council taking a close interest in what hoteliers were doing, or not doing with their own property. How different it is on the Roseland, where the locals really are natives and love their villages dearly. They do not take kindly to outsiders coming from north Cornwall with new ideas! They are prepared to battle every inch of the way about what is going on. In Veryan, which must surely be one of the prettiest, best kept villages in Cornwall, the parish council takes its duties very seriously. Unfortunately in their early years at The Nare the Grays felt they were not always popular with some of the locals — in some quarters they felt they were seen as "foreign upstarts" from the north coast. But some of the councillors with broader views who were also members of Carrick District Council or the County Council were very helpful from the outset — and that helped greatly.

There was a spur of scrubland, mainly brambles, in front of the hotel when the Grays bought it, and they decided to have it cleared, turfed and fenced. Five men worked like beavers for five days to create a pleasant area with seats from what had really been just an eyesore. Several wooden benches were dug into the ground for guests and walkers to sit and enjoy the view and the happenings on the beach below. The men had just finished when a pompous little man arrived, clutching the inevitable clip board — and announced "I represent English Nature. I have come to tell you you can do nothing with your land in front of the hotel without our permission in writing. I have brought the application form for you." Tommie said, in effect, "Well, we've never heard of English Nature and we've just finished clearing that piece of land. You are too late". The man bumbled on, left his application form, and departed. Tommie immediately put the form in his F & F file (file and forget) and no more was heard of that. These days it seems one cannot even clear a bramble patch on one's own land without bureaucratic interference — what are things coming to?

All the family hotels have their own laundry, which makes economic sense, and when the Grays took over The Nare one of the first things they did was install a laundry, which of course immediately overloaded the already dodgy drainage system. In the first two seasons there was an extremely serious drainage problem; raw sewage flowed across the garden and straight on to the beach. The smell was awful. The experts were called in and came up with complicated schemes — and huge estimates, and after many consultations a scheme to build new sewage works at the top of the hill was implemented at a cost of £60,000 (today say £180,000). At last, thought the Grays, that is settled. How wrong they were, it wasn't settled at all; the drainage was to cause them much trouble for years.

Tommie feeding the donkeys.

In 1990 Tommie arranged to have two donkeys from the Donkey Sanctuary at Sidmouth. They were called Nellie and Carly, a pair of benign, docile, middle aged jennies, and they were inseparable. A bucket of carrots was kept in Reception for guests to feed them. One dark wet, windy winter evening the donkeys were missing and a mighty search was launched up and down the road, on the beach and all round the area. No sign of them! Eventually, after three hours, Michael Burt went to the very top of the paddock and there he found poor Nellie trapped with her halter hitched around a post with Carly standing patiently beside her in the wind and rain. They were devoted to each other. Sadly after about four years a problem arose in the paddock with the deadly weed, ragwort; the Donkey Sanctuary insisted on taking them back to Sidmouth, and for a year or two the paddock and donkey shelter stood empty and deserted. Today there is a helicopter pad in the paddock and the donkey shelter is now used by the winter shooting parties for their gun dogs.

For the whole of one winter a young couple stayed at The Nare. The girl came from a well connected family and their bill was paid weekly by her father from her trust fund. They were attractive, agreeable, quiet, and well mannered. During their stay every so often the young man flew to London 'on business' and returned to The Nare the next day. When The Headland Hotel in Newquay opened in March for the next season the couple moved there. In the middle of that summer John Armstrong rang his mother and said "One of our guests was arrested by the police today and carted off in handcuffs!" It was the young man who had been staying at The Nare all the winter. It turned out his 'business' in London had been burglary!

The Nare Gallery came about by chance really; the room was created from what had been just wasted space. Bettye's interest in abstract paintings had begun in the 1950s when Peter Lanyon, a gliding friend of her husband, Michael Armstrong, invited them to a private view of his paintings at the Gimpel Fils Gallery in South Molton Street, London. They went and, although they knew nothing about modern art, when they left Peter's party that evening Bettye said "Well — that was interesting. I really would like to have one of Peter's paintings." Michael gave her one for Christmas that year and her interest in modern art was born. After that they gently collected Lanyons. Tragically Peter Lanyon was killed in a gliding accident in 1964 when he was forty-six years old, but Bettye and Michael remained in touch with his widow, Sheila, and sometimes bought paintings from her. In the late 1960s Bettye had bought some large prints by modern masters in London to adorn the walls of the Edgcumbe Hotel and when it was sold in 1988 all the pictures on the ground floor were excluded from the sale; so the Grays arrived at The Nare in January 1989 with far too many large pictures. They were put in the storeroom and forgotten. Several years later when the new room

Informal directors' meeting in the gallery – Tommie, Bettye and Mrs Burt.

was made, Bettye realised that the high ceiling and good light would make a splendid gallery and the stored paintings were dragged out and the first to be hung in the new gallery. Since then she has spent many happy hours gathering modern pictures for it. That of course goes on to this day. The paintings are a very mixed bag, some are by well known artists, some are merely decorative, but collectively they bring the room to life. It might interest some guests if there were a list, at least of the important ones. Bettye hopes eventually to compile one!

One day Bettye was in Cork Street, London, with her daughter. In one of the galleries she was greeted by an elegant young woman who said "Hello Mrs Gray, you may remember my Grandparents, they stayed at The Nare many times." She named them, Colonel and Mrs B. Bettye remembered them well, and chatted about them for a few moments. When they left she explained to Mary why she remembered Colonel B so well. A few years earlier while staying at the hotel he had caused consternation among the receptionists when he had asked for a chamber pot by his bed (having suffered a stroke). The office staff were aghast — "disgusting", they said — they could not have been more horrified if he'd asked for a rent boy to be sent to his room. However Bettye, like many of her generation, understood about 'pots' and when this request reached her ears she said "Of course", climbed into her loft and produced one of the original pots bought for the little Edgcumbe Hotel in Edgcumbe Avenue, Newquay in 1926, some seventy years before. It is sometimes useful to hoard things. The Nare can be very homely at times!

One winter Sunday afternoon after luncheon there was a telephone call to The Nare. Had they got room for three small two-seater helicopters to land? "Certainly", said the receptionist, but everyone was inclined to think it might well be a hoax. However, sure enough, at 5.30 p.m. three helicopters appeared overhead and landed on the lawn in front of the hotel. Out climbed three young men and three of the most glamorous blondes one can imagine. All the 'heli-guests' were attractive, amusing and friendly and the next morning they invited all and sundry for a flight. They took up guests, staff, and anyone who wished to go for a flip. Guests bought them champagne — everyone had a convivial morning on the terrace. After lunch, they were given a good send off and went on their way. Forty-eight hours later the Grays received a serious letter of complaint from a man who had been staying at the hotel during the visit of the helicopters. He wrote, "... the heli-guests were very disruptive and I had come to the hotel for peace and quiet. Moreover I was outraged by the girls' dress in the evening for dinner." (They wore short micro skirts.) Shocking!

The arrival of the 'heli-guests' circa 1992.

He wrote "You make your staff dress properly and I think you should insist on your guests dressing properly too." Tommie and the other chaps did not share his view — the girls looked gorgeous! and everyone else had thoroughly enjoyed their visit.

From the beginning Bettye and Tommie thought it would be a good idea to have an hotel boat for the guests to charter, skippered by a local boat man. In a burst of enthusiasm they put "Hotel Boat" in the new hotel brochure and in all the advertisements. It didn't come off — they simply didn't get round to arranging the boat and skipper. They then decided the 15 ft Dell Quay Dory which had been in the family for about ten years would have to be the "Hotel Boat" for the time being. (Fortunately, they hadn't said what type of 'boat'!) Every time a guest asked for the boat there was a 'to do' about how the Dory was to be launched. Bettye couldn't understand it for she had coped with it herself several times with a friend and she thought the young porters namby-pamby to make such a fuss. Came the day when the gardener, in his sixties, a landlubber if ever there was one, was asked to launch the boat for a guest. He towed it across the beach with the old tractor, launched the boat — and the tractor, which stuck in the sand and became completely submerged by two or three tides before it could be towed out. The Harbour Master arrived and put a wreckage buoy over it. That was the end of the tractor! The insurance company paid up — £500. The Dory was never launched again from the beach and there was no more talk of an 'Hotel Boat' for several years, but the Grays were still determined that one day there would be one.

There is no doubt taking on a run down hotel and bringing it up to scratch entails much hard work, but it is stimulating, creative and, at the end of the day, satisfying. It is no 'nine-to-five' five-day-a-week job and one has to like it — and like it very much. Tommie, who had been a highly qualified brewer and a top executive in large national breweries dealing with the tenancies of hotels and public houses all his working life, had never been involved in the 'hands-on' management of a small hotel. He could not accept that it was not a nine-to-five five day week job and would get very ratty if tradesmen wanted to see him or Bettye after 5 p.m. or at weekends — or telephoned to talk business out of office hours. He would often ignore a ringing telephone, or even take it off the hook — unlike his wife who was always afraid she might be missing something exciting! but he was always ready to chat to the guests and at 6.00 p.m. every evening he would be in his favourite chair by the window in the bar with a large gin and tonic. To this day that chair is known as Tommy's chair. He was a genial host and often he would be joined by guests. He and Bettye both realised how important the personal touch is to The Nare and were happy to accept it as a way of life, and one which they thoroughly enjoyed.

In 1993, in an effort to jolly the winters along, four-day friendly rubber Bridge Breaks were introduced. They are highly successful and the same guests return again and again to be pampered and enjoy four days bridge in comfortable surroundings with congenial company. They seem to like the relaxed arrangements for the rubber bridge which means they can play morning, afternoon and evening if they wish but are under no pressure to do so. If it is a sunny morning they can decide to walk on the beach and play later in the day. For ten years Trevor and Pat Jones were the very popular hosts, but sadly in 2005 Trevor died and Pat felt unable to carry on on her own and she retired. She kindly introduced their successor, Rob Bell, and he has hosted the Bridge Breaks ever since. They are just cosy, pleasant winter interludes.

In April 1994 the Grays felt they really had achieved something when after a successful AA inspection The Nare was offered 3 Red Stars or 4 Black Stars. They had invested much capital and five years hard work upgrading and improving the hotel and decided they would prefer to have 4 Black Stars as it would be more permanent and advantageous for the hotel in the long term. They were particularly gratified when, with the 4 stars, The Nare was awarded the highest percentage of any 4-star hotel in the south west of England at that time. That was a big step forward and the Grays were delighted, but then Bettye got completely carried away and made a major gaffe.

Determined to take the hotel further up-market she thought it would be a good idea to join 'Pride of Britain', a small consortium of superior privately owned and run hotels offering above average attention and service. Always impetuous and impatient she was keen to get on with it and, ignoring Mrs Burt's wise advice to 'wait until next year', went ahead with her application. The inspectors, three of them, booked at short notice in high season and were given the only available rooms, which happened to be the two worst in the hotel. Everything went wrong and the visit was a disaster. The Nare really wasn't ready for it, there was much more upgrading to be done, and to Bettye's chagrin 'Pride of Britain' turned The Nare down. She was mortified! but she realised that, at that time, they just weren't up to it and she and Mrs Burt settled down determined to carry on improving standards. The truth is that all 'Pride of Britain' hotels are special and they have to be of high quality and give much attention to detail and personal service. Later, much later, Toby Ashworth joined The Nare to Pride of Britain, as the reader will hear.

Of course with hotels it is very much a question of horses for courses. There was a couple who didn't like The Nare. They arrived having booked a de luxe room and were shown to one of the largest and best; it was not to their liking, the décor didn't please them and they were simply not prepared to accept the room. The staff could not understand it — why? Finally, the husband huffed and puffed, drew himself up and stated with great hauteur "You see, we are used to staying at Hilton hotels." That explained everything!

Hotel life is always full of drama. It can be fiendishly hectic, tiresome, exciting, amusing, frustrating, even boring at times but there is always a drama around the corner. One quiet December evening Ronnie Pleydell, one of the few really professional musicians on the Cornish hotel scene, had been booked to play the piano during dinner at The Nare. He arrived early and had a good dinner with a half bottle of red wine in the Gwendra Room before he took to the piano. About an hour later, in the middle of a selection from "My Fair Lady", he fell off his stool — dead. He was carried out and dinner went on quietly in a deeply subdued atmosphere.

A few months later Bettye, walking her dog, found the red Air Ambulance helicopter landing on the beach in front of her house. Oh! What is up now, she wondered? It turned out that one of the young waiters whose bedroom was on the second floor of the new staff block had forgotten his key so decided to climb out of the adjoining window and climb in through his own. There was a sloping roof between the two windows. He lost his grip and fell some twenty-five feet on to the concrete below. He only sustained a broken arm and damaged shoulder. Lucky boy! There is rarely a dull moment in hotels but on the surface all must be serene regardless of what is going on below stairs — or above stairs for that matter!

The Nare is very much an hotel that needs a host as well as a manager and a family presence adds to the atmosphere greatly, so everyone was delighted when Bettye's eldest grandson, Toby Ashworth, decided to join the Grays. He is traditional in his outlook, naturally mannerly and well able to cope with older, and often distinguished, guests, and Bettye's view was that he was the one to take on The Nare. It had been tacitly agreed for some time that eventually he would join his grandmother and Tommie and take over from them, but what had not been agreed was how it should be arranged. It was planned that first he would have a period of training with the Armstrongs at The Headland in Newquay, which he did. He finally arrived at The Nare in October, 1996 and as the reader has heard, immediately got to grips with all the technical and maintenance problems urgently needing attention — particularly the erosion and the drainage, which were still causing trouble. His arrival was a great relief to Mrs Burt; her maintenance manager had recently retired after twenty-five years and she thankfully handed all the technical problems over to Toby, who is a qualified engineer.

Ironically, on the very day that Toby joined The Nare, 14th October, 1996, Tommie Gray had the fall which, in effect, killed him six weeks later. After a complicated operation and three weeks in hospital he was back at the hotel and doing well, zooming around on a Zimmer frame which he was determined to discard before long. After three weeks at home, at six o'clock one evening he asked for a glass of champagne instead of his usual gin and tonic. It was to be his last drink. After a light supper he and Bettye settled quietly for the night at about 10.00 p.m. He went to sleep and he never woke up — shall we be so lucky? Tommie died peacefully in his sleep on 28th November 1996. Poor Bettye! It was indeed a terrible shock for her. She found him dead beside her in the morning, but, for him, surely it was a wonderful way to

Tommie relaxing in the garden, with Ben, the dachshund.

go. He was eighty five. Three days later, her beloved Tibetan spaniel, Bumsie, died too. He was fourteen. Sometimes life knocks one hard.

Tommie left The Nare a lasting legacy. In March 1996 he had had a heart attack; from then on he was unable to garden which greatly upset him but, determined not to give in, he then spent many hours in his greenhouse potting up agapanthus seedlings. When he died the greenhouse was full of hundreds of healthy young agapanthus which were planted out and today The Nare garden is ablaze with them in midsummer and they make an impressive show

But back to the drainage problem, which had proved to be on-going. All through the 1990s The National Rivers Authority and then the new Environmental Health Agency demanded ever higher standards and were given ever greater powers. They kept moving the goalposts! There were testing, testing, testing all the time and The Nare's drainage arrangements were constantly found wanting, in spite of all the money and effort that was being spent, this was the most urgent outstanding problem facing Toby when he arrived was to deal with it. He recalls that during his first week there he had to appear in Court and face the charge of contravening the Clean Water Act. The hotel was fined £1,000 which seemed harsh since expert advice had been sought and heeded regardless of cost. In spite of his constant efforts, in 1998 The Nare was again summonsed for contravening the Act and fined £4,000. Toby and Bettye were at their wits' end. One option seriously considered was to close the hotel laundry and quotations were obtained from a linen hire company. The estimate for dealing with The Nare laundry commercially was £95,000 per annum; that option was <u>not</u> taken up! The drainage at The Nare had probably been a problem ever since the hotel was built in 1929. Of course as the hotel grew busier and the rules were tightened the problem was aggravated. After a three year tenacious battle, in desperation Toby had to call in the up-country 'big boys' and the problem was sorted out at enormous cost, but fortunately Mrs Burt was able to produce a letter she had written to the original firm giving them a free hand do to whatever was necessary to put the system right regardless of cost, and in the end Toby managed to claim back £30,000 from them in an out-of-court settlement.

During his first winter Toby was also struggling to introduce new computer systems into the office, changes the office staff found complex and difficult and were reluctant to accept. Poor Mrs Burt was trying to help Toby find his feet, pacify her office staff and keep the whole place on an even keel. Bettye sat in the White House grieving for Tommie and wondering what next. But with it all, business flourished, the guests were happy and the turnover well up. Happily it gradually became easier and Bettye was much relieved when Mrs Burt and Toby both told her independently it was all falling into place.

The erosion was another unresolved on-going problem that landed on Toby's desk. How long it takes to get anything done in these days of overwhelming bureaucracy! There was a slow-moving erosion problem on the cliff in front of The Nare and in 1993 when the coastal path in front of the hotel became seriously threatened the Grays thought they had better tackle it; they called in the experts. Before long they found themselves caught up in a bureaucratic maze. "A grant can be obtained from the Ministry of Agriculture and Fisheries, who are awash with money" they were told. Seven years later, and more than £100,000 poorer, they were still battling with the problem. There had been site meetings, surveys, tests, and consultations at enormous cost in time and money. The meetings involved solicitors, accountants, structural engineers, surveyors, botanists, geologists, planners, The National Trust, County Council highways department, Carrick Council finance department, English Nature, Plant Life (a less known quango), the Parish Council, the Ministry of Agriculture and Fisheries and Uncle Tom Cobley and all. It had been all talk and <u>nothing</u> positive had happened in all that time. At the many meetings the representatives of these national bodies who had often travelled long distances at great expense to attend seemed not to be there to <u>help</u> the scheme through; they were there simply to guard the interest of their particular outfit and each was fighting his own corner. Since their interests were so diverse, it seemed almost impossible that they could all ever agree about anything. Ultimately one of the major hold ups was about a dock growing on the cliff which was said to be very rare and would be a great loss to the environment if it should disappear — no matter that Tommie Gray had grown hundreds of them easily from seed! One "expert" did suggest quite seriously on the radio that "if it came to it the hotel could be moved back brick by brick" because of the dock — cloud cuckoo land indeed! One cannot help feeling that to some officials the most important thing must be justifying their jobs — it makes life very difficult at times! Toby managed eventually to get the erosion settled too, and what was more he also successfully secured the promised grant to pay for it but it was not until the winter of 2004/5 that the Environment Agency and Cornwall County Council got around to tackling the job. They brought in loads and loads of massive granite slabs, dumped them in the National Trust car park below the White House, and spent most of the winter laboriously massing them at the foot of the crumbling cliff. It was a huge job. Toby Ashworth was also able to reclaim the heavy cost of the professional fees The Nare had paid out over the years.

Once Toby had found his feet the idea of an hotel boat was again on the agenda for now there was an enthusiastic skipper. Toby is a very experienced helmsman; he was in the Royal Navy for six years and had helmed a 37 ft craft for the Navy at Cowes. He had also helmed many off shore races while in the Service, including the Fastnet. Again there were many family discussions about what sort of boat it should be. Should it be a flashy yacht? Or an Admiral's barge type of vessel? The sailors in the family finally decided on a Cornish Crabber to be built at Wadebridge, and she was ordered in autumn 1997 to be ready for the 1998 season. She was delivered to Mylor one wet and windy day in March 1998; a 22 ft Cornish Crabber, a traditional style gaffe rig with four berths. She is white, with tan sails and Bettye, with John, Toby and Henry Ashworth, launched her at Mylor with a bottle of champagne and named her "Maggie O'Nare". They then finished the champagne and ate their pasties on the quay in the drizzle. At last The Nare had its "Hotel Boat"! Maggie O'Nare is skippered by Toby and is available for charter by guests for the day or half day for parties of four or five. £180.00 per half day or £250.00 per full day is charged. She is very popular with the guests and is a great asset to the hotel. Bettye was delighted; that was what she really had in mind originally — it had taken some nine years!

Maggie O'Nare

Toby in Maggie O'Nare – crew Ghillie!

In September, 1998 after another full inspection by the AA the hotel's 4-star rating was confirmed with 77% plus two Rosettes for cuisine; again the highest rating in the south west. Everyone at The Nare was elated. It was a great credit to all concerned, they had all worked extremely hard, and they felt they were once again "top of the pops"! Of course Head Chef, Malcolm Sparks, was particularly gratified about the Rosettes. He and his brigade had made a big effort to achieve them.

In 1998 it was announced nationwide that the following August, 1999 there would be a total eclipse of the sun. It would be a 'once in a lifetime' spectacle and the experts predicted Cornwall would be the best place to see it. Wow! Cornwall got highly excited and, determined to make the most of it went into action. The county spent the entire winter getting ready. Campsite owners and others booked extra fields and Portaloos. Over-spill car parks were arranged. Rents for self-catering were increased — some to double and many hotels raised their charges for the week. Vast amounts of food and drink were ordered — in fact Cornwall prepared for an August bonanza.

Well ahead, an official spokesman was appointed whose brief was to keep the traffic moving. He was remarkably voluble and for months gave the impression nationwide that the Cornish roads were going to be blocked solid, vital services were likely to collapse and essential supplies would surely run out. Unfortunately, there seemed to be no official spokesman to counter that view and make the point loudly and clearly that Cornwall really would be offering the spectacle of a lifetime. The public took fright and the expected hordes simply stayed away. Although in some quarters the event was deemed 'alright on the day' many entrepreneurs burnt their fingers; and for some it must have been a financial disaster — perhaps they were too greedy! The view of one well established, prominent Cornish businessman was that single-handedly the over-zealous official eclipse spokesman had cost his business £100,000, and the county millions in lost revenue from tourism in August 1999. In September 1999 the post mortem about the débâcle still rumbled on. The publicity was surely unbalanced? It seemed Cornwall 'blew it' because there was no official publicity campaign to counteract the dire warnings constantly being given; in fact the message nationwide had seemed to be "don't risk coming". Poor old Cornwall — some think the county made a mighty 'bish' over the eclipse. However, at The Nare on the day all went well. The hotel was full; two helicopters loaded with VIPs flew in, there was a champagne party on the terrace with a jazz band playing in the garden, followed by a sumptuous seafood buffet luncheon in a festive party atmosphere — it was fun and everyone had a splendid time.

One couple came to stay with a neurotic pooch called 'Boyo' — a grey Schnauzer who could NOT be left on his own; so they took it in turns to dine while the other sat in the bedroom with Boyo. When Toby Ashworth realised what was happening he gave the couple a table by the French window leading to the terrace and put a hook on the wall outside so that Boyo could be tied there where he could see his owners while they dined. Everyone was happy — you see, Boyo was their only child!

The next excitement in 1999 was the Millennium which was greeted in great style at The Nare and everyone joined in Toby's programme enthusiastically. The New Year's Eve Dance was a riotous success with a jazz band that played until 1.00 a.m, and there was a fireworks display at midnight. After that were Scottish Reels far into the night. Toby had thoughtfully arranged a practice session for the reels after tea so that people could learn the rudiments of reeling. The Scottish dancing was so successful that it has become a fixture on the New Year's Eve programme, including the rehearsal after tea, and the same guests return again and again for these New Year celebrations.

On New Year's Day 2000 there was a celebratory tree planting to commemorate the Millennium. All guests were invited to plant a tree. The gardeners had dug the holes, shiny spades were provided and about twenty-four guests each planted a British traditional tree; oaks, elms, ash, etc., and the planting was followed by a champagne New Year's drinks party at noon. Nine years later the Millennium grove is well grown and is a pleasant wooded background to the hotel car park.

Mrs Burt gave up the General Management of The Nare on 1st January 2000. It was forty-one years to the day since she had joined Michael and Bettye Armstrong at what was to be the new Edgcumbe Hotel on Narrowcliff. She had loved the hotels from the outset and threw herself in to the life with great enthusiasm. There has been much water under the bridge in those years — sometimes very

Mrs Burt at The Nare on New Year Eve, 1999.

choppy water! Since 1967, when she officially took over the management of the Edgcumbe she had worked tirelessly to maintain and improve standards. John and Mary Ashworth, and John Armstrong, all began their hotel training in the late 1960s at the Edgcumbe under Mrs Burt.

For many years now she has been Bettye Gray's loyal confidante and is very much part of the family. She has made an enormous contribution to the success of the Edgcumbe and The Nare. To adapt the famous words of Mrs Thatcher, "every successful hotelier needs a Mrs Burt". Happily it was not to be "good-bye" when in January 2000 she and her husband moved back to their house in Newquay. Mrs Burt still adores the hotel business and The Nare and was not really ready to put her feet up. She felt, quite rightly, that she had had a big hand in creating it and was proud of the fact that by the time Toby took over The Nare was still the highest rated 4-star AA hotel in the West Country with a turnover of in excess of £3 million. Happily for everyone concerned, she is still involved, and travels from Newquay several days a week. Today she is Toby's Financial Director. She also still manages Bettye's personal monetary affairs.

By 2000 The Nare had come a long way, but it was no larger — it still had its thirty-six bedrooms, but two-thirds of them were large, de luxe rooms, and there were several suites. Space had been found for a gymnasium, steam room and sauna, a beauty clinic, billiards room and a lift from the first floor to the swimming pool on the lower ground floor, but of course there was more updating to be tackled — in hotels one never gets to the end of it.

The first new major project that Toby tackled was the complete rehash of the rather countrified and homely Gwendra Room overlooking the swimming pool and furnished with rattan cane furniture. He called in professional designers, and although at the time his grandmother was somewhat fussed about the cost of it all, it turned out well. The room has a strongly nautical theme. It is stylish with teak furniture and huge blown up black and white yachting photographs on the walls and a six foot model yacht in a glass case. He re-named it 'The Quarterdeck'. The terrace was also enlarged and refurbished with teak chairs and tables. In fact the whole area, including the Gallery, was seriously upgraded.

One day out of the blue a suite was booked at The Nare for an Arab Prince and his entourage. He duly arrived with a secretary and a bodyguard who had an attaché case stuffed with £20 notes chained to his wrist. The visit went well; all their meals were served in their suite at the oddest hours and the air was thick with fluttering £20 notes.

The Arab Prince and his entourage off for a night on the town.

Almost every time a member of staff spoke to him they were given a £20 note. Whilst there the Prince took a fancy to a fresh faced young waiter and kept asking for him to 'be sent up'. The boy, scared out of his wits, had to be banished until he went off duty. One afternoon the Prince phoned reception and ordered a taxi from 3.00 p.m. until 'late'. He also asked for a gay taxi driver who would join them for dinner and a table for four to be booked for them somewhere. A table was reserved at the Pandora Inn, Restronguet Creek. A volunteer taxi driver who fitted the bill was found. When he arrived to pick them up in a large sedan car he was dressed in a full-length fur coat and Trilby hat. Apparently they had a splendid evening. After dinner they went to the Eclipse Club in Truro and then on to Pinkys Club in Headland Road, Newquay. The Prince was well looked after!

Toby is well suited to The Nare and apart from running the hotel he takes his role as host very seriously. He considers it important that he meets his guests and makes them feel welcome. Regrettably, his wife, who is a successful corporate lawyer, does not share his enthusiasm for hotels.

The Nare, like many hotels, has always run a black list of undesirable guests. Happily, it is small. However, when Toby took over he instigated an 'A' list of guests on which are notable people from all walks of life. He considers it important that he and his managers know who is staying in the hotel. In 2001 Labour Central Office contacted The Nare. They wished to make a booking for about four days in the middle of August for the Prime Minister, Tony Blair and his entourage. He and his wife, four children, a nannie, his mother-in-law and four members of his staff — twelve people in all. The hotel was busy and it was near impossible to fit them in — but Toby made a big effort to do so. Negotiations collapsed when it emerged that a huge discount was being asked for on account of what splendid publicity the visit would give the hotel. Toby declined the booking! He was later inundated with messages from people saying, in effect, "Well done, boy!"

Toby Ashworth.
Courtesy: Geoff Hitchens

Diplomatic story told to Bettye by a guest: at a dinner party a woman guest let it be known that she considered her seat at the table belied her exalted status. The seating plan was duly rearranged; she was seated above the salt where she was happy. Later she thanked her host profusely for the re-arrangement. He replied "Oh! Not at all, these things can always be arranged quite easily. You see, the people who matter don't mind and the people who mind don't really matter." How true!

In 2004 Toby tackled an awkward problem — lack of space for manoeuvring cars outside The Nare front door. It was not easy for it entailed moving a twenty foot high bank back some eight or nine feet, cutting a new drive to the entrance and replacing higgeldy-piggeldy steep steps with wide shallow ones. He called in John Battensby, a highly skilled landscape gardener, expert at handling heavy granite. John had landscaped every hotel and house garden for the family for forty years — even the cliff at Watergate Bay. A master in his field, he had become a family friend. Single handedly, and assisted only by one small digger and two boys driving dumpers to keep up with him, he created the magnificent granite wall, some fifteen feet high, without concrete, and now, planted with alpines, it is a gracious back drop to the hotel entrance — a masterpiece and much admired. Sadly, John Battensby died a couple of years later, he was only in his mid-sixties.

Toby feels that the wall is John's memorial at The Nare.

Family-wise 2004 was an eventful year with several exciting and important happenings. In April, Toby and Katie's first daughter was born; Bettye's first great grandchild, John and Mary's first grandchild. Much excitement all round. In September Henry and Sophie's daughter, Olivia, was born amid more family rejoicing, and in December John's elder daughter, Veryan, was twenty-one, and as the reader has heard she had a big party at The Headland. But all through the year there were disturbingly serious family matters brewing. For some time it had been recognized that Bettye's affairs must be sorted out and she was deeply aware that time was not on her side and she must get on with it. Within the family it had long been agreed what would happen, but the difficulty was how to arrange it to everyone's satisfaction.

Throughout the year negotiations, if they could be called that, rumbled on with little success. Eventually, valuers and professional advisers were called in and they, of course, began 'crossing the Ts and dotting the Is' and inevitably what had started as a comfortable family arrangement became a big business deal, to everyone's discomfort. However, by December, 2004 agreement was finally reached and the settlement was signed in Exeter amid a pinch of good, old fashioned, family aggro. It was not a happy day. Sadly it caused deep family divisions and, for Bettye, much personal heartache, but at the end of it she felt she had put her house in order; however she fears she will never be blessed with family peace. Amen.

Toby has gradually put his stamp on The Nare. It is very much an 'up market stamp' and he has done it in his own way. He has introduced private shooting parties and converted the disused donkey shelter into kennels for the guns' working dogs. He has laid a croquet lawn with a landscaped surround and a cedar wood pavilion. He has made a proper helicopter pad which is well used by guests who sometimes just fly in for luncheon, while others just arrive and depart from it. He arranges several wine tastings during the winter, and occasionally cheese tastings and The Nare now has a talented resident artist, Jeanni, who spends much time at the hotel. She sets up her easel and is available to give painting lessons to the guests. She is kept busy. They invariably say she is an excellent teacher and she is immensely popular.

In 2005 Ken Cracknell, the long-term Nare barman, was awarded 'Barman of the Year' title by the RAC and it was well merited. "Why?" the reader may well ask. Ken never forgets a face, always knows the guests' names, what they drink and how they like it — to many regular guests he is their friend. What is more, he is expert at making any

RAC Industry Star
Awards 2005/06

Recognising the brightest stars
in the hospitality industry.

Presented in the category of
Bar Person of the Year

Ken Cracknell
The Nare Hotel, Veryan-in-Roseland, Cornwall

Awarded in recognition of dedication to service
excellence and willingness to go the extra mile
in exceeding customer expectations.

Linda Astbury FHCIMA
Business Manager, RAC Hotels

RAC

Ken's Certificate "Barman of the Year".

Ken with the Countess of Wessex – *Courtsey: Geoff Hitchens.*

drink a guest orders. Is that not the hallmark of a good barman?

An interesting couple stayed twice yearly at The Nare for years. In the summer they arrived in an open 1930s Alvis Speed 20 and in the winter in a glamorous early Continental Bentley saloon. They became friends of Bettye and when his wife died the husband went on coming with his daughter. One June visit she was frightfully concerned, and he seemed to be very poorly, but as usual he booked his favourite room for his September visit, while she wept on Bettye's shoulder, saying "He's booking you know, but he won't be here by September." In September they came as usual, but he was obviously frailer. In November his daughter phoned The Nare and insisted she must speak with Mrs Gray — it was very personal. Bettye composed herself for sad news — not a bit of it, the call was to tell her that Daddy was getting married again and was coming to The Nare for his honeymoon. He did! and they lived happily for a few years. He died aged eighty-seven.

By 2006 The Nare had come a long way and Toby was gratified when he and The Nare were invited to join the exclusive 'Pride of Britain' Consortium — subject to an inspection. The reader has heard how Bettye had tried to join them in 1993 and had been ignominiously turned down. Toby awaited the inspection in trepidation, but when it came, out of the blue of course, it was remarkably laid back. George Goring, Chairman of the well-known Goring Hotel in London, came to dinner, had a look round and a chat with Toby. Then, naturally, he had to report to the Committee and later it was announced that The Nare had been accepted for membership, and so joined the small band of some thirty hotels who are members of 'Pride of Britain', and it is the only one in Cornwall. Toby was elated. It endorsed The Nare's position as 'one of the best' — if not <u>the</u> best! It was certainly a feather in his cap. Today The Nare's AA 4-star rating is 82% — still the highest in the West Country.

In 2006 the hot water system at the hotel began 'playing up' — not enough hot water at times and it became obvious that the boilers would have to be replaced, and what was worse, a new boiler house would have to be built; a huge and costly operation. Toby decided to build the new boiler house and store rooms behind the stone wall surrounding the swimming pool but first, of course, he had to get planning consent. As the site was so near the cliff edge, structural engineers were called in and decreed that piles must be driven deeply into the granite for stability, which greatly complicated the work. Toby then had a brainwave; instead of rebuilding the dreary wall he gave it an interesting façade by designing a row of beach hut fronts which camouflaged the boiler room and store rooms behind. All the original

Beach hut façade backdrop to the swimming pool.

1970s plumbing and pipework for the pool had to be replaced and so Toby completely refurbished the swimming pool, with new tiled surround and dolphin mosaic, glamorous lighting and solar heating. He finally added a hot tub overlooking the beach which is a great success. The swimming pool area, with teak loungers, became what might be called 'properly 4-star' — meaning no plastic rubbish. At the same time Toby joined the 'green club' by putting solar tiles on the roofs of the 'beach huts' and also covering the flat roof of the dining room with solar panels. Later, he proudly showed Bettye the new, spacious boiler room with a meter showing that the solar heating arrangements were working well and The Nare's electricity bill had been reduced by some 30%. The Nare was coming on!

In November 2006 Bettye was invited to a white tie dinner at the Mansion House in London by a distinguished lawyer, a friend, and regular guest at The Nare. When the invitation came Bettye was in Toby's office and she said "He has asked me several times to let him know when I'll be in London; he'd like to take me to luncheon or dinner at his Club, but I have never got round to it; my visits are always so fleeting and hectic." Toby turned on her, quite fiercely, and said "Grannie, I really do think you are churlish. If you were a hundred and two wouldn't you like to have a ninety year old girl to ask out?" Bettye accepted the invitation, went, and had a magical evening.

In 2007 it became law that one cannot smoke inside a public building. In the twilight of a damp Cornish 'mizzle' evening in August, a couple sat huddled under the eaves on the terrace in a howling gale where their after dinner coffee was being brought to them. The girl had no wrap and she shivered. They must be frightfully 'rugged' thought Bettye, and went out to speak to them. Poor dears — they were decadent enough to want a cigarette with their coffee! She then recalled that in the 1920s and 1930s all hotels had a 'smoking room' — even the little twenty bedroom Edgcumbe had one — what was wrong with that?

Bettye, Toby and Sammy in the Gallery.

2007 was also another exciting year at The Nare. In June Toby and Katie's second daughter, Georgiana, was born to everybody's delight. It had been three years since Toby bought the family out and set about improving the hotel and taking it further up-market. In the 2007 edition of the Good Hotel Guide the entry for The Nare Hotel, Veryan on page 325 opened with "Perfect as usual. I still say that this is the best hotel in England." When Bettye read that, soon after her ninetieth birthday, she purred. She thought how proud her husband, Tommie, would have been. They had bought the hotel eighteen years before in the face of strong opposition from Bettye's son and daughter. They had had no need to do it but had just taken it on as an interesting retirement project with the avowed aim of making it the best hotel in Cornwall. It seems that Toby's ambition is to make it one of the best in the country and he is working hard towards that goal. He is still full of ideas — good luck to him! Bettye, who always loved a party and still does, gave a little evening birthday party on the terrace at the White House — with a small jazz band — great fun! It was also a small celebration of the exiting happenings across the road at The Nare.

During 2008-2009 winter further upgrading and refurbishment of bedrooms is planned. Some of the rooms and bathrooms might be called "compact" in 'hotel-speak', which really means small. Doubtless, by spring 2009 they will be vastly improved. Toby is determined to maintain a traditional 'country house' standard of comfort for his guests.

In January 2009, Mrs Burt will have been with the family for fifty years. She has long been a family friend and confidante — not to mention Bettye's right hand. That is an achievement that cannot be allowed to go unnoticed, and a family celebration is planned.

Evening summer party on the terrace of the White House, 2007.

It is a mystery to Bettye 'why', but The Nare has always been a 'hot potato' in the family, and it has caused dissension among some family members. From being the white elephant nobody wanted it seemed to become the jewel in the family crown, but today Bettye comforts herself with the thought that she has managed to hand it over and it is in a safe pair of hands. It was courageous of Toby to take The Nare on — it meant a hefty mortgage — let no one think the hotel was given to him on a plate. It was not. It is now eight years since he took over from Mrs Burt, and she was a hard act to follow, but he has firmly made his mark at The Nare and raised the standards, improved the facilities and increased the turnover by some 89%; the hotel is steadily creeping towards the rarefied atmosphere at the top of the tree. He has many plans for the future, but they do not include making it larger — in fact if anything he plans to take fewer people in greater comfort. There are many regular Nare guests who would appreciate that. Toby Ashworth has confounded his critics and is absolutely determined to build on the reputation his grandmother established. He was once heard to say "The day someone tells me this hotel is not as good as it was in my grandmother's day I shall go home and weep." With that attitude and his wholehearted determination, how can he fail? But he will have to keep his eye on the ball; there is plenty of competition coming along.

Toby, Katy, Cordelia and Georgiana.

Sonia Whittington at Polmaily, 1993 – 2008

Sonia Whittington was always interested in the hotel business and when she left Bedales, did a course on hotel management. She had much of her father in her, and much of her mother — an explosive combination! She is clever and quite one of the most hard-working members of the family, which is saying something: apart from that she has tremendous drive. From the outset it was clear that one day she would set up on her own, and this is how she finally did it. She had married Felix Phillips, a farmer's son from Penzance in 1978 when she was twenty-three. For a while they both worked at Bredon Court, but neither that nor the marriage worked, and in the early 1980s they divorced. He returned to Penzance and Sonia also left to pursue her own interests and in the early 1980s she set up an outside catering business. This she did very successfully with help from her father, although from time to time she needed baling out, but goodness, how hard she worked!

For several years she lived with Julian, and had two children, but the relationship foundered. Outside catering must be one of the most difficult aspects of catering to deal with, and Sonia travelled long distances all over the south west.

She is a seriously good organizer and she had a very up-to-date set up; red and white striped marquees, staff all in red and white striped aprons and straw hats — it was all "some smart". Sonia could often be seen at shows directing the huge operation, looking like a gipsy with her hair hanging down her back and a baby strapped to her with a toddler playing at her feet, but she stuck it out, worked very, very hard. It was successful, but she really found it too heavy going with her young family to cope with as well.

In 1991 she married John Davis and they joined their names, and became known as "Whittington-Davis". They lived in Devon but soon they began to feel the need for a more stable background, for by then they had five children between them. Sonia and John decided to try Scotland because prices are much cheaper than in Cornwall, and there are more grants available to help get businesses going. Also, Sonia was keen to get away from Cornwall and to have a different type of hotel so that hers would not be constantly compared with the other hotels in the family. Family competition can be very keen at times.

She drew the whole of her capital (£150,000) out of Trevelgue against family advice and eventually bought Polmaily House Hotel, by Loch Ness, Drumnadrochit, Scotland, an attractive looking eight bedroom house (six bathrooms) in a mature garden, with eighteen acres consisting of a large paddock and lovely woodlands. It had

Polmaily House Hotel.

beautiful grounds, a tennis court, croquet lawn, outdoor swimming pool, a small lake, and a paddock — very overgrown. It was licensed, and what was very important, it had a spacious three bedroom house attached to the hotel at the back which would provide comfortable living quarters for the family. They never had to face the discomfort of 'tucking away for the summer' as had other members of the family.

Sonia paid £245,000 for it as a going concern, but it was not really a thriving business — its turnover when Sonia and John took it over was £100,000 per annum. They were soon to do much, much better than that. They took over Polmaily House Hotel, by Loch Ness, Drumnadrochit, Scotland, fifteen miles from Inverness, on 10th October 1993 — it was Andrew's first birthday, Natalie eleven years, Hannah eight years, and Neil four years — oh, what courage that must have taken!

On the way to Scotland to take over the hotel the car broke down near Birmingham and they were stranded for ten hours with four children on board — what a nightmare! It must have been a dreadful journey, but it would have taken much more than that to deter Sonia once she had got her teeth into something. She has her father's tenacity. They managed to open for Christmas on 16th December 1993, which brought in some much needed funds.

In the spring of 1994, Sonia hired a truck, put the four children in it, and drove down with them to gather what surplus furniture she could from Bedruthan Steps and Trevelgue. She went on to Trago Mills to buy the many items, including carpets, that can be bought more cheaply there than anywhere. She only stayed a few days — it was no holiday— she then drove the fully laden truck with the four children asleep in the back, right through the night back to Scotland.

It took her twenty four hours; Cornwall to Inverness, some 900 miles. Sonia is certainly a gutsy girl!

When they took over Polmaily House it was very short of lounge space. In 1996 they built a large round garden room which improved the whole hotel enormously. It made a charming room with windows all round and they served breakfast and children's early suppers there. There was a small bar in the corner where guests could enjoy a quiet drink on summer evenings.

Their plan for Polmaily House always was to run a "Nare" type of operation, but more family orientated, and that is exactly what they did. The hotel eventually had fourteen rooms, some of them family suites and when really full they could take twenty-two adults and about eighteen children — a success story, but sadly Sonia and John ran into trouble, they could not work together. Sonia lost interest and turned her attention to Arab horses. It was the beginning of the end. The hotel was sold in 2005, Sonia and John were divorced, and he was paid off. That was the end of Polmaily House Hotel. A sad story indeed: it had lasted twelve years. If only they had built on extra bedrooms it might have ended differently.

At the time of writing Sonia is living with her new husband, Graham, who is a plumber, in the stylish house she built in the grounds of the hotel. Her two sons are at the Blue Coat School at Ipswich and she is still giving her attention to her horses. She is now fifty-two and it really is time for her to settle down. Bettye hopes very much that she will eventually find her niche — and before her money runs out. Poor Sonia, life has not been easy for her; she is hardworking and talented but it is her "stickability" that is in doubt.

Sonia with her children, 2007.

Watergate Bay Beach Complex and The Extreme Academy 1999 – 2008

Henry Ashworth finished his Business Management Course at Oxford Brookes in 1995 and immediately, within a week, took a job with a publishing firm in London. Nine months later he accepted an appointment in Johannesburg when he was head hunted by his London boss to join him in setting up and organising international trade exhibitions in South Africa. His French fiancée, Sophie Déjan joined him there three months later and in September 1997 they returned to France to be married.

After two years in Johannesburg Henry and Sophie, who are both very hardworking and ambitious, decided there would be better opportunities for them to establish their own business in Europe. In spring 1998 they returned to Cornwall, determined to find a project. That, of course, took time and for the 1998 season Henry applied himself to marketing Watergate Bay Hotel, which he did with marked success. Bookings and deposits for 1999 were increased by 100%. Meanwhile they pondered their future. They seriously considered Croatia — too dangerous. Then an hotel in the French ski resort of Chamonix, but that deal did not materialise.

During the 1998 summer Watergate Beach Complex came on the market. The asking price was £500,000. It consisted of a café, a takeaway with a well equipped kitchen, a beach shop, a surf shop with living quarters above which consisted of one large room and a bathroom, and, most important, a large car park. Also included in the package were trading rights for the surfing facilities on Watergate Beach, part of which the Ashworths already owned. Henry and Sophie were immediately interested and appointed an agent to act for them. The negotiations were long-winded and carried out in great secrecy. They did not even view the premises officially, but they eventually bought it well below the asking price. In view of its proximity to Watergate Bay Hotel, already in family hands, and the beach's obvious potential, it surely was a very wise buy? The sale finally went through with completion at the end of the year. Later the vendor was heard saying "I have sold out to a big consortium, and they have very ambitious plans for the beach." Some big consortium — Henry and Sophie Ashworth, both in their twenties! But he was right about the ambitious plans.

The young Ashworths formed a company called Leisure Enterprises Limited, with family directors. They decided to call the new enterprise The Extreme Academy, and its aim was to promote all the modern extreme beach sports which young people are so enthusiastic about today. They took over on 8th January 1999, just as almost eighty years before Henry's great-great uncle, Graham Farmer, had taken over Tolcarne Beach in Newquay. Family history was repeating itself, but it was certainly going to be a very different beach scene in the twenty-first century. No tents, huts, deck chairs, bathing machines or tea trays. Watergate Bay beach was soon to become the local headquarters for exciting, energetic, modern beach sports, with a French style Bistro serving good food alongside. They were both bursting with ideas.

By the time they had bought the property Henry and Sophie were left with very little money with which to put their ideas into practice. Henry set about negotiating all possible financial aid. He arranged an ice cream contract with Nestlés by which the firm provided a marketing fund worth £8,000 over three years. Beach cleaning was obviously going to be a serious problem and to make that easier he managed to persuade SWEB to donate an old Landrover which was about to be scrapped. He did a deal with a coffee supplier who provided the Beach Hut with an espresso coffee machine free of charge. Contact was made with various sporting bodies all over the country and with suppliers, tradesmen, authorities, the locals and everybody and anybody who might possibly be prepared to help get the project off the ground.

The next step was to set up a separate company for the car park so that the car park turnover would not be liable for VAT. Henry then contacted the governing body of the National Power Kite Association (Bigair) and persuaded them to make Watergate Beach the National Power Kite Training Centre for the whole country, offering training courses with expert tuition. He also arranged an agency for The Extreme Sports Academy with Flexifoil, one of the world's leading kite manufacturers.

The next consideration was the catering arrangements. The young Ashworths were both interested in wines, good food, and cooking and were keen to have a good, French style Bistro, with a licence if possible. Bettye was very doubtful whether they would be granted a licence for a café on the beach; there had never been a licensed beach café in Newquay before. However Henry went into action and did his homework thoroughly. He consulted all the local authorities, police, fire officers, etc. and everyone else who might possibly be concerned. When he applied for the licence in April 1999, surprise, surprise, he was granted, not just a restricted restaurant licence as had been expected, but a full licence for the Beach Hut Bistro. What a feather in his cap! The family was delighted for them and of course Sophie and Henry were over the moon. They really felt they were getting somewhere.

They then needed planning permission for a large deck on stilts adjoining the Bistro and bar for outside wining and dining. There was a little delay with the planners, of course, but with excellent co-operation from the builder and a great deal of effort they managed to get the deck erected by June with fire regulations, health and hygiene requirements, etc., all being met. That in itself was an achievement!

They were determined to have the Bistro decorated like a beach hut. They acquired some old pallets then found a brilliant carpenter with imagination, ideas, and an eye for design. He broke up the pallets and slapped them on the walls haphazardly so they looked like driftwood. When colour washed in different colours, they made a splendid, modern, beach hut décor.

Their next headache was getting the Bistro furnished; their money was beginning to run out. Sophie and Henry made a flying visit to Wattiez's enormous warehouse in the wilds outside Peterborough and there during an energetic afternoon scrambling around they managed to unearth tables and other useful bits and pieces. They were also able to gather various items of furniture which were being discarded by the family hotels. A somewhat motley collection, it must be said, but when they had been painted and pushed around they looked just right. The last problem was chairs for the Bistro and that was solved by Henry hiring a van, dashing to Bristol to Ikea, buying them at a lowly bargain price, stuffing them in the van, and driving them back. It was a hard day's work but he returned feeling he had bought well and was very pleased with himself. By the time they opened they had managed to create the colourful, casual driftwood effect they were after and what was important, it was all paid for. The family has never gone in for the "never-never" system.

On 29th June, 1999 the Beach Hut Bistro opened with a flourish. Henry and Sophie hosted an opening party for about sixty people. Everybody who had been involved or who might be remotely interested was there, from the Bank Manager, the Mayor of Newquay, local reporters right down to Granny. There were exotic drinks and delicious food. Just what one would expect, after all, Sophie is French! It got off to a rip roaring start and before long the young were trooping to The Beach Hut in droves.

Beach Hut is launched

RELAX by the beach while the sun goes down on a balmy summer's evening, sipping a pina colada ... or sit warm and snug and watch a fantastic winter storm rage across Watergate Bay.

That was the sales pitch from Henry Ashworth as he opened The Beach Hut on a recent full-tide evening – a venture he and his French-born wife Sophie have been planning since last winter.

Created from the mish-mash of an old beach shop, The Beach Hut, with its bar, sundeck and cascading waterfall, also houses The Extreme Academy, which includes the national kite-surfing training centre, the West Coast Surfari Surf School and the Watergate Bay Boardriders Club.

Henry and Sophie arrived in January, having previously run an event management company in South Africa.

"We got wind of these premises with their own bit of beach becoming available and recognised the possibilities," said Henry, who feels sure there is a good local all-year-round market for the facilities he can offer.

"Local people love the beaches, which is why they live here and there is also the year-round self-catering and holiday trade."

The Beach Hut will try to develop a relationship with as many local hotels as possible, he stressed, though his own family credentials are impeccable – his parents own nearby Watergate Bay Hotel (which they bought as a derelict building in 1968), his uncle and aunt The Headland in Newquay, while a great great uncle was the developer of the Tolcarne Beach in the early 1920s!

The opening reception, attended by Newquay Mayor and Mayoress John and Rachel Weller, gave guests a preview of the facilities, helped along with cocktails and tapas.

The Beach Complex now had the Beach Hut Bistro, a takeaway, two shops, one selling buckets and spades and children's clobber, etc., and the other selling wet suits, beach garb, surf boards, surfing gear and serious kites, and the car park, which was, of course, self supporting. It was essentially a modern enterprise run by young people for young people and there seemed to be a permanent queue at the ice cream kiosk.

The first season from a standing start in a new business is inevitably difficult. New premises, new staff, new everything; one has to feel one's way and the start for the Beach Hut was more difficult than most. The Ashworth's living conditions were haphazard to say the least.

At the very beginning Henry and Sophie and two dogs had to sleep on a fold-up bed that went up into the wall in the small room adjoining their large office which they had divided into two rooms and before they could sort themselves out they had an unexpected visit from the Environmental Health Inspector. It was chaotic and might have been disastrous for they had only one small fridge and they could not yet afford to buy a large one which, of course, they badly needed. When the Inspector came the fresh pasties for that day were stored on the floor on the landing outside the small room. Panic! They shut as many of them as they could in the fold up bed on the wall and the rest were stored under a sheet on the floor in the corner of the room and the two dogs — one an Alsatian — were left in the room to ward the Inspector off. Basil, the Alsatian, barked so ferociously when he appeared he wasn't prepared to enter the room and that saved the day, but what a feast those dogs might have had. Happily Henry soon got hold of a very large fridge — but that visit might have been calamitous!

Henry and Sophie managed to staff the complex for their first season largely by people they had met on the way. The Restaurant Manageress, Sarah, was on the Business Management Course at Oxford with Henry. She saw the season through but sadly she proved to be short on organising ability. He met a chef in Chamonix, the French ski resort, and persuaded him to come to Cornwall. His cooking was good and he stayed for the season but unfortunately his girlfriend, who came with him, found Watergate Bay too quiet and so in October they took themselves off. Luckily the Ashworths had already got their eye on a talented successor and they promptly engaged him and put him in charge of the kitchen. Unfortunately he proved to be highly temperamental and didn't last long.

The young Ashworths were extremely fortunate to be joined by Andrea Wharry, whose parents ran Rosemere Hotel in the bay. She was naturally "sportive", personable and very experienced; she was the International Gladiators' champion on the long running television "Gladiators" series, and that is no mean feat. Andrea and Henry formed a partnership to set up and run the National Power Kite training centre on Watergate Bay beach. They offered two-hour courses and she was the Chief Instructor. She was also in charge of the two beach shops. Andrea was a tremendous asset to the Extreme Academy in the beginning but she went on to bigger things and today she is sponsored by the Extreme Academy for her competitions and record breaking attempts. She is one of the most expert kite surfers in the world.

At the Beach Hut they surrounded themselves with a bunch of attractive, young people who formed a cheery happy team and that gave the whole place an air of gaiety and fun, but it was all under control — well, almost! There were three lifeguards who were costing £600 weekly. That was a heavy burden on Henry and Sophie's slender

The Beach Hut Sun Deck with hatted staff.

resources. One evening Bettye went to see them and when she arrived the sea was like a millpond and Henry said "There is no surfing so I am just going to get the boat and take all my staff water skiing" — surely, a brilliant way to keep a happy atmosphere among one's staff?

Ever since they had returned from Johannesburg Henry and Sophie had been facing the discomforts that most of the family have faced while getting their establishments going — no home of their own. They camped in the barn at Trevithick East for the 1998 summer. For the following winter they moved into his parents' little holiday house, Sea Lodge, at Watergate Bay. When the 1999 summer season began they camped for a while in the small room above the Beach Hut and later managed to rent a nearby converted barn from a friend, which made life a bit more comfortable.

For the 1999 season they were also joined by Sophie's brother, Olivier, from France. He had a degree in Business Management and was a budding accountant. He, of course, was a marvellously trustworthy general factotum and for that season he slept on the premises and was also the night security guard. He used the smaller room on the first floor as a bed-sitting room. He and Sophie's dog, Basil, (who looked like a fierce German Shepherd dog, but Sophie swore was really a Labrador with a Labrador's temperament) made an excellent caretaking and security team. It was an admirable arrangement for their first year.

The major part of their quarters was a large airy office where Sophie spent long hours toiling away. She coped with the accounts, wages, etc., and the mountain of paperwork inflicted on small business these days by the Government with their ever tightening rules and regulations. She is good with figures, very methodical and her talents complemented Henry's well. She kept the finances on an even keel while he dealt with "front of house", marketing, public relations, and the myriad of daily problems that arise. They seemed to work together in harmony but soon Sophie found it too restricting and she gave it up.

One wild August day, with the sea too rough for surfing, Henry, not losing a moment nor missing a trick, took to the beach with the kites in a big way to great effect. That evening he was inundated with enquiries by e-mail about the kiting and one man from Bristol booked himself a course of kiting lessons every month for months ahead. The kiting proved to be a splendid alternative beach sport when the sea was un-surfable.

Henry and Sophie's first season was hectic to say the least; they had to find their feet. One fine day in August they ran out of food completely; their five hundred pasties had gone in a flash — and the cupboard was bare. They had to close for two hours to replenish stocks. They didn't let that happen again!

Henry then endeavoured to set up a non-profit making Environmental Trust for Watergate Bay which he hoped everyone would join. It was to work for the protection of the environment including cleaning the beach and public lavatories and hopefully providing lifeguards to be responsible for the safety of all the people using the beach, and generally to guard the interests of the bay. Unfortunately he didn't manage to get the agreement of all the people concerned and it didn't come off, but it would have been most beneficial to everyone in Watergate Bay.

The ultimate aim of the Extreme Academy was to promote Watergate Bay as the UK's No.1 venue for extreme beach sports, including surfing, surf canoeing, kite surfing, power kite flying, sand yachting, para-gliding and tow-in surfing. Also being considered was another extreme sport from California — street luge racing. Bettye thought this a bit far-fetched. It entailed racing down a road, lying feet first on an elongated skate board. The road, of course, would have to be closed and she thought it must surely be unlikely that it would ever happen in Watergate Bay, considering a previous owner had not even managed to get planning permission to use the skate bowl he had already constructed? But who knew what might happen in the twenty-first century? In the autumn Henry went to Bude and took an instructors' course on Kiting and allied sport and became a qualified instructor which no doubt stood him in good stead.

For the 2000 season it was planned to hold one of the UK's only international kite surfing championships at Watergate Bay. That briefly set the Bay alight!

On the beach, alongside the Beach Hut was "West Coast Surfari" which was, and still is, said to be one of the best surfing schools in the country, and they were working closely with the Extreme Academy. What excitements were in store for Watergate Bay.

With a season behind them the young Ashworths had all kinds of schemes for the Extreme Academy in the pipeline. During the 1999-2000 winter the beach shops and the take-away were sorted out and enlarged. Henry and Sophie hoped that the Beach Hut Bistro would become a venue for local all-the-year-round surfers; they installed a wood burning fire in the corner which set up a good "fug". What could be more appealing to surfers on a cold winter's day after hours in the water than yarning about the "big one they caught or missed" with a hot grog in their hand?

At the end of the 2000 season Henry and Sophie bought a cottage at Higher Tolcarne, St Mawgan in Pydar, but they did not really find it a very congenial place to live; they seemed to have had on-going battles with the planners and with the neighbours over parking and the dogs. They eventually solved that problem by buying the field adjoining their property which gave them a separate drive in and space for parking and exercising their dogs.

Henry sometimes got wild ideas. In 2003 he bought an old London red double-decker bus for £2,000 with the idea of transporting customers to the Extreme Academy to and from Newquay. He somehow persuaded Blackthorne Cider Company to paint it bright blue and plaster it with Blackthorne Cider advertisements, which cost them £6,000. So far so good, but then trouble struck. Not only did the bus have to be driven by a Public Vehicle Licence holder who had to have held that licence for two years, it was not allowed to carry drunks — which was exactly what it had been bought for. However, Henry engaged a militant little 'leftie' unionist as a bus driver — more trouble as it turned out; he wasn't prepared to drive anyone who had had a drink — so the whole scheme collapsed and the bright blue bus stood in the car park for the next two years; eventually it was given to a local bus company. As Henry said philosophically, "Well, one can't win them all!" — but it was a good try.

In September, 2004 Henry and Sophie's daughter, Olivia, was born amid great family rejoicing, and in 2005 there was more excitement to come when during the early months Henry and Will Ashworth spent much time negotiating with the Trustees of the Jamie Oliver Foundation in London in a bid to bring the planned 15 Cornwall

Restaurant to Watergate Bay and it was greatly to their credit that they succeeded in beating two thousand other applicants for it. When it was publicly announced in April 2005 that their bid had been successful the whole family were delighted. It was a feather in their caps and although Henry Ashworth personally was soon ready to move out of Cornwall he must fairly be given the credit for negotiating the deal, which he did, in granny's view, brilliantly, ably supported by William.

Jamie Oliver's "15" Restaurant. – *Courtesy Simon Burt.*

In January 2006 the conversion of the top floor of the Beach Hut to 15 Cornwall, a first class restaurant began. The main aim was to train twenty disadvantaged youngsters in Cornwall every year to become truly top-class chefs. The training plan was very well structured. The

"15" Restaurant showing entrance from car park above. Watergate Bay Hotel can be seen behind.

The Ashworths, Jamie Oliver and the student chefs.
Courtesy Simon Burt.

students began their training in January 2006 and spent the first three months at Truro College. They then had one month's placement in the kitchens of the best restaurants in the county and finally they completed their training under the expert eyes of the Master Chef who is in charge at 15 Cornwall. The whole scheme was funded by the Regional Development Agency and Objective One funds from Europe to the tune of £1,000,000 which was spent on the redevelopment of the first floor of the Extreme Academy and included a new, up to date stainless steel kitchen with equipment which cost £80,000.

The Launch Party was held on 18th May 2006. There were many people there — local dignitaries and tourist 'bigwigs', the bank manager and all the PR and agency people. In fact everybody who had been involved with the project in any way plus everyone in tourism in the county, and of course Jamie Oliver, his team and his parents, who beguiled everyone. They were so proud of their son and yet unassuming about him. Jamie, his No.1 and the two Ashworth brothers all climbed onto a table and had their say. In Bettye's view the whole project is a triumph for Jamie Oliver, Restormel and the two Ashworths. They all worked hard to bring it off. There had been many months of negotiations with the Jamie Oliver Foundation and Henry Ashworth was the instigator. He was keen to lure Jamie Oliver to his Extreme Academy which he had set up in 2002. He was wholeheartedly supported by Betty Hale of Restormel Borough Council who must also be given credit. She showed enormous tenacity for the project. For six months she bombarded the Trust with weekly emails and refused to

William and Henry Ashworth with Jamie Oliver.
Courtesy Simon Burt

take 'no' for an answer; she never gave up. There is no doubt having 15 Cornwall at Watergate Bay is a splendid boost for Newquay's tourism and the Cornish team is to be congratulated. In early 2007 the first wave of students was on its way as fully trained chefs.

So that's how Henry Ashworth's vision for Watergate Bay Beach came about but after a few years he and his French wife Sophie felt restless and found life in Cornwall too limiting, and they were ready to move on. They both have a lively intellect, itchy feet and crave stimulation and change. Henry still has a stake in the Watergate Bay complex, which has now been amalgamated with the hotel and has been taken over by his younger brother William, who became the Managing Director of the whole set up in September 2003 — hotel, shops, Bistro, surf school and car park collectively called "The Complete Beach Life Experience". He seems well able to cope with it and takes it in his stride, and he is firmly supported by his wife, Pix.

In July 2006 Henry and Sophie's son, Alfred, was born. They bought a house in France and Henry accepted the post of an International Director working for Common Purpose, an international charity which helps people in leadership and decision-making positions to be more effective in their own organisations, in the community and in society as a whole. Henry is expert at networking, and his job entails constant trips abroad; he has been to Ghana twice within the space of a few weeks, to Turkey and Hungary briefly and hopefully will soon be working in Switzerland. When asked what is so appealing about the job he replied "The many interesting people I meet". Pressed further he said "I like being a small fish in a big pool and that is what I am." Just so — but he also loves swimming with the big fish!

While Henry grappled with his job Sophie set about putting the house in France in order. They shuffled in in time for Christmas 2006 with Olivia and Alfred, two dogs and a Nannie, but that must have been almost camping because the house was not really habitable at that time; they love camping, anyway! It is about two hours away from Sophie's parents and they are very happy with it. They moved in properly in May, 2007.

Looking back, Henry Ashworth was the first of the family to realize the possibilities and potential surfing had to offer and when he bought the tatty little Beach Café etc. on Watergate Bay beach and started the Extreme Academy with a licensed restaurant in 2003 he set the ball rolling for the big upsurge and interest there has been. Today, although Henry is over the hills and far away, he still has a stake in the business and comes down for directors' meetings from time to time.

Henry and Sophie with Livvy and Freddo.

Trumpers 2002 – 2008

Trumpers, 2002.

In 2000, when Toby Ashworth had taken on the management of The Nare from Mrs Burt, Bettye felt she needed a new project so in 2002 she bought a small block of fully furnished apartments in Porth, with ample parking, and renamed it 'Trumpers'. Mrs Burt, who lived nearby, agreed to manage it for her, and Bettye then had a busy, but enjoyable, couple of years putting them together and re-furbishing them — on a shoe string, of course, in her usual frugal way.

There are five two-bedroom apartments, all named after sea birds. Puffin, Gannet, Tern, Heron and Seagull and having completed those she obtained planning permission to create a small, one-bedroom pad under the eaves for herself, which she called 'The Eyrie' The garden has been landscaped, making several little barbecue corners for tenants to use on summer evenings.

The tenants love them. Mrs Burt runs a sedate establishment, encouraging the young surfers to book elsewhere, and as the number of families and older people coming to Newquay is declining rapidly it is becoming more difficult to fully book. Bettye does not mind in the least, she is not expecting to make her fortune with Trumpers, and is content that it is enjoyed by the people who come. It 'ticks-over' comfortably and appeases her passion for 'putting things together'.

Bettye Gray is now using Tern, a two bedroom apartment on the first floor, for her personal use. She is still disinclined to sit down with her tapestry, and doing Trumpers gives her much pleasure.

A few of the little barbeque corners in the garden.

Watergate Bay Hotel comes to life 2000 – 2008

Mary and John Ashworth had long been ready to retire but they showed much patience in putting no pressure on their sons to return to Cornwall. In October 2000 when William came back to Cornwall and immediately joined Watergate Bay Hotel his parents were delighted, but again showed great restraint and gave him his head, as the reader will hear.

William's return awoke Watergate Hotel from its 'snooze'; it began to come to life. He spent the first winter marketing the hotel and refurbishing it in a minor way, but it was just the beginning of a major shake up. The Head Chef retired after some twenty-five years service and the Restaurant Manager left too. It is likely they both realized the hotel's bumbling days were over and there were big changes afoot. William announced that he wished to be called Will by one and all. He firmly took charge and clearly had a keen determination to modernise the hotel and put it on the map. He was twenty-six years old and embarking on a mammoth undertaking but he was brimming with enthusiasm and ideas.

John and Mary Ashworth again were wise at this point. They appointed a respected and experienced hotelier in his sixties, Chris Skidmore, to be Managing Director. His main role was to guide William and act as a buffer between him and his parents and this worked well for some three years.

During the winter of 2001-2002 the hotel stayed open all the year round for the first time in its one hundred year history. The ground floor public rooms were refurbished in a modern style more in keeping with the image of the Extreme Academy and Beach Hut, which were proving to be highly successful and going great guns.

In 2003 Mr Skidmore retired and during that year was replaced by Mark Grebby, a young, experienced and enthusiastic chap, as General Manager. William Ashworth became Managing Director of the hotel and his first project was to redesign the new wing of bedrooms which already had planning permission. This design was to be much more elaborate and up to date with medium size, wooden floored bedrooms with minimalist modern furniture and elegant bathrooms, and also include flat TV screens incorporating all the latest technology. The new scheme included a lift, large laundry, two conference rooms and a board room but of course it took time for these plans to be re-hashed and in fact the new building with a curving wing facing the sea with eighteen de-luxe rooms was not built until 2003-2004. It really was a massive project. Before they could begin the builders had to dig down

The new curving wing built in 2003-2004.
Courtesy Ben Rowe.

some nine feet into solid rock for the foundations.

The new building was completed by July 2004 with the usual last minute rush. The builders handed over the keys just forty-eight hours before the first guests arrived and the rooms were then booked solidly for the rest of the season. What a scramble it was — but has there ever been an hotel project that wasn't completed like that? Certainly not in this family's story.

Twenty-four hours before the first guests arrived for the new rooms William gave a champagne launch party on the terrace in front of the new wing to which all and sundry who had in any way been involved with the project were invited. Of course the new rooms were on show. It was a warm sunny evening and the chefs produced exotic canapés. There were about sixty people at the party — it was quite an occasion and the guest of honour was Dave Meneer, the Strategic Marketing Director of the Eden Project — who incidentally later became a director of Fifteen Cornwall.

But that was only the beginning; by the autumn of 2004 William had seriously got the bit between his teeth again. During the following winter he completely redesigned the whole of the ground floor of the hotel and laid a slate floor in the hall. He moved the bar from its sea view position and created a quiet, sea view lounge from which children were barred. The ladies' powder room was glamorised. He moved the stairs leading to the Sea Lounge which was renamed the Ocean Room — in fact the concept of the hotel was completely changed. It was no

Living Space – formerly the old ballroom. – *Courtesy Bob Berry.*

longer a traditional stereo type old fashioned, tired, seaside hotel. There was no dreary ballroom, it had been converted into a large open area called the 'Living Space' with a bar, and it is much appreciated by the new breed of young modern guests who now flock to the hotel.

His parents were amazed at how much William managed to achieve in the few winter months from October 2004 to April 2005. They felt at last Cornwall was going to see Watergate Bay Hotel's enormous potential developed. Little had happened there for years. It is not easy to build up a business over a period of years and then step back and watch the next generation completely change its image and style but that is exactly what Mary and John Ashworth did and William is now continuing the good work with their full approval.

One day, Mark Grebby found a dog swimming in the indoor swimming pool. He asked the owner what was the dog doing in the pool? The reply was "Well it is pouring with rain outside and this is the only way I can exercise my dog" and then, of course, strong words from the manager. Another guest arrived at the hotel, plonked a covered cage on the reception desk, and asked "Do you take pets?" "Yes", said the Manager, "we charge £10 a day." He peered into the cage; facing him was a large, plump brown rat — £10 daily — eccentric to say the least!

John Ashworth, for years longing to retire, had spent much effort, time and money refitting and refurbishing a thirty-two foot six berth sloop built of teak called *Inca Rose*, and had been looking forward to the day when he and Mary would be able to sail away and enjoy it.

Sadly that was not to be, as before she could quite shed the shackles of running a 'hands-on' family business he damaged his shoulder and, probably wisely, decided *Inca Rose* was too much for him to cope with and he sold her. Poor John, he had been longing for some serious sailing for thirty-five years — but now he has a Cornish shrimper called *Daisy* which he sails on the Camel estuary. He has also taken up golf, photography, and bird watching with great enthusiasm. Mary is pursuing her life-long interest in botany. She is a Friend of Kew and has attended several courses there on various aspects of botany. Mary and John have been on expeditions to the far corners of the world, led by botanists. As a member of the British Wild Flower Society Mary has won several prizes at national level for her photographs of flowers; she seems to have inherited the Henslow family trait. At last she and John are enjoying their retirement.

In December 2004 William married Pix Bennett, the daughter of a High Court Judge from Sussex and the whole family trooped to their large and glamorous wedding in Pix's village church, All Saints, Highbrook, near Haywards Heath. William and Pix began their married life in a converted barn near St Columb Major. Their first child, a daughter, Tamara to be known as Mara, was born in February 2007 amid great family rejoicing.

Early in 2007 William and Pix Ashworth formed a company which they call "Beach Retreats", a self-catering letting agency. They immediately become letting agents for thirty-one of the thirty-three owners of 'Waves' apartments, the new prestigious development on the

Rosemere re-built – now "Waves" luxury apartments.

site of the old Beach Hotel. The company goes from strength to strength and they now have over fifty exclusive beach properties on their books, and are expecting to grow rapidly over the next year or two. Their target is over two hundred contemporary self-catering retreats, but they will only accept properties of the highest quality and near the sea.

In the winter of 2006-2007 William Ashworth tackled his next major project for the hotel. He completely gutted and then re-designed the two main floors of bedrooms. The rooms were rearranged and given large modern bathrooms. The work was carried out by an excellent team of builders willing to work all day and half the night and they finished on schedule and within budget. William was delighted.

There was one mighty hitch at the last moment. The rooms were fully booked; everything was there, most of it in place, but the Ving cards (electronic keys) for the locks on the doors, which had been ordered in November from Norway, had not arrived which meant the rooms could not be used. Panic! William went into action and threatened all kinds of dire consequences if the keys did not arrive. The locks were then flown from Norway overnight just in time and all was well.

The interiors of the rooms are modern and stylishly designed by Helen Blake of Absolute Design. The rooms now have Ipod docking stations, broadband internet connections and all the other up-to-date wizardry. In short the bedrooms are thoroughly 'with it'. In Bettye's view one of the most startling innovations is that in the best sea-view

Sea View bedroom with bath across the window.
Courtesy Ben Rowe.

rooms William has put the baths in the bedrooms across the window so that guests can sit in the bath with a drink and enjoy the view. What would Great Grannie have thought of that? No doubt the modern generation of guests will love it and Great Uncle Graham Farmer would have said "Well done Boy!"

In the spring of 2007 the squash court was converted into four luxury family suites, but that proved to be a bigger job than had been envisaged. The rear building didn't have the correct footings and so the whole site had to be virtually rebuilt from scratch. It had been planned to open the suites by the spring bank holiday but that wasn't possible. The mains gas water and sewage pipes proved to be in the wrong place and moving them was a major operation which entailed digging deep trenches exactly where the foundations had to go. It delayed the whole job by six weeks. However by 21st July with a struggle and much overtime the suites were ready and were then booked solid for the rest of the season. They all have large bed-sitting rooms, children's bunk rooms, good size bathrooms, well fitted and equipped kitchenettes and all the up-to-date technology; internet connections, DVD players, flip-down televisions in children's rooms, satellite television, etc.

Another bright idea for the 2007 season was the two catering trailers which William bought second hand; one selling ice cream and sited on the private road leading to the beach and the other on the beach selling burgers and hot dogs. The latter had to be towed to and from the beach daily, but they both did a roaring trade.

In July 2007 the hotel and the Extreme Academy held a Surf Relief Festival in aid of young disabled people who yearn to learn to surf. It lasted far into the night. Thousands came and there was something for everybody; six-a-side football, a fancy dress surfing competition, sand castle building and face painting for the children and the Blue Reef Aquarium brought some of its sea creatures and a talk was given to the little ones. A local sky diving club gave a demonstration and five sky divers landed on the beach. In the evening the party really got going: there were four Cornish bands each of whom did a stint. Two large barbecues were set up on the private beach with chefs from the hotel in full whites and bare feet presiding over them. They offered hot dogs (best Cornish sausages) or steak sandwiches which were immensely popular and they sold one thousand before they ran out. On the private beach bare-footed barmen served champagne, wine, and beer and the party went on into the small hours. The hotel guests joined in and had a marvellous time and the Beach Hut had its best day ever. Over £10,000 was raised; it was voted a great success.

Polo on Watergate Bay Hotel Beach, 2007. – *Courtesy Ben Rowe.*

In the summer of 2007 the first ever polo match on a beach in the UK was staged at Watergate Bay. Two teams came down from Somerset. Their eighteen ponies grazed in the paddock in front of William's converted barn with the grooms being housed in quarters nearby. The players stayed in the hotel and the whole event was sponsored by Veuve Clicquot — the champagne flowed. Aston Martin and Frank Knight each sponsored a team. They played with a specially adapted orange ball, lighter than a normal ball and the match was a roaring success.

Polo on Watergate Bay Hotel Beach, 2008. – *Courtesy Bob Berry.*

Watergate Bay Beach circa 1960s showing the sea wall.

Viewing deck built on the sea wall.

The hotel's main deck, which William has built on the sea wall, was the sponsors' hospitality area for their VIPs and hotel guests. Five hundred people were on the beach. In the evening one hundred and fifty corporate guests were invited to the party in the Ocean Room with canapés and a Cornish band, followed by a barbecue around the swimming pool. They partied into the early hours. The tickets were £150 each, but the hotel guests were given free entry for the evening. It was a huge success and a date was pencilled in for a repeat match on the beach in June next year. There was further excitement at Watergate Bay in 2007 when *Echo Beach*, a film series for ITV starring Jason Donovan and Martine McCutcheon about surfing was being made, with the Beach Hut Bistro as the base. It generated much activity, interest and, of course, business.

In autumn 2007 William was granted planning consent to demolish the ugly sports hall and Watergate Villas and to build twenty-seven Eco-friendly two bedroom apartments. He was particularly delighted when his plans were passed first time round and without fuss. The work will begin in January 2009. He had a scale model made of the proposed building and councillors, local businessmen, and Joe Public were invited to view the plans and the model for open consultation of the project. He is particularly proud of the fact that each of the twenty-seven apartments will use no more electricity than two domestic kettles on full time.

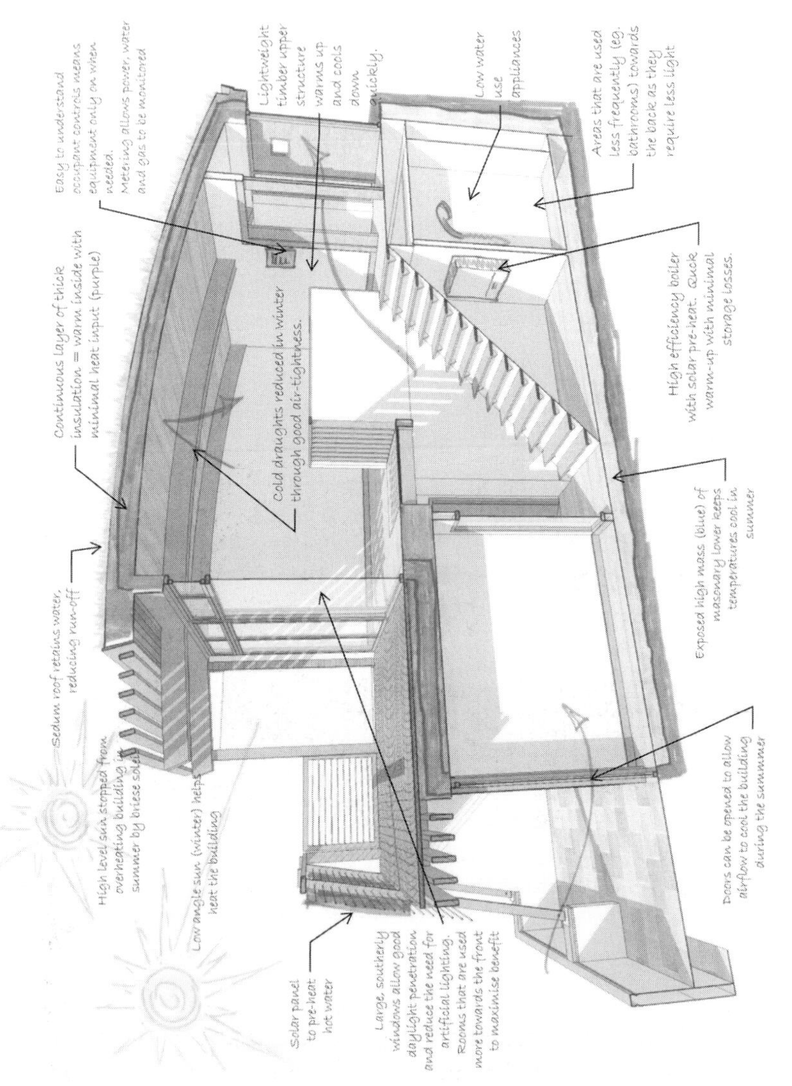

Cross section of one of the eco-friendly two bedroom apartments, for which planning permission was granted.
Courtesy The Architects' Design Group.

In 2008 Watergate Bay Hotel and Extreme Academy won Coutts National Prize for Family Business in the £1-5 million category. They had already won the regional contest and the whole family went to London in June for the National Prize Giving Ceremony. They were over the moon when the winner was announced and Bettye, who was there too, sat and quietly wallowed in reflected glory. They had indeed done well. Will summed it up in his acceptance speech:- *"Being initially shortlisted for the Coutts National Prize for Family Business was a tremendous honour; we were up against some impressive companies and so being named the winner at the award ceremony was an extremely proud moment. The award is recognition of the many years of hard work by our parents and their unwavering belief and courage to stand by and watch as my brother and I took their business apart and put it together in a very different form. Our success is also testament to our hard working staff and in particular our directors who have played a crucial role in transforming the business into what it is today and will no doubt help The Hotel & Extreme Academy to go on and achieve many more great things in the future."* — hear hear!

The Ashworths, Bettye and Judi Blakeburn, Operations Director, and Chris Hugo, Commercial Director, Watergate Bay Hotel & Extreme Academy at the Coutts National Family Business Award evening.

There is no doubt that at thirty-three, the youngest member of the family involved with running the hotels, one might say William has got off to a good start. In the meanwhile John and Mary Ashworth are thoroughly enjoying their retirement and the reflected glory of William's go ahead schemes — and, as Bettye has found, it is a warming potion.

John and Mary are enjoying their well-earned retirement.

From the left are Tamara, Will, Pix and Cicely Ashworth

The Surfing Phenomenon – Newquay late 1990s – 2008

In the last fifty years there have been strong social and economic changes which have affected holiday resorts all over the world and no doubt there will be many more as standards rise and people's horizons broaden. Certainly Newquay has changed. It is no longer the upmarket, elegant, quiet watering hole it was before the Second World War, nor is it the bustling resort for middle class families it became in the late 1940s, but it is now an exhilarating resort for the young and active. Package holidays and cheap world wide travel have had an enormous impact on the tourist industry worldwide. It was clear from the early 1990s that surfing was beginning to get its grip on the town and Newquay was once again facing dramatic changes, but surfing had not yet been recognised or accepted as a serious sport.

In the early days of the surfing era there was a group of keen surfers who descended on Newquay; the impecunious youngsters who teemed into the town at the beginning of the season, many hitch-hiking to get there. They saw it as an escape. They no longer took lodgings or digs in the old fashioned sense of the word. Many of them just took a room for the summer which they shared with a friend, or friends, boys or girls — even three tier bunk beds were acceptable. The rows of small terrace houses at Newquay's western end were known to the surfers as 'bed-sit land' and many youngsters stayed there for the whole season. The boys and girls could surf and laze on the beach all day — free. They could take casual work for an hour or two in the evenings to pay for a few beers, and then party far into the night at the many discos and clubs in the town. It was great fun and it could be done on a shoestring. It was too easy and there were Government benefit schemes encouraging young people to seek work away from home which made it even easier — they, unwittingly, aided and abetted that lifestyle. To some of the youngsters it was the equivalent of the university students' gap year. No doubt they had a wonderful time and made the most of their first taste of freedom, but they did little for Newquay's image or reputation as a family holiday resort. They were inclined to loll around the town in groups and sometimes gangs; they could be rowdy and many of the middle class families who had long been the backbone of Newquay's holiday season drifted away. They didn't like being jostled in the streets by young roughs and toughs

In the late 1990s one or two houses in Headland Road began offering back-packers accommodation for as little as £5 per night with large boards outside proclaiming the fact. Bettye was aghast. What was Newquay coming to? Before the Second World War those houses had been the classiest in Newquay. However, the back-packers' hostels turned out to be the forerunners of the surf lodges which soon began springing up all over the town. The lodges offer dormitory type accommodation, often in bunk beds, showers, storage for surfing paraphernalia and drying space. Some of them have licensed bars and breakfast is often an optional extra. Soon many small hotels copied them and today there are ever more surf lodges; they are Newquay's modern version of the boarding house or small hotel.

Modern youngsters will not be told what time the door is locked, what to eat or when. Their eating habits have changed; these days they 'graze'. If they feel hungry they will buy a burger, pasty or fish and chips and eat it 'on the hoof', or perhaps perched on a wall. Numerous fast food and take-away cafés cater for them and offer cheap, quick 'grub' but it does little to enhance the street scenes. By 2007 there were fifteen late night 'take-aways' in Newquay.

Today surfing is a major sport, it is big business and has completely revolutionised Newquay. No longer is it the simple little pastime it once was, surfing is now accepted world-wide as a serious, skilful sport which gets more sophisticated year by year. In 1999 Plymouth University announced that there was to be a degree course in surfing which would include the science of surfing. Perhaps not the most useful qualification with which to face life, but the students surely enjoy it. International Surfing Championships and competitions are held all over the world and Newquay's surfing beaches, which are among the finest, have been discovered in a big way.

There are three major surfing centres in Newquay where tuition is offered, and various national surfing events are held from time to time. They are at Fistral Beach, run by the Council and facing the Atlantic Ocean and with arguably the most spectacular surf in the country; Lusty Glaze, which is privately owned, surrounded by high cliffs with an Adventure Centre providing adventure activities for all ages and abilities, a Training Centre for first aid, lifeguard training etc. and their Education Centre, run in conjunction with Cornwall College (Plymouth University) offering a Surf Science Foundation Degree; the Extreme Academy adjoining the Watergate Bay Hotel is owned by the Ashworth family and run by William Ashworth, as has already been described in the family story. There are also numerous smaller surf schools in the town offering all grades of tuition and last, but not least, Tolcarne Beach has come to life again too, but today it is all about surfing. Someone recently told Bettye that Tolcarne is their favourite beach for surfing. Apparently it is the way the rollers come in and it has 'Tolcarne Wedge', whatever that may be, for boogie boarders.

The highlights of the season are the various championships and competitions which are held on Fistral Beach, Watergate, or Lusty Glaze from time to time when the professional stars of the world-wide surfing circuit compete. When they arrive with their entourages, cavalcades of followers and vans full of clobber there is a frisson of excitement among the many young, would-be champions. Thousands of visitors from all over England converge on Newquay and at times the town chokes and the traffic grinds to a standstill. Today Newquay is a vibrant, liberated resort for the young. Surely Cornwall's answer to Ibiza or Torremolinos, but it has one enormous advantage over those Continental hot-spots — the surfing. The sun, or lack of it, matters not. Come rain or shine, if the surf is up the surfers are in. Today surf and youth have taken over Newquay and the whole town is geared to their needs. There are twenty six shops selling solely surfing gear and paraphernalia.

Apart from the 'big boys' who travel the world competing in the championships, and the young local fanatics in Newquay who surf all year round and often spend five or six hours a day in the water, thousands of ordinary visitors also come for the surfing. At The Headland Hotel they have enthusiastic 'wrinklies' who return year after year to surf on Fistral Beach. They bring their forty year old wooden belly boards, don their modern wet suits, and surf every day regardless of weather, but these days The Headland also has well-heeled regular guests who come solely for the surfing. They arrive kitted out with the latest expensive surfing gear and the hotel has a flourishing surf shop which is well patronized by the residents.

There was one enterprising entrepreneur in Newquay who bought the nineteen- bedroom St Anne's Hotel, created from two terrace houses in Berry Road, and turned it into a flashy licensed Surf Lodge with palms decked with twinkling lights outside. He managed to accommodate one hundred and nine people and was highly successful until he fell foul of the planners about the sleeping arrangements. He had a near-by back garden full of chalets! Bettye was much amused by this. It reminded her of the six-bedroom guest house on Mount Wise which in 1945 stuffed in seventy-five guests with three sittings for every meal and had people sleeping in houses up and down the road.

One hot sunny Sunday afternoon in August in the late '90s Bettye strolled around the centre of the town; to her it was a revelation. The street milled with young people. Hundreds were standing drinking jammed into the forecourt of the Central Hotel. Outside the Sailors Arms were four uniformed bouncers on duty. The door was open and dance music blared out from the dark interior and the youngsters were pouring in. Fifty years ago on such an afternoon, pubs would have

Central Square August 1999.

been closed, the streets deserted and the mass of holidaymakers would have been on the beaches. Now, apparently, the Sailors Arms is licenced for twelve hundred people, and like others in the town is open all day and half the night. Surely one day the centre of Newquay will burst.

When the Camelot Cinema site was redeveloped in 1999 it really set the ball rolling. The new owners were given planning permission for an Australian Theme Bar. It is a 'walk about' joint with bars, restaurant, and entertainment licensed for two thousand people. It also has a seriously late night liquor licence which allows it to stay open far into the night. From the outset it was an immediate success and, no doubt, helped to endorse Newquay's burgeoning reputation as Cornwall's leading late night 'hot spot'. Of course, others soon followed and there has since been much development and massive capital expenditure in that area of the town. Today Central Square is the hub of modern Newquay's night life.

The Australian Theme Bar, Walkabout, on the site of the old Camelot Cinema - formerly the Pavilion.

Central Square today.

At sundown the centre of the town comes to life; it throngs with thousands of uninhibited youngsters bent on partying far into the night. Shops and cafés are open all hours and there are late night take-aways, many pubs and amusement arcades and nine or ten nightclubs, some with lap dancers and nudes, some licensed until four or five a.m., and to set the scene the main streets are strung from end to end with lights from Blackpool. Newquay is now a magnet to young people; it offers all the excitements that appeal to today's liberated youth. It really has become Cornwall's swinging go-go resort where one can surf all day and dance and drink most of the night and the young adore it. For the moment that is the essence of modern Newquay and, much as the older folk deplore it, it is highly successful and the town is on the crest of a wave — the surfing wave. In modern jargon "Newquay is cool".

In 2007 surf-pods were introduced for the first time. They are plushy, one room apartments with a foldaway bed, shower en suite, a small kitchenette plus storage for surfing gear, drying space and parking. They are for yuppie surfing enthusiasts who need their own pad so that they can have a few days surfing whenever time permits. The first surf-pod was built in Henver Road and others are in the pipeline. Three other small hotels in Henver Road, the Kelsborough, Fort Wayne and Felicia

Cumberland Hotel in Henver Road becoming surf pods.

were also demolished in 2007 and became 'Contemporary Apartments' — whatever they might be! Even Tolcarne Beach has joined the surf craze. Under new owners the beach got going again and today, in 2008, there are well-furnished two-bedroom apartments with bathroom, shower room, kitchen, and lounge/diner, with double doors opening onto a private balcony overlooking the beach and sea. Tolcarne's classic beach huts are listed as one of the attractions as are the Beach Café and the licensed bar/restaurant. Wet suits, surf boards, boogie boards and

Tolcarne Beach and Narrowcliff, September 2008. Note Nagajanka and Bella Vista have gone, and Tolcarne and St Brannocks have also been demolished. The new apartments on the beach, with shops under, can be seen on the right hand side.

deck chairs are all available for hire, and the surfers are once again taking Tolcarne to their hearts. Tolcarne Beach is ready to take a leading place in the newly generated Newquay.

So much for the surfing and the surfers who have completely taken Newquay over — but what of the other hotels that could not be adapted to cater for the surfers? Life for them has not been so easy. While surfing has steadily gained ground over the last ten years other types of tourism in Newquay have not been keeping pace and the number of coach companies bringing parties to the town has fallen. Now year by year fewer coach parties are coming as the companies find more exciting venues for their older passengers. Saga was one of the first companies to pull out of the town and others soon followed; it was inevitable really. At the moment Newquay has little appeal for the 'wrinklies'; it is essentially for surfers and those who enjoy late night clubbing and pubbing.

By the beginning of the twenty-first century some of the hoteliers realised that their properties were worth much more to developers as sites for redevelopment than they were as dilapidated, outdated hotels with rooms they could not fill. Some of the Newquay hotels had fallen behind with improving their standards and the owners found themselves unable to keep up with the demands of the modern holiday makers; for some of them lack of parking became a major problem, and so many owners of the previously highly successful hotels with spacious sites and good sea views applied for planning consent to turn them into residential and holiday apartments.

Tremont Hotel, on Pentire, has been re-developed into 47 private apartments and 12 affordable homes.

Newquay has succeeded in achieving a spectacular turn-around in its fortunes in the last ten years. All the conventional seaside attractions have been swept aside. Gone are the summer shows, the repertory theatre, the cinemas, the flora dances and even the bingo hall — in fact all the public family evening entertainments and many of the old established shops have disappeared. The town is no longer a traditional seaside resort catering for middle-class families. It has little appeal for them although a few are misguidedly still trying to promote it as such. If the present trend continues it seems likely that soon Newquay will be saturated with apartments and there will be a serious shortage of middle of the road hotels — their numbers are dwindling fast.

But what is there for non-surfers? Well, at last Trenance Valley has finally caught up. Apart from the bowling green, tennis courts, and boating lake, which have been there for ever, Trenance Leisure Park now has two swimming pools, 9-hole pitch and putt and crazy golf courses, and the zoo, which has gone from strength to strength, and has won national awards, and is the only zoo in Cornwall. It has recently acquired the large wetland field adjoining and there are plans afoot for further expansion. In 2004 two indoor tennis courts, four floodlit courts and a handsome re-built pavilion and clubhouse were added. There is also now a professionally designed ramp park where youngsters can spin their BMX bikes and skateboards to their hearts'

New indoor tennis courts alongside the Bowling Green at Trenance, 2008.

content. There is a well equipped gymnasium, the two squash courts have been converted into fitness rooms where aerobic classes are held, and last but not least there are plenty of fun things for children and to cap it all — talk of an ice rink. What a boost that would give Newquay! Today there are just two other tourist attractions in the town; 'Blue Reef', a serious aquarium which is on the site of the old Cosy Nook Theatre on the Towan Promenade and 'Tunnels of Time', a small and very minor exhibition depicting Cornish history, at the Newquay Theatre in St Michael's Road where the Repertory Company once played.

One of Newquay's most popular attractions for families is "Dairyland" at Kestle Mill, four miles from Newquay. The Davey family has been farming at Tresillian Barton since 1926 — in fact it was where Peter Whittington was a student farmer in the late 1940s. In the early 1970s the Daveys installed a large rotating milking parlour where the cows stand still and the floor rotates. It was an innovation. In 1975 Rex Davey had the brilliant idea of 'Dairyland' with the idea of showing townsfolk from the industrial Midlands and elsewhere a glimpse of traditional and modern farming methods. Some had never seen a cow; they only knew milk came in bottles. Dairyland was an instant success and families soon flocked to it — and still do. It has an enduring appeal for children of all ages. There is a pets' corner where children can feed and cuddle the animals, hay rides around the farm on the old wagon pulled by a tractor, a museum of Cornish farming artefacts, a collection of ancient tractors, and, of course, Cornish cream teas. Lastly came the 'Bull Ring' a high ceilinged indoor adventure playroom with the latest equipment for children. In fact Rex Davey spent the last thirty years of his life scouring the county for artefacts for Dairyland. It has won many awards and in 2004, aged eighty-six, Rex personally was honoured with the Cornish Tourist Board's highest award for a lifetime's effort for Tourism in the county. "Good on him" as they say in Cornwall — it was very well merited. He died in October, 2007 aged ninety.

In 2005 it was announced that the 2006 Newquay Town Guide would be the last. The Guide had served the town well for most of the 20th Century but for some time it had been losing its impact as, for various reasons, several major hotels had not been using it. Slowly modern businesses had been turning to websites, e-mails, and other modern wonders and sadly the Guide's time had come but, to the older hoteliers, it was an institution and they deplored its demise, but in the modern technological world it had just had its day.

The Radio One Road Show moved to the Barrowfields in 2007 where at the end of July there was a massive jamboree with DJs, and well known bands and thousands of excited youngsters had a ball. It officially ended at 11.00 p.m. when the hyped-up young, in party mood, dashed to the clubs and pubs in the town for a night of frivolity and fun. It fits in well with today's visitors to Newquay.

In the spring of 2008 seven hundred Iranian Muslims celebrated the Persian New Year at Trevelgue Holiday Park. It was voted a success but there were some complaints from locals who considered the 5.30 a.m. call to prayer disturbed the peace of the neighbourhood. Apparently people from as far away as St Columb Minor could clearly hear the call to prayer over the loud hailer every morning, lunch time, and evening.

For some years the start of the giddy season in Newquay, also based at Trevelgue Holiday Park at Porth, has been the 'Run to the Sun'. It is held over the spring bank holiday weekend and attracts thousands of youngsters in their VW Beetles and custom built cars. They marshal at various up-country service stations on the A30 and travel in convoy to Newquay, sometimes forming a cavalcade five miles long and really taking over the town. They then have a weekend of hectic festivities tearing about in their cars and partying far into the night. They have a wonderful time, of course, but can be over-exuberant and the Police are out in force while local residents have to take cover. But for the motoring enthusiasts it is no doubt a great weekend.

Newquay today is in the melting pot. The entrance to the town is unsightly; there are many empty sites where hotels have been demolished, several building sites with cranes reaching to the sky and

Philema Hotel – once Thelema School, Pentire undergoing re-development.

Mount Wise Hotel – one of the first to be demolished at the beginning of the 21st century. Now known as Horizons, a development of 30 two-bedroom apartments, it was in the news early in 2008 as a deserted second-home project with one sole resident, an 83-year-old great-grandmother.

other major hotels closed and boarded up awaiting planning permission for redevelopment. Soon there will be a serious dearth of hotels, there are less than fifteen sizeable ones left in the town at the time of writing. Large firms of developers from up-country have moved in: they have millions to invest and they seem to be taking the town by storm. One firm has twelve major projects in the pipeline, and another has eight. Literally hundreds of luxury apartments are being built, many costing £500,000 and more and several good restaurants are being opened in the town.

2008 has been an exciting year in the major redevelopment of Newquay. Almost weekly there have been announcements and planning applications for demolishing and redeveloping

Advertising the new development on the site of Graham Farmer's Tolcarne Hotel, and the adjoining St Brannocks on Narrowcliff.

the sites of many of the long established hotels. The old Victoria Hall, for years a cinema and lately a bingo hall, is being re-developed as a multi-screen cinema. It is due to open for the 2009 season and will be a great asset for Newquay — bravo — at last!

Today's financial climate must cast a shadow over some of the ambitious plans on the drawing board and one wonders whether some will be held up. Already one of the large firms of developers in the town has called in the receiver. It is to be hoped the major schemes will not be delayed; Newquay is not a pretty sight at the moment.

The airport, too, is undergoing major expansion. Until recently, Newquay's little civilian airport had been struggling for years, run by private companies from just a corner of the enormous St Mawgan airfield. Although it has one of the longest, widest runways in the country, its use by civilian aircraft has always been somewhat limited. Facilities within the airport building have been minimal. It still has no Customs and when needed Customs Officers have to come from Padstow, but all that could be about to change. The RAF, who has occupied the major part of the airfield since the Second World War[1], are scheduled to move in December 2008. Cornwall County Council has recently taken the civilian airport over and already the facilities are being vastly improved. They have received millions of pounds from the EU, Objective One, Government, and the Regional Development Agency. Already a new arrival lounge has been built and the car park is getting ever larger, a new control tower is being built and the runway is being re-surfaced to accommodate the modern airliners. The road

Newquay Airport new entrance.

[1] It has been the headquarters of RAF Search and Rescue and it flies rescue helicopters from there.

2008 destinations on offer and prices.

leading to the airport from the A30 has been widened. Business is growing with flights to ever more destinations and there is no doubt that now Newquay Airport will go from strength to strength and provide a vital link bewteen Newquay and the rest of the world. Newquay Cornwall Airport will be Cornwall's chief gateway to and from the big wide world 'ere long. It is to be hoped that its arrival on the world stage will be without the débâcle of the recently-opened BA's Terminal 5. In the face of the dire warnings about the state of the economy in this country in 2008, hopefully the planned extensions to the airport and its services will not be unduly delayed. They are surely vital to Cornwall's future prosperity.

Major changes in Newquay
Some of the family hotels have disappeared:

Nagajanka Boarding House 1912 – where it all began 1908.

2008 getting Bella Vista incorporated Nagajanka – now the site is to be redeveloped as apartments.

Graham Farmer's Tolcarne Hotel, circa 1936.

2008 – getting ready for re-development as apartments.

When the Armstrongs sold it in 1958.

Now part of the Eliot Hotel, Edgcumbe Avenue

Just before it was sold by the family in 1987.

2008 – re-development is under-way.

Beach Hotel, formerly Rosemere, in mid 1980s.

Now "Waves" luxury apartments. Note Tregurrian Hotel, adjoining, has been demolished to be rebuilt as apartments.

Edgcumbe, Narrowcliff 1989.

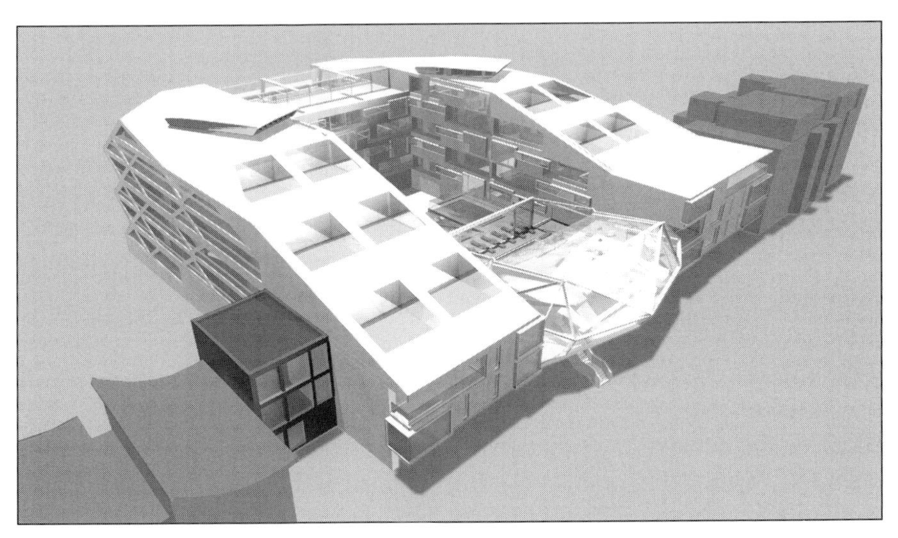

Design of 'Coast', on the site of The Edgcumbe Hotel, and Kilbirnie, Narrowcliff, 2009
Courtesy: Richard Hywel Evans Architecture & Design Ltd.

Other prominent hotels which have changed use or been demolished are:

Ambassadors Hotel, Mount Wise	retirement apartments
Beachcroft in Cliff Road	Travel Lodge with Aldi supermarket on ground floor
Beaconsfield, Harbour Crescent	awaiting a make over
Bewdley, Pentire	apartments
Cumberland	surf pods
Felicia Hotel, Henver Road	apartments
Fistral Bay, and Trecarne, Pentire	apartments (one huge site)
Fort Wayne/Kelsborough, Henver Road	demolished – awaiting redevelopment
Hilgrove Road Filling Station	apartments and Tesco Express on ground floor
Mount Wise Hotel, Mount Wise	apartments
Nance's Showroom (formerly Astor Cinema)	apartments and affordable housing
Newquay Pearl, Quintrell Downs	Travel Lodge
Pebble Hotel, Henver Road	apartments
Philema, Pentire	apartments
Porth Bay Hotel, Porth	apartments
Riviera Hotel	apartments
Rocklands, Narrowcliff	apartments
St Brannocks Hotel (and Tolcarne)	awaiting re-development to apartments
The Chough Inn, Porth	apartments
Tredragon	demolished – 'Scarlet' luxury hotel being built to open 2009/10
Trelawney Hotel, Edgcumbe Avenue	nursing home
Tremont, Pentire	apartments
Trenance Hotel, Harbour Crescent	apartments
Waters Edge Hotel, Pentire	apartments
Westward Ho! Hotel, Headland Road	apartments
Windsor Hotel, Mount Wise	apartments

Postscript

It is quite clear that the third and fourth generations of my family have inherited an enthusiasm for hotels and tourism. At the time of writing they are all forging ahead with exciting plans for the expansion of their hotels and tourist enterprises.

The Armstrongs at The Headland are planning a multi-million pound Conference Centre with underground parking, while their young family members are training at first class hotels up-country.

At Mawgan Porth the Whittingtons are busy with their plans for the new luxury thirty-six bedroom hotel they are building on the site of the Tredragon Hotel, which has already been demolished.

At Watergate Bay the Ashworths are building twenty-seven luxury apartments and there are exciting plans afoot, yet to be disclosed.

At The Nare at Veryan there are no plans to enlarge it but the hotel holds its position as the highest rated in the West Country and the accent is on making it ever more comfortable — and exclusive!

Interestingly all five Cornish hotels at present owned by members of the family are aimed at an entirely different market, and each of them in their turn has won national acclaim and accolades. How fortunate I am to still be able to take a keen interest in the activities of the younger members of the family. I am immensely proud of them and their achievements.

The end!

Bettye's family at her 90th birthday party.
From the left: Sophie Ashworth, William Ashworth, Henry Ashworth, John Ashworth, Katie Ashworth, Pix Ashworth, Morwenna Armstrong, George Armstrong, Toby Ashworth.
Sitting: Veryan Armstrong, Bettye, Mary Ashworth and Sammy.
Unfortunately, John Armstrong was in hospital at the time.

Acknowledgments

My story is told — not quite 'warts and all' but I ask my family's indulgence in what, some may deem, the odd indiscretion. My apologies to anyone who feels they have been inaccurately portrayed. I have simply told the story as I remember it, and I do stress it is only my personal view of how it all came about, and what happened on the way.

I must thank Lady Mary Holborow for kindly writing the Foreword for this book. I am also most grateful to my friends and family who have helped me recall my long story, and lastly, but certainly not least, I am seriously indebted to Coral Pepper who has encouraged and supported me far beyond the call of duty for the last three years. She has spent hours sorting my often jumbled notes with infinite patience. When I wrote *Oh! My dear life* I said that it would never have seen 'light of day without Coral's help and support'. This time I can go further — much further! This book would by now be at the bottom of the sea, but for Coral's encouragement and determination — thank you, Coral.

Bettye Gray
November 2008

FAMILY TREE

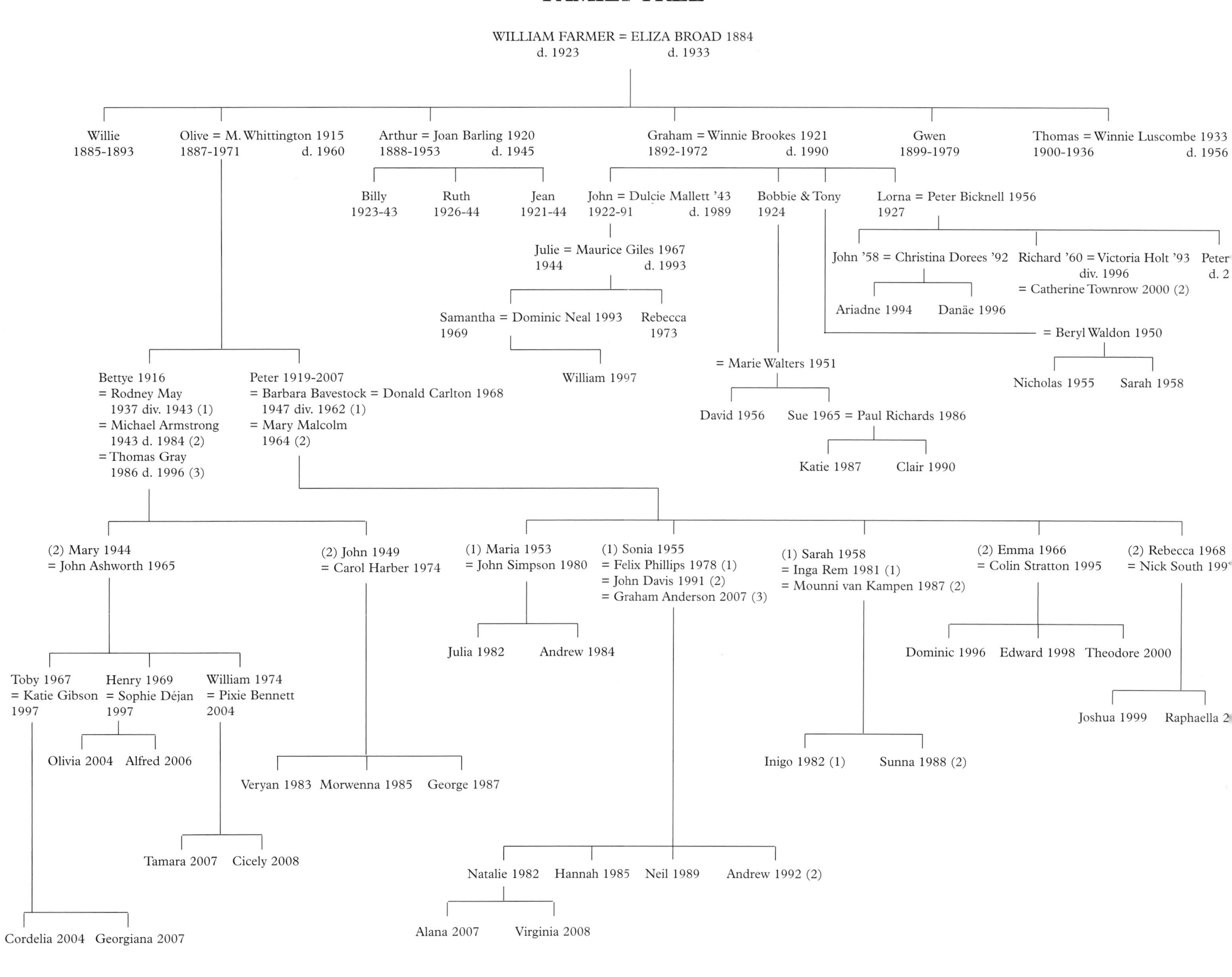
WILLIAM FARMER = ELIZA BROAD 1884
d. 1923 d. 1933
Willie
1885-1893
Olive = M. Whittington 1915
1887-1971 d. 1960
Arthur = Joan Barling 1920
1888-1953 d. 1945
Graham = Winnie Brookes 1921
1892-1972 d. 1990
Gwen
1899-1979
Thomas = Winnie Luscombe 1933
1900-1936 d. 1956
Billy
1923-43
Ruth
1926-44
Jean
1921-44
John = Dulcie Mallett '43
1922-91 d. 1989
Bobbie & Tony
1924
Lorna = Peter Bicknell 1956
1927
Julie = Maurice Giles 1967
1944 d. 1993
John '58 = Christina Dorees '92
Richard '60 = Victoria Holt '93
div. 1996
= Catherine Townrow 2000 (2)
Ariadne 1994
Danäe 1996
Samantha = Dominic Neal 1993
1969
Rebecca
1973
= Beryl Waldon 1950
William 1997
= Marie Walters 1951
Nicholas 1955
Sarah 1958
Bettye 1916
= Rodney May
1937 div. 1943 (1)
= Michael Armstrong
1943 d. 1984 (2)
= Thomas Gray
1986 d. 1996 (3)
Peter 1919-2007
= Barbara Bavestock = Donald Carlton 1968
1947 div. 1962 (1)
= Mary Malcolm
1964 (2)
David 1956
Sue 1965 = Paul Richards 1986
Katie 1987
Clair 1990
(2) Mary 1944
= John Ashworth 1965
(2) John 1949
= Carol Harber 1974
(1) Maria 1953
= John Simpson 1980
(1) Sonia 1955
= Felix Phillips 1978 (1)
= John Davis 1991 (2)
= Graham Anderson 2007 (3)
(1) Sarah 1958
= Inga Rem 1981 (1)
= Mounni van Kampen 1987 (2)
(2) Emma 1966
= Colin Stratton 1995
(2) Rebecca 1968
Julia 1982
Andrew 1984
Dominic 1996
Edward 1998
Theodore 2000
Toby 1967
= Katie Gibson
1997
Henry 1969
= Sophie Déjan
1997
William 1974
= Pixie Bennett
2004
Joshua 1999
Olivia 2004
Alfred 2006
Inigo 1982 (1)
Sunna 1988 (2)
Veryan 1983
Morwenna 1985
George 1987
Tamara 2007
Cicely 2008
Natalie 1982
Hannah 1985
Neil 1989
Andrew 1992 (2)
Cordelia 2004
Georgiana 2007
Alana 2007
Virginia 2008

THE FAMILY HOTELS

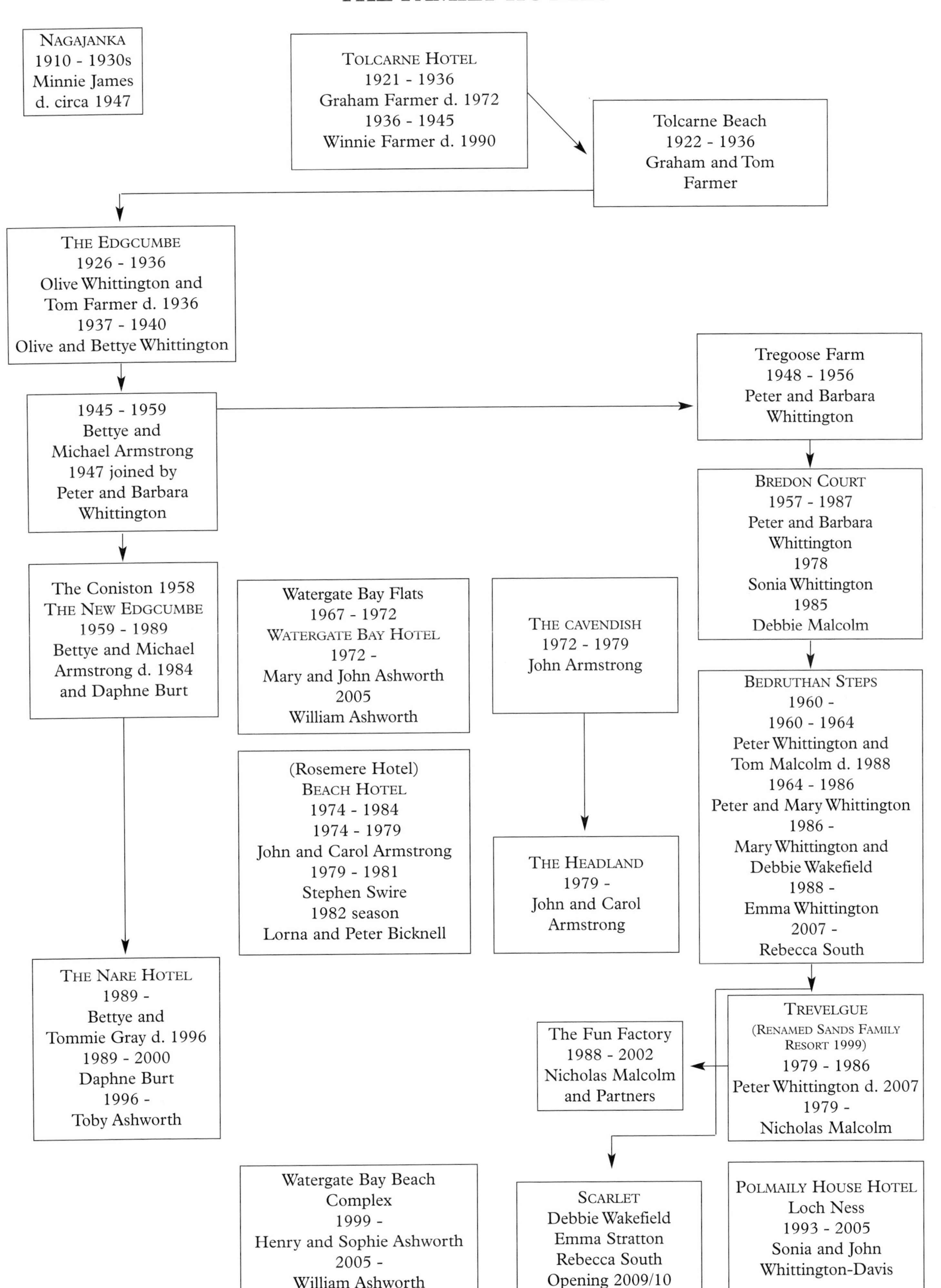